The '60s
FOR
DUMMIES®

by Brian Cassity and Maxine Levaren

WILEY

Wiley Publishing, Inc.

The '60s For Dummies®

Published by
Wiley Publishing, Inc.
111 River St.
Hoboken, NJ 07030-5774
www.wiley.com

WILEY

About the Authors

Brian Cassity: Brian Cassity is an assistant professor of history at Kapi'olani Community College who specializes in 20th-century history, specifically the Vietnam War.

Maxine Levaren: Maxine Levaren is a writer, a personal success coach, a passionate traveler, and a lifelong adventurer. Although she hates to admit it, she remembers the 1960s well, looks back on them with nostalgia, and views herself as an unrepentant hippie. She lives in San Diego with her two dogs, Senji and Bandit.

Dedication

Brian Cassity: My deepest thanks go to my wife, Kathy, and my son, Liam, both of whom inspired me to finish this project. Their love, patience, and understanding with my long hours at the computer made this work possible. I dedicate this book to them.

Maxine Levaren: This book is dedicated to my three greatest fans, Jean Haren, Michael Bruce Iritz, and Stuart Allen Iritz.

Authors' Acknowledgments

Though writing a book is a solitary endeavor, publishing one is definitely a team effort. As such, we would like to thank the editors at Wiley Publishing, Tracy Boggier, who helped birth this project, Mike Baker, who kept us on the straight and narrow, and Kristin DeMint, for her way with words. Their efforts proved invaluable in bringing this work to publication. Also, appreciation to our family and friends for their support and tolerating our absence and distraction during the last few months.

Publisher's Acknowledgments

We're proud of this book; please send us your comments through our Dummies online registration form located at www.dummies.com/register/.

Some of the people who helped bring this book to market include the following:

Acquisitions, Editorial, and Media Development

Project Editor: Mike Baker

Acquisitions Editor: Tracy Boggier

Copy Editor: Kristin DeMint

Editorial Program Assistant: Courtney Allen

Technical Reviewer: Jeremi Suri

Editorial Manager: Christine Meloy Beck

Editorial Assistants: Hanna Scott, Melissa S. Bennett

Cover Image: © Abbie Enneking/2005

Cartoons: Rich Tennant (www.the5thwave.com)

Composition Services

Project Coordinator: Shannon Schiller

Layout and Graphics: Carl Byers, Barry Offringa, Erin Zeltner

Proofreaders: Leeann Harney, Carl William Pierce, TECHBOOKS Production Services

Indexer: TECHBOOKS Production Services

Special Help: Chad R. Sievers

Publishing and Editorial for Consumer Dummies

    Diane Graves Steele, Vice President and Publisher, Consumer Dummies

    Joyce Pepple, Acquisitions Director, Consumer Dummies

    Kristin A. Cocks, Product Development Director, Consumer Dummies

    Michael Spring, Vice President and Publisher, Travel

    Kelly Regan, Editorial Director, Travel

Publishing for Technology Dummies

    Andy Cummings, Vice President and Publisher, Dummies Technology/General User

Composition Services

    Gerry Fahey, Vice President of Production Services

    Debbie Stailey, Director of Composition Services

Contents at a Glance

Introduction 1

Part 1: Acting Presidential: Viewing the Decade from the Top 7
Chapter 1: The Times They Are A-Changin' 9
Chapter 2: Enter JFK: A New Era 21
Chapter 3: LBJ and the Great Society 45
Chapter 4: Richard Nixon: Cold War Warrior 67

Part 11: Marching toward Freedom: The Civil Rights Movement 83
Chapter 5: Establishing a Firm Foundation 85
Chapter 6: Sitting, Riding, and Marching for Freedom 101
Chapter 7: Embracing Black Power 125

Part 111: Fighting for Peace: Vietnam and the Antiwar Movement 143
Chapter 8: Welcome to Vietnam 145
Chapter 9: Speaking Out against the War 169
Chapter 10: Shifting the Burden: Leaving Vietnam 193

Part 1V: Starting a Revolution: Social Upheaval and Angst 211
Chapter 11: Leaning to the Left 213
Chapter 12: I Am Woman: From the Frying Pan into the Fire 231
Chapter 13: Protesting for Equality and Pushing for Change 251

Part V: Tuning 1n, Turning On, and Dropping Out: Transforming American Culture 265
Chapter 14: Far Out: The Counterculture 267
Chapter 15: A Long, Strange Trip: Music in the 1960s 283
Chapter 16: Exploring Pop Culture 303

Part VI: The Part of Tens 323

Chapter 17: Ten Years of Hit Songs 325
Chapter 18: Ten Movies to Take You Back in Time 331
Chapter 19: Ten Things You Could Get for $1 337

Appendix: Taking a Trip through Time 341

Index 345

Table of Contents

Introduction 1
    About This Book 1
    What You're Not to Read 2
    Conventions Used In This Book 2
    Foolish Assumptions 2
    How This Book Is Organized 3
        Part I: Acting Presidential: Viewing the Decade from the Top 3
        Part II: Marching toward Freedom: The Civil Rights Movement 3
        Part III: Fighting for Peace: Vietnam and the Antiwar Movement ...4
        Part IV: Starting a Revolution: Social Upheaval and Angst 4
        Part V: Tuning In, Turning On, and Dropping Out:
           Transforming American Culture 5
        Part VI: The Part of Tens 5
    Icons Used In This Book 6
    Where to Go from Here 6

*Part 1: Acting Presidential: Viewing
the Decade from the Top* 7

  Chapter 1: The Times They Are A-Changin' 9
    Surveying the Political Landscape 10
    Viewing Issues in Black and White 11
        Setting the stage 11
        Pushing for change 12
        Getting radical 13
    Fighting the War in Vietnam — At Home and Abroad 13
        Wading in chin deep 14
        Beginning the slow withdrawal 15
    Fighting for Equality 15
        Joining the student movement 15
        Changing society's views of women 16
        Fighting for Latino rights 16
        Rallying around American Indian issues 17
        Sowing the seeds for gay pride 17
        Giving voice to the silent majority 17
    Living a New Way 18
        Creating a youth counterculture 18
        Rocking to the music 19
        Stylin' in the '60s 19
        Turning to entertainment 19

Chapter 2: Enter JFK: A New Era 21

Inspiring America: Kennedy and the Power of Rhetoric 22
  Fulfilling the Kennedy family heritage:
      Young, rich, and Catholic 23
  Joining the 1960 presidential race 24
Exploring Camelot 25
  Filling the White House with glamour 26
  Recruiting Kennedy's "whiz kids" 27
  Pushing New Frontier domestic policies 28
  Expanding the boundaries of the frontier 30
  Supporting the civil rights movement 31
Fighting in the Cold War 32
  Attempting to overthrow Castro: The Bay of Pigs fiasco 34
  Watching the Berlin Wall go up 36
  Managing the Cuban Missile Crisis 36
  Easing tension: The 1963 Limited Test Ban Treaty 40
  Entering the quagmire: The growing
      U.S. commitment to South Vietnam 40
Detailing a Fateful Day in Dallas 41
  Capturing a suspect 41
  Deliberating on the assassin: The Warren Commission 42

Chapter 3: LBJ and the Great Society 45

Learning the Game: Early Service in the House and Senate 46
  Congressman Johnson 48
  The senator from Texas 48
  Presidential desires and vice-presidential opportunities 48
The Unexpected Promotion: The Death of JFK 49
  Carrying forth the torch 50
  Finding an agenda: The unconditional War on Poverty 50
  Applying a label: The Great Society 51
The 1964 Presidential Race 52
  Shifting to the right: Republicans react 52
  Holding onto the left: Johnson campaigns 54
  Emerging victorious 55
Back to the Great Society and the War on Poverty 56
  Pushing Kennedy's Civil Rights Act 57
  Establishing the Voting Rights Act 57
  Ensuring educational opportunities 58
  Addressing medical problems with Medicare 60
  Fighting poverty and making changes on multiple fronts 61
Guns or Butter? The Tragedy of Vietnam 62
  Escalating the war 63
  Looking shady: Johnson's credibility gap 63
  Smothering the dream: The Tet Offensive 65

Chapter 4: Richard Nixon: Cold War Warrior 67

Getting Started: Nixon's Early Life 68
    Redbaiting his way to the top 68
    Winning the vice presidency 71
    Losing the presidential race 73
Taking Another Shot: The 1968 Race 73
    A year of change and turmoil 74
    The silent majority speaks 75
Taking the Presidential Reins 76
    Pursuing peace with honor 76
    Achieving success with foreign policy 79
    Focusing on the domestic front 80
Running for Reelection 82

**Part II: Marching toward Freedom:
The Civil Rights Movement** 83

Chapter 5: Establishing a Firm Foundation 85

The Post–Civil War Era and Jim Crow 85
Demanding a Place in American Society 87
    Stepping out on the frontlines 88
    Claiming first place 89
    Gaining freedom through song and stage 90
    Working within the government 92
Enduring the Brutality of Racial Violence 93
    The aim and end of lynch mobs 94
    The murder of Emmett Till 94
Integrating the Schools 95
    Exposing the fallacy of separate and equal 95
    Desegregating Central High School 96
Rosa Parks and the Bus Boycott 97
    Staking a claim to her seat 97
    Boycotting the buses 98
The Civil Rights Act of 1957 99

Chapter 6: Sitting, Riding, and Marching for Freedom 101

Preaching Nonviolence: Dr. Martin Luther King Jr. 102
    Keeping the faith 102
    Embracing peaceful protest 103
    Gaining worldwide recognition 103
    Facing dissention in the ranks 104
    Dying young 105
Opening the Lunch Counters: The Sit-In Movement 106

Making Alphabet Soup: CORE, SCLC, SNCC, and NAACP 108
    The granddaddy of civil rights organizations: The NAACP 108
    Bringing whites to the fight: CORE 110
    Fighting with faith: The SCLC 111
    Mobilizing students: The SNCC 113
Going on a Road Trip: Freedom Rides 113
Shaking the Nation: Turning Points in 1963 115
    The Battle of Birmingham 115
    The murder of Medgar Evers 117
    The March for Jobs and Freedom 117
    The murder of four girls in a Birmingham church 118
Heating It Up: Freedom Summer 120
    Continuing drives to get out the vote 120
    Providing competition with an alternate Democratic Party 121
    Learning equality in Freedom Schools 122
    Coping with three Klan murders 122
The Civil Rights Act of 1964 123

Chapter 7: Embracing Black Power **125**
Marching from Selma to Montgomery 126
Winning the Voting Rights Act 127
Rioting in the Cities 128
    The Watts Riots 128
    The Detroit Riots 129
    The Newark Riots 130
    Investigating the riots 131
    Reacting to King's murder 131
Pressing for Economic Empowerment 131
    The Chicago Freedom Movement 132
    Operation Breadbasket 132
    The Poor People's Campaign 133
Being Black and Proud 134
    Joining the Nation of Islam 134
    Asserting black power on campus 137
Fighting with the Black Panthers 138
    Devising and implementing programs 139
    Resisting the law with violence 140
Black Empowerment: The Legacy of the '60s 142

**Part III: Fighting for Peace: Vietnam
and the Antiwar Movement** *143*

Chapter 8: Welcome to Vietnam **145**
Enter America: The Last Chapter of the Long Vietnamese Struggle 145
    Continuing the colonial effort: The French in Indochina 147
    Creating two Vietnams: The Geneva Conference 148
    Building a nation: The developing quagmire 149

Drawing the battle lines 151
Facing a crisis of leadership in the South: The Coup of 1963 152
Americanizing the War 153
Inheriting the conflict: JFK's legacy to LBJ 154
Dealing with the conflict: The presidential campaign of 1964 154
Wading in deep: The Tonkin Gulf incident 155
Committing U.S. Troops: Shifting from Advisors to Combatants 157
Relying on air superiority: Rolling Thunder I 158
Fighting a different kind of war 159
Relying on body counts 160
Understanding the cold war concerns
of maintaining a limited war 161
Failing to win hearts and minds 162
The Tet Offensive of 1968 164
Diverting attention at Khe Sanh 165
Surprising the U.S. with the real attacks 166
Assessing the aftermath: A military
victory and a political defeat 167

Chapter 9: Speaking Out against the War **169**
The Diversity of Dissent 170
Beginning with the peace movement 170
Participating in the student movement 172
The Emerging Antiwar Movement 173
Spreading the word with teach-ins 173
Holding early marches and demonstrations 174
Initiating civil disobedience 174
Following the lead of the Buddhist monks 174
Turning Up the Heat 175
Resisting the draft 176
Making diplomacy a personal mission 179
Buying media coverage 181
Joining the fray: Civil rights and the antiwar movement 182
The Turning Point in 1968 183
Confrontation in Chicago 184
Witnessing "a police riot" 184
Trying the Chicago Eight 186
Winding Down the War 187
The Moratorium of October 1969
and the November Mobilization 187
Death on campus 188
Problems within the military 189
The Winter Soldier Investigation 190
The VVAW 190

Chapter 10: Shifting the Burden: Leaving Vietnam **193**
The Aftermath of Tet 194
Seeking negotiations with North Vietnam 194
Electing a new president in 1968 195

Playing the Cold War Card 196
Taking Initial Steps Toward Vietnamization 198
Reassuring South Vietnam 198
Withdrawing U.S. troops 198
Negotiating with the North 199
Feeding the Protest Fires 200
Eliminating Communists: The Phoenix Program 200
Hitting the press: The My Lai Massacre 201
Widening the War 202
Moving into Cambodia 203
Relying on the ARVN in Laos 206
Coming to a Head: The Easter Offensive 207
Clearing the Last Hurdles to Peace 209

Part IV: Starting a Revolution: Social Upheaval and Angst 211

Chapter 11: Leaning to the Left 213

Left Wing of the American Eagle: Liberal and
Socialist Politics before the 1960s 213
The Palmer Raids 214
Pinks and reds in the 1930s and '40s 215
McCarthyism and the Communist hysteria 215
Birthing the New Left 216
What were they fighting for? 217
Protesting with direct action 219
Fighting for Free Speech 220
Berkeley activism before '63 — HUAC 221
Striking for civil rights 221
Exercising freedom of speech 222
The sit-in at Sproul 223
Berkeley meets the Haight 225
. . . and Oakland 226
People's Park 226
Participating in Student Society 228
Participatory democracy and direct action 229
Knowing which way the wind blows — the Weathermen 229

Chapter 12: I Am Woman: From the Frying Pan into the Fire 231

Exposing the Feminine Mystique 232
Looking to the Government with Mixed Results 234
Establishing a commission and legislating equal pay 234
Including women in the Civil Rights Act of 1964 236

Coming Together to Build a Movement 237
    Organizing to take a stand — NOW 237
    Making waves for working women 238
Getting Radical 240
    Bringing the movement to the national stage:
      Miss America 1968 241
    Raising consciousness 242
    Using the "L" words: Liberation, love, and lesbianism 244
Getting It On: The Power of the Pill 245
    Embracing planned pregnancy 246
    Unleashing female sexuality 246
    Banning birth control: The Catholic Church weighs in 248
Facing a Backlash: Men and Women Fight Back 249
Leaving a Legacy 250

Chapter 13: Protesting for Equality and Pushing for Change **251**

¡Sí, Se Puede! Cesar Chavez and Latino Activism 251
    Moving from the fields to the picket line 252
    Brandishing the boycott 253
Leaving the Reservation 255
    Breaking into Alcatraz 255
    Taking AIM into the 1970s and beyond 258
Opening the Closet Door 259
    Coming out 259
    Rioting at the Stonewall bar 260
Preserving the Status Quo: The Conservatives 261
    Fighting the Communist conspiracy: The John Birch Society 262
    Stumping for segregation 263
    Speaking to the silent majority 263

Part V: Tuning In, Turning On, and Dropping Out: Transforming American Culture **265**

Chapter 14: Far Out: The Counterculture **267**

Defying Convention: Alternate Lifestyles before the Hippies 268
Being In and Loving In 269
    Showing hippie style 270
    Quitting your day job and hitting the road 271
    Living cooperatively 271
    Making love (not war) 273
    Letting the spirit move them 274
    Getting political: Peace and equal rights 275
    Rebelling through writing: The underground press 275

Flying with Lucy in the Sky with Diamonds: Drugs and the
Counterculture 277
Day-tripping with LSD 277
Burning grass 279
Flower Power: Haight-Ashbury and the Summer of Love 280
Blood on the Flowers: The Manson Murders 281

Chapter 15: A Long, Strange Trip: Music in the 1960s **283**

This Ain't Your '50s Rock 'n' Roll 283
The World before the Beatles 284
Goin' surfin' 284
Getting down in Motown 285
Reliving history with folk music 287
The British Invasion 289
Ladies and gentlemen, the Beatles 290
Like the Rolling Stones 292
Singing with the Revolution 294
Watching through a purple haze: Psychedelic rock 294
Marching to the music: Rock protests 295
Coming Together and Falling Apart: The Music Festivals 297
Flower power at Monterey 297
The big one: Woodstock 298
A day of violence and music: Altamont 301

Chapter 16: Exploring Pop Culture **303**

Stylin' in the '60s 303
Reinventing women's wear, from Jackie to Twiggy 304
Saying goodbye to plain and white: The men and the mods 305
Hanging loose, hippie style 306
Whiskers, sideburns, and the long and short of hair 306
Bringing Society to the Big Screen 307
Revisiting popular themes and characters 307
Confronting social and political issues 309
A Hair-Raising Experience: The '60s Make It to Broadway 311
Reflecting Life on the Small Screen 312
Late-night talk shows 312
A new kind of variety show 312
The vast wasteland: '60s sitcoms 313
An immediate look at the news 314
Poking Serious Fun: The New Comedians 314
Hitting the Books 315
Topping the charts 315
Embracing the Playboy philosophy 316
Changing Perspective: Pop, Op, and Psychedelic Art 316

Playing the Game 317
    The dynasties 317
    The underdogs 318
    International politics at the Olympics 319
    The Greatest: Muhammad Ali 319
Walking the Talk 321

Part VI: The Part of Tens 323

Chapter 17: Ten Years of Hit Songs 325

1960 325
1961 326
1962 326
1963 326
1964 327
1965 327
1966 328
1967 328
1968 329
1969 329

Chapter 18: Ten Movies to Take You Back in Time 331

Malcolm X 331
Ali 332
Dr. Strangelove, or: How I Learned to
  Stop Worrying and Love the Bomb 332
Thirteen Days 332
The Green Berets 333
Hamburger Hill 333
Platoon 333
Good Morning, Vietnam 333
American Graffiti 334
The Graduate 334
Easy Rider 334
Woodstock: 3 Days of Peace & Music 335

Chapter 19: Ten Things You Could Get for $1 337

Three Gallons of Gas 337
20 First-Class Postage Stamps 337
A Hamburger with Fries, Salad, and Dessert 338
A Gallon of Milk (And Other Groceries) 338
Ten Razor Blades (And Other Toiletries) 338

Enough Aspirin for 50 Headaches (And Other Meds) 339
Numerous Copies of Your Favorite Magazine or Newspaper 339
A Paper Dress (For You, Not a Doll) 339
A Home Decoration or Two 340
A Six-Pack of Beer 340

Appendix: Taking a Trip through Time *341*

Index *345*

Introduction

● ●

*T*he 1960s were a turning point in the United States. It was decade of change and turbulence that had enormous impact on people's lives, even up to today. In almost every phase of life, from the political to the social to the cultural, you can still see the impact of these ten years.

From the beginning of the decade to the end, the mood of the country changed, from the hopeful optimism of John F. Kennedy's New Frontier to disillusionment that came with the Vietnam War. People began to question long-held assumptions and beliefs. It was a time to get involved, and activists found a variety of subjects to pursue, ranging from the issue of equality — be it for African Americans, Hispanics, women, or gays — to issues of personal conduct and community expectations. Though these issues weren't all solved in the decade, the willingness and courage to confront them represents a clear advance in the ongoing development of the nation.

Even now, more than 40 years later, few people are neutral about the '60s. Many people applaud the movements that changed people's lives (and, possibly, regret that some didn't have a greater impact). Other people blame the '60s for everything from moral turpitude to corrupt politicians. If these ten years can still stir up that kind of emotion, you know there are some stories to be told. And that's what *The '60s For Dummies* is all about.

About This Book

This book is designed to be a factual, interesting, and fun trip through the 1960s, giving you an overview of these fascinating years. Although filled with facts and information, this book isn't your standard sleep-inducing historical treatise. We deal with some serious topics, but we also have a really good time along the way.

As a history professor and a professional writer, we try to present the facts in an unbiased manner. But we have to admit that we're both fans of the '60s. One of us (and we won't tell you who) remembers the protests, wore tie-dyes, listened to the music, and saw *Hair!* on Broadway. The other wanted to live the '60s. For many of the same reasons that many people enjoy visiting this decade, we find it fascinating. We're also somewhat nostalgic about the heady optimism that many folks shared during the early years of decade. We understand the importance of the issues that came to the forefront, and we appreciate many of the changes that came about during these years.

What You're Not to Read

If you're short on time or you don't need *all* the details, you can skip the text marked by a *Technical Stuff* icon and the text formatted in a sidebar (paragraphs inside shaded boxes). This material is certainly interesting, but you can still understand the subject at hand without reading it.

Conventions Used In This Book

We use the following conventions throughout the text to make everything consistent and easy to understand.

- *Italic* is used for emphasis and to highlight new words or terms that we define in the text.
- **Boldfaced** text is used to indicate keywords in bulleted lists or the action parts of numbered steps.
- `Monofont` text is used for Web addresses.
- Sidebars are shaded gray boxes that contain text that's interesting to know but not necessarily critical to your understanding of the chapter or section topic.

Foolish Assumptions

We wrote this book with you, the reader, in mind. We've strived to provide you with just the sort of information you're looking for. To do so, we've made a few assumptions about you. If one or more of the following descriptions sounds familiar, you're in the right place:

- You want to find out more about the history of a time that continues to shape American life today, but you're not a social scientist or a historian. You want accessible and interesting information about the decade's cultural changes, protest movements, and politics.

✔ You *think* that you remember the '60s. If so, we think that you'll find yourself saying, "Hey, I forgot about that" a lot.

✔ You *know* that you don't remember the '60s — because it was before your time. In this case, you'll be saying, "Oh, so that's where that started."

✔ History wasn't necessarily your favorite subject in school — but if it was, that's great, too.

✔ You compulsively buy every book you see that sports a snazzy yellow and black cover.

✔ In addition to the more serious stuff, you want a healthy dose of offbeat trivia and fun information on pop culture — television, movies, music, the hippie scene, and more.

How This Book Is Organized

We've organized *The '60s For Dummies* so that you can easily find out whatever you want to know about the 1960s. To give you a quick view of what's where, here's a rundown.

Part 1: Acting Presidential: Viewing the Decade from the Top

Part I is the most chronological part of this book. First, you get an overview of what happened during the '60s and how the decade impacted later years. Then, you can see what happened during the administrations of four very different leaders (about whom no one was, or is now, very neutral) — Dwight D. Eisenhower, John F. Kennedy, Lyndon B. Johnson, and Richard Nixon.

Part 11: Marching toward Freedom: The Civil Rights Movement

Part II deals with events that changed the lives of all Americans — the civil rights movement. Starting in the mid-1950s and reaching its peak during the '60s, the civil rights movement fought to ensure equal rights for African Americans. Focusing on the southern states, where all aspects of life were segregated — from schools to buses and lunch counters to restrooms — the movement worked to eliminate the indignities and lack of opportunities associated with being regarded as second-class citizens.

This part begins by giving a brief overview of life before the civil rights movement. In the process, we cover some of the events that provided a foundation for the movement as it hit its stride in the sixties. Then we discuss the events that changed everything — the freedom rides, civil rights marches, lunch counter sit-ins, and civil rights legislation. We talk about the leadership of the civil rights movement — from Martin Luther King Jr., who was fully committed to nonviolent protest, and later black leaders, such as Malcolm X, Stokely Carmichael, and the Black Panthers, who believed that using violence was sometimes necessary to achieve their goals.

Part III: Fighting for Peace: Vietnam and the Antiwar Movement

Part III deals with the pivotal event of the 1960s — the Vietnam War. Vietnam was the first war fought on TV — and therefore the first one that the American public viewed up close and personal. The war forced many Americans to rethink their views of patriotism and the presidency.

Part III talks about how and why the United States became involved in a civil war half a world away. Like many other world events, this war didn't start overnight. Even before World War II, Indochina was an embattled area, and with the advent of the cold war, this area, which the United States determined must remain a bastion of democracy, became disputed. However, U.S. involvement and the escalation of the war were based on misinformation that eventually led to the protests that tore the country apart. Finally, as much as getting embroiled in Vietnam was a long, drawn-out affair, getting out proved to be slow and difficult and wasn't actually achieved until the mid-1970s.

Part IV: Starting a Revolution: Social Upheaval and Angst

The '60s were marked by protest. The civil rights movement mobilized many students, who were touched by the injustices against blacks. Students joined the freedom rides and other protests in order to integrate public facilities in the South and ensure that all Americans had the right to vote. This movement inspired many young people to protest other injustices — most notably the Vietnam War.

However, the war and civil rights weren't the only things that inspired protests — women, Latinos, American Indians, and gays and lesbians all demanded to be regarded as equals under the law. And the New Left groups weren't the only ones to be heard from during the '60s — many people liked the way everything was during the "good-old days" and protested the way they saw the country was going.

Part V: Tuning In, Turning On, and Dropping Out: Transforming American Culture

Music, fashions, theater, television, and choice of lifestyle — few things remained unchanged through the turbulent '60s. Hippies questioned the wisdom of living lives of quiet desperation and looked for ways, both spiritual and chemical, to reach new levels of awareness. The music scene underwent huge changes. The rather tame rock 'n' roll of the 1950s got injections of soul, the British invasion, and drug-induced psychedelic music to create a whole new sound. Also, because of the huge social movements, and especially the protests against the Vietnam War, political, protest music came to the forefront. And the '60s saw the rise of another phenomenon — the rock festival, a la Woodstock.

The '60s also saw a fashion revolution — miniskirts, mod style, and hippie threads went into the mainstream, and by the '70s, a variety of styles were everywhere (and women even started to wear pants!). Theater, movies, and comedy also began to reflect the changes taking place, but the largest of these changes was television — which brought everything, from the Vietnam War to JFK's funeral, and from Bobby Kennedy's and Martin Luther King Jr.'s assassinations to Woodstock, into living rooms all over the United States.

Part VI: The Part of Tens

This section contains some fun and interesting information about life in the '60s. You can turn to these pages for a year-by-year view of the pop charts for a dose of nostalgia and to trace the changing face of music throughout the decade. We also include a description of ten movies that capture many different aspects of the decade. So, when you're done reading about the civil rights movement or Vietnam, for example, you can head out to the video store to get an entertaining and engrossing visual perspective of the events. Finally, we include a chapter on ten things that you could buy for a buck in the '60s. (Wait until you see the gas prices!) At the end of the Part of Tens, you can find an Appendix that contains a timeline of the 1960s.

Icons Used In This Book

This icon indicates a piece of information that's key to understanding the 1960s.

This icon lets you know that we're uncovering the roots of the trials and tribulations, events, movements, and changes in 1960s American society. If you want to know where it all started, this is where to look.

This icon highlights interesting, humorous, or otherwise noteworthy quotes.

This icon indicates information that isn't crucial to understanding the events we describe, but it can add to your knowledge of the topic, it's often rather fun, and it would be useful if you ever decide to try out for *Jeopardy!*.

Text with this icon alerts you to statistics or other hairy details (that you may or may not care about).

Where to Go from Here

Like the 1960s, *For Dummies* books buck the conventional norms. So, you don't have to read this book from cover to cover in order to get the most out of it (although you can if you want, and we think it makes for some pretty interesting reading). You can tune in or drop out anywhere along the way and still get a good idea of what was happening with the subject that you're interested in. Check out the Table of Contents to find what interests you, and turn to that chapter or section. For example, if you're a Nixon fan, you can turn directly to Chapter 4 to see what Dick was up to in the '60s. Or, if you're here for the music, you can flip to Chapter 15. To get a bird's-eye view of what was going on in the United States from 1960 to 1969, check out Chapter 1, which is an overview of the decade, or the timeline Appendix at the back of the book.

In each chapter, you can find a bit of background of what led up to the events that we discuss. Then we tell you what happened — the "who, what, why, when, where" and sometimes how. Finally, we tell you why anyone cares — that is, the impact that the events had and continue to have today.

Part I

Acting Presidential: Viewing the Decade from the Top

The 5th Wave   By Rich Tennant

OCT. 1960: THE LAST KENNEDY–NIXON DEBATE

"I think Dick could have used some makeup."

In this part . . .

You can tell the overarching story of the 1960s like any historical tale by taking a look at the political side of life — the major figures and events that helped shape the decade. And that's what we do in this part. We survey the playing field by exploring the presidencies of the decade, along with the successes, trials, and tribulations the United States went through with these men during the decade.

Political life of the 1960s was full of contradictions — the decade started out with Republican President Dwight Eisenhower leading the country. It was a time of peace, prosperity, and conformity. It was what people referred to as "the good-old days" — everyone seemed to be content, and no one wanted to make waves. Then, in November 1960, Democrat John Kennedy was elected president — the youngest man and the only Catholic ever elected to the nation's highest office. In spite of cold war concerns, it was a time of hope and optimism. But Camelot ended with an assassin's bullet, and Vice President Lyndon B. Johnson, a good-old Texas glad-handing politician, took over. His style was completely different, but Johnson continued, and actually expanded, Kennedy's domestic programs to boost civil rights and end poverty. But the U.S. presence in Vietnam, which expanded to a full-blown war under the Johnson administration, was his undoing, and in 1968, Richard Nixon was elected, in large part because of his law-and-order platform and his vow to end the Vietnam War.

Chapter 1

The Times They Are A-Changin'

In This Chapter

▶ Governing the United States, from Eisenhower to Nixon

▶ Uniting a nation: The civil rights movement

▶ Dividing a nation: The Vietnam War

▶ Claiming various rights: Protests of the '60s

▶ Creating new lifestyles

The 1960s were a time of change, but just as importantly, they were a time of hope. Despite all the turmoil (the decade was certainly turbulent), everyday people thought that they could change the world. Activists are still around today, but in no decade since the '60s (and early '70s) were people so committed to putting themselves on the front line, sometimes even in physical danger, for what they believed. The '60s were also a fun, wild kind of time, ripe with individuality. Musicians, fashion designers, artists, and writers all experimented with creating new kinds of art and human expression. And young people experimented with new ways to live, breaking away from their parents' lifestyles, which they believed were conformist, materialistic, and often stifling.

Television also came into its own in this decade — no longer was it just a novelty that people used in order to watch Milton Berle once a week, but it reflected some of the social changes that were rapidly taking place. Most importantly, for good or bad, TV brought the news right into peoples' living rooms. American citizens saw it all — the civil rights movement, dogs and policemen attacking peaceful protesters, inaugurations and assassinations, a walk on the moon, war (and antiwar protests), and the hippie lifestyle. As a result, almost every American was affected by what was going on in society. And even today, Americans (and not only the baby boomers who lived through the '60s) are affected by the events of the decade.

Surveying the Political Landscape

When most folks hear the phrase "the 1960s," they immediately think of hippies, war protestors, and other images of rebellion and experimentation, and for good reason. But these connotations don't completely reflect the decade. Even amidst civil rights demonstrations, antiwar protests, new fashions, new music, and changing lifestyles, many people still went to work each day, returned to their homes each night, raised children, and lived altogether conventional lives.

Comparing the political landscape of the presidential administrations versus these mental images can also appear strange, as the presidential bookends of the decade were Dwight Eisenhower, the general who led the Allied invasion of Normandy to end World War II in 1945, and his conservative vice president, Richard Nixon. In between these two Republican administrations, however, the United States went through eight hopeful, inspiring, terrifying, and violent years under the leadership of John F. Kennedy and Lyndon B. Johnson.

- ✔ **Dwight "Ike" Eisenhower (1953–61):** January 1, 1960, was ushered in under President Eisenhower's administration, which many observers saw as a bland, white-bread administration that concentrated on maintaining the U.S. prosperity and presenting a strong challenge to the growth of Communism worldwide. Ike seemed like the elderly father seeking to guide and care for his children.

- ✔ **John F. Kennedy (1961–63):** John F. Kennedy was the youngest man ever to be elected to the office, and Americans saw his presidency as the beginning of a new era. In his inaugural address, he asked the country to join him in helping the United States reach its potential. Kennedy asked Americans to help end poverty in Appalachia and discrimination against blacks in the South, to create new allies overseas by participating in the Peace Corps, and to land a man on the moon by the end of the decade. The civil rights movement (see the "Viewing Issues in Black and White" section, later in this chapter) and the violence that often met it pushed Kennedy to address the issues and call on Congress to pass legislation to ensure civil rights for all Americans.

  Kennedy's administration also saw the country through some difficult times. The cold war heated up as Eisenhower's plan to overthrow Castro in Cuba led to the Cuban Missile Crisis, when the United States and the Soviet Union came very close to a nuclear war. Though the incident passed, the cold war continued, and the United States started down that painful path that became the Vietnam War. You can read about these events and the rest of the Kennedy years in Chapter 2.

- ✔ **Lyndon B. Johnson (1963–69):** Following President Kennedy's assassination in 1963, his domestic and international agendas were left to his vice president and successor, Lyndon Johnson. Johnson vowed to push Kennedy's agenda, especially in the area of civil rights, but he also expanded Kennedy's vision by pressing his Great Society programs, using his political prowess (some called them strong-armed tactics) to initiate the War on Poverty; to create a Medicare program for the elderly; to support funding for education, housing, and jobs; and to pass civil rights and voting rights legislation.

Johnson also inherited an increasingly complicated mess in Vietnam that would force him into a no-win position — a war that he couldn't afford to lose but couldn't win. This undeclared war had two devastating effects on his administration. The funds necessary for the war sapped funds from his Great Society programs, and an expanded military draft resulted in antiwar protests, which eventually eroded Johnson's reputation and credibility. In 1968, he announced that he wouldn't run for a second full term as president. Chapter 3 covers Johnson.

✔ **Richard Nixon (1969–74):** Amidst the disarray in the Democratic Party, and with the support of the *silent majority* (Americans who were uncomfortable with the turbulent changes taking place in the nation), Nixon was elected in 1968 on the promise that he could bring peace with honor and restore law and order to the country. However, the Vietnam War didn't end until 1973, and the antiwar protests continued (on and off) until then.

Nixon's administration changed the world in both negative and positive ways. The Watergate scandal eroded whatever faith the American public still had in their elected officials. But Nixon's foreign policy genius also had a lasting impact — in 1972, he opened relations with mainland Communist China. (See Chapter 4 for more on Nixon's road to the White House and his tenure as president in the '60s.)

Viewing Issues in Black and White

The civil rights movement of the 1960s had lasting effects on American society. Although many African Americans still face racism, the situation has changed considerably since the '60s. But change didn't come without struggle. The decade saw peaceful protests that often turned violent, murders of civil rights workers and innocent victims, as well as urban rioting and destruction. Although race relations in the United States have a long way to go, significant progress has already been made.

Setting the stage

The struggle for freedom and equality for African Americans dates back to the very beginnings of U.S. history. Even though the end of the Civil War in 1865 brought the *promise* of freedom for those people held in bondage, the attainment of true freedom and equality was fleeting at best. For a while after the Civil War, the North forced the southern states to stop the blatant discrimination, yet when Reconstruction ended, southern states began passing Jim Crow Laws, designed to prevent blacks from voting and keep them segregated from whites in schools and other public and private facilities. In northern states, although segregation wasn't legally mandated as it was in the South, it still existed, in the form of racially segregated neighborhoods and the prejudice blacks faced.

In the face of continued oppression through the first half of the 20th century, African Americans formed organizations to help press for equality and assist rural blacks to adjust to the urban environment. This push for equality gained tremendous momentum in 1954, when the nation's highest court ruled that segregation was illegal. Soon after, a seamstress named Rosa Parks refused to give up her bus seat to a white passenger in Montgomery, Alabama. This simple act began the yearlong Montgomery Bus Boycott (which gained blacks the right to equality in public facilities) and also brought Rev. Martin Luther King Jr. (one of the boycott's leaders) to national prominence. In Chapter 5, we cover the Montgomery Bus Boycott, along with other individuals, organizations, and events (including Supreme Court rulings, the integration of previous segregated schools in the South, and the passage of the Civil Rights Act of 1957) that provided a foundation for the civil rights movement in the 1960s.

Pushing for change

Encouraged by the successful Montgomery Bus Boycott, and with the help of strong leaders such as Martin Luther King Jr., Ralph Abernathy, and others, students organized nonviolent protests. Throughout the South, students organized sit-ins to integrate lunch counters, freedom rides to integrate bus terminals, and protest marches and demonstrations to insist on equal access to public facilities. The Ku Klux Klan, law enforcement officials, and ordinary citizens often met these peaceful protests with violence. Although life for southern blacks was always dangerous, many in white America began to become aware of the level of violence for the first time, especially after four girls were killed in a church bombing in Birmingham, Alabama, in 1963.

Even President Kennedy was appalled by the violence, compelling him to propose comprehensive civil rights legislation. To press for support for the civil rights bill, civil rights organizations joined together to coordinate a huge march on Washington, D.C., where Martin Luther King Jr. gave his famous "I have a dream" speech. (For more information, head to Chapter 6, where you can read all about King and the civil rights movement in the first half of the decade.)

In 1964, civil rights organizations held Freedom Summer, an all-out voter registration drive in Mississippi. This peaceful demonstration was again met with violence as three civil rights workers were killed. Responding to this violence, as well as the fear that blacks would become more militant, President Johnson pushed for passage of the Civil Rights Bill of 1964, which enforced equal voter registration and prohibited discrimination in all public facilities.

Even after the civil rights bill passed, the protests continued. In 1965, a march from Selma, Alabama, to the state capital of Montgomery was met with police and Klan violence and therefore again awakened the nation. The Voting Rights Act, which put teeth into the 15th and 19th Amendments, passed as a result — see Chapter 7.

Getting radical

Despite the progress made, American society still had inequalities, especially regarding education, economic disparity, and substandard housing. Furthermore, the gains made by the civil rights movement raised blacks' expectations, and they became impatient with nonviolent protest. The mid- to late '60s were marked by more strident protests, at times culminating in urban riots such as the Watts Riots in Los Angeles. The rise of black militants, such as the Black Panthers, was a direct response to the slow progress in the movement. Many blacks were no longer willing to passively resist police violence and wait for white America to give them their rights. They were willing to fight, violently if necessary, to take their rightful place in their country, as we discuss in Chapter 7.

Fighting the War in Vietnam — At Home and Abroad

Another event that profoundly affected life in the 1960s was the Vietnam War. The United States first got involved in the conflict because the French were allies during World War II. Perhaps more importantly, because of the cold war with the Soviet Union, the United States had a vested interest in keeping Vietnam anti-Communist. Therefore, after the Vietnamese drove the French out of Southeast Asia, Vietnam was divided. The United States, fearing a Communist takeover from the north, offered its support to the South Vietnamese nationalist government of Ngo Dinh Diem. However, Diem wasn't an especially popular leader. He was inflexible, his administration was corrupt, and he alienated many peasants, who were attracted to North Vietnam's leader Ho Chi Minh, a man whose ideals and programs were more attractive to the ordinary Vietnamese people.

As a result, South Vietnam increasingly depended on U.S. support to shore up Diem's government. At first this support was mainly money and a few military advisors, but as Diem faced more challenges to his authority, he requested more assistance, placing the United States on the path into the quagmire. The first sizeable increase was in 1961, when President Kennedy sent 8,000 advisors, including the elite Green Berets, to train and assist the South Vietnamese military.

By 1964 some Americans began to be concerned about the growing U.S. involvement in Vietnam. Therefore, in his campaign speech, President Johnson reassured Americans that he wouldn't send "American boys to do the job that Asian boys should do" for themselves.

Wading in chin deep

Although in 1964 Johnson ran for president promising peace, he believed he was compelled to keep a strong military presence in Vietnam in order to keep Communism from taking over Southeast Asia. This strategy, which continued the dominant cold war thinking, included sending ships into the Tonkin Gulf to gather intelligence and training and supporting the South Vietnamese. These events, which we discuss in Chapter 8, were pivotal in drawing the United States much deeper into the conflict.

In August 1964, a minor (and much disputed) confrontation occurred in the Tonkin Gulf. Given sketchy information, especially about the American and South Vietnamese role in provoking the incident, Congress enacted the Tonkin Gulf Resolution, which gave the president the power to respond to aggression however he felt was necessary. This resolution provided all the justification that Johnson needed to escalate the conflict in Vietnam. Then the U.S. role shifted from being advisors to actual combatants, and the number of troops began to increase exponentially up through 1968.

As the war in Vietnam escalated in the mid-1960s, students organized antiwar protests at home. Disaffected college students weren't the only ones who rallied. Clergymen, parents, executives, and senior citizens — a cross-section of American citizens — protested against the war that they believed was unjust and couldn't be won. The war undermined President Johnson's Great Society plans, and the dissention over it actually caused Johnson to withdraw from the presidential race of 1968. For more on the antiwar movement, see Chapter 9.

By 1967, insurgency was increasing in South Vietnam, and to take advantage of it, the North Vietnamese designed an offensive during the Tet (Lunar New Year) holiday in January 1968. Hoping to force an end to U.S. bombing missions, the North Vietnamese offered to negotiate if the United States stopped bombing — however, at the same time, they planned diversionary actions to allow them to start an offensive against South Vietnamese cities. Attacks took South Vietnamese and U.S. troops by surprise. They even pulled off a successful raid on the new American embassy in Saigon. For the full story of the Tet Offensive, turn to Chapters 8 and 10.

One of the largest impacts of the Tet Offensive was on the American public. With scenes of the conflict on TV almost every night, citizens watched the war in their living rooms and were dismayed with what they saw. Increasing dissatisfaction with the racial disparities within the ranks (blacks made up a disproportionately large portion of the combat soldiers, and consequently suffered more deaths and wounds) as well as the elimination of student draft deferments gave a poignant focus for many, helping to expand the antiwar movement. The antiwar movement not only affected the people at home but also caused a growing cynicism among the troops in Vietnam.

Beginning the slow withdrawal

Nixon was elected president on the expectation and hope that he could end the war. Using an approach called *Vietnamization,* he began to shift more of the responsibility for fighting the war to the South Vietnamese while seeking a negotiated settlement that was favorable to U.S. interests. (We discuss these Vietnamization efforts in Chapter 10.) However, the quick end wasn't meant to be. In fact, Nixon actually widened the war into Laos and Cambodia, hoping to eliminate sanctuaries for the North Vietnamese in order to place greater pressure on the North Vietnamese to agree to U.S. terms. However, the greatest effect of this move was to intensify the antiwar sentiment at home.

Although Nixon continued to reduce the number of troops and press for negotiations, the war wasn't officially over until 1973, with the fall of Saigon coming two years later. The United States lost not only the war but also the faith of many of its citizens in their government.

Fighting for Equality

Encouraged by the successes of the civil rights movement, other groups were motivated to look at their lives and work to improve them. Students pressed for free speech, and women campaigned for equal opportunities. In addition, farmworkers staged strikes and boycotts to press for better wages and working conditions, American Indians fought to reclaim their independence, and gays and lesbians worked for acceptance in American society. At the same time, however, those who preferred the good-old days also made their positions known (and had a lot of popular support) during the '60s. You can get the whole scoop on the latter four groups in Chapter 13, but we give you the basic rundown here.

Joining the student movement

University students were no longer content to accept whatever the authorities decreed — especially concerning nonacademic matters. For example, in Berkeley, students demanded the right to voice and promote their political opinions, in defiance of the administration (which was allegedly motivated by their ties to local business as well as the military-industrial complex). Because of the administration's overreaction, simple protests escalated into full-scale conflict, culminating in the protesters' occupation of Sproul Hall for three days. Eventually, with the faculty's support, the Berkeley free speech movement (FSM) achieved its goals, but by then the activist students had found another cause — protesting the Vietnam War.

With Students for a Democratic Society (SDS), the Berkeley students organized antiwar protests all over the United States. Although they didn't end the war, they made the American public more aware of what was going on in Southeast Asia and effectively forced President Johnson from office. In what was probably the fiercest antiwar protest, they demonstrated at the 1968 Democratic National Convention in Chicago (see Chapter 9). For more on the FSM, the SDS, and the ins and outs of the student movement, see Chapter 11.

Changing society's views of women

One of the groups whose protests had perhaps the farthest-reaching effect was the women's movement. In the early 1960s, most middle-class white women catered to their husbands and cared for their children, believing that domesticity was the path to their ultimate fulfillment. However, with the publication of Betty Friedan's *The Feminine Mystique* in 1963, many women began re-examining their lives and considered whether life offered more than just being housewives. Chapter 12 chronicles how the women's movement started and progressed throughout the decade.

In 1966, a group of women formed the National Organization for Women (NOW) to fight for employment opportunities and equal pay. However, the organization's focus broadened to include fighting for reproductive rights, promoting quality child-care options, opposing racism and sexism, and promoting legislation to help control domestic violence. Feminism also took a radical turn toward the end of the decade, when women objected to being looked at as sex objects, and some even decided that men were unnecessary for a satisfying life, turning to lesbianism as a viable lifestyle.

Fighting for Latino rights

Hispanics also demanded their rights. Cesar Chavez organized farmworkers to demand the right to unionize in order to get a living wage and decent working conditions. Using the nonviolent tactics promoted by Gandhi and Martin Luther King Jr., they coordinated strikes, protest marches, and a nationwide boycott on grapes, which called America's attention to the plight of farmworkers.

Rallying around American Indian issues

American Indians also rebelled against their ill treatment. Their land had been stolen, their heritage had been debased, and instead of being respected as the first Americans, they were marginalized, forced to live on the worst lands, with inferior school systems and almost no social support. To call attention to their needs, they protested with the occupation of Alcatraz Island in the San Francisco Bay from 1969 through 1971. Russell Means, who participated in the occupation of Alcatraz, founded the American Indian Movement (AIM), which continues to advocate for American Indians to this day.

Sowing the seeds for gay pride

Homosexuals also advocated for their rights during the '60s, both peacefully and militantly. Because of the women's movement as well as Alfred Kinsey's book, *Sexual Behavior in the Human Male,* the public became more aware of gays and lesbians in American society, but it took the Stonewall Riots in 1969 (when the police raided a gay bar in New York's Greenwich Village and the community retaliated) to mobilize the gay rights movement. Today, gay pride parades (oftentimes to mark the anniversary of the Stonewall Riots) take place in cities all over the United States, and gays and lesbians are recognized (if not always accepted) throughout America.

Giving voice to the silent majority

Of course, some people wanted to go back to the good-old days, when men were men, women were women, and society didn't have any shades of gray (or black or brown). The segregationists had their spokesmen, most notably Governor George Wallace of Alabama, and Bull Connor, the racist police chief of Birmingham.

Conservatives, led by intellectuals such as William F. Buckley, pragmatists, such as Barry Goldwater, and rabid right-wingers, such as Robert Welch and the John Birch Society, were also vocally opposed to government social programs, such as Johnson's Great Society. Frustrated by the civil rights movement, social programs, and the antiwar protests, the conservatives finally made their voices be heard in 1968, when Nixon and his vice president, Spiro Agnew, became the spokesmen of the "silent majority."

Living a New Way

Culturally, the '60s were also a decade of change. Hippies not only questioned conventionality but also acted out a different lifestyle, rejecting their parents' middle-class lifestyle. Fashions took daring new directions, as women's skirts became shorter, men's hair became longer, and everyone's clothes became more flamboyant. The '60s also saw an explosion of music styles, embracing folk, rock, surf, soul, and protest music. New movements emerged in the arts, and movies, theater, books, comedy, and television began to reflect the changes in society.

Creating a youth counterculture

Young people challenged everything — marriage and family, sexuality, the relevance of their education, patriotism, the evils of drugs — you name it, they questioned it and embraced alternative ways of being. Many young people rebelled against the morals and standards of the 1950s, and some adopted the hippie lifestyle. Why did they make such a drastic change? Perhaps because they thought that their parents' lives were so conformist and sterile, because they believed that materialism didn't buy happiness, or maybe because, removed from economic struggles or a world war, they just had to do something different.

Free love, long hair, tie-dye, sex, drugs, and rock 'n' roll were the most obvious signs of the lifestyle, but those characteristics were just on the surface. The love wasn't just the sexual kind; the hippies believed in sharing with their friends — whether it was food or a joint. Often hippies lived communally, whether in apartments in the Haight-Ashbury neighborhood in San Francisco or in rural communes to be closer to nature.

Hippies also wanted to expand their consciousness, and to do so, they not only experimented with marijuana and LSD but also explored different religious traditions. To a large extent, the hippies weren't interested in politics but were angry enough about the Vietnam War to join the protests in the late '60s.

Rocking to the music

Perhaps one of the greatest cultural changes of the '60s was in the field of music (see Chapter 15 for more about the '60s music scene). Although rock music started in the '50s, it took on a whole new dimension the following decade. Influenced by jazz, blues, and soul, the British Invasion influenced American music back from the other side of the pond, beginning with the Beatles in 1964. The Rolling Stones and other British groups continued to shape rock music throughout the decade.

However, other, purely American influences affected the '60s music scene as well. Folk music, the surfer sound, and Motown, which brought black music to white audiences, were widespread during the '60s. The drug culture and antiwar sentiments also affected the music — the psychedelic sound and protest songs were popular. And all these styles were heard during the huge '60s rock festivals — Monterey and Woodstock, which reflected the hopeful mood of "making love, not war," and Altamont, which showed the dark side of the hippie culture.

Stylin' in the '60s

Almost nothing remained unchanged during the '60s. Fashion revolted against the status quo of design, with women wearing miniskirts, bikinis, see-through blouses, or — on the other end of the spectrum — pantsuits. Men also broke out of their conformist fashion image; even "establishment" types added colorful clothes, with bright shirts and wide ties. Men began wearing their hair longer, and women cut theirs shorter or ironed it straight, and by the end of the decade, whites as well as blacks grew big Afros. (See Chapter 16 for more on how the '60s influenced fashion.)

Turning to entertainment

New movements in visual art, such as pop art, op art, and psychedelic art, became popular during the '60s. In the theater, although established forms of drama and musicals continued, a new show, *Hair! The American Tribal Rock-Love Musical,* reflected the hippie, antiwar culture of the late '60s. Movies also both took the traditional route and echoed the times — huge epics and historical dramas, such as *Lawrence of Arabia, Dr. Zhivago, A Man for All Seasons,* and *A Lion in Winter* were top hits, and people loved *Mary Poppins* and *The Sound of Music.* In addition, movies such as *Dr. Strangelove* and *James Bond* reflected cold war concerns, and *Bob and Carol and Ted and Alice* showed the changing sexual morality of the '60s.

But perhaps the greatest change and influence was due to television. The '60s brought events such as presidential debates, Kennedy's funeral, civil rights struggles, and the Vietnam War (as well as antiwar protests) into American living rooms. No longer did people have to visualize what was going on after reading words in a newspaper — with TV, they saw the events that occurred, almost in real time.

TV also reflected the way many people lived. By the mid- to late '60s, television started to portray blacks in similar roles as whites, women were depicted as independent and single with careers of their own, and comic and variety shows, such as *Rowan and Martin's Laugh-In* and *The Smothers Brothers Comedy Hour,* mirrored '60s fashions. (See Chapter 16 for more about popular culture and society in the decade.)

Chapter 2

Enter JFK: A New Era

In This Chapter

▶ Following JFK from the cradle to the White House

▶ Beginning the presidency by bringing hope to the nation

▶ Continuing the cold war

▶ Ending the Kennedy era

*I*n his 1961 inaugural address, President John F. Kennedy called upon a new generation of Americans to step forward and play their part in creating America's future, stating, "Ask not what your country can do for you; ask what you can do for your country." Many young Americans who were attracted to Kennedy's youth and vigor answered his call.

Following eight years of the steady though unexciting Dwight Eisenhower administration, Kennedy's election set a new tone. He promised to get America moving again through vigorous governmental activism both at home and abroad. In his inaugural address, Kennedy discussed his vision for American activism worldwide, declaring, "Let every nation know, whether it wishes us well or ill, that we shall pay any price, bear any burden, meet any hardship, support any friend, oppose any foe to assure the survival and the success of liberty." Thus the 1960s began with high expectations, or as one British journalist put it, "the politics of expectation."

Though Kennedy cultivated new expectations, many of the social problems that arose in the sixties had been developing under the surface for decades. Indeed, though many historians talk of the new era of the 1960s, it must be seen, to some extent, as a reaction to the 1950s cold war fight against the Soviet Union and the spread of Communism. Some of the most controversial and tense moments of the sixties arose in part because of ongoing inequities at home and because of entrenched assumptions of cold war ideology that defined the thinking of the age. Kennedy's call for activism helped bring social problems to the surface and initiated a decade of social turbulence.

Kennedy's youth and vigor, the brutality of his assassination, and a prevailing sense by Americans that they were robbed of a great leader who was remolding America into a revitalized nation have all contributed to the incredible

Kennedy mystique. The eternal question "What if?" lingers on regarding his life, and it's difficult to get a true assessment of America's martyred president's accomplishments. Though Kennedy's record is incomplete, he did handle some tremendous challenges. Yet his true legacy is the spirit of hope that he brought forth in America, which is nearly impossible to measure. John Kennedy will be forever young in the memories and imaginations of the American people.

Inspiring America: Kennedy and the Power of Rhetoric

In his acceptance speech at the 1960 Democratic National Convention, John F. Kennedy (see Figure 2-1) demonstrated his rhetorical power when he stated, "We stand today on the edge of a new frontier — the frontier of unknown opportunities and perils — a frontier of unfulfilled hopes and threats." As an avid fan of American history, Kennedy understood the special appeal that the idea of the frontier had always held for Americans. It suggested excitement, adventure, opportunity, and change, all of which held the promise of new hope and growth. One of Kennedy's greatest strengths was his ability to move people to action through rhetoric. The nation, having settled into the patterns of the postwar era following the end of World War II in 1945, was ready for a change.

Figure 2-1:
President
John F.
Kennedy.

*Courtesy of the Library of Congress,
Prints and Photographs Division*

Fulfilling the Kennedy family heritage: Young, rich, and Catholic

Born on May 29, 1917, and raised in Boston, Massachusetts, John F. Kennedy had a privileged childhood as the second son of one of the richest men in America, Joseph P. Kennedy. He attended the finest private schools and studied briefly at Princeton before moving on to Harvard University. Kennedy's grandfather had been the mayor of Boston, and his father had served in President Franklin Roosevelt's cabinet and later became the U.S. ambassador to Great Britain. Though Joseph Kennedy had hopes that his oldest son, Joseph Kennedy Jr., would fulfill the family heritage in politics, his son was killed during a World War II bombing mission in 1944. Thus John F. Kennedy, urged by his powerful father, became destined for a career in politics.

During World War II, Kennedy tried to join the army but was rejected because of a chronic back problem. Undaunted, Kennedy then joined the navy and served as the commander of a torpedo gunboat. During the war, Kennedy distinguished himself in combat and became a hero by rescuing a wounded sailor after a Japanese destroyer rammed his PT boat. His record as a war hero would serve him well in his future political life.

Kennedy entered politics shortly after World War II ended, following a family history of political service in the Democratic Party. Running on his record as a war hero, Kennedy easily beat his Republican rival in 1946 and was elected to the U.S. House of Representatives at the age of 29. As a Congressman, Kennedy was reelected in 1948 and again in 1950. In 1952 Kennedy ran for the U.S. Senate against a powerful Republican incumbent named Henry Cabot Lodge Jr. Under his father's guidance, Kennedy built up his reputation with a well-financed and engineered public relations campaign and ultimately beat Lodge by a very narrow margin.

As a senator, Kennedy continued to hone his political savvy and rhetorical skills. But he suffered a major setback when he became hospitalized with further back troubles in 1954. Suffering from Addison's disease, Kennedy spent the next two years in and out of the hospital. While spending so much time in bed, Kennedy had his aide, Theodore Sorenson, ghostwrite his famous book, *Profiles in Courage,* which expressed his admiration for politicians who risked their careers to pursue ethical goals. The book earned Kennedy the Pulitzer Prize and national acclaim.

As Kennedy struggled with his health problems, he also found time to think deeply on his political beliefs, coming up with the central ideas that would become his political platform in the 1960 presidential race. Returning to the Senate after his back improved, Kennedy began to shape his political destiny by calling for civil rights legislation, improved funding for education, healthcare for the elderly, urban renewal, a stronger military, a space program, and a plan to contain the spread of Communism worldwide. In 1957 Kennedy became a member of the Senate Foreign Relations Committee, where he supported the further development of U.S. nuclear missile technology and economic aid to third-world countries as a means of stopping the spread of Communism. This early experience with foreign policy shaped his views on the subject that he later dealt with as president.

Joining the 1960 presidential race

When Kennedy entered the presidential race in 1958, he faced several problems. His opponent, Eisenhower's vice president, Richard M. Nixon, was much more well known and had enjoyed a rapid rise to power in the Republican Party. Though Kennedy had entered politics in 1946, the same year as Nixon, Nixon was much more successful in gaining his party's attention because of his aggressive tactics. Solidly probusiness and anti-Communist, Nixon had built a powerful reputation as a fierce and sometimes savage opponent (see Chapter 4 for more on his take-no-prisoner approach to politics). His aggressive style served him well, and by 1950 Nixon was one of the most requested Republican speakers in the country. His reward was to be selected as Dwight D. Eisenhower's vice presidential candidate in 1952.

Thus, by 1960, Nixon was older, more experienced, and more well known than Kennedy. Further, serving as Eisenhower's vice president for eight years, he campaigned as Eisenhower's heir who would continue the policies of the popular president. Yet Eisenhower himself wasn't very supportive of Nixon's presidential aspirations.

When asked by the press which major policy decisions Nixon had helped create during his tenure as vice president, Eisenhower sarcastically retorted, "If you give me a week, I might think of one."

Kennedy's other challenges were that he was young and Catholic. But he successfully turned his age into a powerful asset by practicing "new politics," emphasizing his style, personality, and youthful charisma over issues of policy. And recognizing that some Americans feared that a Catholic president could result in the pope ruling the country, Kennedy handled concerns about his faith with forceful candor. Speaking before the Houston Ministerial Association in 1960, Kennedy directly addressed the role of his faith as president, telling the Protestant crowd that he believed that the separation of church and state in America was absolute and that "no Catholic prelate would tell the president — should he be a Catholic — how to act and no Protestant minister should tell his parishioners for whom to vote."

The Kennedy-Nixon debates: Politics in the television age

Kennedy benefited from Richard Nixon's decision to debate with him on television. Though many have criticized Nixon for agreeing to appear with his less prominent opponent, the technology was new, and an opportunity to reach many more people was very enticing. Some 70 million Americans watched the first-ever televised debate, and many were moved by what they saw.

Nixon, who had just been released from the hospital, still suffered from a bad knee infection and thus looked sickly. He perspired heavily under the hot studio lights; his skin looked pale and his face unshaven, showing his perpetual five o'clock shadow. By contrast, Kennedy looked vigorous, calm, cool, and collected as he gave crisp answers to the questions. Kennedy won the debate, and as polls showed, his popularity rose immediately afterward. The power of image was demonstrated as most people who watched TV concluded that Kennedy had won, but most of those who had listened to the debate on the radio concluded it was a victory for Nixon.

The narrowest of victories

During the campaign, Kennedy recognized that his support for civil rights would cost him votes in the South, where racial discrimination was the norm, and he sought to offset the loss by wooing black voters. Thus, when Martin Luther King Jr. and 50 other protestors were arrested in Atlanta for trespassing at an all-white restaurant, Kennedy intervened on King's behalf by calling the judge in the case and persuading him to release King. Kennedy also chose his vice president well, selecting Lyndon B. Johnson from Texas, who had a reputation for his ability to get legislation passed in Congress.

When the election was complete, Kennedy had edged out Nixon by only 118,574 votes out of the 68 million votes cast. Though the electoral vote was a clear win for Kennedy, 303 to 219, this margin didn't show just how close the vote had been in many states. The popular vote was 49.7 percent for Kennedy to 49.6 percent for Nixon. Kennedy narrowly won by pulling together a coalition of diverse segments of the Democratic Party.

Exploring Camelot

At the age of 43, Kennedy was the youngest person ever elected president. The inaugural ceremonies set the tone for his presidency, with a theme of youthful enthusiasm and vigorous promise. Kennedy was handsome and charismatic, and his wife, Jackie, was glamorous and beautiful. Together they would define the Kennedy style. Kennedy's Harvard education and his robust ambition and enthusiasm made many people feel that the era was exciting and new. Though he was plagued with health problems, he concealed them from the public. Kennedy seemed strong and powerful, creating a feeling of optimism that had been sorely missed due to the fears of the cold war world.

Kennedy's youth, vigor, and style created a feeling that almost anything was possible. As president he was eager to begin addressing the problems of the country. The young fresh faces that Kennedy chose for his cabinet and advisors suggested a real change from Eisenhower's more conservative group of wise old men. Kennedy created a "politics of optimism" by calling on young Americans to step up to the challenge of leadership in America. He found a focus for his domestic policies in his theme of the New Frontier, which suggested opportunity and potential. His New Frontier program promised to "get America moving again" by stimulating economic growth through the manipulation of fiscal policy.

Filling the White House with glamour

The Kennedys brought a new vitality to the White House. (Figure 2-2 shows the glamour couple.) Youthful, idealistic, attractive, and with a young family (siblings John Jr. and Caroline), they were easy for many Americans to relate to. Eisenhower, Truman, and Roosevelt seemed old by comparison, often coming across as fatherly or grandfatherly in demeanor. Yet Kennedy and his wife seemed to many people like members of their own generation, creating the impression that when he spoke of the nation and said "we," all Americans were part of that "we."

The origins of the Camelot connection

The Kennedy years have often been referred to as "the years of Camelot." Though this yearning for a return to some golden era has been deeply idealized because of Kennedy's assassination, the idea has a connection to his life. The popular Broadway musical *Camelot* opened on December 3, 1960, and became an immediate success. Its popularity was in part due to the stars, such as Julie Andrews, Richard Burton, and Robert Goulet. Frederick Loewe composed the music, and Alan Jay Lerner, a Harvard classmate and friend of Kennedy, wrote the lyrics and book. According to Jackie, the title tune, *Camelot*, was a favorite of the president, and they had regarded it as an unofficial theme of his administration. In an interview with *Life* magazine a few days after Kennedy's assassination, Jackie stated, "I'm so ashamed of myself — all I keep thinking of is this line from a musical comedy." According to Jackie, President Kennedy had loved the tale of the Knights of the Round Table from early childhood and favored an idealistic view of history replete with heroes. Linking JFK with Camelot, Jackie Kennedy remarked, "There'll be great presidents again . . . but there'll never be another Camelot."

Figure 2-2:
Kennedy style at Buckingham Palace: Prince Philip, Jackie Kennedy, Queen Elizabeth, and President Kennedy.

©Bettmann/CORBIS

The fact that the Kennedy clan had been poor immigrants only three generations before gave hope to many blue-collar workers and immigrants. The Kennedys embodied the American dream and made many feel that much was possible. When Jackie gave an interview, her answers to questions seemed like responses that many young Americans might give, instead of coming across as motherly or condescending. Yet Kennedy's professional manner and his self-confidence also appealed to many in the older generation. The sense of glamour grew as the first couple threw glittering social parties attended by Nobel Prize winners, artists, musicians, intellectuals, and movie stars. The Kennedys filled the White House with a sense of energy, exuberance, and excitement.

Recruiting Kennedy's "whiz kids"

Another aspect that set the Kennedy administration apart was his selection of cabinet members and advisors. Kennedy surrounded himself with people of talent. He wanted the best and brightest in his administration, people who would create a tough, pragmatic, thoughtful, and vigorous government that could take on any problems. Accordingly, his staff comprised 15 Rhodes Scholars and several famous authors. When picking his national security people, Kennedy chose a team of the best minds around: a proud, tough-minded bunch of self-proclaimed "hard-nosed realists" and World War II veterans. He recruited both people he knew personally and those he learned about through their successes:

✔ **Secretary of State Dean Rusk:** Rusk had distinguished himself in the State Department.

✔ **Secretary of Defense Robert McNamara:** McNamara was the first president of the Ford Motor Company who wasn't a member of the Ford family. He was one of the new, young whiz kids who embraced the latest in technology.

- ✔ **Attorney General Robert Kennedy:** The only controversial appointment that Kennedy made was appointing his own brother, Robert, to be the attorney general, because it was the first time a president had appointed a brother to his cabinet.

- ✔ **Secretary of the Treasury C. Douglas Dillon:** A Republican banker, Dillon was appointed secretary of the Treasury in a move designed to reassure conservative business owners.

- ✔ **Press Secretary Pierre Salinger:** Salinger had established his career in journalism, coming to the attention of Robert Kennedy after his series of articles on Jimmy Hoffa.

- ✔ **National Security Advisor McGeorge Bundy:** Bundy was a Harvard political-science professor. His brother, William Bundy, also served as a Kennedy advisor and was one of the architects of the Vietnam War.

- ✔ **White House Historian and Advisor Arthur Schlesinger Jr.:** This famed Pulitzer Prize–winning historian became one of Kennedy's speechwriters and advisors.

- ✔ **Undersecretary of State George Ball:** Ball was one of the more experienced men on the Kennedy team. His past work at the Farm Credit Administration, the Treasury Department, the Land Lease Administration, and the World War II Strategic Bombing Survey all prepped him for his role as U.S. Undersecretary of State.

Pushing New Frontier domestic policies

The expansive vision of leadership and service that Kennedy brought to the White House ran into difficulty at home. The lack of a clear mandate from his election hampered Kennedy from the start. He couldn't rally enough public support for the domestic agenda of his New Frontier program. A conservative alliance of southern Democrats and Republicans killed much of his legislation regarding societal reform. This conservative coalition blocked Kennedy's efforts to increase federal aid for education, to create Medicare to provide health insurance for the elderly, and to create a department of urban affairs. The Senate crushed his initiatives on unemployed youth, migrant workers, and mass transit systems.

Meeting with mixed results

In the spring of 1962, U.S. steel firms implemented major price increases after the steel unions accepted modest pay raises. Angered over the predicted effects of such a move in a society already suffering from economic recession, Kennedy lashed out publicly against the steel firms, stating that their decisions promoted private power and profit over the needs of the public.

The president pressed for congressional intervention, ultimately forcing the steel mills to make some concessions on prices. This soured relations between Kennedy and big business, because of business resentments over government interference. In May after the crisis ended, the stock market plunged in the greatest drop since the Depression. Kennedy received the blame for the decline.

Kennedy did, however, score a few victories in Congress. He succeeded in passing a modest increase in the minimum wage. His Housing Act also passed, providing about $5 billion over four years for public housing, urban renewal projects, and community development. Congress passed an increase in Social Security benefits, funds for sewage treatment plants, and loans to redevelop distressed areas. Kennedy's greatest legislative victory was the passing of the Trade Expansion Act of 1962, which led to tariff reductions averaging 35 percent between the U.S. and the European Common Market.

Funding space travel

One program that won congressional support was a vast increase in spending for the National Aeronautics and Space Administration (NASA). Following the Soviet Union's success with *Sputnik I,* the world's first satellite, in 1957, the U.S. had created the Mercury space program. With the space race on, American popular interest rose as well. Though the Russians launched the first man into space, Yuri Gagarin in April 1961, the U.S. matched the feat one month later when Alan Shepard became the first American in space. Then, beating the Soviets to the next milestone, U.S. astronaut John Glenn manned the first space mission to orbit Earth in February 1962. (Check out Glenn and Kennedy in Figure 2-3.) American interest in space reached new heights when Kennedy proposed that the nation challenge itself to land a man on the moon within the decade. Though Kennedy never lived to see it, NASA accomplished just that in 1969 (see Chapter 4).

Figure 2-3:
President Kennedy with astronaut John Glenn in Cocoa Beach, Florida.

COCOA BEACH PARADE

Courtesy of NASA

Expanding the boundaries of the frontier

Kennedy's New Frontier extended beyond his domestic policies to include a variety of international outreach efforts. International aid and nation-building programs also fulfilled the need to continue improving the United States' international stature as the leading capitalist nation. The focus was to promote capitalism and keep struggling nations from falling under the influence of the Soviet Union, which also supplied aid for the same reasons.

Spearheading the Peace Corps

One of the first opportunities for Americans to participate in creating this extended New Frontier was the Peace Corps. Created in 1961 and headed by Kennedy's brother-in-law, Sargent Shriver, the Peace Corps embodied the call to public service that Kennedy had announced in his inaugural address. Thousands of men and women, most with college educations, eagerly went to third-world nations to help build water systems, roads and bridges, hospitals, and schools, all designed to spread democracy and ensure that troubled nations remained within the American camp and away from Communist influence. As such, this group was an important tool in the cold war struggle.

Cutting taxes with Keynesian economics

As Kennedy sought a solution to the economic recession started under Eisenhower, he began to shift his stance on a balanced budget. Though formerly committed to a balanced budget, Kennedy began to listen to his more liberal advisors, who suggested a Keynesian approach to economic growth.

John Maynard Keynes was one of the most important figures in the history of economics. His basic idea was simple and straightforward. In order to keep up the employment rate to protect and promote consumer demand, a government should undertake deficit spending. Though it appeared counterintuitive to spend money that it didn't have, the reality was that by spending, the government could stimulate growth and avoid the dangerous cycle of less investment, leading to more layoffs, which led to even less demand and further layoffs. The growth created by the spending would generate greater tax revenues that could be used to pay off the debt created by the deficit spending. Thus the idea is that a government could spend its way out of a depression.

Over the summer of 1962 Kennedy's advisors finally convinced him to give this theory a try. Kennedy proposed a $13.5 billion cut in corporate taxes over a three-year period. Ironically, conservatives refused to accept the basic theory that budget cuts would stimulate growth. Foes of the plan kept it within the committee, where it died before coming to a vote by the full Congress.

Providing aid to developing countries

As a part of the same thrust by which he created the Peace Corps, Kennedy pushed for economic aid to developing countries. The State Department's Agency for International Development distributed foreign aid to third-world nations, including surplus agricultural products distributed through the Food for Peace program. In Latin America, the Alliance for Progress provided money for food, medicine, education, and housing. America was reaching out to help shape the world in the ways Americans thought it should develop.

Supporting the civil rights movement

Some of the most important developments of the 1960s occurred in civil rights. Pressure for change regarding segregation laws had mounted in the 15 years following the end of World War II. When Kennedy became president, his margin of victory was so slim that he was reluctant to alienate any segment of the Democratic Party. Fearing a loss of support among southern Democrats, Kennedy took a cautious approach to the growing civil rights movement. Yet over time, as it became clear that the civil rights movement held widespread support in the black community, Kennedy began to shift his views and undertook active support of the movement.

Acknowledging statewide protests

The civil rights movement began to shift into high gear in 1960 when four black college students in Greensboro, North Carolina, staged the first sit-in at a Woolworth's lunch counter (see Chapter 6). Because many restaurants refused to serve blacks, young men and women undertook sit-ins as peaceful protest against the discrimination. Young people simply sat down at lunch counters and waited for service that never came. It was a move to attain the moral high ground while generating sympathy for the cause. When the story hit the press, it motivated others to join similar protests. Within a week, six more towns in North Carolina had sit-ins, and within two months, sit-in demonstrations had spread to 54 cities in 9 states.

In 1963, Martin Luther King Jr. organized a series of nonviolent protests in Birmingham, Alabama. Television, which had made such an impact in the Nixon-Kennedy debates (see that section earlier in this chapter), again made a difference as televised coverage of the protests showed reasonable, compliant young blacks being attacked by police dogs, shocked with cattle prods, sprayed with fire hoses, and hit with tear gas. The American public was uncomfortable with images that affected them in ways that print media couldn't match. Kennedy himself, prodded by his brother Robert, concluded that simply enforcing the existing statutes wasn't enough; new legislation was needed to address the situation.

In 1963 Kennedy told the nation that racial discrimination "has no place in American life or law." Kennedy threw his support behind a civil rights bill aimed at ending segregation in schools and discrimination at public facilities. Southern Democrats quickly blocked the bill from coming to a vote.

Watching the movement sweep the nation

Kennedy took the issue to the American public on June 11, 1963, when he stated: "If an American, because his skin is black, cannot enjoy the full and free life which all of us want, then who among us would be content to have the color of his skin changed and stand in his place? Who among us would be content with the counsels of patience and delay?" Kennedy empowered the Justice Department, which his brother, Attorney General Robert Kennedy led, to implement desegregation with federal authority. Many blacks hailed Kennedy's speech as a "second Emancipation Proclamation."

The same night of Kennedy's historic speech, the president of the Mississippi chapter of the NAACP, Medgar Evers, was gunned down. Evers's assassination accelerated the already powerful civil rights movement onto the national stage. On August 28, 1963, 250,000 black and white demonstrators met for a rally at the Lincoln Memorial in Washington, D.C. Here, Martin Luther King Jr. gave his most famous and memorable "I have a dream" speech to the gathered crowd. Television coverage of the event displayed the power and eloquence of King's speech. Yet of even greater impact was the image of blacks and whites together at the protest, showing the nation that the issue was a moral crusade and not a split between white and black Americans. (We cover all the key events of 1963 in detail in Chapter 6.)

In September 1963, a Baptist church in Birmingham was bombed on a Sunday morning, instantly killing four little girls and injuring numerous others. The stalled investigation and the continued racial violence served to push the civil rights movement forward, yet Kennedy wouldn't live to see it to fruition, as he was assassinated only two months after the Birmingham bombing.

Fighting in the Cold War

Though his New Frontier platform contained a long list of domestic social reforms, Kennedy was also deeply interested in foreign affairs. Throughout the 1960s the cold war loomed ominously in the background; its presence shaped the options and decisions of America's leaders. The fear of a cataclysmic nuclear war was ever present and dominated thinking in regard to foreign policy. Though the United States and the Soviet Union were locked in a dangerous competition over which government system should be allowed to shape the world, direct confrontation was too frightening to consider. Thus the cold war was fought through a long series of *proxy wars,* in which the U.S. backed one side and the Soviets backed the other, yet the two superpowers never fought each other directly.

HISTORIC TRIVIA

The Green Beret

The distinctive hat worn by the U.S. Army Special Forces units was originally designed by Special Forces Major Herbert Brucker in 1953. Though the army refused to authorize its use, Special Forces soldiers began to use the distinctive "green beanie" for field exercises. When President Kennedy visited Fort Bragg in October 1961, he approved of the special headgear, noting that the Special Forces had a unique mission within the military and thus it was appropriate for them to have a special symbol to distinguish them from the rest of the military. The army acquiesced, and the Green Beret has become the recognized symbol for and common name of the U.S. Special Forces Units.

TECHNICAL STUFF

Proxy wars of the cold war era included wars in Korea, Vietnam, Angola, Nicaragua, and Afghanistan. Often the U.S. or the U.S.S.R. would fight directly in the conflict, yet never against the other superpower. For example, the U.S. fought in Vietnam, but the North Vietnamese received arms, supplies, and logistical assistance from the U.S.S.R. The opposite was true in the war in Afghanistan in the 1980s, when the Soviets sent troops into Afghanistan and the U.S. provided arms, supplies, and logistical support to the Afghani mujahedin.

The need to stand up to the Soviets without directly fighting them with troops created a fierce arms race. During the 1960 campaign, Kennedy campaigned on the needs to strengthen the U.S. military and to address the *missile gap* — the idea that the U.S. was falling behind the Soviet Union in the race to create a nuclear arsenal. Yet after Kennedy was elected, he found the missile gap to be a myth.

Kennedy believed in the cold war policy of containment as a means to stop the spread of Communism. In contrast to Eisenhower's "New Look" policy, which emphasized using nuclear weapons at the expense of conventional weapons, Kennedy's defense strategy was based on his concept of *flexible response,* which focused on deterring all wars, conventional and nuclear. As part of this new strategy, Kennedy immediately began making large budget requests for expanding the conventional military forces. The flexible response strategy was designed to deter any direct attacks by the Soviet Union. To prepare for the complications inherent in the wars of national liberation that were arising in some third-world countries, Kennedy chose the military doctrine of *counterinsurgency,* which focused on training foreign governments to win local guerrilla wars. The U.S. Special Forces, often called the Green Berets, were formed based upon this strategy and began creating and testing counterinsurgency techniques.

Attempting to overthrow Castro: The Bay of Pigs fiasco

When Kennedy took office, he also discovered that the CIA was training Cuban émigrés to invade Cuba as part of ongoing operations designed to dislodge Fidel Castro as leader of Cuba (check out Castro in Figure 2-4). In 1960, during the last year of the Eisenhower administration, the CIA actively worked to find a way to undermine Castro, who had taken control of Cuba in 1959 and launched a campaign against U.S. control in Cuba and influence in Latin America. The charismatic leader promised Cubans he would break their economic dependency on the U.S. and reduce American influence in Cuba overall by restructuring Cuba both economically and politically as a Communist nation, which would better meet the needs of the Cuban people. As economic relations soured in 1960, Castro increasingly accepted help from the Soviet Union.

Figure 2-4:
Fidel Castro.

©Roger-Viollet/Topham/The Image Works

Plotting Castro's demise: Let me count the ways

In 1960, the CIA under Eisenhower began to make plans to discredit or assassinate Castro. In 1960 alone, records show that the CIA concocted a variety of plans, ranging from the absurd to the deadly. A few examples include

- ✔ Spraying Castro's broadcast studio with a chemical that would produce similar effects to having taken LSD

- ✔ Coating his shoes with thallium salt, a powerful depilatory that would cause his hair and beard to fall out

> ✔ Treating a box of Castro's favorite cigars with the deadly botulinum toxin
>
> ✔ Attempting to hire Cuban underworld assassins
>
> ✔ Developing poison pills designed to dissolve in Castro's drink

Though some of the plans were discarded for their absurdity, others were attempted, but none of them worked. By January 1961, President Eisenhower, in the very last days of his administration, broke U.S. diplomatic relations with Cuba over the growing alliance between Castro and the Soviet Union. As Kennedy entered the White House, he inherited a situation of growing importance and shrinking options.

Invading Cuba: The Bay of Pigs

Operation Mongoose was the name of the Eisenhower administration's plan to train and equip 1,500 Cuban nationals to invade Cuba and initiate the revolution that would sweep Castro from power. The idea was that Cubans would rally to the cause and spontaneously rise up against Castro after the invasion began. The invasion was scheduled for April 1961, three months after Kennedy became president. He was briefed on the operation and approved it, not wanting to appear weak against the spread of Communism.

Part of the plan was to have "Cuban" bombers, supported by fighter planes in on the action. The bombers had been U.S. military equipment before they'd been given to the anti-Castro revolutionary movement. The fighter planes were from the U.S.S. Essex aircraft carrier. U.S. "civilian pilots" were to fly the fighters, which had all U.S. insignia painted over.

The April 17, 1961 invasion was an operational disaster. The unmarked U.S. support fighters from the Essex arrived an hour earlier than the bombers, due to a misunderstanding over which time zone was used to coordinate the attack. With no bombers to support, the U.S. planes withdrew. When the bombers arrived an hour later, two were immediately shot down by Castro's air force. The 1,500 Cuban commandos hit the beach at the Bay of Pigs with no air cover and suffered tremendous losses from the Cuban planes. At this point, U.S. military commanders urged Kennedy to send in U.S. air support, yet Kennedy refused because it had become clear by that point that mission was a failure.

What a failure it was. The Cuban people hadn't spontaneously risen against Castro. Some 1,100 men were captured, and the United States was exposed to the world attempting to overthrow a sovereign government. Some people faulted Kennedy for going along with such a reckless plan in the first place, while others faulted him for not having enough courage to send in the U.S. planes to support the ground invasion. Either way, America's young president didn't get off to an auspicious start. His first attempt to stand up to the Soviet menace was a clear failure.

Watching the Berlin Wall go up

Two months after the Bay of Pigs fiasco, Kennedy met Soviet leader Nikita Khrushchev in Vienna, Austria. The meeting was set to discuss the future of Berlin, which had been divided and jointly occupied by Soviet and U.S. Allied forces since the end of World War II. The issue was a sore spot for the Soviets, because some 2.6 million Germans had fled into the U.S.-controlled sector of the city to escape life under the Communist system. In this tense meeting, Khrushchev attempted to intimidate Kennedy into withdrawing from Berlin by issuing him an ultimatum, but Kennedy held his ground, and the two men didn't achieve a permanent solution.

When he returned to the U.S., Kennedy desired to show his resolve to the Soviets. He therefore asked Congress for an additional $3 billion in defense appropriations and called up National Guard and Reserve units. His reaction worked, as the Soviets chose not to escalate the situation and instead solved their problem by erecting the Berlin Wall around West Berlin, sealing off the East German escape hatch. The wall was 96 miles long and 12 feet high, topped with barbed wire. The Soviets also set up machine gun emplacements to discourage any further attempts at escape. The wall became a powerful symbol of the tensions of the cold war.

Managing the Cuban Missile Crisis

In the year following the Bay of Pigs disaster, Fidel Castro worked to strengthen his country's ties to the Soviet Union. Castro's support for Communist revolution in Latin America continued to make him a thorn in the side of U.S. policymakers. Because of this tension, both Castro and Khrushchev believed that a U.S. invasion of Cuba was only a matter of time. In May 1962, Soviet military personnel completed their plans for a nuclear missile defense of Cuba. The plan also called for Russian technicians and 42,000 Russian troops. Khrushchev's decision to place nuclear missiles in Cuba was based on several objectives:

- ✔ Deter an American invasion of Cuba.

- ✔ Keep Cuba, which had been building relations with China, within the Soviet sphere of influence.

- ✔ Give the Soviets greater leverage to bargain with the U.S. over the still uncertain future of the divided city of Berlin.

- ✔ Balance the U.S. nuclear missiles that had been deployed to Turkey in early 1962.

Castro, of course, wanted the missiles to serve as a deterrent against further U.S. military action against Cuba. Though Castro wanted to make the missile agreement public immediately, Khrushchev opted to keep it a secret until the missiles were fully operational. He knew that the reaction from America would be shock and outrage. But he figured that operational missiles would deter any U.S military response out of fear of starting a nuclear exchange. Because his missiles were only 90 miles from the U.S. coast, they'd be able to hit targets across the East Coast and throughout most of the Midwest.

Soviet plans called for the deployment of 24 medium-range R-12 ballistic missiles and 16 intermediate-range R-14 ballistic missiles, all equipped with nuclear warheads.

Spying on the Soviets

Following the Bay of Pigs fiasco, the CIA continued to closely monitor Cuba, looking for any opportunity to oust Castro. On September 21, 1962, the Defense Intelligence Agency (DIA) reported that one of its assets had sighted a truck convoy carrying 20 missile-shaped objects, each 65 to 70 feet long. The U.S. government knew that the Soviets were setting up defensive surface-to-air missiles (SAMs), but this sighting raised the possibility of a more ominous situation. On October 9, Kennedy approved an overflight of a U-2 spy plane to investigate the report. Heavy cloud cover delayed the flight until October 14, and by then a leak about the possible missiles had occurred, allowing Republican senator Kenneth Keating to announce that he had evidence of six nuclear missile sites in Cuba.

The October 14 U-2 flight lasted six minutes and produced 928 photographs that revealed clear evidence of Soviet missile sites. Upon seeing the photos the following morning, Kennedy called a meeting of his Executive Committee (ExComm) on national security. Thirteen men were present at this meeting with the president, including Vice President Lyndon Johnson, Attorney General Robert Kennedy, Secretary of State Dean Rusk, Secretary of Defense Robert McNamara, CIA Director Marshall Carter, several undersecretaries, General Maxwell Taylor, and several aerial photography experts. After reviewing the evidence and weighing the implications, ExComm outlined options for a U.S. response. By the end of the meeting, Kennedy decided that the U.S. had to get rid of the missiles. The group had created four options, each with different advantages and risks:

- ✔ An air strike against the missile sites in Cuba

- ✔ A wider air strike against a variety of targets in Cuba

- ✔ A naval blockade of Cuba to stop the arrival of any more Russian missiles and supplies

- ✔ An invasion of Cuba

Kennedy adjourned the meeting to allow his advisors to develop a plan for each option. On October 18, the committee met again to discuss new photographic evidence showing five separate missile sites, including the launch pads for nuclear missiles. This evidence convinced the military leaders to call for a full-scale invasion of Cuba, yet other voices such as McNamara and former U.S. ambassador to the Soviet Union Llewelyn Thompson urged Kennedy to seek a diplomatic solution before turning to military options. Kennedy agreed with McNamara and Thompson, fearing that failure to attempt a diplomatic solution would make any unannounced air strikes similar to Japan's 1941 attack at Pearl Harbor.

The meeting on October 18 didn't rule out military action, yet it did establish that some sort of blockade and diplomatic attempt would be necessary before resorting to military options. One of the grave concerns was that an invasion of Cuba could set off a Soviet seizure of Berlin, which could escalate into a nuclear exchange in which there would be no clear winner.

Taking a diplomatic approach

Kennedy continued to consult quietly with a variety of U.S. leaders, including former presidents Hoover, Truman, and Eisenhower. On Monday, October 22, Kennedy addressed congressional leaders first and then went on television to announce the crisis to the American people. Watched by over 100 million Americans, Kennedy explained that the Soviet Union had created a nuclear strike capability in Cuba that could hit U.S. East Coast cities. Kennedy went on to condemn the Soviets for lying about supplying Cuba with only defensive weapons.

The president explained that the U.S. couldn't tolerate such a threat and that he had ordered Navy ships in the waters around Cuba to begin a quarantine blocking further Soviet ships from reaching the island. Kennedy demanded that the Soviets remove the missiles immediately, stating that failure to do so would result in U.S. military action against Cuba. Finally, Kennedy stated that "it shall be the policy of this nation to regard any nuclear missile launched from Cuba against any nation in the Western Hemisphere as an attack by the Soviet Union on the United States, requiring a full retaliatory response upon the Soviet Union." Americans who remember the Cuban Missile Crisis recall that they expected that they could die within a week.

Khrushchev's response stated that Kennedy's actions represented a "serious threat to peace" and that the U.S. quarantine was a "gross violation of . . . international norms." Khrushchev warned Kennedy that his reckless actions could lead to "the catastrophe of thermonuclear war." By October 24, Kennedy and his advisors felt that they were on the brink of a tremendous catastrophe. The U.S. military had been moved to Defense Condition 2, the last stage of readiness before all-out war. The lack of clear response from

Khrushchev left them still divided between immediately using military force and continuing to delay in order to keep diplomatic negotiations open.

The problem was that each passing day brought the missiles one day closer to being fully operational. Further, they were on the verge of the first test of the quarantine just as Soviet freighters with submarine escorts were approaching the U.S. Navy quarantine line.

Concluding the crisis

The first major break in the crisis came amidst a tense ExComm meeting on October 24 when news arrived from naval intelligence that the Soviet ships had turned back and weren't attempting to cross the quarantine line. Though the Soviets had backed down, the crisis wasn't over until the missiles were removed.

The next day, Kennedy and Khrushchev exchanged harsh letters, each accusing the other of escalating the situation. As a dozen Soviet ships turned around and started back to the Soviet Union, the issue of the existing missiles remained unresolved. On October 26, in a long and rambling letter to Kennedy, Khrushchev proposed that both sides step back from the brink of destruction. He offered to remove the Soviet missiles from Cuba if the U.S. would pledge to not invade or support any invasion of Cuba. The next day, a more polished letter from Khrushchev arrived with the same proposal, yet with an added demand that the U.S. withdraw its 17 Jupiter missiles deployed in Turkey. That same afternoon a Russian surface-to-air missile hit an American U-2 spy plane over Cuba, downing the plane and killing the U.S. pilot. The Joint Chiefs again pressed for a military response, yet Kennedy still held on to hope in terms of Khrushchev's olive branch.

Kennedy sent word to Khrushchev that he would promise not to invade Cuba in exchange for Soviet withdrawal of their missiles in Cuba. He didn't mention the U.S. missiles in Turkey in his response, yet he sent a private message to Khrushchev stating that he would be willing to remove the Jupiter missiles after four or five months had passed, to avoid the criticism that the U.S. had abandoned Turkey because of Soviet pressure. (The U.S. decision to remove the missiles was made easier because submarine-launched Polaris nuclear missiles could perform the same function.) The Soviets would have to agree to keep the Jupiter missile deal a secret, or the U.S. would withdraw the offer. In this secret communication, Kennedy warned Khrushchev that he needed a response within 24 hours, because he feared that with the Cubans shooting at U.S. planes, the situation could spin out of control.

Khrushchev discussed the situation with the Soviet Presidium (the governmental body of the U.S.S.R.) and concluded that accepting Kennedy's agreement was in the best interests of the Soviet Union and world peace. Khrushchev broadcast his acceptance over Soviet radio on October 28. He made no mention of the Jupiter missile deal, and the U.S. quietly withdrew the missiles a few months later as promised. The Cuban Missile Crisis was over. Kennedy had steered a difficult path between standing firm and knowing when to negotiate. Most historians today agree that these 13 days in October mark the most dangerous moment of the whole cold war.

In the wake of the crisis, the U.S. and the Soviet Union worked to ease the tension and avert future possible confrontations. The U.S. agreed to sell excess wheat to the Soviet Union, and a hot line was established between Washington, D.C., and Moscow. Further, the U.S. also removed its Jupiter missiles from Italy and Britain.

Easing tension: The 1963 Limited Test Ban Treaty

In the summer of 1963, Kennedy announced that the U.S. was participating in direct talks with the Soviet Union aimed at reducing cold war tensions. Concluded in July and formalized in September, the 1963 Limited Test Ban Treaty was an agreement to end above-ground testing of nuclear weapons. Though it didn't end underground nuclear tests, it was nonetheless a step in the right direction.

Entering the quagmire: The growing U.S. commitment to South Vietnam

When Kennedy took office in 1961, U.S. commitment to South Vietnam had already been well established (for details, see Chapter 8). Cold war fears had driven the U.S. to support the French after World War II until their defeat in 1954. After the collapse of the French, the U.S. actively supported the independent government of South Vietnam. By the time Kennedy entered the White House, the U.S. had already spent about $1.5 billion supporting South Vietnam and had over 700 advisors in the country assisting in building their army.

Under Kennedy, the U.S. commitment to the region grew exponentially. By 1963, the U.S. had 16,000 men in South Vietnam. Kennedy, ever fearing Republican taunts of being weak on Communism, oversaw this U.S. expansion, trying new counterinsurgency techniques designed by U.S. Special Forces troops. (For details, see Chapter 8.) No one knows just how far

Kennedy would've taken the U.S. into the Vietnam conflict, because his life was cut short by assassins' bullets that November. The major ground and air war would fall to Lyndon Johnson.

In September 1963, Kennedy publicly declared that the South Vietnamese would win or lose the war themselves and the U.S. role would be advisory. In October, he announced his intention to withdraw American forces from Vietnam by the end of 1965. This proclamation has prompted a dispute among historians today. Some argue that Kennedy had seen the coming quagmire and was attempting to pull back from it, but others maintain that it was a political maneuver and had no bearing on Kennedy's long-term plans for Vietnam. Without the emergence of any new evidence, this difference of opinion will continue without resolution, much like the dispute over who killed John F. Kennedy.

Detailing a Fateful Day in Dallas

Though his first two and a half years in office were tumultuous, Kennedy still looked forward to reelection in 1964. He went to Dallas on November 22, 1963, in an attempt to help heal some of the rifts in the Texas Democratic Party; he knew he needed to win Texas as part of his reelection strategy. As Kennedy and his wife rode through the parade route in Dallas in an open convertible, Kennedy was shot in the head and neck by a sniper. He died 30 minutes later at Parkland Hospital.

Capturing a suspect

Within hours of Kennedy's death, the story broke that Kennedy's assassin, a 24-year-old loner named Lee Harvey Oswald, had been captured. The press reported that Oswald, a lone gunman, had shot the president from the sixth floor window of the Texas Book Repository and then successfully fled the building. He was later confronted by a Dallas police officer, whom Oswald shot and killed. After he was caught, Oswald was held incommunicado for almost two days.

While in custody, Oswald persistently proclaimed his innocence, asserting that he was the patsy of the assassination. Oswald's history itself is somewhat bizarre — he served as a U.S. Marine and then lived in the Soviet Union for three years before returning to the United States with a Russian wife. The mystery of who shot JFK grew deeper when, two days after the assassination, Oswald was gunned down at point-blank range while in custody of the Dallas police (see Figure 2-5). The man who gunned him down was Jack Ruby, a Dallas nightclub owner with ties to the Mafia.

Figure 2-5:
Jack Ruby
shoots
Kennedy
assassin
Lee Harvey
Oswald on
November
24, 1963.

©Topham/The Image Works

Deliberating on the assassin: The Warren Commission

Lyndon B. Johnson became president immediately after Kennedy's death. On November 29, 1963, one week after the assassination, Johnson established a presidential commission to investigate the murder. Unfortunately, the commission, which came to be known as the *Warren Commission* (led by Chief Justice Earl Warren), decided to operate in secrecy. Their report identified Oswald as the lone gunman who killed Kennedy.

Almost immediately, opposition developed regarding the commission's conclusions. Questions arose about the testimony of the hospital physicians who had tended the dying Kennedy, who described wounds that had come from the front and back. Eyewitnesses claimed to have heard a second set of shots coming from behind the grassy knoll in Dealy Plaza. Along with problems in assessing Oswald's abilities and motives in carrying out the crime, these questions persisted.

Though the Warren Commission concluded that Oswald operated alone, in 1968, a congressional committee on the assassination concluded that Kennedy was likely killed by a group of conspirators. The truth about who killed Kennedy will probably never be known to everyone's satisfaction. The sheer volume of literature on the subject attests to the fact that Americans are still deeply divided over this issue.

Who killed JFK?

Though no one knows whether the full truth about JFK's killer or killers will ever emerge, it's interesting to speculate who may have had a motive to assassinate the president. The following list demonstrates the difficulties in conclusively identifying the assassins because each of the groups had reasons to want to get rid of Kennedy, and each represents substantial power and the capability of doing so:

- Members of the CIA, who were severely criticized after the Bay of Pigs fiasco, blamed Kennedy for not sending the air support (see the "Invading Cuba: The Bay of Pigs" section earlier in the chapter). After the disaster, Kennedy severely curtailed their powers and expressed his belief that the agency was out of control and needed to be restructured.

- Members of the Cuban American community, who felt betrayed by Kennedy and deprived of an opportunity to retake Cuba due to the botched Bay of Pigs invasion.

- The Soviets, who had been forced to back down in the Cuban Missile Crisis.

- The Mafia, which had been under investigation by Attorney General Robert Kennedy.

- Southern extremists, who deeply resented Kennedy's attempts to push for civil rights.

- Cold warriors, who may have feared that Kennedy was pulling the U.S. out of Vietnam.

This is not to say that any of these groups participated in a conspiracy, yet even the congressional investigation of 1968 concluded that Oswald didn't act alone. The co-conspirators, if they do exist, have apparently gotten away with their terrible crime.

Chapter 3

LBJ and the Great Society

In This Chapter

▶ Paying dues: Life in the House and Senate

▶ Watching the presidency land in Johnson's lap

▶ Securing a victory through a successful campaign

▶ Promoting a Great Society at home

▶ Making a mess in Vietnam

Following Kennedy's assassination, Vice President Lyndon Baines Johnson (LBJ) was immediately sworn in as president aboard the presidential plane, Air Force One, as it winged its way out of Dallas heading for Washington, D.C. Though this moment represented the pinnacle of Johnson's long and illustrious political career, he didn't reach his goal in the way he'd dreamed.

Extremely different in style from Kennedy, Johnson brought his own style and political savvy to the office (see Figure 3-1 for a portrait of LBJ). Though not the smooth, handsome, polished politician that Kennedy was, Johnson was a fierce competitor, a tireless worker, a skillful negotiator, and a genuinely amicable man. When, in 1964, he ran as a presidential candidate in his own right, his political skills proved effective, and he won the highest office in the land in the manner in which he'd always dreamed — in a landslide vote.

When Johnson became president, the United States received a bold and ambitious leader. As a self-made man from a poor background, he saw his father rise in power and status through Texas politics. And he never forgot his roots, working to make the government responsive to the needs of the American people. A tremendously driven man, Johnson used his energy, strength, and unique ability to negotiate compromise to fulfill Kennedy's New Frontier idea of energizing the nation to embrace the new challenges of the age, and go beyond it to create his own legacy with the Great Society program, aimed at ending poverty and racial inequality.

In many ways Johnson's Great Society was an outgrowth of Franklin Roosevelt's New Deal legislation. Johnson admired Roosevelt and consciously worked to model himself as a similar reformer. Just as he'd hoped, his Great Society changed America as legalized segregation disappeared. And the myriad federal funding projects, though often criticized for being too much or too little, have provided Americans with significant opportunities that only became possible with the new funding.

However, Johnson's administration was imperfect, failing to live up to the promises of the Great Society. Perhaps such great strides to reform the nation were destined to fall short of their promise. The growing war in Vietnam clearly undermined Johnson's lofty goals, gobbling up the funds that could've been put to good use at home. The president saw the funds being whittled away but felt he couldn't stop it amidst his fears of becoming the first U.S. president to lose a war. For Johnson, the thought of losing the Great Society was nearly unthinkable. Yet the thought of losing the war to the Communists was *totally* unimaginable. Ultimately, he was forced to bear the former to avoid the latter. And had the Vietnam War not proved to be Johnson's undoing, one wonders just how much he could've accomplished.

Figure 3-1:
President
Lyndon B.
Johnson.

*Courtesy of the Library of Congress,
Prints and Photographs Division*

Learning the Game: Early Service in the House and Senate

Though Johnson came from the South (Stonewall, Texas, to be exact), he wasn't a stereotypical conservative southern politician. Born in 1908 and raised in much humbler circumstances than Kennedy, Johnson attended public schools and went to Southwest Texas State Teachers College in San Marco. After graduating in 1930 with a Bachelor of Science degree, Johnson taught grade school for a year in Cotulla, Texas. There, he worked closely with disadvantaged Hispanic children and saw firsthand the problems of the poor.

Lady Bird Johnson

Born Claudia Alta Taylor in Karnack, Texas, in 1912, the future wife of LBJ received the nickname Lady Bird as a baby after her nursemaid stated, "She's pretty as a lady bird" — the nickname just stuck. After her mother died in 1917, she was raised by her father, Thomas Jefferson Taylor, an aunt, and the household servants. As a child she developed a deep love of nature — later, as first lady, she channeled her energies into preserving the country's natural beauty. As Lady Bird grew up, her father taught her a great deal about running a business, and she went on to earn a Bachelor of Arts from the University of Texas. In 1934, she met Lyndon Johnson in Austin. Though he was living in Washington, D.C., at the time, Johnson courted Lady Bird with telegrams, letters, and phone calls. On his next trip to Texas, Johnson proposed, and Lady Bird accepted, stating, "Sometimes Lyndon simply takes your breath away."

Married on November 17, 1934, Lady Bird became Johnson's confidante, assistant, and political cohort. When Johnson went off to serve in the navy during World War II, his wife helped to keep his congressional office running.

She did the same thing in 1955, when Johnson was recovering from his heart attack.

When Johnson became president, Lady Bird assumed her duties as first lady without feeling a need to compete with the glamour that Jackie Kennedy had brought to the White House. Instead, she established her own style of Texas hospitality in White House social affairs. As first lady, she created the "First Lady's Committee for a More Beautiful Capital," which she later expanded to a national focus. She also participated in Johnson's Great Society programs, with a special interest in the Head Start Program for disadvantaged children.

In 1968, after Johnson retired from political life, he and Lady Bird returned to Texas, where the former president later died in 1973. Lady Bird went on supporting her husband through his legacy. Since retirement, she has returned to her early love of nature, serving as an active supporter of The Lady Bird Johnson Wildflower Research Center, which she founded in 1982, trustee of the National Geographic Society, and the matriarch of the Johnson business interests that she and her husband established.

In 1931, following his father's interest in politics, Johnson became secretary to Texas Democratic congressman Richard Kleberg and moved to Washington, D.C. Over the next four years, he found his true calling in politics, as he worked to build political alliances and contacts. Drawn to the backroom struggles that are prominent in democratic governments, Johnson began to learn the fine art of building consensus. He had a natural ability to find the political mainstream — a trait that would serve him well in his years of public service.

On November 17, 1934, Johnson married Claudia Alta Taylor in Austin, Texas, while traveling there on business. After a whirlwind romance spanning between Washington, D.C., and Austin, Johnson married Taylor who became affectionately known as Lady Bird Johnson. They later had two children, Lynda Bird and Luci Baines.

Congressman Johnson

Developing a reputation as a young, promising star, 27-year-old Johnson was appointed by President Franklin Roosevelt in 1933 to head the Texas National Youth Administration. During his two years in this position, Johnson participated in the New Deal programs, helping young people find opportunities for work and schooling in the Depression era. He also worked to build support for launching his political career in Texas, which paid off in 1937 when he successfully ran for a Texas seat in Congress. As a congressman, Johnson backed Roosevelt's New Deal legislation, championing public works projects, social aid, and public power programs. When World War II broke out, Johnson became the first congressman to enlist, entering the U.S. Navy, and serving in the war in the Pacific in 1941. When Roosevelt recalled members of Congress from active duty in the same year, Johnson returned to continue his support of Roosevelt's foreign and domestic policies.

The senator from Texas

Johnson set his sights higher than Congress in 1948, running for a Senate seat against one of the most popular former governors in Texas history. In a bitterly contested race, Johnson won by a mere 87 votes. Though his opponent cried fraud and sued in court, Johnson prevailed, jokingly referring to himself as "Landslide Lyndon."

Using his skills of negotiation, conciliation, and intimidation, Johnson thrived in the Senate. In 1951, at the age of 44, he became the youngest Senate minority leader in Democratic Party history. When he was reelected in 1954, the shift in political power in the Senate made him the majority leader. In his years in the Senate, Johnson kept his position by supporting the Texas oil and natural gas interests, participating in the *redbaiting* of the era (accusing and attacking people for being Communists or having Communist sympathies), and consistently opposing civil rights legislation. Johnson created strong ties to his southern counterparts by opposing all civil rights issues up until 1957, when he began to have higher aspirations once again.

Presidential desires and vice-presidential opportunities

In the late 1950s Johnson began to plan his presidential bid. Realizing that his Senate record was highly conservative, Johnson sought to broaden his appeal to increase his chances for a bid. The answer to the question of whether Johnson's shift in 1957 was because he desired to soften his image or because he was going back to his roots within the New Deal ideology is unclear. Whatever his motivations, that year Johnson began to support civil rights legislation playing a crucial role in the passage of the 1957 Civil Rights Act. Though this change was a savvy attempt to widen his support, many Northern Democrats still saw him as a small-time southern politician. Johnson didn't campaign actively for the presidency before the American people, instead seeking brokered deals for support, as he had done so successfully as a senator. At the Democratic National Convention in 1960, John F. Kennedy was chosen as the Democratic candidate for president on the first ballot.

For Johnson the vice presidency was a tragedy, for he never liked to be anything less than the best. He'd spent 23 years in Congress and had become one of its most powerful and skillful leaders, yet he was forced to accept the second seat on the party's ticket. Despite his personal feelings, Johnson campaigned for Kennedy with his usual gusto and commitment, bringing in the southern states that Kennedy needed to win.

When Kennedy presented his new, youthful administration, Johnson felt more akin to Dwight Eisenhower than to the new wunderkind that made up Kennedy's "best and brightest." Kennedy worked hard to keep Johnson satisfied without letting Johnson overshadow him as president, because Kennedy was younger and less experienced. Keeping the powerful vice president in check without losing his valuable help assuring Southern support in the next presidential election was a delicate balancing act. Kennedy, recognizing that Johnson had been the legislative father of the space program, gave him an important role as chairman of the National Aeronautics and Space Council. Johnson was also given travel assignments as vice president helping him hone his diplomatic skills. His trip to Vietnam as vice president proved useful to him later when he was making his policy decisions. Kennedy also made Johnson the chair of the new Committee on Equal Employment Opportunities.

The Unexpected Promotion: The Death of JFK

The tragedy of John F. Kennedy's assassination only 36 months after his election catapulted Johnson to the position he'd aspired to attain. Amidst national grief, Johnson stepped up and provided a calming model of leadership. On the day of the assassination, Johnson stated simply, "I will lead, and I will do the best I can." (Figure 3-2 shows Johnson taking the oath of office.)

Though Johnson couldn't match the energy and passion that Kennedy had created, his experience and professional yet fatherly demeanor soothed a nation that was traumatized by the events in Dallas (head back to Chapter 2 for more information on the assassination of JFK).

Figure 3-2: Johnson takes the oath of office aboard Air Force One, with Jackie Kennedy looking on.

Carrying forth the torch

Based upon Johnson's years leading the Senate, domestic policies quickly became his prime focus. He announced that Kennedy's cabinet would remain as his cabinet and that the legislative initiatives Kennedy had started, which were currently stagnating in congressional committees, would now be passed. Johnson made good on his promises. Managing the political infighting associated with the passing of Kennedy's legislative program was one of his greatest strengths.

Although Kennedy hated political wrestling and wrangling, Johnson was in his element. He summoned reluctant or obstructive senators and congressmen to the White House to give them what was known as the "Johnson treatment," from his days in the Senate: He sought to overpower and intimidate them into accepting his will. Johnson was a master of this aggressive tactic of both speech and body language and was able to force most men to demur under his relentless onslaught of analogies, facts, threats, and promises. His long and distinguished service in Congress gave him the tools he needed to jump-start Kennedy's legislative programs, and they soon began to pass under his aggressive leadership.

Finding an agenda: The unconditional War on Poverty

By the end of 1963, the year before Johnson's election, Congress passed a foreign aid bill along with a plan to sell wheat to the Soviet Union. Yet, looking at foreign aid packages raised questions about the needs of American citizens.

In 1964, the Council of Economic Advisers issued a report stating that about 20 percent of the American population was living below the poverty line — this estimate amounted to 9.3 million families living on less than $3,000 per year for a family of four.

In his first State of the Union address in 1964, Johnson explained, "Unfortunately, many Americans live on the outskirts of hope, some because of their poverty and some because of their color, and all too many because of both."

Johnson made tax reduction and civil rights legislation his top priorities, yet as he mulled over them, he had an epiphany. He decided to declare unconditional war on poverty in America. The timing of this move was brilliant; much the same as in the Progressive Era at the turn of the century, when a rising middle class began to show compassion for the plight of the poor, the middle class in the postwar world had prospered and was ready to begin to address some of society's problems.

Searching for a theme for the upcoming elections, Johnson put together the Economic Opportunity Bill as his vehicle for the War on Poverty. It included a wide range of programs, such as

- The Work Study Program to help poorer college students

- The Job Corps Program for troubled inner-city youths

- The Government Loan Program to help businesses willing to employ the chronically unemployed

- The Government Grant Program for farmers and rural businesses

- The Community Action Program, designed to give the poor a say in how the War on Poverty would be conducted in their neighborhoods

- A domestic Peace Corps program called Volunteers In Service To America (VISTA)

Taking over Kennedy's unfinished agenda, Johnson was now forging ahead, going much further in his bold plans for revitalizing America. Johnson told his advisors he wanted a plan that was big and bold and would make a real impact on the nation. He planned to fund his program through revenues from corporate taxes, which were surging following Kennedy's $10 billion tax reduction that Johnson signed into law in 1964. The tax cuts put money back into the economy in the form of investment and consumer demand. As a result, America entered a long, sustained economic boom.

Applying a label: The Great Society

Johnson continued to search for the great theme for his presidential run in 1964. In March, when asked whether he'd chosen a slogan such as the New Deal or the New Frontier, Johnson replied that he hadn't had a chance to work on that yet but noted that everyone likes the idea of a better deal. Though Johnson didn't like to label himself, he did describe himself on several occasions as a prudent progressive.

The truth was that Johnson was wracking his own brain and pressing his advisors to find a theme that would go beyond Kennedy's vision and define his own ideology. He needed a vision that was bold, daring, and aggressive — one that would establish the Johnson legacy for future generations. The idea was to identify the era in which the United States transitioned from a prosperous nation to one that focused on quality of life as well as quantity of money and possessions for all American citizens. Eric Goldman, a Princeton historian and part of the LBJ brain trust, suggested using the title of a Walter Lippmann book, *The Good Society*. Richard Goodwin, a Johnson speechwriter, changed the idea to the Great Society and drafted a speech with the new theme. The goal of the Great Society was to promote greater opportunities for prosperity and happiness for all Americans.

Johnson was immediately taken with it, seeing it as a way for him to fulfill the promise of Franklin Roosevelt's New Deal, which had focused on reorganizing society to create greater equity and fairness. In a graduation address in Ann Arbor, Michigan, Johnson tried out the rhetoric for the first time. The crowd interrupted his speech with applause 29 times. Johnson was euphoric; he'd found his theme and his legacy.

The 1964 Presidential Race

In the 1964 presidential election, Johnson was established as the Democratic candidate from the very beginning. He chose Hubert Humphrey of Minnesota as his running mate. The Republican Party was shifting to the right, driven by a perceived need to distinguish the party from the positions of the Democrats. The Republicans' choice of Barry Goldwater created a situation in which voters would choose between the consensus-building politics of Johnson or the much more extreme calls for action of Goldwater. Following the upset and disorientation created by the assassination of Kennedy, the country desired peace and continuity.

Shifting to the right: Republicans react

Johnson's Great Society program provoked a strong reaction among the conservative Republicans, who felt that their party had moved too far toward the center, making them a mere echo of the Democrats. Thus, as a reaction to the perceived liberal drift in the party, many conservatives began to pull for dogmatic varieties of conservatism, such as the aristocratic intellectual new conservatism of the *National Review* magazine as articulated by William F. Buckley, or the more extreme views of the John Birch Society (see Chapter 13).

Barry M. Goldwater: Extremist on the right

Ultimately, the struggle between moderate and conservative factions in the Republican Party resulted in the party's shift to the right. By 1960, an extreme conservative named Barry Goldwater had emerged as the leader of the Republican Right. Goldwater, a millionaire department-store owner and senator from Arizona, had been preparing for the 1964 election by building his extreme right-wing agenda. He placed his agenda in his 1960 book, *The Conscience of a Conservative.* Running for president in 1964, Goldwater called for

- An abolition of the graduated income tax
- The sale of Roosevelt's Tennessee Valley Authority
- A change in Social Security to make it voluntary
- An end to government interference in the economy
- An end to federal aid to education
- An aggressive bombing campaign against North Vietnam
- Federal opposition to forcing civil rights issues

Goldwater was a blunt man who was interested in promoting a right-wing ideology but lacked the subtleties of successful politicians — he came across as harsh and authoritarian. On record, he stated that he favored withdrawing U.S. recognition of the Soviet Union. He also stated his belief that local military commanders should be given the authority to use their atomic weapons against the Soviet Union, stating, "Let's lob one into the men's room of the Kremlin." As if that insensitive remark wasn't enough, he called welfare recipients people with "low intelligence and little ambition." He also expressed his strong opposition to civil rights legislation.

The melee at the Republican National Convention

In June, at the Republican National Convention in San Francisco's Cow Palace, Goldwater's biggest rival was fellow Republican Nelson Rockefeller. Though a poll on the eve of the convention showed that, on eight out of ten issues, Americans felt sharp disagreement with Goldwater, the candidate's conservative supporters dominated the convention. When Rockefeller addressed the convention, he was heckled by Goldwater supporters who yelled and jeered, shaking cowbells and blowing horns. When Rockefeller criticized the crowd for using "Communist and Nazi methods," they just increased their savage attacks. When Goldwater took the floor, he felt no need to hold back, saying that his opponents saw the nation in fundamentally wrong ways. He accused them of promoting collectivist thinking and undermining the American way of life. He expressed his commitment to freedom, explaining that the goals of the extreme right that he represented couldn't be compromised.

In his speech at the Republican National Convention, Goldwater went on to say, "Extremism in the defense of liberty is no vice! . . . Moderation in the pursuit of justice is no virtue!"

Holding onto the left: Johnson campaigns

Prior to the June Republican National Convention, Johnson had deeply worried about his election chances. An insecure man, he excessively worried about his weaknesses. He feared that in the event of a strong run from Nixon, Rockefeller, or Goldwater, he'd be seen as a Texas-style backroom brawler, unlike the suave man Kennedy had been. To counter this image, his promoters had pictures taken of Johnson strolling in the White House gardens holding his wife's hand, quietly reading books, and bowling with his daughter. The images were designed to promote the image of an intelligent, thoughtful family man. And as he dealt with President Kennedy's memory, he was also forced to deal with Robert Kennedy's vice presidential ambitions.

Drinking, driving, belching, and abusing

As Johnson's promoters strove to create a nationally appealing image of their candidate, Johnson often undermined their best efforts. In one incident, he treated reporters to some Texas hospitality, including taking four reporters on a tour of his ranch in his Cadillac, beer in hand, at speeds over 90 miles per hour. When *Time* magazine published the account, it showed a reckless Texas cowboy playing fast and loose with the rules — not a good image for a presidential hopeful. The second incident occurred less than two weeks later, while the White House was still denying the speeding incident. Johnson was photographed and described in the press as lifting up his two pet beagles by the ears, making him appear crude and heartless.

Johnson's fears of being outclassed had some truth to them; the fact that he often displayed behavior unbecoming of a president was an open secret in Washington. Johnson was well known for shouting at his aides in public and calling them into the bathroom while he was "on the throne." Further, he surprised reporters who were visiting him at his ranch by candidly discussing the sex life of bulls, urinating in public, and belching while gulping down highballs.

Although Johnson's behavior gave his supporters much to worry about, opinion polls still predicted that he'd have a comfortable win in November. After the Republicans chose Goldwater for their candidate, Johnson's aides worried less, yet Johnson still fretted.

Handling the Bobby problem

As Johnson considered his options for a running mate, one obvious choice was Bobby Kennedy. He had a solid reputation and wouldn't overshadow the presidential candidate. Yet the problem was that Johnson and Kennedy simply didn't like each other. Johnson was also concerned that a victory with Kennedy as his running mate might bring speculation that Johnson couldn't have won re-election without riding on Kennedy coattails. For Bobby, although he disliked Johnson, he knew that serving as vice president was a likely path for him to ascend to the presidency following Johnson.

Johnson hoped that Bobby would decline without incident, but Bobby didn't. However, after Goldwater became the Republican candidate, Johnson learned, through the polls, that his choice of running mate probably wouldn't make a difference, so he invited Bobby in for a chat. In this meeting Johnson clearly told Kennedy that he saw him as a liability because of his work on civil rights legislation, and that he wouldn't choose him as a running mate. He went on to tell Kennedy that his time would come and that he should work to promote him in the election. Johnson ended up choosing Minnesota senator Hubert Humphrey as his running mate, though he worried that Hubert talked too much and was too exuberant.

Emerging victorious

IN THEIR WORDS
"Four score and seven..."

Though polls showed Johnson with a very comfortable two-to-one margin over Goldwater, he still believed that he had to attack his opponent. When Goldwater came out with the slogan, "In your heart, you know he's right," Johnson's public relations team responded, "In your guts, you know he's nuts." The Democratic candidate created a strong anti-Goldwater campaign that hounded his opponent on a daily basis.

Probably Johnson's most decisive move was to hire the ad agency Doyle, Dane, Bernbach (DDB) to prepare television and radio spots, which finally destroyed what little chance Goldwater may have had. In perhaps the most significant attack ever made, DDB came up with the Daisy Ad, in which a little girl is in a field picking petals off of a daisy and counting to ten. In the background, the voiceover is a man counting down from ten to one. When the man gets to one, you see a startled look on the girl's face and then a closeup of her eye, in which you see the mushroom cloud of a nuclear explosion. The announcer's voice cuts back in and states, "These are the stakes — to make a world in which all of God's children can live, or to go into the dark. Vote for President Johnson on November 3. The stakes are too high for you to stay home." DDB ran a series of other attack ads — some of them variations on the daisy ad, and others attacking Goldwater for his threats to Social Security.

By late September, the ads began to really pay off, as Johnson surged forward to take a three-to-one margin over Goldwater. The Republicans fought back with a smear campaign of their own, suggesting that Johnson had participated in corrupt business practices. Late in the campaign, the Republicans felt they'd found a weakness in the Johnson administration when a moral scandal erupted over presidential aide Walter Jenkins, who was arrested and charged with indecent sexual behavior at a YMCA. The Republicans pressed the case as a sign of moral failure in the Johnson administration. Johnson, however, deftly handled the potentially damaging situation. Jenkins immediately resigned, and Lady Bird discussed her concern over him in an interview in which she noted the tremendous strains he'd been under since the assassination of JFK. The Jenkins situation created no lasting effects, and on November 3, Johnson thoroughly trounced Goldwater to win reelection.

Goldwater carried only his home state of Arizona and five states of the Deep South. Johnson won the electoral vote 486 to 52, and the popular vote 43,129,484 to 27,178,188.

Back to the Great Society and the War on Poverty

Johnson's strong presidential victory gave him his mandate for the Great Society program. Because the Democrats had also won clear majorities in both the House and Senate, Johnson was ready to push forward. He was a pragmatic man who wanted more than the liberal dream of doing good; he wanted solid legislative measures that would directly address issues of education, housing, public transportation, and health. So he set up 14 separate task forces, each staffed with experts whose jobs were to identify the nation's problems and then to suggest concrete measures to solve each one. The groups were to do their work in secrecy, because Johnson believed that leaks about social policies during the Kennedy administration had fostered public debate, making it more difficult to pass such legislation.

As Johnson geared up to pass his Great Society reforms, many of which form the social programs that people readily recognize today, he cautioned his staff to press on at every occasion, without creating an image of massive reform for fear of creating a backlash. In manipulating Congress, Johnson was in his element. He began his legislative push by honoring Congress and the individual lawmakers as great Americans who worked and sacrificed for the good of the nation. Though his program of flattery didn't work on all his critics, it did have the desired effect of setting the tone for his legislative thrust. Further, he instructed his staff to do everything possible to bolster congressional egos, including knowing all the legislators and returning their calls within ten minutes whenever feasible. These measures all helped groom Congress members to be receptive to new ideas.

Pushing Kennedy's Civil Rights Act

Following Kennedy's assassination, Johnson felt a compelling need to drive the former president's Civil Rights Act through Congress without letting it be diluted in any way. He recognized that the civil rights movement was becoming more militant and being met with more violence, particularly after the fierce battles over the Freedom Rides and the violence in Birmingham. Johnson felt that he needed to act before violence and unrest intensified, and he also felt that he owed it to Kennedy's memory to get the bill passed. Within weeks of his inauguration, Johnson decided to get it passed before the end of summer. Though civil rights advocates were suspicious of this southerner wanting to push their legislation through, over time, many learned to trust his intentions.

As a southerner, Johnson knew that segregation had done more than just separate whites and blacks in the South; it had also separated the South from the rest of the nation. Johnson believed that this bill would help heal the wounds of Kennedy's assassination and benefit the South by allowing it to better integrate with the rest of the United States. Getting the legislation passed was a challenge that tested Johnson's powers of compromise and persuasion. Though there were fears that the Republicans would make this a partisan issue, they overwhelmingly supported the legislation, and in fact, Republican Senate Minority Leader Everett Dirksen helped push the bill through Congress. The real resistance was more of a regional division than a partisan issue. Pressing House members, he guided the bill to passage by a margin of 290 to 110 on February 10. He then turned his efforts to the Senate, where he expected greater opposition. A determined filibuster by southern senators delayed the bill until June 10, when Johnson's relentless pressure on everyone he could reach paid off, with the Senate passing the bill 71 to 29. Johnson signed the bill into law on July 2, 1964.

The law was a landmark in American race relations. Among the myriad other details, the bill outlawed racial, sexual, or national origin discrimination in employment and public accommodations. The Civil Rights Act of 1964 ultimately resulted in the desegregation of schools and public facilities throughout the South. (For more details on the provisions of the act, see Chapter 6.)

Establishing the Voting Rights Act

Although the 15th Amendment was supposed to have guaranteed voting rights for blacks, the efforts by civil rights organizations to register black voters under the Freedom Summer project of 1964 had led to violent confrontations in the South (see Chapter 6 for the details).

Martin Luther King Jr. and the Southern Christian Leadership Conference chose Selma, Alabama, as the ideal place to make their stand, because it had a reputation as one of the most oppressive cities of the South. A series of televised brutal police attacks on demonstrators, which culminated with the events of "Bloody Sunday" during a planned march from Selma to Montgomery, horrified much of America (for a complete account of the Selma protests, see Chapter 7). The national reaction to the event was what Johnson had been waiting for; he sent the Voting Rights Act to Congress two days later.

When Johnson took his bill to Capitol Hill, he made one of his finest speeches, declaring

> What happened in Selma is part of a far larger movement, which reaches into every section and state of America. It is the effort of American Negroes to secure for themselves the full blessings of American life. Their cause must be our cause, too. Because it is not just Negroes, but really it is all of us, who must overcome the crippling legacy of bigotry and injustice. And we shall overcome.

After a moment of stunned silence, contemplating the fact that the president had just quoted the unofficial anthem of blacks and civil rights groups, almost every member of Congress responded with a standing ovation. In the Senate, southern senators organized a filibuster that delayed the bill, yet on May 26, it passed by an impressive 77-to-19 vote. In the House, conservatives worked to water down the bill, but Johnson supporters were able to keep it in its original form, passing the House 333 to 85 on July 9. Johnson signed the Voting Rights Act into law on August 6, 1965.

The impact of the Voting Rights Act was almost immediate, as southern states were forced to register black voters. Increased black votes resulted in a greater black representation in state legislatures, as well as in Congress. This act became the most influential piece of civil rights legislation since Reconstruction. (For more details on the impact, see Chapter 7.)

Ensuring educational opportunities

When it came to establishing priorities, Johnson saw the expansion of educational opportunities as one of his administration's top priorities. He was convinced that education was the ticket to raising people out of poverty, an idea that was largely based upon his own history. In turn, he believed that federal funding of education would solve the problems of overcrowded schools and underqualified teachers.

Providing more money for schools

On January 12, Johnson sent a message to Congress, calling on them to create a national goal of "full educational opportunity." In his message, he laid out his plans to double federal spending on education from $4 billion to $8 billion. He reminded Congress that America spent seven times more on welfare, prison, and reform on students who had dropped out and gone bad than it did on youths who remained in school and completed their educations.

Johnson guided his bill, called the Elementary and Secondary Education Act (ESEA), through Congress in a masterful way. He wisely avoided the religious issues by making funding available to both public and private schools. To rally support, Johnson met with National Education Association leaders and paid a symbolic visit to the Office of Education. He and his aides kept a daily count on congressional votes, and he pressured noncompliant House and Senate leaders with multiple phone calls, administering the Johnson treatment wherever needed (see the "Carrying forth the torch" section for the details on Johnson's persuasive tactics). His work paid off on March 26, with the House voting for the bill 263 to 153.

With this victory in hand, Johnson pressured the Senate to pass the same bill without modifications in order to avoid the need for a conference committee that could undermine or change the bill. Though some Republicans complained that the president's pressures were undermining the congressional prerogative in legislation, the Senate passed the bill on April 9 by a vote of 73 to 18. In just 87 days, Johnson had successfully shepherded a multibillion-dollar piece of legislation dealing with fundamental issues of education through both houses of Congress. The real victory was that such a bill would've been blocked over the issue of segregation, yet this issue had been settled with the earlier passage of the 1964 Civil Rights Act. Another major component of Johnson's Great Society had fallen into place.

Making college more accessible

Johnson also sought to take his ideas regarding the value of education to the college level. In November 1965, Johnson signed the Higher Education Act (HEA) at his alma mater, Southwest Texas State University. This bill provided federal funding for library acquisitions and more library specialists. This bill also provided federal funding for scholarships, loans, and work-study programs for students. The tremendous effects of this legislation were obvious within five years, as the nation saw a dramatic rise in the number of students seeking college degrees. In 1950, only 15 percent of 18- to 21-year-olds were attending college. By 1970, this number rose to 34 percent, and by 1990 the number reached 52 percent. Much of this increase is due to the HEA.

Funding the arts

In addition to his push for educational funding, Johnson was successful in creating the National Endowment for the Arts and the National Endowment for the Humanities. Though Johnson seemed an unlikely champion of the arts, he believed that scholars and artists "are the creators and keepers of our vision," and that "the creative and performing arts constitute a real national treasure." As such they played an important part in the project to create the Great Society. These programs provided funding for artists and scholars for work that helped expand, define, and interpret the nation's cultural heritage. The National Endowment for the Arts has funded many public art projects, including bringing Shakespearean productions to smaller communities and supporting a variety of performers and musicians to make their work and talents more accessible to the American people. The National Endowment for the Humanities has funded scholars and students, making educational opportunities available to a variety of people through research grants and scholarships.

Addressing medical problems with Medicare

During Johnson's first months in office, he sent a message to Congress calling on its members to make modern medical practices available to all Americans. He called for four reforms:

- ✔ Health insurance for the elderly
- ✔ Better and more hospitals
- ✔ Greater funding for mental health
- ✔ Funding research to find cures for cancer, heart disease, and strokes

Johnson's own heart attack at the age of 46 made the issue of health very important to him. The commission that he'd created to study the health issues reported that a $2.8 billion program would bring victory over diseases such as cancer, heart disease, and strokes, which accounted for nearly three-fourths of the country's deaths in 1962.

Buoyed by this information, Johnson asked Congress to fund a Regional Medical Program (RMP) to deliver federal funding to research hospitals. His request was met with fierce opposition, particularly from the American Medical Association (AMA), which feared that government-operated hospitals would threaten the existing system of private healthcare. Congress buckled to pressures from the AMA and passed a significantly watered-down version of the RMP that was no threat to the AMA. Johnson's attempts to gain more and better hospitals were also opposed by the insurance lobby and the AMA who feared that state-owned hospitals would lead the country down the path toward socialized medicine. Though some funding for mental health was included in the Medicare/Medicaid bill, this too was limited.

In 1965, Johnson made his Medicare proposal to provide health insurance for the elderly his top priority. He was intent on getting it passed while he still enjoyed such a strong position with Congress. Though he did everything he could to press the issue forward, the president quickly ran into opposition from conservative Republicans and the AMA, each of whom came up with alternate plans to address the need. Republican senator John Byrnes hatched an idea called "Bettercare"; the AMA produced its own, dubbed "Eldercare."

Though both plans covered fewer American seniors, they did provide more comprehensive coverage. Johnson outmaneuvered the opposition by incorporating the strong features of both competing plans into his Medicare plan. Medicare was to have three levels:

- ✔ Hospital insurance under Social Security
- ✔ A voluntary insurance program for doctors' bills
- ✔ A medical welfare program for the poor seniors, administered by the states, to be called Medicaid

Johnson lobbied heavily for the new legislation to pass, and though it ran into heavy resistance in the Senate and took over 500 minor amendments, Congress passed the Medicare Act on July 28. Though Johnson believed that the AMA couldn't resist the new law without damaging the organization's reputation with the American public, he left little to chance and met with AMA leaders to be sure that they'd be on board with the program. Over the next ten years, Medicare became a highly popular entitlement that no politician dared oppose.

Fighting poverty and making changes on multiple fronts

In early 1965, many of Johnson's Great Society programs were already up and running. The Office of Economic Opportunity was the centerpiece of the "War on Poverty," administering a number of programs including the Job Corps, the Volunteers in Service to America (VISTA), the Neighborhood Youth Corps, Community Health Centers, the Foster Grandparents program, the Legal Services program, Senior Centers, Summer Youth programs, and the Aid to Families with Dependent Children program, (AFDC), all of which were operating as part of the Great Society. The central idea was to push programs that could end American poverty by addressing the unmet needs of many of the nation's poor. By February, 44 states had local antipoverty programs in place, with plans for the last 6 states to open by June. VISTA had over 8,000 volunteers, and over 4 million people were receiving government aid from AFDC.

Yet for Johnson, this progress was only the beginning. In February he asked Congress for an additional $1.5 billion to expand the programs to ensure that poor children received good educational opportunities and that the poor had access to good legal counsel. In response, Congress passed the Head Start Program, aimed at giving disadvantaged children the opportunity to enter schools on an equal level as the more fortunate children. Congress also funded the Upward Bound Program, which helped poorer children prepare for college.

Johnson also pushed a new immigration bill through Congress in 1965. This new immigration policy abandoned the quota system. The president signed the bill into law on Liberty Island in New York Harbor, with Ellis Island visible in the background. The new law was designed to treat all nationalities and races equally by creating hemispheric ceilings stipulating that no more than 20,000 could come from each country each year. The new act also gave priority to family members of American residents.

To boost economic growth, Congress passed the Public Works and Economic Development Act, which was aimed at revitalizing areas of the country where industry had faded away and urban blight had set in. For the larger urban areas, Johnson saw a need for a government office that could deal with the variety of problems facing the community. Johnson backed a plan to create the Department of Housing and Urban Development (HUD), which would coordinate construction, community services, and social benefits. HUD's goal was to beautify American cities, eliminate slums, and facilitate the growth of services, ranging from parks to sewers to water supplies.

In 1965 Johnson also pushed for legislation for stricter controls on pollution, along with a Highway Beautification Act that would limit billboards and highway eyesores such as junkyards. In these matters, Johnson ran into real opposition from the chemical, automobile, and billboard lobbies, who feared that such laws would impinge on their business practices and their bottom lines. With much political arm-twisting, Johnson was able to get these laws passed, though in significantly watered-down versions. Nevertheless, he accepted the limitations, noting that these new laws would be a good start.

Johnson also passed the Highway Safety Act and the Traffic Safety Act, creating safety standards for automakers and highway design. He pushed to create a new department to oversee the work of numerous smaller entities with the field of transportation. The Department of Transportation (DOT) was to oversee the Federal Aviation Authority (FAA), the Commerce Department's transportation division, the Civil Aeronautics Board (CAB), the Maritime Administration, and the Transportation Safety Board of the Interstate Commerce Commission. Though industry and labor objections kept the Maritime Administration out of the DOT, the bill was signed into law on October 15, 1966. Johnson complained that leaving the Maritime Administration out of the DOT was a mistake, but there was little he could do about it. Fifteen years later, Congress came to agree with Johnson and reorganized the department accordingly.

Guns or Butter? The Tragedy of Vietnam

As Johnson was building his Great Society, the Vietnam War grew rapidly in terms of the number of troops and the cost of the war. When Johnson took over after Kennedy's assassination, 1,600 U.S. advisory personnel were in South Vietnam. Each U.S. president since Harry Truman had tried to spend as little as possible on South Vietnam, yet just enough to keep it from falling into the hands of the Communists. At first, Johnson had hoped to continue this trend in order to promote the Great Society programs, but beginning with his decisions to escalate the war in 1965, the situation overseas began to slide out of his control.

The war expenditures for 1965 were controllable but showed a growing trend toward becoming an unmanageable burden. By 1966, the U.S. government was spending over $22 billion on the Vietnam War and only $1.2 billion on the War on Poverty. This harsh reality created Johnson's terrible dilemma of whether the U.S. should invest in "guns or butter." In assessing the war, Johnson later explained to his biographer, Doris Kearns Goodwin, that creating the Great Society was his true love, but it was the Vietnam War that undermined his greatest dreams for America.

Escalating the war

In his attempts to not lose South Vietnam, Johnson was forced to engage and eventually escalate the conflict. His legal justification for fighting the war lay in the Tonkin Gulf Resolution, passed by Congress in 1964. (See Chapter 8 for greater detail.) Though Congress had never formally declared war, the resolution itself gave Johnson full authority to "take all necessary measures to repel any armed attack against the forces of the United States and to prevent further aggression." Armed with this sweeping power, Johnson and his staff began a long series of escalations in South Vietnam in 1965.

Although Johnson's desire to fulfill the dream of the Great Society was still his primary focus, he felt that the U.S. couldn't afford to lose in the cold war struggle. In retrospect, Johnson's decision to Americanize the war seems curious given his domestic agenda, yet it was consistent with his predecessors' foreign policy positions. Containment theory, initiated under Harry Truman, had been embraced by Eisenhower and reiterated by Kennedy in his famous "bear any burden" speech. Johnson had little choice but to follow these precedents and be sure that he wasn't the one to lose to the forces of Communism. Though he had to keep the U.S. in the cold war game, he also knew that he must not press forward so fast that he'd provoke the Chinese or the Soviets into direct confrontation.

Looking shady: Johnson's credibility gap

While Johnson was well aware of the "guns or butter" dilemma of the Vietnam War versus the Great Society, the lack of a clear way out of the problem caused him to continue his balancing act while looking for a solution. By 1966, the strategy was still working, with his domestic policies still moving forward, albeit at a much slower pace than in 1965. Polls showed American public support for Johnson's handling of the war, with two-thirds of Americans viewing the stand in Vietnam as essential. As General William Westmoreland and the

Joint Chiefs of Staff pressed Johnson for more troops and broader latitude in the bombing campaign, Johnson repeatedly resisted their requests, oftentimes in violent outbursts in which he accused them of trying to trigger World War III. Then, after the heat of the moment passed, Johnson felt compelled to grant the next escalation.

Because the war in Vietnam was the nation's first televised war, Johnson remained keenly aware of public perceptions and was careful to manage the war before the American people. Though the Tet Offensive of January 1968 is seen as the turning point of American public opinion about the war (see the "Smothering the dream: The Tet Offensive and LBJ's decline" section, later in this chapter), this belief is only understandable in the context of the Johnson credibility gap, which had developed over the previous two years.

As the war escalated, the Johnson administration and the U.S. military had been careful to show the American public that the war was progressing and that the U.S. was taking great measures to fight the insurgents while minimizing civilian casualties and human suffering. U.S. airpower pounded military targets of concrete and steel, thereby defeating the aggressors while preserving the idea that the U.S. was winning the hearts and minds of the Vietnamese people. As for the greater cold war issues fueling the conflict, the American public heard only one side of the story from the American press, which generally reported what the military showed them.

Little did America know, however, that trouble was brewing under the surface of the war front. Taken together, some gray areas formed the seeds of Johnson's credibility gap, which played a significant role in the interpretations of the events of 1968. Questions about the Tonkin Gulf incident (see Chapter 8 for more information on the Tonkin Gulf incident) began to plague Johnson, ultimately culminating in a Senate investigation of the matter. In addition, a series of private fact-finding missions to North Vietnam and attempts to negotiate an end to the war were reported in the press, embarrassing the administration and giving the American public reason to be suspicious that what they were hearing from the government was not the whole truth. (See Chapter 9 for more on these nongovernmental trips to Vietnam.)

Johnson also created new examples of his duplicity. Because of his desire for secrecy and to be the first to tell the American public about his decisions and accomplishments, he became more willing to mislead the American people. In a March 9, 1967 news conference, when a reporter asked Johnson if he was looking for a replacement for American Ambassador to Vietnam Henry Cabot Lodge, Johnson stated that there was no truth to the rumor. But within days, Johnson named Ellsworth Bunker as Lodge's replacement, prompting complaints from the press that Johnson had again purposely misled the American people.

In an attempt to cover the gaffe, the White House press secretary explained that Johnson was technically correct when he said he wasn't looking for a replacement because he had already found one. Though this situation seems somewhat trivial in itself, the fact that it occurred in the midst of the turmoil created by revelations from private missions to Vietnam gave it added prominence in the minds of many Americans. The debate it sparked reveals Johnson's accelerating credibility gap. Lack of progress in the war and continued requests for more money and troops multiplied the questions many Americans were beginning to seriously struggle with.

Smothering the dream: The Tet Offensive

The Tet Offensive of January 1968 was the North Vietnamese attempt to break the stalemate of the war with a bold offensive that had several important goals:

- ✔ Cause greater financial strain on the U.S. by forcing them to either further extend troop and equipment commitments or to withdraw in the areas that they could not hold

- ✔ Demonstrate the limitations of American military power to the South Vietnamese in hopes of driving a wedge between the two governments

- ✔ Demonstrate American vulnerability to attack anywhere in Vietnam

- ✔ Spark a popular uprising in the South, which would lead to either a coalition government or a northern victory

When the Tet Offensive occurred in January 1968, Americans were shocked to see that the war they'd been told was nearly over was suddenly out of control. Though the offensive was a military loss for the Viet Cong and the National Liberation Front, it strongly shifted U.S. public opinion regarding the war. (See Chapter 8 for more on the Tet Offensive.) Americans were dismayed that this type of offensive could happen in a war that they had so thoroughly been led to believe that they were winning. Many began to question whether the war could ever be won. Johnson's growing credibility gap had laid the foundations for the American public to interpret the Tet Offensive, an American victory on the battlefield, as a negative turning point in the war.

Major newspapers and magazines began running antiwar editorials and urged a withdrawal in the wake of Tet. Even Walter Cronkite, one of the most respected television anchormen in America, expressed doubts that the war was winnable. Johnson's approval polls, which had hovered near 65 percent before Tet, fell to a 35 percent approval rating. The Great Society Program had been undermined by the financial realities of the war; in 1968 the U.S. was spending approximately $322,000 for each Communist killed in Vietnam, while the War on Poverty was spending only $53 per person.

Johnson's support had clearly eroded, and on March 31, 1968, President Johnson announced that he wouldn't run for reelection. The man of great ambition no longer believed the war was winnable.

Chapter 4

Richard Nixon: Cold War Warrior

• •

In This Chapter

▶ Tracking Nixon from childhood to the presidential debates

▶ Grabbing the presidential brass ring

▶ Reviewing President Nixon's successes and failures

▶ Securing and forfeiting a second term

• •

*W*hen Richard Milhous Nixon was elected president in 1968, he inherited a nation that was divided over the issue of the Vietnam War. By the time he left office in 1974, he left the nation stunned and disillusioned. Under Nixon, the United States entered a new era that set the stage for the rise of new conservatism. Nixon's desire was to reverse the trend of growing federal power and begin the shift of power, money, and regulation back to the states. Though he was unable to fulfill this agenda in his years as president, he did lay the foundations for the shift to the right, particularly through his appointments to the U.S. Supreme Court.

The Watergate scandal forced Nixon to resign his role as president and ended his political career, yet his five and a half years as president allowed him to significantly shape American history. For Nixon, politics were more than a gentleman's game — political life was a war in which only victory counted in the long run. However, paranoid and powerful, he went far beyond the boundaries of ethics and law, ultimately bringing about his own downfall.

Because his presidency ended so poorly, Nixon is a difficult president to assess. He was a man of extremes. Some credit him with a skillful ending of the Vietnam War, while others criticize him for prolonging the conflict. His skills at foreign diplomacy were superb, and his achievements were great, particularly those with China and the Soviet Union. Yet his achievements are all tarnished by his complicity in the Watergate scandal. His abuses of presidential authority served to undermine himself and the high office, yet they also led to new safeguards designed to stop future abuse. Without a doubt, Nixon was one of the most controversial presidents in U.S. history. Figure 4-1 gives you a face to put with the name.

Figure 4-1:
President
Richard M.
Nixon.

Courtesy of the Library of Congress,
Prints and Photographs Division

Getting Started: Nixon's Early Life

On January 9, 1913, Richard Milhous Nixon was born in Yorba Linda, California. The second of five sons, Nixon had a relatively simple childhood. The Nixons were simple Quakers who worked the area citrus groves. At the age of nine, Nixon's family moved to Whittier, California, where his father operated a gas station and store. As an early sign of his future occupation, Nixon competed in debate on the national level while in high school.

Nixon attended Whittier College, majoring in history and graduating second in his class. He earned a scholarship to study law at Duke. After graduating from law school in 1937, he practiced law for a small firm in Whittier where he met his future wife, Thelma Pat Catherine Ryan (see the "Mrs. Nixon: St. Patrick's babe of the morning" sidebar for more on the first lady). They married in 1940 and later had two daughters, Julie and Tricia.

When World War II broke out in December 1941, Nixon was drawn to Washington, D.C., where he worked in the Office of Price Administration. There he learned to dislike bureaucratic red tape. Nixon enlisted in the U.S. Navy in the summer of 1942 and served in the south Pacific with the Naval Air Transport. Discharged in 1946 at the rank of lieutenant commander, Nixon returned to California, where he embarked on his political career path.

Redbaiting his way to the top

Upon Nixon's return from naval duties, local Republican Party leaders in California recruited him to run against long-time Democrat Jerry Voorhis in the 12th Congressional District. Nixon leaped at the opportunity, exclaiming his willingness to serve the party vigorously on a platform of "practical liberalism," which promised a more efficient, less intrusive form of government, which he believed was the answer to the New Deal liberalism of President Franklin D. Roosevelt and the Democrats.

Looking for an issue to exploit in the election, Nixon researched Voorhis' past to find that he was a Socialist during the 1920s and '30s and had supported major unions and the idea of government-owned businesses. Taking advantage of developing cold war fears (see Chapter 2 for an introduction to the cold war), Nixon immediately branded Voorhis as a Communist. Though Voorhis had the advantage of being the incumbent in his fifth term, Nixon played on the fact that the American public was tired of governmental regulations associated with the New Deal and with restrictions on consumption to help with the war effort. In 1946 many Republicans campaigned successfully on the slogan "Had Enough?"

During the campaign, Voorhis made the mistake of engaging Nixon in a series of debates, a foolish move because Voorhis was already well known, and Nixon wasn't. In addition to raising the issue of Voorhis' Socialist past, Nixon showed that the incumbent congressman had introduced only one bill that had passed in Congress over the previous four years. These two issues undermined Voorhis, leading Nixon to win his first election at the age of 33. Nixon's accusations that Voorhis was a Communist were at least partially responsible for the victory.

Mrs. Nixon: St. Patrick's babe of the morning

Thelma Catherine Ryan was born in Ely, Nevada, on March 16, 1912. Because she was born on the day before St. Patrick's Day, her father called her his "St. Patrick's babe of the morning." The name Pat stuck with her throughout her life. Pat's road wasn't an easy one. Her family was poor. At the age of 13, she lost her mother, and her father passed away only five years later. Following her father's death, Pat finished high school and enrolled in Fullerton Junior College, earning her way as a janitor. After a brief stint in New York, she returned to the West Coast in 1934, finishing her bachelor's degree at the University of Southern California. Pat took her first job as a high-school teacher in Whittier, California, where at a play tryout, she met a young attorney named Richard Nixon who was also performing in the amateur theatrical group she'd joined. He told her on their first date that he was going to marry her, which he did on June 21, 1940.

After her husband was elected president in 1968, the first lady championed volunteerism and pushed programs such as the Right to Read program and attempts to create new recreational areas in poorer neighborhoods. Though she suffered through the Watergate affair, Pat remained poised and dignified. She died at home of cancer in Park Ridge, New Jersey, on June 22, 1993, just a few months before her husband. They're both buried in Yorba Linda, California.

Redbaiting (the practice of discrediting someone by attacking and denouncing them as a Communist) and the pursuit of Communists (both real and fictional) became a road to greater power for Nixon within Congress and later the Senate.

Hunting down the Communists on HUAC

After he landed a seat in the House, Nixon increased his visibility, serving on the Herter Committee, which helped implement the Marshall Plan for aid to Europe (the Marshall Plan was a financial assistance program to aid and stabilize European nations to lessen the chance of them shifting toward Communism), and on the House Education and Labor Committee. Because he'd established himself as a staunch anti-Communist, Nixon secured a position on the House Un-American Activities Committee (HUAC), investigating Communist connections within the American film industry.

Originally established in 1938 as a special investigating committee of the U.S. House of Representatives charged with finding German Americans involved with the Nazi movement, HUAC shifted its focus to issues that it considered un-American propaganda after the war ended. The post-war focus was on Communism and the desire to root out any Communist themes in Hollywood films. HUAC helped create the blacklists against left-leaning screenwriters, which ruined many careers even though most of the charges were later proved unfounded. As the investigations broadened, some people avoided the questioning by simply leaving the country (such as Charlie Chaplin, who fled to Switzerland). The committee lasted into the 1970s, investigating leaders in the New Left movement but to much less effect as young witnesses, such as Abbie Hoffman, had a lot less to fear from the investigations than did the successful screenwriters of the 1950s.

Pursuing Alger Hiss

Nixon's reputation as a dedicated anti-Communist got a huge boost from his dogged pursuit of the Alger Hiss case. Alger Hiss, president of the Carnegie Endowment for International Peace, had served the Truman administration in the State Department. When a former Soviet agent accused Hiss of passing secrets to the Soviets, he sued for libel. His accuser, Whittaker Chambers, produced microfilms of the documents he claimed Hiss had passed to him. Though the statute of limitations had expired for trying Hiss on espionage charges, he was convicted of perjury in the case. The Alger Hiss case was damaging to the Truman administration and to Democrats in general, and at the same time, it brought Nixon important national exposure, helping him move from the House to the Senate.

Reaching for the Senate: Taking on the Pink Lady

In 1950 Nixon set his sights higher, running for Senate against Democrat Helen Gahagan Douglas. Nixon employed his well-honed redbaiting tactic, accusing Douglas of being a Communist (or at least a Communist sympathizer) and comparing her voting record in the Senate to the only openly pro-Communist member of Congress. Nixon called Douglas the "Pink Lady" and printed anti-Douglas fliers on pink paper. With the growing cold war fears of the era, Nixon's pink paintbrush worked again — he won the seat by over 650,000 votes.

Winning the vice presidency

In 1952, Republicans believed they had a strong chance to retake the White House for the first time in over 20 years. Republican candidate Thomas E. Dewey's 1948 challenge of President Truman resulted in a very narrow defeat; thus, with their hopes raised from the strong showing, the Republicans were organizing early for the 1952 elections. Having gained a great deal of exposure for his part in the Alger Hiss case, Nixon was a rising star in the Republican Party. After much debate, Dwight Eisenhower, who had beaten out Robert Taft for the Republican nomination, called on Richard Nixon to serve as his running mate. Eisenhower, the former general who served as the allied commander in Europe during World War II and as head of NATO after the war, had a strong reputation in the East, and Nixon's popularity in the West would help balance the ticket.

Doggone clever: The Checkers speech

Almost immediately after being selected as Eisenhower's running mate, Nixon found himself in a tremendous controversy. On September 18, 1952, the *New York Post* published an article under the headline "Secret Nixon Fund." The inside header of the story proclaimed, "Secret Rich Men's Fund Keeps Nixon in Style Far Beyond His Salary." The truth behind the press? Nixon had let rich California businessmen, eager to promote Republicans, contribute to a fund that he used for travel expenses, postage, and phone bills during his time as a congressman and senator. Though technically legal, the fund was shady, particularly because the Eisenhower campaign had been accusing the Truman administration and Democrats of financial corruption.

Amid rumors that Eisenhower would ask Nixon for his resignation, Nixon decided to take the issue to the people and await their reaction. The Republican National Committee put up $75,000 for a 30-minute television spot on September 23. Nixon's speech that night saved his political career. In 30 minutes, he disclosed his entire financial picture. He explained the fund and gave a detailed picture of how it worked, emphasizing that his family wasn't rich — they were just like other ordinary Americans.

In the speech, Nixon said, "Pat and I have the satisfaction that every dime that we have got is honestly ours. I should say this, that Pat doesn't have a mink coat. But she does have a respectable Republican cloth coat, and I always tell her she would look good in anything."

During his brief TV spot, Nixon praised Eisenhower's leadership and called upon the audience to decide whether he should resign. Nixon insisted that he'd done no wrong, yet the most powerful portion of the speech didn't concern his financial information; rather, what moved Americans nationwide was his explanation about a dog his family had received as a present.

Nixon stated, "One other thing I probably should tell you, because if we don't, they'll probably be saying this about me too, we did get something — a gift — after the election. A man down in Texas heard Pat on the radio mention the fact that our two youngsters would like to have a dog. And, believe it or not, the day before we left on this campaign trip we got a message from Union Station in Baltimore saying they had a package for us. We went down to get it. You know what it was. It was a little cocker spaniel dog in a crate that he'd sent all the way from Texas. Black and white spotted. And our little girl — Tricia, the 6-year-old — named it Checkers. And you know, the kids, like all kids, love the dog and I just want to say this right now, that regardless of what they say about it, we're gonna keep it."

Nixon's speech (now known as the Checkers speech) worked, and the overwhelming response was positive. His talk about his finances was frank, and his idea to let the American people decide whether he'd done anything wrong helped his case. He seemed honest and sincere, and the part about his children and the dog hit close to home for many Americans. Nixon kept the dog, Eisenhower kept Nixon, and they went on to an easy victory in 1952.

The anti-Communist heat is on: Goodwill ambassadors

As a two-term vice president, Nixon, along with his wife, Pat, became Eisenhower's goodwill ambassadors to the world. In 1953 the Nixons did an extensive tour, Asia, meeting with major leaders and establishing a rapport with them that would later serve Nixon well as president.

The Nixons' journey to South America in 1958, however, was a different story — there, they met fierce protests of their presence in Lima, Peru, and in Caracas, Venezuela. Venezuelans had overthrown a military dictator named Perez Jimenez the year before amidst cries that he had sold out Venezuelan interests to American businesses. Jimenez and his entourage had been allowed to escape to the U.S., which strengthened the cries of corruption of both Jimenez and the U.S. Amidst such a charged atmosphere, pro-Communist forces found it easy to enflame anti-U.S. sentiment. In Caracas, they were spat upon by an angry mob at the airport, and later, their limousine was pelted with rocks, shattering windows and injuring several staff members and Venezuelan officials. The incident reaffirmed Nixon's anti-Communist stance. His calm composure at the press conference after the attack heightened his reputation at home as a man willing to stand up to extremists.

Nixon had one more moment in the spotlight as vice president in 1959, during an official visit to the Soviet Union. There, while visiting the American Exposition and standing in the kitchen of an American model home at the exhibition, Nixon and the Soviet leader Nikita Khrushchev got into a fierce debate over the merits of capitalism and Communism. Commonly referred to as the "kitchen debate," neither side won. Yet Nixon again gained admiration at home for standing up to the Communist leader.

Losing the presidential race

In the 1960 presidential election, Nixon believed that his opportunity to realize his lifelong ambition had finally arrived. As the Republican frontrunner, Nixon was nominated in the first ballot at the convention. Things looked good for Nixon. In the presidential race his Democratic opponent, John F. Kennedy, had much less experience than he did, particularly in foreign affairs.

The polls showed that both candidates were very close, yet the handsome and youthful Kennedy held an advantage because Nixon had to defend Eisenhower's policies and was thus open to attack on more issues. Another decisive factor was the series of four televised debates between the two candidates. These presidential debates were the first ever to hit the home screen, so no one could've predicted the results. Kennedy moved ahead in the polls and beat Nixon by the narrowest of margins (for more information on the debates and the election results, see Chapter 2). He spent the next year writing a book entitled *Six Crises,* based on six events in his own life. The book allowed him to sort through his loss and move on.

By the time *Six Crises* was finished, Nixon had already decided to run for governor of California in 1962. Though he pushed hard to beat Democrat Pat Brown, he lost the election by 297,000 votes out of 6 million. Nixon's tried-and-true recipe for defeating opponents by branding them as soft on Communism failed this time, because voters didn't see the larger picture of Communism as a significant issue for a state governor.

Taking Another Shot: The 1968 Race

After his defeat in the 1962 governor's race, Nixon moved to New York to resume his practice of law. He continued to serve the Republican Party behind the scenes, campaigning for Barry Goldwater in 1964 and many local Republicans. By late 1967, Nixon was again a likely presidential candidate. His Republican opponent was Ronald Reagan, who had also built his fame in California politics.

For his second presidential bid, Nixon again used Communism as an important theme, but this time he began to use a slightly different tone. The Tet Offensive of 1968 (see Chapter 8) had taken him by surprise as much as it had President Lyndon B. Johnson, because it revealed that the strategy of continued escalation in the Vietnam War hadn't produced victory. This reality called into question Nixon's long-held belief on taking a firm stand with the Communists, which forced him to rethink his strategy about the war.

On March 5, 1968, in a speech at an American Legion Hall in Massachusetts, Nixon stated, "I pledge to you, new leadership will end the war and win the peace in the Pacific." Having stumbled on this phrase, Nixon recognized its importance as good rhetoric.

When asked later the same day how he'd win the peace in Vietnam, Nixon explained his belief that Johnson had placed too much emphasis on the military side of the conflict and not enough on the nonmilitary aspects. He went on to explain that good relations with the Soviet Union could create leverage with the North Vietnamese and help win the peace. This speech showed a real shift in Nixon's beliefs. Instead of calling for victory, Nixon was calling for an honorable peace.

A year of change and turmoil

Throughout his campaign, Nixon attacked Johnson for the growing violence of the antiwar movement, asserting that Johnson's problem was in blaming everyone except the protesters for the violence. Nixon also cautioned that government needed to move more swiftly to stop the planners of violence. His reasoning was that riots are generally spontaneous events, but the recent antiwar violence had been planned, making them more like all-out war. Nixon had finally found his winning issue and his new voice.

On March 16, 1968, buoyed by signs that Johnson was vulnerable, Robert Kennedy, the brother of JFK and a New York senator, announced his candidacy for president. When Johnson withdrew from the presidential race on March 31, Nixon was shocked. With Nixon certain of his own nomination and Johnson out of the race, the only question was who he would face as the Democratic nominee. Eugene McCarthy, Robert Kennedy, and Hubert Humphrey were the most likely candidates. Nixon realized that with Johnson gone, he needed to shift his platform because new leadership became a nonissue and his former focus on the president's problems was no longer relevant.

But before Election Day 1968, three violent events changed the political landscape and the face of America.

> ✔ **The assassination of Martin Luther King Jr.:** Only four days after Johnson announced that he wouldn't seek reelection, James Earl Ray, a small-time criminal, shot and killed Martin Luther King Jr. in Memphis on April 4. Nixon wondered whether he should attend the funeral because spontaneous riots had broken out following the assassination, and he'd been campaigning on a platform of law and order. He finally decided to make the trip. He flew to Atlanta to pay his respects to the King family. (See Chapter 6 for a brief biography of King.)

- ✔ **The assassination of Bobby Kennedy:** On June 4, as Nixon watched the California Democratic Primary, it became clear to him that he'd be facing Robert Kennedy and not Eugene McCarthy, as California had been a critical test of McCarthy's support. But before the evening was over, Kennedy was assassinated, and Nixon again had to change much of his strategy. He'd feared the Kennedy mystique and felt that Kennedy would be a hard opponent to beat. With Kennedy out of the way, Nixon would face Hubert Humphrey. Not only was Humphrey far less charismatic than Kennedy, but he was also vulnerable because he was Johnson's vice president and thus was seen as a part of the quagmire of Vietnam. (For more information on the effect the Vietnam War had on the election of 1968, see Chapter 10.)

- ✔ **The Chicago Riots:** In August, the Democratic National Convention was held in Chicago. Following the April riots over King's assassination, Chicago Mayor Richard Daley warned that he wouldn't tolerate lawlessness and disruption. Nevertheless, riots broke out, and police used tear gas, horses, and batons to dominate the protesters. Press cameras filmed the action. The Democrats nominated Hubert Humphrey, who was heavily associated with Johnson's Vietnam War strategy, yet the whole scene in Chicago was eerily reminiscent of the Vietnam fiasco — the Democratic Party and its policies were in disarray. (See Chapter 9 for more on the Chicago Riots.)

The silent majority speaks

By contrast to the Democratic convention, the Republican National Convention in Miami went smoothly. The delegates nominated Nixon over New York governor Nelson Rockefeller and California governor Ronald Reagan. Nixon chose Spiro Agnew, governor of Maryland, as his running mate. In the November presidential elections, Nixon and Agnew captured a narrow victory by about 500,000 popular votes, although the Electoral College was more strongly weighted toward Nixon at 301 to 191. As a clear sign of the backlash against the civil rights advances, George Wallace, campaigning as an independent, won in Arkansas, Louisiana, Mississippi, Alabama, and Georgia.

By the time of Nixon's election, the numerous social movements unleashed in the 1960s had already changed many of the attitudes and ideas of American social life. Yet as these changes gained momentum, so too did the backlash against change. By the late '60s, the white working class and the middle class were both working to regain control of the nation. Many of these Americans felt that the nation had become caught up in anarchy, permissiveness, and narrow self-interests, which had put small minority interests ahead of the greater interests of the majority. This group of people made up the *silent majority* that elected Nixon and Agnew. Motivated by a desire to end the violence, strife, and bloodshed, this new force was determined to regain some sort of equilibrium. Though they disagreed with much of the liberal agenda and turbulent events of the decade, they did agree that ending U.S. involvement in

Vietnam was a top priority. The nation now looked to a man associated with the stability of the '50s to restore law and order and lead the nation into peace with honor.

Taking the Presidential Reins

When Nixon took office in January 1969, his most important mission was taking care of the Vietnam quagmire. But he also had other foreign policy issues to take care of, so he gathered advisors to help him achieve his goals. The major players in the Nixon administration were Attorney General John Mitchell, who was a rich municipal bonds dealer in Nixon's old firm; H.R. Haldeman and John Ehrlichman, who handled domestic policies; Henry Kissinger, who dominated foreign policy as national security advisor (even though William P. Rogers was secretary of state); and Melvin Laird as secretary of defense. Nixon's inner circle was all white, all male, and all Republican. Unfortunately, Nixon wasn't equally interested (or successful) in domestic matters, and most of his proposals were stalemated in Congress.

Pursuing peace with honor

Nixon's most passionate interests had always been in foreign policy. Though he named William Rogers as secretary of state, the real architect of his policy was National Security Advisor Henry Kissinger (see Figure 4-2). Nixon believed that the war in Vietnam had driven Johnson from office and thus realized that in order to secure reelection to a second term, he had to succeed where Johnson had failed.

Throughout his election campaign, Nixon had promised "peace with honor." He saw success couched in the larger context of worldwide diplomacy, which included establishing rapport with the Soviets and the Chinese. Though Nixon finally succeeded in extricating the U.S. from Vietnam in 1973, another 20,000 young American men, as well as millions of Vietnamese peasants, lost their lives before he did so.

Nixon's primary plan was to shift the burden of the war away from U.S. combat troops and onto the South Vietnamese troops. Calling it "Vietnamization," Nixon wanted to quell the antiwar upheaval at home by steadily reducing the U.S. presence in Vietnam. This slow release, in turn, bought time for Nixon's diplomatic push to undermine Soviet and Chinese support for the North Vietnamese to have a significant effect (for greater detail, see Chapter 10). His foreign policy met with the following successes:

✔ He reduced troop presence from a peak of 540,000 in 1969 to 50,000 in early 1973.

✔ In 1969 he established a draft lottery system that eliminated many of the draft system's earlier racial and economic inequities (see Chapter 9).

✔ By 1973 he did away with the draft entirely, establishing the all-volunteer army that the U.S. still uses today.

Figure 4-2: Henry Kissinger (left), the brains behind Nixon's foreign policy.

©Topham/The Image Works

The clock is ticking

In addition to shifting the war burden onto South Vietnamese troops, Nixon pushed for a negotiated settlement in Vietnam by using the "carrot and stick." This entailed the use of rewards and punishments to secure an agreement acceptable to the U.S. Although he was willing to negotiate, Nixon also demonstrated that he was ready, willing, and able to punish the North Vietnamese with a vigorous bombing campaign (for more on this campaign, called Operation Linebacker, see Chapter 10). At the same time, Nixon was aware that the clock was ticking. If the antiwar movement perceived that withdrawal was too slow or was half-hearted or insincere, protests would rise up again. However, if he withdrew too fast, it would encourage the North Vietnamese to press in their attacks.

Further, the military itself began to have severe problems as soldiers openly expressed their desires to not be casualties in a lost cause. Between 1969 and 1971 there were 730 reported instances of *fragging*, where a soldier would toss a grenade into his commanding officer's foxhole or bunker as a means to stop him from being so willing to engage the enemy. Drug abuse also rose significantly, with four times more troops hospitalized for it than for combat wounds in 1971 alone.

At home, news of the My Lai Massacre and the Cambodian incursion also made the antiwar crowd flare once again (see Chapter 10). The protests over these problems led to more demonstrations including the ones at Kent State University in Ohio and Jackson State University, both of which resulted in the deaths of students (see Chapter 9). These events only served to inflame the unrest even more. In response, the silent majority began attacking students for their protests, such as when students clashed openly with construction workers in New York. For Nixon, all these pressures continued to remind him that the clock was running on the Vietnam War.

The truth is out there

The political situation at home became more critical in June 1971 when the *New York Times* began publishing excerpts of what has come to be known as the *Pentagon Papers.* At first, the Nixon administration successfully stopped publication for 15 days, until the Supreme Court gave the newspaper the right to resume. The *Pentagon Papers* revealed a secret Defense Department study of early U.S. involvement in the war. Leaked to the press by former Defense Department official Daniel Ellsberg, the study confirmed what many critics of the war had already suspected.

The publication showed that the American public hadn't been told the whole truth regarding the Tonkin Gulf incident in 1964, the alleged North Vietnamese attack on U.S. naval vessels in the Gulf of Tonkin, which the Johnson administration had used as a pretext for escalating U.S. participation in the war (see Chapter 8 for all the details). Further, the report showed that contingency plans for America's entry into the war were already in place when Johnson went before the nation promising that he wouldn't send combat troops to Vietnam. Though the *Pentagon Papers* dealt only with events up to 1968 (and therefore condemned Kennedy and Johnson more than Nixon), Nixon fought their publication on the grounds that their release was a threat to national security, but his attempts failed. His stance on the papers and his secret expansion of the war into Laos and Cambodia (see Chapter 10 for details) only served to make many Americans feel that he was no more trustworthy than Johnson had been.

For Nixon, the leak of the *Pentagon Papers* put him on the path to greater difficulties, because his response was to put together his team of shady White House "plumbers" to stop leaks in the White House — the team that would eventually lead to his demise. It was this group of officials, many of them former CIA personnel, who broke into the Democratic National Headquarters in the Watergate Hotel in the early '70s, initiating the scandal that ultimately forced Nixon to resign to avoid impeachment. (See the sidebar "The infamous Watergate scandal," later in this chapter, for more info.)

Achieving success with foreign policy

Nixon's foreign policy goals were much broader than Johnson's had been. He saw the key to the war in Vietnam in separating the North Vietnamese from their sponsors of China and the Soviet Union. Further, Nixon hoped that by working with both the Chinese and the Soviets, he could play them against each other and widen the already existing gap between the two interpretations of Communism. Nixon's strategy yielded powerful results for both goals, enhancing the U.S. negotiating position with the North Vietnamese and increasing U.S. power in the cold war.

✔ **Establishing relations with China:** One of Nixon's greatest successes as president came from his creation of diplomatic relations with China. Since Communist China was established in 1949, the U.S. had refused to recognize the new Communist nation, instead insisting that nationalist government in Taiwan was the rightful Chinese government.

Nixon's historic trip to mainland China in 1972 ended 20 years of Chinese isolation from the U.S., with both sides agreeing to scientific and cultural exchanges. They also discussed resuming trade and the possibility of reconciling the two Chinas. The U.S. and China established unofficial embassies, which lasted until 1979 when formal recognition and proper embassies were established. Today China is one of the strongest trading partners of the U.S., a feat for which credit is owed to the diplomatic brilliance of Nixon and Henry Kissinger.

✔ **Easing tensions with the Soviets:** In 1972 Nixon announced that he'd visit the Soviet Union. Since 1969, Nixon had negotiators working on an agreement with the Soviets, aimed at limiting each country's arsenal of nuclear missiles. This work came to fruition three years later, when Nixon met with Soviet Premier Leonid Brezhnev and established *détente* (an easing of tensions) between the two superpowers, both of them signing the Strategic Arms Limitation Treaty (SALT I). The treaty didn't end the arms race, but it helped stabilize it, producing dialogue aimed at future cooperative agreements. At this meeting, the two nations also made trade agreements, including the U.S. deal to sell one-quarter of its national wheat crop to the Soviets.

✔ **Working toward Middle East peace:** Although efforts for diplomacy in the Middle East were less spectacular than the achievements in China and the Soviet Union, the U.S. did make advances toward Middle East peace. Though Kissinger's efforts were appreciated in the Arab capitals, he wasn't able to broker a major peace accord. He did, however, lay the groundwork for the peace accords created later under the Carter administration.

Focusing on the domestic front

Nixon's domestic successes were much more modest than his foreign policy achievements, largely because he faced a Congress where both the House and the Senate remained under Democratic control. One bright spot occurred on July 16, 1969, with the launch of Apollo 11, when the U.S. fulfilled John F. Kennedy's dream to place an American on the moon before the end of the decade. Figure 4-3 shows Neil Armstrong walking on the moon.

Figure 4-3:
The Man on
the Moon.

Courtesy of NASA

Attempting to push back civil rights

Though Nixon said that the U.S. should steer a middle path between segregation forever and integration now, in actuality he worked hard behind the scenes to block the renewal of the Voting Rights Act of 1965 and vetoed the Voting Rights Act renewal that Congress passed despite his objection. (Congress overrode his veto; see Chapter 3 for more on the Civil Rights Act of 1964 and the Voting Rights Act of 1965.) Nixon also worked to delay the forced integration of schools in Mississippi.

The U.S. Supreme Court opposed Nixon's attempts to delay desegregation by ordering Mississippi schools to do so immediately. The Nixon White House was clearly antiblack in its outlook and strove to roll back civil rights advances of the Kennedy and Johnson administrations. Sixty-five lawyers within the Justice Department signed a letter of protest against the Nixon administration's stance on civil rights issues.

When desegregation orders began to be implemented in the North, many families rose up to complain that their neighborhood schools were being undermined. Nixon asked Congress to put a halt to forced bussing programs. The

House went along with this scheme, but a *filibuster* (an action in which senators literally talk a bill to death to avoid it coming to a vote before the bill expires) in the Senate blocked Nixon's attempts to get his antibussing bill through. However, the High Court (which was already becoming more conservative through Nixon's appointments) weakened some civil rights legislation through cases such as *Bakke v. The Board of Regents of California,* which restricted the use of racial quotas in admissions systems.

Facing opposing legislation by the Democratic Congress

Though Nixon sought to roll back many of the gains achieved under Johnson's Great Society programs, he faced a Democratic Congress that opposed much of his agenda. Even during the Nixon administration, the Democrats passed several important new laws:

- Voting rights for 18-year-olds in national elections
- Increased funding for food stamps
- Social Security benefits indexed to the inflation rate
- Clean Air Act and water pollution bills
- Campaign finance reform with the Federal Election Campaign Act

Battling economic malaise

Oddly, in the late '60s and early '70s the U.S. economy was suffering from a recession and inflation at the same time. Usually during a recession, inflation isn't a problem, yet the odd conditions of the day created this new problem. The costs of the Vietnam War tended to overheat the economy, fueling inflation beginning in 1967. By 1973 the inflation rate had risen to 9 percent, and in 1974 it rose to 12 percent. Meanwhile, the Dow Jones Industrial Average fell 36 percent between 1968 and 1970. In 1968, unemployment was 3.3 percent, yet by 1970 it had risen to 6 percent.

Economists dubbed the strange problem as *stagflation.* To address this new problem, Nixon tried old remedies. First, he tried to reduce the federal deficit by raising taxes and cutting the budget. When Democrats in Congress refused to cooperate, Nixon called on the Federal Reserve Board to raise interest rates in hopes of reducing the money supply. However, this elevation caused the stock market to collapse, creating the Nixon recession of 1969.

Creating the Environmental Protection Agency

In the late 1960s, many Americans began to take an interest in the environment. After the Democrats in Congress passed legislation regarding water and air pollution, Nixon issued an executive order to create the Environmental Protection Agency, which consolidated existing agencies and created federal guidelines for air pollution, water pollution, and toxic wastes.

Running for Reelection

By 1972, Nixon's foreign policy victories made him the clear frontrunner in the election. His only real fear was from Independent George Wallace, the governor of Alabama. As a third-party candidate, George Wallace didn't have a chance to beat Nixon, yet he could've played the spoiler by shifting conservative votes away from the Republican candidate. This potential problem disappeared on May 15, 1972, when Wallace was shot and left paralyzed below the waist, forcing him to withdraw from the race.

The Democrats nominated South Dakota senator George McGovern, who was swept into the position by the expansion of minority and women voters. Though McGovern was the antiwar candidate, this attribute mattered little because the Vietnam War was rapidly winding down. At the polls Nixon was reelected, capturing 520 electoral votes to McGovern's 17. Less than two years later he was forced to resign from office due to the Watergate scandal (see the corresponding sidebar).

The infamous Watergate scandal

During the 1972 election, the Watergate scandal erupted. The White House "plumbers," a team that Nixon had put together to stop the leaks in the White House (see "The truth is out there" section in this chapter), had become the key players in CREEP, the Committee to Re-Elect the President. These men zealously pursued their goal of reelecting Nixon by disrupting the Democrats in any way they could. Their most outrageous act was breaking into the Democratic National Headquarters in the Watergate Hotel in order to search for any information on the Democrats that could give the Republicans the edge in the election. Through their own ineptitude, a group assigned to actually pull off the caper was caught in the act. Subsequent investigations led authorities to CREEP, and eventually, all leads led back to the White House.

Though no evidence suggests that Nixon ordered the break-in or even knew about it beforehand, he clearly worked hard to cover up the crimes. Though Nixon used every trick he could think of to thwart the investigation, including using the CIA to undermine the FBI investigation and refusing to hand over key evidence to prosecutors, his own recordings made in the Oval Office helped prove him guilty of the coverup. In July 1974, the House Judiciary Committee voted to recommend three articles of impeachment: obstruction of justice, abuse of power, and defiance of Congress. Realizing that impeachment and conviction was imminent, Nixon resigned as president on August 9, becoming the only U.S. president to resign from office. Vice President Gerald Ford took Nixon's position as president and promptly pardoned him of all crimes, even though he stated before he took office that there would be no pardon. Ford's excuse was that pardoning the former president was for the good of the nation.

Part II
Marching toward Freedom: The Civil Rights Movement

The 5th Wave   By Rich Tennant

"I marched in Selma, Montgomery, and D.C. But I'm not marching on a bleach company because their bottle contains the message 'whites only'."

In this part . . .

In a decade filled with defining movements and moments, the push for civil rights puts as large of a stamp on the decade as any other. But the struggle for freedom and equality has deep roots in American history, and to best understand the movement in the 1960s, you need to take a brief look at its foundation. Although what we call the civil rights movement can be dated to the 1954 Supreme Court ruling that struck down segregation and Rosa Parks' decision in 1955 to refuse to give up her seat on the bus (and the Montgomery Bus Boycott that followed), the struggle for racial equality (which continues to this day) may have been the most important event of the decade. Not only did the movement result in the elimination of segregation in public facilities and enforcement of voting rights for all Americans, but it also sparked protests in many other areas (such as antiwar protests, women's rights, American Indian rights, and gay and lesbian rights).

After taking a look at the foundation, we examine the movement in the early sixties. In the beginning, the civil rights movement pushed forward using the philosophy of nonviolent protest. Advanced by Martin Luther King Jr., the civil rights movement brought about an appreciation of politicians and the American public for the plight of African Americans in the South. However, many blacks became impatient with the movement's progress and unhappy with the role of whites in the movement. We wrap up this part by exploring the latter part of the decade including King's assassination and the increased militancy of the movement, some corners of which supported separatism rather than integration, and advocating violence when necessary, especially in self-defense.

Chapter 5

Establishing a Firm Foundation

In This Chapter

▶ Uncovering the roots of segregation

▶ Making their presence known

▶ Staring down hatred and violence

▶ Integrating public schools

▶ Boycotting the buses

▶ Supporting civil rights with legislation

*T*he civil rights movement, which began during the late 1950s, was a defining event of the 1960s. The recognition of equality and the extension of rights to African Americans that are taken for granted today were the direct result of monumental actions undertaken by America's black community and their supporters during the sixties. But changes don't take place in a vacuum — especially when they're as important as those resulting from the civil rights movement. So, to fully understand the events of the '60s you need to take a look at how the U.S. and the black freedom struggle got to that point.

In this chapter, we take a quick look at a post–Civil War push for equality and the stiff resistance that delayed its realization. We then turn our attention to times and events much closer to the 1960s — the United States after World War II, especially in the 1950s, as events in that decade established the path the would lead the civil rights movement through the '60s. Gradually, in the second half of the 20th century, blacks began to push again for the promise that America was supposed to fulfill.

The Post–Civil War Era and Jim Crow

From their sale in Africa to the horrific trips across the Atlantic Ocean and their enslavement throughout the New World, blacks have fought to be treated with dignity and equality under the law. Even after the Civil War ended in 1865, and the addition of the 13th Amendment to the Constitution in 1865, which freed all slaves, blacks weren't equal members of American society. For the most part, whites refused to treat blacks as equals; even the Northern states housed a great number of whites who were hostile, scornful, and fearful of blacks, even if they didn't express it as openly or violently.

To make it possible for blacks to vote and also bring the southern states back into the Union, Congress implemented a Reconstruction Act, which lasted from 1866 to 1877. Under Reconstruction, the southern states were placed under military rule and were required to meet strict conditions in order to be readmitted to the Union, including ratification of the 14th Amendment, which granted full citizenship to blacks, and the 15th Amendment, which insured the right to vote (for men only, just as it was for whites). Almost all the southern states refused — they saw Reconstruction as a humiliating effort to destroy their way of life and wouldn't ratify the amendments. Only through the use of the Force Acts (enacted between 1870 and 1875 and imposed penalties on Southerners who tried to obstruct the Reconstruction program) as well as the presence of northern troops, were southern states forced to comply on the issue.

Southerners opposed Reconstruction with the Ku Klux Klan and other similar organizations. In the beginning, the Klan consisted of local groups of armed men who terrorized blacks (and violently dispensed "justice" outside the realms of the law) in almost all southern communities. The Klan rode in the dead of night, hidden by white robes, and burned crosses to announce their presence. But crosses weren't the only things they burned — they torched houses, dragged folks out of their homes, and administered whippings and lynchings. One of their main objectives was to keep blacks away from the polls and thus reclaim political powers for whites.

In 1871, Congress passed an anti-Klan bill (one of the Force Acts), and the Klan all but disappeared until 1915, when a "new" Klan remerged. This revamped Klan added white supremacy, anti-Semitism, anti-Catholicism, and anti-Communism to its menu of hate.

However, blacks made some important headway during Reconstruction:

- ✔ **They hit the books.** When freed Southern blacks got the opportunity to go to schools (a right that was routinely denied to slaves), people of all ages took advantage of the opportunity to become literate.

- ✔ **They ran for office (and won).** Black men became involved in local, state, and national government.

- ✔ **They made some bread and bought some dirt.** Or, if you prefer the non-'60s-slang version, they took advantage of opportunities to acquire land and secure employment.

Amidst a highly disputed presidential election of 1876 between Democrat Samuel Tilden and Republican Rutherford B. Hayes, the two political parties made a corrupt bargain. The disputed election went to Hayes after Southern Democrats agreed to accept the Republican win if the North pulled its troops out of the southern states, which in turn ended Reconstruction in 1877. With northern troops gone, the southern states began to roll back the gains made by blacks in the post–Civil War period.

Southern leaders created *Jim Crow Laws* to keep blacks and whites separate. These laws, which remained in effect until they were overturned during the last half of the 20th century, prohibited interracial marriage and segregated schools, restaurants, transportation, and other public and private facilities. Though denying blacks the right to vote was illegal, southerners used *poll taxes* (an amount that had to be paid before an individual could vote) and literacy tests to weed out black voters. Poor whites who couldn't read were often exempt from such requirements due to loopholes purposely placed in the laws. White southerners began reclaiming their power, and by the end of the decade, most of the gains for blacks had been lost.

In 1896 the U.S. Supreme Court ruled in the *Plessy v. Ferguson* case that "separate but equal" facilities weren't contrary to the 14th Amendment to the Constitution, which guaranteed civil rights to all citizens. *Segregation* (the separation of people according to race) clearly made schools, drinking fountains, and restaurants separate, yet the government did little to ensure that the facilities were equal. For the most part, all "equal" meant was that facilities existed, and the facilities for blacks were routinely inferior. Few changes were made until the 1954 Supreme Court ruling of *Brown v. Topeka Board of Education* case, which required desegregation (see the section "Exposing the fallacy of separate and equal," later in this chapter).

Demanding a Place in American Society

Up through World War II, blacks remained on the margins of the larger American society. Because of white prejudice, getting a good education or a high paying job was difficult if not impossible, which left blacks out of the mainstream and, therefore, mostly invisible to the white community. After World War II, however, blacks became far more visible to the larger white society in the United States, due in part to their service to the country. In this section, we detail how some folks took advantage of whatever opportunities were available and, in the process, challenged stereotypes and fought against unequal treatment. Of course, the following groups, individuals, and actions are by no means the whole story. They do, however, provide a glimpse into what it took to achieve large-scale success in the decades before the sixties.

Stepping out on the frontlines

From the time blacks came to the colonies, they fought alongside their white neighbors. From fighting for freedom in the Civil War to playing an instrumental role in shaping the American West as "buffalo soldiers" (fighting Mexican revolutionaries, American Indians, and outlaws and repairing buildings, stringing telegraph wire, and protecting the men who built the railroads), African Americans have a long history of displaying valor for a country that didn't accept them as equals. Even when fighting for their country, it was common for blacks to be in separate military units. Often, their quarters and supplies were inferior, their white leaders were inexperienced, and they were thrown into the most dangerous missions.

Up through World War II, the U.S. military remained segregated, but the contributions of black troops were becoming harder to ignore. To prove that they were equal to white soldiers, black soldiers volunteered for some of the most dangerous missions, and that, along with the exploits of the Tuskegee airmen and protests of their separate and unequal treatment, brought black fighting men to the attention of the public and eventually led to the integration of the military.

With the formation of the famed 66th Air Force Flying School at the all-black Tuskegee Institute the heroism of African American soldiers was ready to take center stage. Throughout the war, the 99th Squadron, the first group of men trained at the Tuskegee Institute, racked up an impressive number of victories with strikes against German forces in Italy. Unlike contributions in earlier wars, the squadron's victories, as well as the indignities of fighting in a segregated army, garnered the attention of correspondents. Despite their success, many people criticized them, which made them work even harder — they felt that they had to be better and braver than whites, because their performance would affect all other blacks in the military.

After the impressive performance of the Tuskegee Airmen and other black regiments, the War Department and the federal government reexamined their policy of maintaining a segregated military, and in 1948, President Truman issued executive orders that mandated "equality of opportunity" in the U.S. armed forces (and not integration, as is commonly and mistakenly thought). In spite of President Truman's orders, segregated units existed as late as the Korean War (1950 to 1953).

Although an integrated military has offered a wealth of opportunities to blacks and other minorities, it came at a large cost. In the Vietnam War, as well as the Gulf War in the 1990s and the War in Iraq shortly after the turn of the millennium, blacks and other minorities were represented in a large proportion. Although the Vietnam War (see Chapters 8, 9, and 10) involved a military draft, whites were better able to take advantage of deferments. After the draft was abolished, recruiters began targeting minorities in poor communities, offering them education as well as a feeling of belonging and dignity. Consequently, a larger proportion of blacks and other minorities die in war than whites.

Claiming first place

At one time, blacks were almost completely excluded from participating in sports together with whites. In the 21st century, sports are seen as an almost completely integrated field of dreams. In the 1960s, not only did black athletes make their mark on the playing fields, but they also spoke up for issues affecting larger society. Jim Brown, who played with the Cleveland Browns from 1957 to 1965, spoke out on civil rights issues, and Muhammad Ali (see Chapter 16) took a stand against the Vietnam War.

Making the Majors

Baseball was America's pastime, but until 1947, it existed in two parallel universes — black and white. Blacks were excluded from Major League Baseball; instead, they had leagues of their own: the Negro National League (formed in 1933) and the Negro American League (established in 1937). The Negro Leagues had a roster of celebrity players, such as Satchel Paige and Josh Gibson, who could equal, if not surpass, the most celebrated stars of the American and National Leagues.

Jackie Robinson, infielder for the Brooklyn Dodgers, was the man who broke the color barrier. In 1945, while playing in the Negro Leagues, he caught the attention of Dodgers' owner Branch Rickey, who signed Robinson to the Montreal Royals, a Dodgers' farm team. On April 15, 1947, Robinson was called up to the major leagues and made his first appearance at Ebbets Field in Brooklyn. Although he was often snubbed by teammates and harassed by fans and opposing teams, he persevered, playing a great game and earning respect (although sometimes grudgingly) from players and fans. Robinson knew his worth and refused to be grateful to the white men for his opportunities; as such, whites often criticized him for "not knowing his place." After Jackie Robinson, baseball — and, in fact, all sports in America — was never the same.

In 1946, Kenny Washington became the first African American to play in the NFL for the Los Angeles Rams. And in 1950, Chuck Cooper joined the Boston Celtics, becoming the first African American in the NBA.

Racing to the finish line

In 1936, the Olympic games were played in Nazi Germany. These games, Hitler hoped, would prove to the world that the Aryan race was superior and that the Germans would take the lion's share of the medals. However, Jesse Owens, track star from Ohio State, disproved Hitler's theory. Owens won the 100-meter dash, the 200-meter dash, and the broad jump. In spite of his accomplishments, Owens' race prevented him from cashing in on his fame and prowess. In the 1930s, no company would offer an endorsement contract to a black athlete, so he had to resort to racing in exhibitions against other people, animals, and even vehicles.

Wilma Rudolph was another Olympic track star who overcame poverty and racism to become a top athlete. A childhood survivor of scarlet fever and polio, she was determined to excel, playing basketball and running track in high school and college. In the 1960 Olympic games in Rome, Rudolph earned the title "World's Fastest Woman" by winning gold medals for the 100-meter dash, the 200-meter dash (setting an Olympic record), and as part of the 400-meter relay team (setting a world record).

Gaining freedom through song and stage

Blacks have always been prominent in the field of music, although mainly in the black world, in the genres of jazz and blues. However, some pre-sixties entertainers not only crossed the color line, but crashed through it, making powerful friends and enemies along the way. Here are just a few of those entertainers — all of them, in their own way, fought racism rather than accept the status quo.

Opening night at the Lincoln Memorial

Born in 1902, classically trained opera singer Marian Anderson was acclaimed, mostly in Europe, for her concert performances. When she returned to the United States, Anderson performed at benefits for Howard University (a black institution in Washington, D.C.), singing to larger crowds each year. In 1939, the university was forced to look for a larger venue for its annual benefit, mostly because of Anderson's fame. They tried to lease Constitution Hall from the Daughters of the American Revolution (DAR) but were turned down, ostensibly because it was booked; however, the DAR was known for refusing to rent to blacks.

Both black and white citizens were outraged that an acclaimed artist such as Anderson couldn't perform at Constitution Hall. In fact, the outrage reached all the way to the top of D.C. power — First Lady Eleanor Roosevelt resigned from the DAR in protest, writing about her decision in her column *My Day,* which was published in newspapers across the country. To find a place for Anderson's concert, Secretary of the Interior Harold Ickes arranged for her performance at the Lincoln Memorial. On Easter Sunday, 1939, she sang in front of Lincoln's statue, an impressive and enduring image of an effort to protest racism and discrimination at the highest level of government.

Making popular music

Blacks also made their mark in jazz and popular music during the '50s and early '60s. Nat "King" Cole moved from the world of jazz to popular music during the 1940s, and during his career, broke a number of barriers. In 1948, he was the first black jazz performer to have his own radio show, and in 1956, was the first black entertainer to have a weekly show on network TV. However, the show was cancelled in 1957, because national sponsors didn't want to invest in a "black" show.

Ray Charles was another musician who embraced a variety of musical genres. From the late '40s until his death in 2004, Ray Charles performed jazz, gospel, country, R&B, pop, and rock 'n' roll, and attracted fans across color lines. Charles took a public stand against racism by refusing to play in segregated venues, and he supported civil rights in the '60s.

Taking the stage and speaking out

From 1924 until 1947, Paul Robeson was a famous performer. Robeson was a singer, accomplished athlete, author, and actor — but through much of his life, his political activism often eclipsed his talent. Son of a slave and educated as a lawyer, Robeson loved performing and appeared in several of Eugene O'Neill's plays, including *Emperor Jones,* and gave impressive performances in Shakespeare's *Othello.* But Robeson was as dedicated to social ideals as he was to performing, and he actively fought racism and fascism at home and abroad. He counted people such as Eleanor Roosevelt, W. E. B. DuBois, Lena Horne, and Harry Truman among his friends.

During the Red Scare of the 1950s, marked by fear of Communism (see Chapter 11 for more about McCarthyism), Robeson was considered as a threat to American democracy because of his visits to the Soviet Union and his questioning of why blacks should support a government that treated them poorly. When the House Un-American Affairs Committee condemned him, the State Department revoked and confiscated his passport. Eight years passed before it was restored and he was again able to travel abroad. However, today people remember him as one of the African American performers who used his intelligence, talent, and fame to help others.

Creating a cultural center — the Harlem Renaissance

As a center of black culture, writers, artists, and performers thrived in Harlem in the 1920s and '30s. The movement was collectively called the New Negro Movement and later referred to as the Harlem Renaissance. Langston Hughes, Countee Cullen, Zora Neale Hurston, and W. E. B. DuBois are among the best-known writers of the period. Black theater and the visual arts flourished as well. The Cotton Club was a showcase for some of the best black entertainers of the day, including Josephine Baker, Lena Horne, Cab Calloway, Duke Ellington, and Bessie Smith.

However, the Harlem Renaissance wasn't just about the arts and culture — it was also about Black Nationalism. Many of the artists and writers supported Marcus Garvey (a leader who promoted separatism for blacks and repatriation for all immigrants to their countries of origin to preserve their heritage), a more positive self-image, and a more positive image among the white community (which didn't affect many white Americans, who had no concept of black life).

Working within the government

After Reconstruction and before the civil rights movement of the 1960s, few blacks were involved in government. One controversial congressman, Adam Clayton Powell, definitely made his presence and opinions known, and because of it, aroused the ire of his colleagues in Congress. Ralph Bunche, who worked for peace on an international scale, and Thurgood Marshall, who argued the *Brown v. Topeka Board of Education* case in 1954, were two other African Americans at the top levels of government.

Reaching Capitol Hill

Adam Clayton Powell Jr., a New York preacher and politician, could make things happen. In 1944, he was elected as the first post-Reconstruction black congressman. While in Congress, Powell fought for civil rights and worked for desegregation. Some of his more important accomplishments include the integration of whites and blacks in House of Representatives facilities, the accreditation of black reporters to the House of Representatives, and the desegregation of the U.S. Naval Academy.

Powell also fought to ban poll taxes and tried to attach antidiscrimination clauses to most *appropriations measures* (the allocation of money for some specific purposes). But Powell wasn't popular with all his colleagues, and in 1967, he was accused of misusing government funds and was refused his seat in the House. He took his case to the Supreme Court, which vindicated him, and cited racism as the reason for the trumped-up charges; however, his reputation was just about ruined by all the media coverage. But in 1969, Powell regained his seat, which he used to protest the Vietnam War.

Working for world peace

Ralph Bunche, an educator, scholar, and diplomat, gained international fame through his work at the United Nations. He participated in drafting the U.N. charter and worked for colonial nations that were pressing for self-government. His most important work was as the U.N. mediator on Palestine, where he negotiated an armistice between Israel and the Arab nations. For this achievement, Bunche was awarded the Nobel Prize for Peace in 1950.

Taking it all the way to the Supreme Court

Thurgood Marshall was the first African American to sit on the U.S. Supreme Court, beginning in 1967. Though nowhere near as vocal or charismatic as some other black activists, he accomplished a great deal working through the courts. A lawyer from a middle-class family in Baltimore, Maryland, Marshall concentrated on civil rights cases for most of his career, both in private practice and as counsel for the National Association for the Advancement of Colored People (NAACP). As a lawyer, his most famous and important case was *Brown v. Topeka Board of Education* (see the "Exposing the fallacy of separate and equal" section, later in this chapter), which ruled that segregated education was illegal. Marshall argued 32 cases before the Supreme Court, winning 29.

President Kennedy appointed Marshall to the Second Circuit Court of Appeals in 1961, and in 1965, President Johnson appointed him Solicitor General. Then, on June 13, 1967, Johnson named him to the Supreme Court. When Johnson appointed Marshall as Solicitor General, he said that it was "the right thing to do, the right time to do it, the right man, and the right place."

Although some black leaders later condemned Marshall for his moderate views on integration rather than pressing for black power, he believed that integration was the only way to achieve equality and justice in American society. He was also convinced that integration could only be achieved through the law — peaceful protest excited passion and gathered publicity but accomplished little, and violent revolution and continued racial separation would only aggravate racism.

As a Supreme Court justice, Marshall consistently supported liberal causes. Besides promoting integration, he advocated women's rights, reproductive freedom, and affirmative action. He consistently opposed the death penalty. As Republican presidents occupied the White House and more conservative justices joined the court, Marshall was often part of the minority opinion, but he persisted in advocating the causes that were important to him. Even when his health began to fail, Marshall resisted resigning as long as possible, in order to maintain a liberal presence in the court.

Enduring the Brutality of Racial Violence

Fear often brings about violence. And whites, especially in the South, probably had good reason to fear blacks — their population was large, and they justifiably resented their treatment at the hands of whites. So whites not only made sure that blacks stayed away from them, but they lashed out, often violently, against them.

The aim and end of lynch mobs

Many people say that the Ku Klux Klan, with their robes, masks, and burning crosses, existed mainly to terrorize and intimidate blacks. However, their actions were actually much more brutal — they often beat, whipped, and tortured their victims. However, *lynching* (an execution by hanging, by a mob) was the most brutal of all. The years from the end of Reconstruction (1877) to the beginning of the Great Depression (1929) saw the greatest number of lynchings, mostly in the southern states, although it continued, on a much lesser scale, into the 1960s.

However, lynching wasn't the exclusive province of the Klan, as other white supremacist organizations utilized the same tactics. Often, ordinary citizens banded together to form a mob and acted as police, judge, jury, and executioner, sometimes for relatively minor infractions, and sometimes for no reason at all. Lynch mobs preferred doling out their punishments in public places in order to inspire fear among the black community. But blacks weren't the only victims of lynching — whites who protested vigilante justice were also targets of mob rule.

Lynching wasn't limited to hanging. Often the mobs stripped, whipped, beat, dismembered, and burned their victims. Whites often lynched blacks in order to control the black population through fear and terror and to eliminate competition for economic and political power.

The murder of Emmett Till

To a large extent, lynching was America's dirty secret. Many white Americans had no idea it was going on, and if they did, they preferred to ignore it. However, in 1955 the lynching of a teenager in Mississippi brought the horror of racism, in its most extreme form, to the forefront of American consciousness.

Emmett Till, a 14-year-old from Chicago, was visiting relatives in Mississippi in the summer of 1955. As teenagers do, he was hanging out with friends in front of a local store. His friends dared him to talk to a white woman, and he did, bidding goodbye to the store owner's wife. Several days later, two white men rousted him out of his uncle's house, and three days later, his mutilated body was pulled from the Tallahatchie River.

Till's mother had his body shipped back to Chicago, and pictures of her son were all over the media. People all over the country were horrified, even southern whites. However, the worst horror was yet to come — despite overwhelming evidence, Till's murderers were acquitted.

More than perhaps any other incident until that time, the murder of Emmett Till united blacks — those living in the North, though many miles from Mississippi, saw how vulnerable they were. And whites, some for the first time, were forced to see the injustice and brutality of racism.

Integrating the Schools

Up through the 1950s, many American public schools were segregated by race. Southern states drew the line with local legislation confirmed by the 1896 Supreme Court case *Plessy v. Ferguson,* which determined that separate public facilities were constitutional as long as they were equal. Although the decision was originally made in a case about segregated railroad cars, local laws applied the principle to almost all other public facilities, including restaurants, theaters, restrooms, recreational facilities, and public schools.

Exposing the fallacy of separate and equal

In 1954, the *Brown v. Topeka Board of Education* case was brought before the Supreme Court, contending that by their very nature, no separate facilities could be considered equal. Following the court's ruling, the rest of the century was marked by issues relating to school integration.

The case came about in 1951 when a black man, Oliver Brown, wanted to send his daughter Linda to the elementary school closest to her home, a white school in Topeka, Kansas. When he tried to enroll her, the principal refused. Brown asked the local NAACP to represent him and they agreed, because it was a great opportunity to pursue a school desegregation case.

At first, the case went before the Federal District Court in Kansas. The Board of Education argued that segregated schools realistically prepared blacks for a life of segregation, but Brown's lawyers claimed that separate schools implied inferiority. Although the court heard and largely agreed with arguments contending that separate schools were implicitly unequal, they upheld the board's right to keep Topeka's schools segregated, because of the precedent set by *Plessy v. Ferguson.*

When Brown and the NAACP, led by lawyer Thurgood Marshall (see the "Taking it all the way to the Supreme Court" section), appealed to the Supreme Court on October 1, 1951, the case was combined with other cases challenging school segregation. The Supreme Court heard the case several times between 1952 and 1954 before reaching a decision. Finally, on May 17, 1954, the court overturned the "separate but equal" doctrine because it violated the 14th Amendment to the Constitution, mandating that schools be integrated with "all deliberate speed."

Chief Justice Earl Warren read the unanimous decision, which said, in part, "Does segregation . . . in public schools solely on the basis of race, even though the physical facilities . . . may be equal, deprive the children of the minority group of equal educational opportunities? We believe that it does. Separate educational facilities are inherently unequal."

Brown v. Topeka Board of Education was hailed as a great victory for integration, but the long-term results didn't reflect the initial euphoria. "All deliberate speed" was very loosely interpreted, and many communities instead exercised the principle of "all deliberate deliberation." Also, even in states where segregation hadn't been legally mandated, schools reflected their segregated communities. The Brown decision caused minorities to question these "de facto" segregated schools, which often were in old, inferior buildings and had inexperienced teachers and fewer funds to spend on textbooks, labs, and other educational materials.

In 1970 a federal judge in North Carolina ordered school busing in an effort to end de facto segregation (which resulted from racially segregated neighborhoods rather than from schools segregated by law). A year later, the Supreme Court upheld the use of busing to achieve integration. In 1974, when a judge mandated busing in Boston, protests and violence were as vocal and violent as some of the protests in the South during the 1960s.

Desegregating Central High School

Almost immediately after *Brown v. Topeka Board of Education,* the school board of Little Rock Arkansas announced that it would begin to implement the new law, and by 1957 made plans to gradually desegregate the public schools. They planned to integrate the high schools first, followed by the junior high and elementary schools. Everyone expected that the plan would go smoothly because the University of Arkansas's law school had been integrated since 1949, and seven of its eight state universities were desegregated by 1957. In addition, many other public facilities, such as transportation, parks, and libraries, were already integrated.

However, Arkansas governor Orval Faubus didn't get with the program. A confirmed segregationist, he was dead set against integrating the schools, and on September 2, called out the Arkansas National Guard to prevent nine black students from entering Little Rock Central High School. However, the troops were withdrawn on September 20 when a federal injunction prohibited using the National Guard to prevent integration.

In each state, the National Guard is commanded by the governor and can be called out in cases of natural disaster or civil unrest. However, in cases of national emergency, the president can mobilize the guard and put it under federal control.

On September 23, police surrounded the school and escorted the nine black students inside. However, after the anti-integrationists found out that the blacks were inside, they began to storm the school. Fearing mob violence, the administration got the nine black students out of the building.

Finally, the state of Arkansas realized that they needed federal help. On September 24, Little Rock mayor Woodrow Mann sent a telegram to President Eisenhower requesting troops. Eisenhower federalized the Arkansas National Guard to remove them from Faubus's control, and the next day, under protection of Arkansas National Guard and 1,000 members of the 101st Airborne Division of the United States Army, the nine black students entered Little Rock Central High School. In spite of the apprehension of students, parents, faculty, and administration, integration of Central High School went better than expected. Most people were determined to obey the law, and few incidents occurred. In spite of angry citizens and the governor, Arkansas desegregated its schools. Faubus was reelected as governor six times and became more moderate over the years. However, in 1965, after passage of the Voting Rights Act, which enabled more blacks to vote (see Chapter 7), Faubus was defeated and was never reelected.

Rosa Parks and the Bus Boycott

One day, a simple act by one young woman helped set the wheels of the civil rights movement in motion. Although blacks have worked for their freedom and equality since they arrived in the United States, Rosa Parks's civil disobedience and arrest changed the focus of the movement, from solely relying on the courts to gain equality to rejecting and protesting their treatment in segregated states.

Staking a claim to her seat

On December 1, 1955, Rosa Parks, a seamstress from Montgomery, Alabama, got on a bus to head home from work. Though she hated the indignity of the seating arrangement, she went to the back of the bus, which was the only place where blacks were allowed to sit. However, blacks were required by law to give up their seats in the back if a white person asked.

In 1955, the back of the bus was considered the *colored* section, a term that was considered polite, if somewhat demeaning. Through subsequent decades, *Negro, black,* and *African American* became the preferred terms.

On that fateful day, when the front (white) section of the bus filled up, a white man asked Parks to give up her seat in the back, and she refused. Contrary to popular legend, she didn't refuse just because she was tired. Rather, she was sick and tired of being treated like a second-class citizen. When she refused to give up her seat, the white bus driver threatened to call the police, but she held her ground. The police arrived and Parks was escorted to the police station, where she was fingerprinted and then released on bail after talking to an NAACP lawyer (see Figure 5-1).

Figure 5-1:
Rosa Parks and one of her attorneys, Charles Langford.

©*Bettmann/CORBIS*

Rosa Parks didn't become an activist because of this incident. By 1955, she was already working for civil rights. She was active in the Montgomery Voters League, an organization established to help blacks pass the literacy tests designed to keep them from registering to vote. She was also involved in the NAACP, and she had already recognized and begun to protest the indignity of segregation. Whenever possible, she avoided elevators and buses, preferring to walk or climb stairs rather than be treated as inferior.

Rosa Parks wasn't the first African American to be arrested for refusing to give up her seat on a Montgomery bus. But, by the time of her arrest, anger and resentment about their humiliating treatment roused blacks to action.

Boycotting the buses

The day after Rosa Parks's arrest, the word went out among Montgomery's black community. The Women's Political Council decided to protest her mistreatment by organizing a bus boycott to begin on December 5, the day of Parks's trial. However, the plan wasn't to keep the boycott small — Martin Luther King Jr. and others in Montgomery's black community formed the

Montgomery Improvement Association (MIA) to continue boycotting the buses until the segregation laws were changed. The main objective of the boycott was to end segregation in the Montgomery public transportation system and also to hire black bus drivers in Montgomery.

Although the MIA expected the boycott to be a success, it exceeded their wildest expectations. Almost all of Montgomery's black community avoided the buses, walking, taking cabs, organizing carpools, and even riding mules to get to where they were going. Often, whites refused to be without their domestic workers and drove them back and forth to work.

The boycott lasted for 382 days, costing the bus company a great deal of money, but the city refused to give in. Boycott leaders filed a federal lawsuit against Montgomery's segregation laws, claiming that the city violated the 14th Amendment. On June 4, 1956, a federal court ruled that the segregation laws were unconstitutional, but Montgomery county lawyers appealed. The boycott continued until November 13, when the Supreme Court declared the Montgomery segregation laws illegal.

During the boycott, the authorities made numerous arrests. At one point, the police arrested groups of blacks waiting for carpool pickups. On February 21, 1956, a grand jury declared the boycott illegal, and 115 boycott leaders were arrested.

After the Supreme Court decision was officially received in Montgomery, the boycott ended, and the buses of Montgomery, Alabama, were no longer segregated. However, Rosa Parks's refusal to give up her seat, followed by the yearlong bus boycott, had far-reaching results. Blacks in other southern cities realized that if protest worked in Montgomery, it could work elsewhere, and they began to protest segregation in their own towns. Also, because of his role in the Montgomery Bus Boycott, Martin Luther King Jr. gained national prominence and rose to the forefront of the civil rights movement (see Chapter 6 for information on his life).

The Civil Rights Act of 1957

The first significant civil rights legislation since 1875 was the Civil Rights Act of 1957, passed during the Eisenhower administration. Although President Dwight Eisenhower never actively supported integration and civil rights (he believed that laws couldn't change people's beliefs), he did support the Civil Rights Act, possibly as a reaction to the public's outcry against the violence in Little Rock, Arkansas (see the "Desegregating Central High School" section earlier in the chapter). The main focus of the Civil Rights Act was to support and enforce voting rights for blacks by creating a nonpartisan division of the Justice Department to monitor and report on civil rights abuses. The bill provided for

- ✔ Creation of a bipartisan Commission on Civil Rights to study racial discrimination and recommend remedial legislation.

- ✔ Enhancement of the Civil Rights Section of the Justice Department.

- ✔ Empowerment of the attorney general to secure court injunctions in civil rights cases so that they could be heard in federal court.

- ✔ Increase in the power of the Justice Department to seek injunctions against anyone interfering with the right to vote.

From the beginning, passing the act was difficult. Southern senators did their best to take the teeth out of the bill. However, Northern Democrats and Republicans wanted the Civil Rights Act to pass, in part to secure black and liberal votes in the next election (without losing the white southern vote).

Lyndon Johnson, a Democrat and the Senate majority leader (see Chapter 3), had to straddle the fence on the Civil Rights Act to preserve party unity as well as his political career. He didn't want to alienate the southerners in the party, who opposed the bill, but he also wanted to cultivate the black and liberal vote. With his superb skills at negotiating compromise, he managed to get a civil rights act passed without alienating either side.

Even after the Civil Rights Act passed, it was difficult to enforce. Because most violations occurred in the South, where only whites served on juries, violators were rarely prosecuted. As such, some black leaders saw the bill as simply a lame concession to their community, since the law was virtually unenforceable. However, if for no other reason, the bill was important for its symbolic value. The Civil Rights Act of 1957 was the first civil rights legislation since Reconstruction and was the basis for later laws, including the Civil Rights Act of 1964, which not only expanded the scope of the law but also provided for better enforcement (see Chapter 6).

Chapter 6

Sitting, Riding, and Marching for Freedom

In This Chapter

▶ Inspiring the movement — Dr. Martin Luther King Jr.

▶ Refusing to budge at lunch counters

▶ Organizing to fight for freedom

▶ Standing firm while traveling south

▶ Mixing hope and despair: The events of 1963

▶ Targeting Mississippi with Freedom Summer

▶ Legislating equality once again

The civil rights movement wasn't a single event, but collectively it was one of the most important events of the 1960s and perhaps of the entire 20th century. Seeking to undo the evils of slavery and the injustices of the post–Civil War South, the movement's initial focus was integration of public facilities. With peaceful protests inciting violent backlashes, coupled with the fact that television brought the movement into the living rooms of America, whites learned about the injustices suffered by black Americans.

In this chapter, we take a look at the civil rights movement during the first few years of the 1960s. During those years, until 1964, the movement was dominated by the nonviolent principles of Martin Luther King Jr., the most famous civil rights leader. You can see how African Americans capitalized on the success of the Montgomery Bus Boycott by conducting sit-ins at lunch counters, carrying out freedom rides to integrate interstate transportation, creating organizations to work for desegregation, challenging segregation in the most segregated states in the nation, and marching on Washington, D.C., to make all Americans aware of the need for integration and civil rights legislation. And you can see some of the movement's goals realized with passage of the Civil Rights Act of 1964.

Preaching Nonviolence: Dr. Martin Luther King Jr.

One of the most influential people of the civil rights movement, and certainly the man most folks think of when they consider civil rights in the 1960s, was Dr. Martin Luther King Jr. (see Figure 6-1). Although King was by no means the only one driving the push for equality, his leadership skills in mobilizing protesters and his stirring speaking style brought many to join the drive toward equal rights. He also brought the concept (and practice) of nonviolent civil disobedience as the preferred path to protest to the American scene.

Figure 6-1:
Martin Luther King Jr. at the March on Washington.

©Bettmann/CORBIS

Keeping the faith

Throughout King's public life, his message was always firmly rooted in his deep religious faith, which was only natural because he was the son and grandson of Baptist preachers. An outgrowth of his upbringing was a talent for public speaking. Whether in the religious or the political arena, King was gifted with the ability to inspire people and spur them to action.

Born on January 15, 1929, King grew up and was educated in Atlanta, Georgia, graduating from Morehouse College with a degree in sociology in 1948. Continuing the family tradition, he went on to Crozer Theological Seminary in Upland, Pennsylvania, graduating with a Bachelor of Divinity degree in 1951. He then went on to Boston University, where he received his PhD in systematic theology in 1955.

In February 1948, while he was attending Crozer, King was ordained at the Ebenezer Baptist Church in Atlanta, where he became co-pastor with his father. After he received his PhD, he got his first congregation of his own at the Dexter Avenue Baptist Church in Montgomery, Alabama. It was here that he first burst on the national scene as one of the leaders of the Montgomery Bus Boycott (see Chapter 5).

Embracing peaceful protest

While studying at Crozer, King attended a lecture about Mahatma Gandhi and how he applied the principles of passive resistance to oppose British colonial rule in India from 1915 until British rule ended in 1947. King learned that armed insurrection invites attack — instead, he advocated boycotts and non-violent civil disobedience, teaching people that even if they're met with violence, they shouldn't retaliate. In 1959, King traveled to India to meet with Gandhi's followers and became even more committed to the principles of nonviolence. Throughout his life, King believed that peaceful protest was the best (and, in his opinion, the only) way to achieve the goals of integration and equality for blacks in America.

Not only was nonviolence in agreement with King's religious principles, but he also believed that such protests were the strategy that would win the support of white Americans, especially if the protests were met with violence from racists. He was correct: Though widespread support didn't come quickly, when protests were shown on national television, America saw southern sheriffs greeting peaceful demonstrators with attack dogs and fire hoses. Many Americans saw, for the first time, how blacks were being victimized by the lawmen that were supposed to support the law.

King was instrumental in forming the Southern Christian Leadership Conference (SCLC), which trained people in methods of nonviolent protest. In Greensboro, Atlanta, Birmingham, Selma, and all over the South, King marched with protesters and was arrested time and again for civil disobedience. But King was not the only one to promote the principles of peaceful protest; the Congress of Racial Equality (CORE), founded in 1942, also believed in passive resistance to achieve their goals (see the "Making Alphabet Soup: CORE, SCLC, SNCC, and NAACP" section later in this chapter.)

Dr. Martin Luther King Jr. said, "The old law of an eye for an eye leaves everybody blind."

Gaining worldwide recognition

After his leadership role during the Montgomery Bus Boycott in 1955 and 1956, Dr. Martin Luther King Jr. became nationally recognized as a civil rights leader. Throughout his career, he met with presidents Eisenhower, Kennedy, and Johnson to keep the fight for civil rights legislation at the forefront of their national agendas.

Perhaps King's most visible moment was the March for Jobs and Freedom in Washington, D.C., on August 28, 1963, where he gave his famous "I have a dream" speech. This event was organized as much to support the push for civil rights legislation as to protest the segregation and racism that made new legislation necessary. Initially, Kennedy tried to convince King not to hold the march, but he knew that the march would be important to the cause. King's instincts were correct — the march drew more than 200,000 people, both blacks and whites, and was, up until that time, the most important civil rights demonstration in history. After this march, which was covered on television, the movement gained momentum.

After Kennedy's assassination, President Johnson fought for passage of the Civil Rights Act. On July 2, 1964, he signed it into law (see "The Civil Rights Act of 1964" section at the end of this chapter), and on August 6, 1965, the Voting Rights Act, which ensured that all citizens would be able to vote, regardless of race, was enacted (see Chapter 7).

Responding to people who said that prejudice couldn't be legislated away, King responded, "Morality can't be legislated, but behavior can be regulated."

In 1963, King was named *Time* magazine's "Man of the Year," and on October 14, 1964, he won the Nobel Peace Prize. King turned over the prize money (more than $50,000 at the time) to be used to further the civil rights movement. At age 35, King was the youngest man, the second American, and the third black man to receive the Nobel Peace Prize.

Facing dissension in the ranks

Although King awakened the conscience of the nation, not everyone agreed with his principles or his tactics. By the mid- to late '60s, some African Americans became more impatient and confrontational, believing that integration wasn't the answer and that they had to fight (even violently, if necessary) to get what they wanted. Malcolm X, a leader of the Black Muslims, felt that the races should remain separate to allow them to preserve their culture. Others, such as H. Rap Brown, Stokely Carmichael, and the Black Panthers, promoted Black Nationalism (see Chapter 7 for more about the Black Muslims, the Panthers, and the drive for black power). King, however, remained true to his principles, believing that black separatism was as dangerous as white separatism.

In the late '60s, King also drew criticism because of his opposition to the Vietnam War. Although he avoided the issue through 1966, he then declared that the United States had been wrong from the beginning of the war and encouraged young men to become conscientious objectors. One consequence of his position was that LBJ, who had supported King and the civil rights movement, felt betrayed. *Time* magazine (which had earlier named him "Man of the Year") as well as the *Washington Post* condemned his position, feeling that he was giving support to the enemy. Interestingly, by 1968, a year after King's "Beyond Vietnam" speech in 1967 (see Chapter 9), King's position was the majority, and many Americans no longer supported the war in Vietnam.

Dying young

Ironically for a man who preached nonviolence, King was no stranger to being the target of aggression. During the Montgomery Bus Boycott his house was bombed, and in 1958, while autographing his book *Stride Toward Freedom,* he was stabbed in the chest. He received many death threats over the years, but he claimed to be unafraid because he felt that personal consequences weren't that important. Ironically, on the day before he was assassinated, King gave his "I've been to the mountaintop" speech, which expressed his thoughts about and foreshadowed his own death.

After President Kennedy's assassination, King expressed his concern that unfortunately the country's climate condoned men who expressed their disagreement through violence and murder. At that time, he also said that he believed he'd be assassinated before his 40th birthday. That prophecy proved to be true. On April 4, 1968, while in Memphis, Tennessee, to support a sanitation workers' strike, James Earl Ray, a high school dropout, petty criminal, and self-proclaimed racist, shot and killed King. At King's funeral in Atlanta, about 200,000 people marched behind his casket, which was on a sharecropper's wagon pulled by mules.

The FBI almost immediately identified Ray as King's assassin and chased him from place to place until they apprehended him in England. He confessed, and in May 1969, was sentenced to 99 years in prison. However, Ray recanted his confession three days later, claiming he was coerced, and put forth a theory that there was a government conspiracy and coverup — an opinion that King's son, Dexter, as well as Jesse Jackson, support.

In the short term, the aftermath of King's murder was one he would've despised; blacks were so enraged about the assassination that they rioted in protest in 100 cities, and more than 10,000 people were arrested (see Chapter 7). However, his long-term legacy highlights the progress of blacks in American life. Public facilities throughout the South were integrated (or at least they weren't legally separated), and white America began to think about race in a different way. Because of his efforts, which resulted in more black voters, blacks gained a foothold in government: Edward Brooke became a senator from Massachusetts, Thurgood Marshall became a Supreme Court justice, Carl Stokes and Richard Hatcher were big city mayors, and Shirley Chisholm became the first black congresswoman.

A powerful enemy: J. Edgar Hoover

FBI director J. Edgar Hoover and the rest of the FBI were never comfortable with Martin Luther King Jr. To them, nonviolent protest had a suspicious, almost un-American air about it (or about any protest against government, for that matter). Hoover felt that King and the civil rights movement were instigated by Communists and what Hoover called "outside agitators," who were stirring up discontent among blacks and the poor. Unfortunately, some of King's supporters had Socialist and Communist ties, which gave the FBI a rationale for pursuing King.

Hoover worked with the House Un-American Activities Committee (HUAC), a committee in the House of Representatives whose mission was to fight Communism wherever they saw it (see Chapter 11) to paint King with a pink paintbrush, but the accusations never stuck. So Hoover went after King personally by delving into his personal life and attempting to blackmail him into stopping his activism. However, none of Hoover's attempts much affected King's work or his legacy.

Opening the Lunch Counters: The Sit-In Movement

On February 1, 1960, Congress of Racial Equality (CORE) (see the section on civil rights organizations "Making Alphabet Soup: CORE, SCLC, SNCC, and NAACP" later in this chapter) organized four black college students, who conducted the first lunch counter sit-in in Greensboro, North Carolina. The basic plan for a *sit-in* evolved into a standard operating procedure: Black students went to a lunch counter and ask to be served. If they were, great — they moved onto another location. If not, they waited until they were served or until the store closed. If they were asked to leave, they politely refused, and if they were arrested or forcibly removed, another group of students was waiting to take their place. Most protesters were extremely calm, polite, and well dressed, so their appearance wasn't objectionable (other than their black skin, of course). However, the locals did object by harassing and taunting the protesters. Figure 6-2 shows a lunch counter sit-in.

Although almost all restaurants and lunch counters (casual restaurants where customers were served from behind a counter) in the South were segregated, Woolworth's was a good choice because it wasn't just a luncheonette. At the time, it was the largest national five-and-ten-cent store. Woolworth's always welcomed people of all races to buy cosmetics, toys, and other miscellaneous items in their stores, but in the South, blacks couldn't eat at Woolworth's.

On the first day, nothing much happened — the four students sat at the lunch counter and were never served (they were largely ignored), so they stayed until closing. But the students wanted a reaction and publicity, so they recruited more students to come to Woolworth's. Throughout the next week, more students continued occupying the Woolworth's counter until it was so crowded that almost no one else could fit. The results were mixed — the sit-in attracted local reporters, which ensured that they'd receive publicity. However, the manager temporarily closed the store, leaving the students to find another all-white lunch counter to occupy.

Figure 6-2:
A sit-in at an all-white lunch counter.

©Bettmann/CORBIS

Black students all over North Carolina caught on to the idea, and throughout the next week they held sit-ins in Winston-Salem, Durham, Raleigh, Charlotte, Fayetteville, High Point, Elizabeth City, and Concord. Representatives of CORE went to southern campuses to recruit more students, organize the sit-ins, and teach protesters how to conduct themselves — to always be polite, not disrupt business, and not react to any insults. It didn't take long for the protests to spread to other states. By the end of February, seven southern states had hosted sit-ins, and by the end of April, almost 50,000 students had participated in sit-ins all over the South.

Northern students, both black and white, supported the southern sit-ins by boycotting chain stores, such as Woolworth's, that remained segregated in the South. Suddenly, the unfairness became a growing concern. Although the first sit-ins were fairly peaceful, later in February, in Nashville, Tennessee, protesters were attacked by a group of white teens, resulting in the arrest of the black students for disorderly conduct while the white teenagers were released.

Despite violence and arrests, the sit-ins continued. By 1961, more than 70,000 people had participated (and more than 3,000 were arrested). Even after the Civil Rights Act of 1964 became law, segregation continued in parts of the South, so the sit-ins continued as well. Sit-ins weren't limited to lunch counters; throughout the '60s, protesters used this strategy to integrate movie theaters, bus stations, and other public facilities. These acts of defiance emphasized that passing laws wasn't the only way to achieve the goal of desegregation — protests could be effective, too.

Making Alphabet Soup: CORE, SCLC, SNCC, and NAACP

Although they all had the same goals, several important associations were involved in the civil rights movement. These organizations started at different points in the 20th century and didn't always agree on methods, but in the early to mid-1960s, they worked together to end segregation and ensure that blacks had the right to vote. But there were distinctions between the groups. Some such as the NAACP tended to be more conservative and wanted to work within the system, and on the other end of the spectrum, SNCC preferred a more direct approach, and didn't particularly worry about white sensibilities. However, they did join together to accomplish common goals, such as the March for Jobs and Freedom in 1963.

The granddaddy of civil rights organizations: The NAACP

The National Association for the Advancement of Colored People (NAACP) is the oldest national organization to promote the welfare of African Americans. Established in 1909 to promote equal rights and eliminate racial prejudice in the U.S., the NAACP worked to advocate voting rights, gain equality in education and employment, and achieve impartial treatment under the law. In the beginning, the NAACP had three main areas of focus:

- Fight Jim Crow (segregationist) Laws such as those that allowed separate public facilities for blacks and whites (see Chapter 5)
- Make people aware of the horrors of lynching
- Enforce the 15th Amendment to the Constitution, which guarantees the right to vote

Other important goals were to oppose racist government appointees, such as the nomination of John Parker as a Supreme Court Justice in 1930. Throughout their history, they also spoke out about films that glorified racism, such as *Birth of a Nation* in 1915, and TV shows that showed derogatory black stereotypes, such as *Amos and Andy* in 1951.

The NAACP sought not only to improve the image of blacks in film and on television, but also to promote greater opportunities for blacks in the entertainment industry. The NAACP Image Awards, which began in 1968 and continues to date, celebrates black entertainers as well as filmmakers who present positive images of blacks.

One of the NAACP's most important divisions was the Legal Defense and Educational Fund (LDF), founded in 1940. Spearheaded by Thurgood Marshall, who was later appointed to the Supreme Court, the LDF argued school integration cases before the Supreme Court, the most famous and far-reaching of which was the *Brown v. Topeka Board of Education* decision, which mandated integration of public schools. (Check out Chapter 5 for a discussion of this decision.) LDF lawyers were also active in other ways:

Activism in the city — the Urban League

In order to improve the conditions of blacks who moved to northern cities in the Great Migration during the late 19th and early 20th century, the Committee on Urban Conditions Among Negroes was established in New York City on September 29, 1910. These new arrivals came north because of bad crops, rampant poverty, and Jim Crow laws, as well as the need for unskilled labor in northern cities and better living conditions. Although there was also poverty and discrimination in northern cities, they still earned more money than they did at home. The organization helped the new arrivals adapt to urban living and overcome poverty and the lack of educational and economic opportunities. By 1920, the committee merged with several other urban organizations to form the National Urban League.

From the beginning, the Urban League was an interracial organization (founded by Ruth Standish Baldwin, the widow of a railroad tycoon and Dr. George Edmund Haynes, the first black man to earn a PhD from Columbia University) that helped blacks gain better access to recreation, housing, healthcare, and education. However, the league's greatest push was in the area of employment. To create new opportunities for blacks, they boycotted firms that wouldn't hire them. They also pressed to have blacks included in New Deal programs (government programs designed to provide employment and stimulate economic growth during the Great Depression from 1929 to 1933), and worked to get them admitted into labor unions. Although the league didn't actively participate in the civil rights protests of the '60s, it consistently worked behind the scenes to ensure equal opportunities for all Americans, focusing on economic and educational progress.

✔ They defended several civil rights leaders, including Ralph Abernathy, Fred Shuttlesworth, and James Meredith when they were arrested during protests.

✔ They pursued employment discrimination cases and pushed for affirmative action.

✔ They defended Rosa Parks after her arrest, and the organization was active in the Montgomery Bus Boycott in 1955.

The group was so effective that the state of Alabama prohibited them from operating within the state. (The Supreme Court eventually overturned this state law.)

By the mid-1960s, however, the NAACP was no longer the most influential civil rights organization. Although they continued to support the sit-ins, freedom rides, marches, and voter registration drives, other organizations, such as CORE, SCLC, and SNCC, rose to the forefront of the movement. These younger organizations often mocked the NAACP as too establishment, middle-class, and obsolete, but the organization is still active today.

Bringing whites to the fight: CORE

In 1942, a group of students in Chicago banded together to form the Congress of Racial Equality (CORE) to fight segregation and racism by using nonviolent resistance, including sit-ins, jail-ins, and freedom rides. From the beginning, CORE attracted both blacks and whites, and its members were mostly college students. Its first leaders were two University of Chicago students: George Houser, who was white, and James Farmer, who was black.

CORE's first efforts were sit-ins, conducted to protest segregation in public facilities. Later that year, the organization went national. Farmer, along with Bayard Rustin, traveled around the country recruiting new members. By the end of the 1940s, CORE was successful at integrating public facilities throughout the northern states.

Although CORE kept working to end segregation, by the late '50s the organization was stagnating. However, with the Montgomery Bus Boycott, which used the nonviolent methods that CORE advocated, the organization was again in the forefront of the civil rights movement. CORE participated in the lunch counter sit-ins, freedom rides, and voter registration drives. But by the late '60s, CORE was again in crisis. Although they still advocated interracial membership, some black members didn't want to be restricted to nonviolent methods of protest. In 1966, Farmer stepped down as leader, and when Floyd McKissick, who embraced the concept of black power, took over the organization, it became more militant. Although not advocating violence, it was accepted if nonviolent methods weren't successful.

Fighting with faith: The SCLC

Although the Southern Christian Leadership Conference (SCLC) didn't become an official organization until 1957, its roots were in the Montgomery Bus Boycott of 1955 and 1956 (see Chapter 5). The boycott, a huge and successful nonviolent protest, was organized and executed by the Montgomery Improvement Association (MIA), led by Martin Luther King Jr. and Ralph Abernathy.

Unsung heroes of the movement

One of the oldest civil rights leaders was A. Philip Randolph, who formed the first black labor union in 1925, the Brotherhood of Sleeping Car Porters. Throughout his life, Randolph worked to help the black working class and was also instrumental in the fight to end segregation in the military. Randolph was one of the organizers of the March on Washington for Jobs and Freedom in 1963.

Bayard Rustin was an active member of CORE and one of the founders of SCLC. Born a Quaker, he was a committed pacifist who believed in nonviolent protest. Although he actively worked in the civil rights movement, he was forced to work in the background because he was gay, and no one wanted his sexual orientation to discredit the movement. However, later in life, he openly worked to promote gay rights.

Another SCLC leader who had a huge impact on the civil rights movement was Rev. Fred Shuttlesworth. One of the leaders of the 1963 demonstrations in Birmingham, Alabama, he was arrested and jailed along with Dr. King. Although he was injured and hospitalized during the worst moments of the protests, he convinced King to keep on, regardless of police resistance.

After the boycott ended, the MIA and other protest groups met to form an organization to coordinate peaceful protests throughout the South. During a meeting in Atlanta in January 1957, King, Abernathy, Fred Shuttlesworth, and Bayard Rustin (of CORE) officially formed the SCLC. The new organization's initial announcement stated that civil rights were essential to democracy and that segregation must end. They pledged that the SCLC would be open to anyone regardless of race, religion, and background. Rather than seek individual members, the SCLC coordinated local civil rights organizations throughout the South. They also committed to nonviolent protest as their primary strategy and taught their members how to passively resist arrest and violence with the least injury to themselves.

Throughout the '60s, the SCLC was at the forefront of the civil rights protests throughout the South, participating in the protests in Birmingham in 1963, Freedom Summer in 1964, and the Selma to Montgomery march in 1965. The SCLC was also instrumental in organizing the March on Washington for Jobs and Freedom in 1963.

Although the SCLC lost some of its influence during the late '60s as the civil rights movement became more militant, it still exists today, working to end discrimination, promote voter education and registration, and advocate nonviolent conflict resolution.

Fighting violently: The Deacons for Defense

During CORE's 1964 campaign to desegregate public facilities in Jonesboro, Louisiana, local black men began to guard the CORE activists. They decided to form an armed defense group, called the Deacons for Defense, in order to protect civil rights activists from white supremacists. This working-class organization was unwilling to wait for an end to the injustices of racism and instead wanted to defend themselves, especially against the Ku Klux Klan.

In Bogalusa, Louisiana, in 1964, the Deacons armed themselves against Ku Klux Klan violence, which provoked more terrorism against blacks, including the murder of a white policeman. Eventually, the federal government intervened,

compelling the local government to abide by the Civil Rights Act of 1964. However, in the process the Deacons attracted the FBI's attention, which called them a dangerous black group.

By 1966, the Deacons became embroiled in the rifts that were forming in the civil rights movement. After James Meredith was shot and wounded, the NAACP, SCLC, and the Urban League still wanted to continue nonviolent, interracial protest, while CORE and SNCC wanted to restrict the demonstration to blacks and invited the Deacons for Defense to protect the marchers. Although they faded from the scene by 1972, the Deacons were a large part of the shift from nonviolent protest to black militancy.

Mobilizing students: The SNCC

Two months after the first lunch counter sit-in in Greensboro, North Carolina, students in Raleigh formed the Student Nonviolent Coordinating Committee (SNCC; usually pronounced *snick*) with the objective of coordinating, supporting, and publicizing the sit-ins.

SNCC's first chairman was Marion Barry, who later became the mayor of Washington, D.C.

Throughout the rest of the decade, however, SNCC, along with the rest of the civil rights movement, widened its focus to fight all racial oppression in any form. With its youthful, interracial membership, SNCC actually overshadowed some of the more established civil rights organizations, such as the NAACP and SCLC, during the late '60s. They were a major participant in the freedom rides, the 1963 March on Washington for Jobs and Freedom, Mississippi Freedom Summer, and the Mississippi Freedom Democratic Party, which focused on education and voting rights for blacks.

However, over the next few years, many SNCC activists began to lose patience with nonviolent protest and civil rights legislation and believed that equal rights could only be achieved by more direct and militant means. In May 1966, Stokely Carmichael became the leader of the organization. At first, he said that blacks should be able to use violence in self-defense, but later he began advocating the initiation of violence in order to fight oppression. Under his leadership, SNCC got rid of the organization's white members. In June 1967, Carmichael left SNCC to join the Black Panther Party (see Chapter 7). Although SNCC renounced the philosophy of nonviolence in the late '60s, Martin Luther King Jr. and the SCLC originally supported the student organization.

In 1969, SNCC officially changed its name to the Student National Coordinating Committee to reflect its more militant focus.

Going on a Road Trip: Freedom Rides

Although the concept of freedom rides began with CORE in 1947 to emphasize the Supreme Court decision outlawing segregation in interstate travel, it took SNCC and the 1960s to bring freedom rides to the national consciousness. During the freedom rides, blacks and whites rode busses through the South to challenge local laws that segregated interstate travel.

The first freedom ride of the decade began on May 4, 1961, when the Supreme Court extended its desegregation of interstate travel beyond the actual buses to bus terminals as well. A group of 13 students, black and white, left Washington, D.C., in two buses, a Trailways bus and a Greyhound bus, headed for New Orleans. The group made it through Virginia and North Carolina without incident, but at the Greyhound depot in Rock Hill, South Carolina, a mob attacked the group as they entered the white waiting room. Police intervened, and the group was admitted to the waiting room.

The trip through Georgia was uneventful, but the Greyhound bus was stopped in Alabama when a mob surrounded the bus, slashed the tires, and set the bus on fire. Not discouraged, the ride continued. However, in Anniston, Alabama, one bus driver wouldn't move the bus until the group segregated itself, and the other bus was burned (but the riders caught another bus and continued on.) They finally headed to Birmingham, where more violence waited for them, hospitalizing some of the riders. After that, they found no bus that would take the integrated group. The first freedom ride of the '60s was over. Figure 6-3 shows the freedom riders and their burnt-out bus.

Figure 6-3: Freedom riders watch a bus that was set on fire in Anniston, Alabama.

©Bettmann/CORBIS

Although the first freedom ride didn't reach its destination, the riders vowed to continue and organized a ride from Nashville, Tennessee, through Montgomery and Birmingham, and on to Mississippi. They made it as far as Birmingham, where they were jailed and run out of town by Police Chief "Bull" Connor (more about him in the section "The Battle of Birmingham," later in this chapter). President Kennedy worried about violence against the freedom riders and insisted that the governor of Alabama guarantee their safety. However, a mob was waiting in Montgomery, and along with the students, newsmen and cameramen were beaten in a riot that went on until police used tear gas to disperse the crowd (which had grown with onlookers and supporters for both sides in the melee). Undeterred, the group rode on to Jackson, Mississippi, where they were arrested for using white restrooms and waiting rooms. They spent the night in jail.

For the freedom riders, the violence and arrests just seemed to strengthen their resolve. The mob violence that the rides provoked served to gather support from northern blacks and many whites as well.

Although Martin Luther King Jr. offered moral and financial support for the freedom rides, he didn't actually participate in the rides himself, because he believed they were suicide missions. His failure to join the rides caused some SNCC members to question his leadership, and was one factor in the beginning of a rift between the more traditional and more militant black leaders.

Shaking the Nation: Turning Points in 1963

The year 1963 was pivotal for the movement. In Birmingham, Alabama, police violently opposed peaceful protest, and later that year, segregationists bombed a Birmingham church, killing four black girls. In Mississippi, civil rights worker Medgar Evers was murdered in cold blood. On a more hopeful and optimistic note, civil rights organizations banded together and organized the March on Washington for Jobs and Freedom, designed to promote equal opportunity, end segregation, and support passage of civil rights legislation.

The events in Alabama and Mississippi turned many people, who were previously unaware of the evils of segregation and the intensity of racism, in favor of the civil rights movement, and the March on Washington for Jobs and Freedom emphasized the massive support for civil rights at all levels of American society.

The Battle of Birmingham

In the beginning of 1963, Dr. Martin Luther King Jr. and other black leaders decided to concentrate their efforts on what they considered to be one of the most segregated large cities in the United States — Birmingham, Alabama. However, no one thought it would be easy — George Wallace had just been elected governor on a segregationist platform and was determined not to let the protesters take over his city (for more on George Wallace, see Chapter 13). In addition, the Birmingham Ku Klux Klan was supposedly one of the most violent chapters in the country, so the demonstrators had their work (and their strength of will) cut out for them.

Ralph Abernathy and King went to downtown Birmingham on April 12 and were arrested for defying Police Chief Bull Connor's order prohibiting demonstrations. When protestors staged a large demonstration, Connor, in a show of force, set vicious police dogs on the protestors, turned the fire hoses on them, and had them beaten with clubs. Some historians speculate that Connor's overt racism and brutality prompted so much outrage that it hastened the passage of the Civil Rights Act of 1964.

President Kennedy interceded to get both Abernathy and King freed. However, while in custody, King wrote "Letter from Birmingham Jail" and had it smuggled out. In this letter, addressed to fellow clergymen who doubted the wisdom of his actions in Birmingham, King explained that though some considered him an outside agitator, he believed that as an American, he wasn't an outsider in Birmingham or anywhere else in the country. Further, King emphasized that he was in Birmingham because the city housed injustice and that as an SCLC leader, he was compelled to fight injustice wherever it occurred. Finally, he addressed the clergymen's opinion that he should be patient and negotiate instead of engaging in direct action, saying that blacks had been told to "wait" for too long, and the time for action had come.

After King was released from jail on April 20, SCLC began planning the next phase of the demonstration. On May 2, a large group of children joined the protest. The plan was to attract the media and embarrass the city of Birmingham. After King gave a speech at the 16th Street Baptist Church, the march moved downtown, but Connor and his policemen were waiting, and they arrested more than 900 youngsters. The next day, approximately 1,000 more children more joined the march, but this time Connor didn't stop at mere arrests.

The police attacked the marchers — which included all those children — with fire hoses, clubs, and attack dogs. Thanks to the media, Americans all over the country saw youngsters being savagely beaten, but Connor wouldn't be stopped. The following day, Connor again ordered an attack, but because of the number of young children involved, firemen refused to turn on the hoses, and many of the police wouldn't participate in the violence. This time, Connor had to settle for making arrests.

Finally, on May 10, the city of Birmingham responded to pressure from the federal government and the weight of world opinion (as well as the fact that they had no more room in the jails) and agreed to desegregate. However, the Ku Klux Klan and other white segregationists were furious and went on a rampage, rioting throughout the city and bombing black churches, businesses, and homes. King's brother's home, the motel where King was staying, and the SCLC headquarters were among the buildings destroyed.

In response to the racism and violence that tarnished America's image throughout the world, Kennedy agreed to push civil rights legislation through Congress, saying, "Race has no place in American life or law."

The murder of Medgar Evers

Medgar Evers was a Mississippi native who worked for civil rights and paid for them with his life. After graduating from Alcorn State College in Lorma, Mississippi, he applied for admission to the segregated University of Mississippi Law School, but his application was rejected. This caused the NAACP to become involved in the desegregation efforts at Ole Miss, and although Evers never gained admittance, he was instrumental in getting James Meredith admitted in 1962.

Although his first post-graduation job was selling insurance, Evers's real passion was to improve the lot of poor black families in Mississippi. In 1954, he joined the NAACP and became Mississippi's first field officer, responsible for forming local chapters and organizing desegregation efforts throughout the state. In this position, he fought to enforce the desegregation mandated by *Brown v. Topeka Board of Education* (see Chapter 5). He also pressed for enforcement of black voting rights and encouraged blacks to boycott merchants who discriminated against them. Evers's activism provoked death threats, but he wouldn't be deterred from his work. However, on June 13, 1963, he was shot in the back when he got out of his car.

Police had no problem finding the culprit, because the shotgun that killed Evers (complete with fresh fingerprints) was found in the bushes; Byron de la Beckwith, owner of said fingerprints and an active white supremacist, was arrested. Although the prosecution submitted hard evidence against him, including the fact that he publicly stated that he wanted to kill Evers, two all-white juries deadlocked, and Beckwith seemingly got away with murder. However, in 1989, new information indicating that the juries may have been tampered with prompted a new trial. On February 5, 1994, a jury of blacks and whites found Beckwith guilty, sentencing him to life imprisonment.

The March for Jobs and Freedom

As protests intensified, President Kennedy realized that without an effective civil rights law, desegregation wouldn't occur "with all deliberate speed." As far as black Americans were concerned, the nation's response to *Brown v. Topeka Board of Education,* which declared that "separate but equal" facilities were unconstitutional, was agonizingly slow, and neither state legislatures nor Congress seemed willing to press for enforcement. Finally, on June 11, 1963, Kennedy proposed a bill that would ensure equal protection under the law for all Americans.

To publicize the bill and support its passage, A. Philip Randolph (see the sidebar "Unsung heroes of the movement") called for a massive march on Washington for jobs and freedom, inviting people and groups of all races and religious persuasions to participate. Passing a civil rights bill was so important that all civil rights groups, including the NAACP, CORE, SCLC, SNCC, and the Urban League, joined together to organize the march. (Malcolm X and the Black Muslims opposed the march, calling it the "farce on Washington.") Although the main objective of the march was the passage for civil rights legislation, other goals were to

- Eliminate segregation in schools and other public facilities
- Protect protesters from police brutality and vigilante justice
- Implement a public-works program to provide jobs
- Prohibit discrimination in hiring
- Raise the minimum wage
- Establish self-government for the District of Columbia, which had a black majority

Although President Kennedy introduced the Civil Rights Bill, he originally opposed the march, because he was worried that a white backlash might actually strengthen resistance to civil rights legislation. However, after he realized that the march would go on with or without his backing, he supported the effort.

On August 28, 1963, more than 250,000 people (approximately one-fifth of them white) united in Washington for the March for Jobs and Freedom (see Figure 6-4). Not only civil rights leaders but also clergymen, union leaders, and entertainers such as Sidney Poitier; Marlon Brando; Marian Anderson; Joan Baez; Bob Dylan; Mahalia Jackson; Peter, Paul, and Mary; and Josh White joined the demonstration and entertained and addressed the crowd.

The March for Jobs and Freedom was the largest demonstration ever seen in Washington until that time and had extensive television coverage. Probably the most stirring, inspirational, and famous speech of the entire civil rights movement took place at that march: Dr. Martin Luther King Jr.'s now-familiar "I have a dream" speech.

The murder of four girls in a Birmingham church

Unfortunately, despite King's inspiring words and the hope and enthusiasm created by the March for Jobs and Freedom, in September, one of the worst acts of violence occurred during Sunday services in a black church in Birmingham.

Figure 6-4:
The March
for Jobs and
Freedom.

©Flip Schulke/CORBIS

Angered over a federal court order mandating desegregation of Birmingham public schools (and encouraged by Governor George Wallace's defiance of the order; see Chapter 13), segregationists bombed several places in Birmingham over the next several months. Bombing seemed to be the violence of choice in Birmingham — between 1947 and 1955, more than 50 bombings occurred, earning the city the nickname "Bombingham."

However, the worst of these attacks was the bombing of the 16th Street Baptist Church on September 15, 1963, killing four young girls — Denise McNair, Carole Robertson, Cynthia Wesley, and Addie Mae Collins — who were preparing for Sunday school in the church basement. The angry black community rioted in protest (in spite of King's plea for nonviolence), and the authorities retaliated with their usual tactics — attack dogs, fire hoses, beatings, and arrests, but in the end, the bombing strengthened the resolve of civil rights protesters.

King led the eulogy for three of the four girls, and the horrible death of innocent children even prompted many of the whites of Birmingham to attend the memorials. National outrage prompted the FBI to investigate the bombing, particularly because the Birmingham authorities showed little enthusiasm for prosecuting the offenders, even though they knew who the perpetrators were. Based on their findings, the FBI office recommended that the suspects be prosecuted, but the FBI leader J. Edgar Hoover wouldn't allow evidence to go to the federal prosecutor, and in 1968, the FBI closed the case. Not until 1977 was one of the bombers convicted. The other two were finally convicted in 2000.

Heating It Up: Freedom Summer

For many blacks, the desegregation of schools and other public facilities was an important goal, but equally important was the enforcement of the right to vote for all Americans. Many white southerners, afraid that the large black populations would overturn Jim Crow Laws if they were allowed to vote, put up impossible roadblocks. *Poll taxes* (an amount that had to be paid before an individual could vote) and literacy tests virtually prohibited blacks from voting, although technically their right to vote, guaranteed by the 15th Amendment, was legally enforced.

To address this and other crucial issues, Freedom Summer was launched in 1964 in a state that was the most notorious for denying blacks the right to vote: Mississippi. Organized by CORE, the NAACP, and SNCC, volunteers — largely students — signed up to go to Mississippi to help blacks with voter registration and to challenge the all-white Democratic Party in the state. In addition, they would work to establish schools to teach reading and math to young black children and to open community centers that would provide legal and medical help to poor blacks.

To prepare for their summer in Mississippi, volunteers (the majority of whom were white middle-class students) attended an orientation, where they were coached on some of the problems they might face, such as arrest, jail, or even death. Freedom Summer volunteers were required to bring $500 for bail money.

SNCC's James Forman, who addressed the volunteers, told them to go to jail without argument or protest if they were arrested, because "Mississippi is not the place to start conducting constitutional law classes for the policemen, many of whom don't have a fifth-grade education."

Continuing drives to get out the vote

Since the 1950s the NAACP (and later SCLC and SNCC) had organized registration drives in the South to help blacks to register to vote. However, because of literacy tests, poll taxes, and outright intimidation by whites, these drives had limited success. Then, in 1962, an organization of civil rights groups, the Council of Federated Organizations (COFO), was established. In 1963, COFO staged the Freedom Vote, a mock election in Mississippi designed to demonstrate that blacks wanted to vote and would cast their ballots if allowed. (White segregationists in Mississippi tried to justify preventing blacks from voting by stating that they really didn't want to vote anyway.) The Freedom Vote began by holding a mock convention to select candidates for state office, and aided by volunteers, blacks registered to vote. On Freedom Vote's Election Day, almost 80,000 blacks cast their ballots for the integrated ticket.

SNCC organized Freedom Summer of 1964 to take advantage of the momentum and enthusiasm created by the Freedom Vote. However, some dissention filled the air while the event was in the works — some black leaders feared that white volunteers would take over the movement. Others were concerned about the possible violence that would meet the racially mixed group of volunteers. (In later years, SNCC and CORE became all-black organizations. See Chapter 7 for more information about the segregation of the civil rights movement.)

Providing competition with an alternate Democratic Party

One of Freedom Summer's objectives was to challenge the regular Democratic Party of Mississippi. To do so, they established the Mississippi Freedom Democratic Party (MFDP) to win seats at the 1964 Democratic National Convention.

Although the MFDP candidates lost their bid to become delegates to the convention, they sent a delegation to Atlantic City anyway and presented their credentials. This initiative was a problem for President Johnson, who was up for re-election on a Democratic platform and was trying to maintain the support he'd gained by supporting civil rights legislation without completely losing the Southern Democrats, many of whom were committed to maintaining white supremacy.

Needing to diffuse the racial tensions at the convention, Johnson and his supporters offered a compromise, which would give the MFDP two nonvoting seats. However, MFDP refused the offer and kept up the defiance throughout the convention, trying a variety of tactics to get seated on the convention floor, including borrowing badges and occupying empty seats. After the 1964 convention, discouraged about working in the mainstream Democratic Party, the MFDP became more radical. They invited Malcolm X (see Chapter 7) to speak at their next convention and opposed Johnson's policy in Vietnam.

In the 1964 presidential election, Johnson took a hit, as white Mississippi Democrats took a position that rejected the national Democratic Party's civil rights platform, which pledged to end segregation and enforce voting rights and openly supported Barry Goldwater, the Republican candidate who supported states' rights and opposed civil rights legislation.

Learning equality in Freedom Schools

During Freedom Summer, volunteers established the Freedom Schools, which more than 3,000 students attended in towns throughout Mississippi. Although most of the students were teenagers, some of them were also children who hadn't yet started school. Besides teaching traditional subjects such as remedial reading and math, one goal of the Freedom Schools was to create a curriculum that was relevant for their students and would also prepare them for becoming equal voting citizens in the future. Therefore, the Freedom School curriculum included black history and the philosophy of the civil rights movement. Essentially, the Freedom Schools were the youth division of the Mississippi Freedom Democratic Party.

Coping with three Klan murders

As volunteers learned during orientation, participating in Freedom Summer was risky business. White supremacists actively opposed the volunteers, bombing and setting fire to black churches, schools, and businesses. Volunteers, both black and white, were routinely arrested, and many were beaten by segregationist mobs or racist police officers. (One of the things that infuriated the segregationists was the sight of blacks and whites together.)

However, the murder of three civil rights workers was the most blatant act of violence of the summer of 1964. On June 21, James Chaney, a local black volunteer, and Andrew Goodman and Michael Schwerner, two northern white students, went to investigate a church bombing near Philadelphia, Mississippi. Stopped and arrested for traffic violations, they spent several hours in jail. When they were released later that day, it was the last time anyone saw the three young men alive. Even after they were reported as missing, local authorities ignored the disappearance, stating that they staged their own disappearance to gain publicity for the movement.

The next day, the FBI got involved in searching for the three young men, but their bodies weren't found until six weeks later. Chaney died as a result of a brutal beating, and Goodman and Schwerner each died from a single gunshot to the chest. On October 13, the FBI arrested 18 men, but state prosecutors, citing lack of evidence, refused to take the case. Therefore, the federal government was forced to charge the suspects with federal conspiracy and civil rights violations. At trial, seven men were convicted, seven were acquitted, and three received mistrials. The longest sentence for the three murders was a mere six years.

Testimony indicated that the Neshoba County police, who had earlier arrested the three volunteers, alerted the local Ku Klux Klan when the men were released from jail. Samuel Bowers, Imperial Wizard of Mississippi's Ku Klux Klan, was found guilty of giving the order to kill Schwerner. However, years later, he admitted that he covered up the fact that Ray Killen, a Baptist minister and Klan organizer, was the main conspirator in the murders (and said that he was proud of giving the testimony that allowed Killen to go free). In 1998, Bowers was sentenced to life in prison for the 1966 murder of NAACP leader Vernon Dahmer. And in 2005, a Mississippi jury found Killen guilty on three counts of manslaughter for the 41-year-old crime.

The murders of Chaney, Schwerner, and Goodman gained even more support for the civil rights movement and called attention to the goals of Freedom Summer. Eventually, this influential summer not only led to the Voting Rights Act of 1965 (see Chapter 7) but also gave southern blacks the power to enforce the right to vote, which gave them the motivation to become more politically active. However, the media attention and outrage also caused a rift within the movement; many blacks believed that the attention and indignation was only because two of the victims were white. Blacks also began questioning the role of whites in the movement, especially when whites assumed leadership roles. The black community noted that although the FBI found the bodies of three lynched blacks while searching for Chaney, Schwerner, and Goodman, these victims received hardly any media attention.

The Civil Rights Act of 1964

As the most important civil rights legislation since Reconstruction, the Civil Rights Act of 1964 abolished discrimination in public facilities, government, and employment. With a few strokes of the pen, this act nullified the Jim Crow Laws that were prevalent in the South for almost a century. The Civil Rights Act of 1964 was the product of JFK's increased support of civil rights as time went on and LBJ's willingness to take up the fight for legislation after Kennedy's death. (For more on Kennedy and civil rights, see Chapter 2; for more on Johnson's fight to pass the bill, see Chapter 3.)

The Civil Rights Act of 1964 took aim at discrimination and segregation throughout society:

- **Voting:** It mandated equal voter registration.

- **Public accommodations:** It prohibited discrimination in any public accommodations engaged in interstate commerce (which included not only transportation but also hotels, motels, restaurants, theaters, and so on). This effectively made all Jim Crow Laws, which supported segregation, illegal.

- **Public schools:** It enforced the desegregation of public schools.

- **Federally funded programs:** It authorized the withdrawal of federal funds from programs that practiced discrimination. For example, no segregated school would receive federal funding.

- **Employment:** It outlawed discrimination in employment based on race, national origin, sex, or religion and included the Equal Employment Opportunity Commission to enforce this provision.

Chapter 7

Embracing Black Power

· ·

In This Chapter

▶ Marching across Alabama in protest for voting rights

▶ Getting impatient and aggressive in the movement

▶ Fighting for the down and out

▶ Banding together and creating pride

▶ Taking matters into their own hands: The Black Panthers

▶ Seeing progress since the 1960s

· ·

*I*n the mid- to late 1960s, in spite of the progress made, such as the Civil Rights Act of 1964, there was still much left to be done. Despite the laws guaranteeing the right to vote (the 15th Amendment and the Civil Rights Act of 1964), enforcement was lax. There were still few black voters in the South, and the civil rights movement was largely unsuccessful in breaking through white resistance to black voter registration. Martin Luther King Jr. and the Southern Christian Leadership Conference (SCLC) decided to focus on the issue, and in January 1965, they began a voter registration drive in Selma, Alabama, which was the prelude to the historic Selma to Montgomery march that ultimately resulted in the Voter Registration Act.

But by 1965, some blacks were getting impatient and feeling dissatisfied with the civil rights movement. They were outraged by the fact that peaceful demonstrations were met with violence, and that, according to Dr. King and other leaders, they were still expected to remain nonviolent. Many people felt that, at the very least, they should be free to defend themselves. Others felt that more radical means to achieve their goals were justified. More militant blacks were also infuriated at what they saw as whites taking over their movement. Some even decided that integration wasn't a worthwhile goal and that blacks should remain separate and take care of their own.

Marching from Selma to Montgomery

In early 1965 in Selma, Alabama, less than 1 percent of eligible black voters were registered. At the request of local leaders, King and the SCLC began to organize and lead voter registration drives. But they quickly found their efforts thwarted because the registrar's office was only open twice a month, and it often had a reduced staff. In response, protesters marched, and King, along with several others, was arrested. Although the mayor, who was just elected by promising nonviolence, had asked Police Chief Jim Clark to peacefully control the protests, the police used clubs and cattle prods against the demonstrators.

Motivated by this response and the need to press for voting rights, as well as the recent killing of Jimmy Lee Jackson during a protest against the imprisonment of an SCLC leader in Marion, Alabama, the SCLC and the Student Nonviolence Coordinating Committee (SNCC) joined together to organize a march from Selma to the state capital, Montgomery.

On March 7, 1965, protesters set out on a march from Selma to Montgomery, demanding voting rights across Alabama. Though Governor George Wallace had banned the march, the protesters went ahead with the plan. As they crossed the Edmund Pettus Bridge over the Alabama River, leading out of Selma, they met 50 state troopers and dozens of Clark's deputies, who were authorized by Wallace to block their path and order them to turn back. When the protesters refused, the mounted officers charged (and sometimes trampled) the marchers, whipping them with bullwhips, beating them with clubs, and driving them back across the bridge under a cloud of tear gas. Much of the event, called Bloody Sunday, was captured by the press and televised on the evening news.

In response to the police brutality, King called for another march two days later, and people from all over the country, motivated by televised scenes of Bloody Sunday, came to Selma to support the marchers. Before the protesters started out, they tried to get a court order to prevent police from blocking their path, but instead, the judge issued a restraining order prohibiting them from marching over the bridge. As a compromise, Dr. King altered the march to go as far as the Edmund Pettus Bridge, where they prayed and then turned around and returned to Selma.

Finally, a federal judge ruled that King's planned march to Montgomery could go on, and on March 21, accompanied by the Alabama National Guard, marchers crossed the Edmund Pettus Bridge. Five days later, King and the rest of the group (including Rosa Parks, John Lewis, Roy Wilkins of the NAACP, Whitney Young of the Urban League, Philip Randolph, Ralph Bunche, Bayard

Rustin, and other leaders of the civil rights movement), which had grown from about 3,000 to 25,000 marchers, triumphantly reached Montgomery, ten years after the movement began there with the bus boycott.

Winning the Voting Rights Act

Prompted by the voting rights protests in Birmingham (see Chapter 6) and Selma and the violence that met this effort, President Johnson sent the Voting Rights Act to Congress two days after Bloody Sunday. Although voting rights were supposed to have been guaranteed by the 15th and 19th Amendments, legislation was needed to put teeth into the earlier laws. Because of public outrage after the violence in Selma, the Voting Rights Act quickly passed Congress, and on August 6, 1965, Johnson signed it into law.

The law had immediate and far-reaching effects. By the end of 1966, only four of the former Confederate states still had less than 50 percent of eligible black voters registered. By the 1968 election, black registration in the Deep South averaged 62 percent. (In fact, by 1968, voter registration had almost doubled in most southern states.) This change began to shift the political landscape, as southern politicians began to have to consider the impact of this strong new group of voters. As a result, a whole new generation of "enlightened politicians" emerged in the South.

Passing and repealing laws

Though perhaps not as far-reaching as the Civil Rights Act of 1964 and the Voting Rights Act of 1965, all three branches of government acted to further racial equality.

✔ **Executive Order 11246:** In 1965, LBJ signed this order that prohibited discrimination by federal contractors or subcontractors. But the more controversial portion of the order required some employers to take positive steps, "affirmative action," to recruit minorities. In 1967, Executive Order 11246 was amended to include women.

✔ *Loving v. Virginia:* In 1967, the Supreme Court ruled that state laws prohibiting interracial marriage were unconstitutional. At that time, 16 states banned interracial marriage, (and until 2000, Alabama still had a clause in its constitution that barred these marriages).

✔ **Civil Rights Act of 1968:** This legislation is also known as the Fair Housing Act. It prohibits discrimination in housing based on race, color, national origin, religion, sex, or familial status. Also, in response to urban unrest, the act contained an antiriot provision.

Rioting in the Cities

Looking at the violence against peaceful protesters in Birmingham, Selma, and other southern cities, many blacks were becoming disillusioned with the principles of passive resistance. In spite of the Civil Rights Act of 1964 (see Chapter 6) and the Voting Rights Act of 1965, many felt that they were still the underclass in American society and that changes were needed, by whatever means were necessary.

Despite legislation and some changing attitudes in white America, blacks were well aware that they were economically and socially worse off than whites. They faced not only discrimination but also a lack of opportunity and unfair treatment at the hands of the police. It was only natural (if not necessarily justifiable) that in the mid- to late '60s, this disillusionment and despair exploded into violent action in the form of urban riots.

The Watts Riots

As with many urban disturbances, the riots in the Watts district of Los Angeles began with a rather routine incident, a traffic stop. On August 11, 1965, a young black man named Marquette Frye, who'd had one too many drinks, was stopped by a Los Angeles police officer. At first, nothing out of the ordinary happened — the young man tried to talk his way out of a ticket and even joked with the officer. But as a small crowd gathered, Frye's protests got louder and more insistent, and the officer called for backup.

Frye resisted arrest, shouting that they'd have to kill him before he went to jail. Frye's anger spread to the growing crowd, and many began cursing and spitting at the policemen. In the end, the officers arrested Frye and a number of onlookers. Although the mob was angry, the whole incident might have ended there, until a young man broke a bottle. The sound of breaking glass inflamed the crowd, and within minutes, people gathered weapons — bottles, rocks, and so on. What began as a nonincident escalated into a riot.

The Watts Riots lasted for six days, during which homes and businesses were destroyed and looted. The rioters' anger and violence were directed mainly at white businesses, as well as the Los Angeles police. When National Guardsmen and police came into the Watts district to contain the insurrection, some rioters used firearms against them. After the riots ended, 34 people were dead, more than 1,000 were injured, and approximately 4,000 had been arrested. No one knows exactly how much property damage resulted from the riots — the numbers vary from $50 million to $200 million.

Why did the riots happen? That was the question on everyone's minds when all was said and done. Los Angeles wasn't the Deep South with Jim Crow Laws, and the Ku Klux Klan wasn't burning crosses on lawns. But communities were still segregated, and police often dealt far more harshly with African Americans than with others. Governor Pat Brown named a commission to study the riots, and its members identified several reasons for the spontaneous eruptions of violence:

- ✔ The police often targeted blacks for no reason, such as walking through a white neighborhood.
- ✔ Segregation and discrimination in black neighborhoods had created years of pent-up anger.
- ✔ Los Angeles had inner-city problems, such as substandard housing, unemployment, and inferior schools.
- ✔ Blacks had rising expectations (and subsequent disappointments) due to the civil rights movement.
- ✔ Many people were becoming impatient with nonviolence as a way to solve problems in the black community.

The Watts Riots further divided Americans on racial issues. Militant blacks saw the riots as a way to improve their lot. Moderates, both black and white, felt that the riots destroyed more than they accomplished. Conservative whites thought that urban rioting was a sign that changes in race relations were happening too fast and thus causing the problems.

A week after the riots, Dr. Martin Luther King Jr. went to Watts to see the devastation. He addressed the crowd but was booed and heckled by people who felt that rioting accomplished more than passive resistance. Although King still condemned violence, he recognized the desperation and frustration that led to the destruction in Watts, and afterwards he went to Chicago to find out firsthand about urban poverty (see "The Chicago Freedom Movement" section, later in this chapter).

In a sense, the Watts Riots had a negative effect on California's blacks, because the liberal governor, Pat Brown, was defeated in the next election by his conservative challenger, Ronald Reagan, who ran on a platform of law and order and blamed Brown for the riots.

The Detroit Riots

As in Watts, the 1967 Detroit Riots started with a relatively minor incident when police raided an after-hours club in a black neighborhood. Because it was an unlicensed bar, the police arrested everyone, while outside, a crowd gathered and started vandalizing and looting nearby businesses. Within two days, the rioting had spread over much of the city, and the National Guard, accompanied by airborne units, was called in. But the riots continued for five days, and in the end, 43 were dead, and more than 1,100 injured and 7,000 arrested. As in Watts, poor living conditions were part of the underlying cause, but Detroit also had several unique situations.

- ✔ **Housing:** Urban renewal projects had been causing the destruction of thriving black neighborhoods, as areas were bulldozed to make way for freeways. Houses in black neighborhoods, though often more run-down than those in white neighborhoods, actually cost more, and blatant discrimination prevented blacks from moving into more desirable areas.

- ✔ **Auto-industry jobs:** Although many blacks in Detroit were economically better off than blacks in other American cities, they made less than their white coworkers, many of whom were also employed in Detroit's auto industry. In addition, increasing factory automation often led to more black workers being laid off than their white counterparts.

In addition to these inequalities, ongoing police harassment and brutality was a major reason for the riots. In Detroit, police targeted blacks, often stopping and arresting them for minor infractions. They were insulting and physically abusive, often out of proportion to the alleged offenses. At times, police beat their detainees so brutally that they died of their injuries, and in several instances police actually shot people in the back of police cars.

Fanning the flames of dissatisfaction were local militants who told their followers that whites would never share their power, that the civil rights movement was a failure, and that only self-determination and separatism would improve their lives.

When H. Rap Brown, national director of SNCC, visited Detroit in 1967, he told the crowd that if Motown didn't come around, "we are going to burn you down."

The Newark Riots

In 1967, rioting also erupted in Newark, New Jersey, for many of the same underlying reasons as it did in Detroit and Watts. However, unemployment in Newark was epidemic, as many industries had left the city for a variety of reasons. Just as in Detroit and two years earlier in Watts, the riots were sparked when several white policemen arrested a black man, and the situation began to escalate. One aggravating factor in Newark was that although blacks made up a large portion of Newark's population, they were underrepresented on the police force and almost nonexistent in city government.

This time, the cause of arrest was so minor it was ridiculous, especially considering the violence that followed. John Smith, a cabdriver, was stopped, interrogated, and arrested for driving around a double-parked police car. En route to the precinct, the arresting officer gave him a severe beating. The story of the arrest spread through the community, and a crowd gathered outside the precinct, waiting for an update. Although Smith was taken out through a back door and sent to a hospital to treat his wounds, the rumor spread that he'd died.

Infuriated, the crowd threw rocks and bottles at the precinct, and police soon dispersed them. However, after the mob started running through the neighborhood, they began breaking into stores and looting them. The mayhem eventually spread from the neighborhood into downtown Newark. The New Jersey State Police and National Guard troops were mobilized to put down the riot, but their involvement actually worsened the situation. After six days of vandalism and violence, 23 people were dead, 725 were injured, and close to 1,500 had been arrested.

Investigating the riots

On July 28, 1967, President Johnson appointed a National Advisory Commission on Civil Disorders in order to understand the causes and possible solutions to eliminate urban rioting. After seven months, they released the *Kerner Report* (named for the commission's chairman, Illinois Governor Otto Kerner), which concluded that the nation was headed for two separate and unequal societies unless the government took action to end segregation and poverty in the cities and recommended legislation to create jobs and improve housing in predominantly black ghettos.

Reacting to King's murder

After the murder of King on April 4, 1968 (see Chapter 6), riots erupted in more than 100 cities, with the most destructive ones in Chicago, Baltimore, and Washington, D.C. Local police, federal agents, and the National Guard were sent to deal with the insurrections. The looting and destruction actually hit black homes and businesses particularly hard, because the rioting took place in mostly black neighborhoods.

Pressing for Economic Empowerment

After viewing the destruction in Watts, King and the SCLC realized that in spite of the progress of the civil rights movement in the areas of desegregation and voting rights in the South, economic inequality throughout the country would continue to plague blacks. Although equal access to public facilities and the right to vote would spell progress, and improved educational opportunities would mean a better future, King believed that something had to be done to improve blacks' lives right then and that nonviolent protest was still the correct way to create better lives for poor people of all races.

The Chicago Freedom Movement

Dr. King decided to begin the protest in Chicago, a city that had a large black population, an activist black clergy, the support of powerful leaders, including some strong labor unions, and a large liberal white community. In 1966, King launched the Chicago Freedom Movement, a coalition of civil rights organizations dedicated to ending discrimination and providing equal housing and full employment for blacks. Some white residents of Chicago, who feared that blacks would erode property values in their neighborhoods and compete for their jobs, put up fierce opposition to the movement.

Unfortunately, King and other leaders of the Chicago Freedom Movement soon realized that the methods they used in the South, such as marches, sit-ins, and boycotts, wouldn't work in the North, where prejudice lay just below the surface but was often just as strong as it was in the South, and racial discrimination was rampant. The community met the protesters with violence, throwing rocks, overturning cars, and setting cars on fire. The explosive racism of some of Chicago's whites was discouraging, and King began to believe that although equal employment, education, and housing were necessary to bring blacks fully into mainstream American society, these objectives might be just "a distant dream."

The Chicago Freedom Movement forced some whites (many of whom had supported the civil rights movement in the South) to face an uncomfortable truth about themselves. Alabama, Mississippi, and Georgia weren't the only places where racism flourished — prejudice existed everywhere, perhaps even in their own minds.

Operation Breadbasket

Founded in 1962, Operation Breadbasket, an arm of the SCLC, was an organization dedicated to improving economic conditions in the black community. One of its missions was to distribute food in poor communities in 12 American cities. It also encouraged blacks to patronize black businesses and to boycott companies that discriminated against them. In 1966 Reverend Jesse Jackson, an up-and-coming civil rights leader, was head of the Chicago branch.

Dr. King considered Operation Breadbasket one of the outstanding successes of the SCLC. Through its efforts, more than 2,000 new jobs were created, and two black-run banks were established in order to serve the community.

A new leader emerges: Jesse Jackson

The leader of the Chicago branch of Operation Breadbasket (and the man who later rose to lead the national organization) was Reverend Jesse Jackson. Jackson was a charismatic and impassioned orator. However, his forceful personality and tendency to say whatever was on his mind also made him many enemies throughout his career.

After an impoverished childhood, Jackson attended the University of Illinois on an athletic scholarship and later graduated from North Carolina Agricultural and Technical State College, where he became involved in the civil rights movement. Jackson attended the Chicago Theological Seminary and was ordained a Baptist minister in 1968.

Jackson participated in the 1965 march from Selma to Montgomery and then became involved in the SCLC. In 1971, he left to form his own organization, Operation PUSH (People United to Serve Humanity), which continued Operation Breadbasket's goal of economic empowerment for blacks. Jackson ran for the Democratic nomination for president in 1984 and 1988 but didn't succeed, partly because of the racial divisions in the country but also because of his controversial positions, such as his support for the Palestinian Liberation Organization (PLO), his association with Louis Farrakhan (leader of the Harlem Mosque of the National of Islam from 1965 through 1975), and his anti-Semitic remark that referred to New York as "Hymietown."

Jackson has been an activist and advocate for African Americans and other minorities. In 1984, he formed the National Rainbow Coalition, an organization dedicated to having all races work together, which, in 1986, merged with PUSH to form the National Rainbow/PUSH Coalition (RPC). Using the tools of demonstrations, as well as influencing legislation, the RPC supports affirmative action and equal rights, economic development and job opportunity, an end to discrimination in housing, and fair representation of minorities in the media.

The Poor People's Campaign

In 1967, King and other leaders of the SCLC launched the Poor Peoples' Campaign to apply the principles of nonviolence to the goals of educational and economic advancement of minorities. However, Dr. King also recognized that poor people of all races had issues and needs in common.

Although some people in the SCLC thought that King's agenda was overly ambitious, he planned a march on Washington to press for economic equality, including funds dedicated to achieving full employment, a guaranteed annual income, and adequate low-income housing. As part of his commitment to economic equality, King went to Memphis to support and march with the black sanitation workers, who were striking for better pay and working conditions. Little did King know this event would be his last mission — on April 4, 1968, he fell victim to an assassin's bullet and never saw his plans for a Poor People's March come to fruition.

The last act of the Poor Peoples' Campaign was Resurrection City, which lasted from May 14 through June 24, 1968, planned and organized by Rev. Ralph Abernathy. Designed to be an interracial protest against poverty (and a memorial to the work of Dr. King), the event hosted more than 2,000 poor people of all ages and races (including urban street gangs), who camped on the mall near the Lincoln Memorial in a collection of makeshift huts and tents. The protest started out hopefully as the protesters lived together in Resurrection City. However, tourists and many white residents avoided the area for fear of crime.

Hope faded when rain turned Resurrection City into a sea of mud, and optimism disappeared entirely when Robert F. Kennedy, one of the heroes of the civil rights movement, was assassinated on June 5, 1968, in Los Angeles. The anger and despair devastated Resurrection City, and when violence erupted within the camp, police invaded and fired tear gas into the crowd.

Reacting to the amounts of tear gas fired into the camp, Abernathy said it was "worse than anything I ever saw in Mississippi or Alabama."

In the rioting that ensued after the camp was shut down, a number of black businesses were destroyed, the city lost more than 2,500 jobs, and new businesses were reluctant to come into the area. The hope of the Poor People's Campaign and Resurrection City was gone.

Being Black and Proud

Black pride and the need for blacks to control their own destiny didn't start in the 1960s. Even before the Civil War, blacks were interested in their history and celebrated their culture. In the early 20th century, Marcus Garvey worked to make blacks aware of their history and instill a sense of pride in their accomplishments, and beginning in the 1930s, the Nation of Islam, taught blacks that by joining together they could help their communities and have a voice in their own futures.

Joining the Nation of Islam

Although white America didn't hear much about the Black Muslims until the 1960s, the Temple of Islam, later to be renamed the Nation of Islam and also known as the Black Muslims, was founded in 1930 in Detroit by W. D. Fard (also called Wali Farad). Fard believed that because Christianity was a white man's religion used to enslave blacks and keep them in their place, blacks should become Muslims. Fard based the new movement on a mixture of Black Nationalism and the belief in Allah as God. He firmly believed that integration and assimilation with the white community wasn't a worthwhile goal and that instead, blacks should work toward an effective, separate society. One of the main demands of the Nation of Islam was self-determination, which they believed would best be achieved by either an independent black state in America or a return to Africa.

By the 1960s, the Nation of Islam was actively looking for recruits to join their cause. They disagreed with the drive for integration, backed by the mainstream civil rights movement, because they believed that by banding together and working within their own communities, they could achieve their goals.

Finding community in faith

In one sense, finding blacks to adopt the new religion was easy, because it expressed all the anger and frustration of being treated as second-class citizens. Especially among black prisoners, who were outcasts on the margins of society, the Nation of Islam provided a sense of pride and the hope that by embracing its principles, blacks could have control over their own destiny.

Belonging to the Nation of Islam also gave members a feeling of community. By adhering to the strict codes of behavior, such as avoiding pork, tobacco, alcohol, drugs, and extramarital sex, they also had the feeling of kinship with other Muslims and a pride in following a moral code. This bond was reinforced because they were discouraged from having much contact with whites.

Even among those who disagreed with the Black Muslim idea of separation of the races, the movement made African Americans aware of their strength and added to their empowerment.

Following the leadership of Malcolm X

A young ne'er-do-well who was imprisoned for burglary in 1946 and son of a minister who believed in black nationalism, Malcolm Little had lived with the injustices of white America since he was a small child. The Ku Klux Klan had threatened the Littles and burned down their home. After Rev. Little was murdered (reputedly by the Black Legion, a white racist group similar to yet more violent than the Klan), the Little family went on welfare, and the children often lived in institutions and foster homes.

Dressed for success

Although the Black Muslims were among the most radical of all black organizations, they were the most conservative looking. Men dressed in dark suits, white shirts, and ties, often wearing fedoras (hats with a crown and a brim), and women wore headscarves, long dresses, and no makeup. This appearance had the triple effect of instilling self-respect, commanding authority, and telling mainstream American society that they were serious about their goals.

This childhood left Malcolm ripe for transformation. In prison, he learned about the Nation of Islam and dedicated himself to learning about Muhammad and his teachings and to faithfully following Islam. When he was released from prison in 1952, he met Elijah Muhammad, leader of the Nation of Islam, officially joined the movement, and adopted the name Malcolm X. (Black Muslims took the last name *X* because they wanted to get rid of their slave names, which were often the surnames of their owners.)

Malcolm X was a dedicated follower of the Nation of Islam and studied under Elijah Muhammad in Chicago, after which he organized a mosque in the Windy City and then went to New York City to head the mosque in Harlem, one of the largest black communities in the United States.

An outstanding orator, Malcolm X quickly became one of the leaders of the Black Muslim movement. Even as Martin Luther King Jr.'s nonviolent protests were gaining headlines and white sympathizers, the separatist Black Muslim movement was gaining adherents among blacks who believed that integration wouldn't improve their lives. Instead, Malcolm X advocated black self-sufficiency, including creating their own community projects and opening and supporting black businesses.

With Malcolm X as a spokesman, the Nation of Islam gained a lot of press, especially because he vocally disagreed with King's methods of protest. He believed that violence was necessary for blacks to defend themselves. Mostly, Malcolm X and the Black Muslims advocated a separate black society, believing that whites were essentially evil, racist, and corrupt. Suddenly, whites who were reluctant (and in some case outright unwilling) to integrate with blacks were furious that some blacks were contemptuous of mainstream American society and had no desire to assimilate. Malcolm X didn't even want blacks to vote — he believed that to do so would be to participate in a racist and decadent system.

Malcolm X's appeal and leadership qualities were among his greatest assets, but they also were a problem, because they incited jealousy as well as conflict with his former mentor, Elijah Muhammad. Malcolm's outspokenness was also a cause of conflict. His remark that President Kennedy's assassination was only the "chickens coming home to roost" offended even some of his supporters; Elijah Muhammad suspended him and forbid him to speak in public for 90 days. Malcolm's strict adherence to the religious prohibitions of Islam also made him overtly critical of Elijah Muhammad, who interpreted these laws rather loosely in his personal life.

Because of these differences, in 1964, Malcolm X split from the Nation of Islam and formed a new organization, the Muslim Mosque, Inc. He still believed that blacks should take an active voice in determining their own destiny, but after a pilgrimage to Mecca, where he met Muslims of all races, he backed off from the idea of a completely separate black society, realizing that a black nation or a return to Africa was an ideal, not an immediate possibility for most black Americans. He therefore thought that blacks should work within the system for better jobs and economic opportunity.

After addressing a crowd in Harlem on February 21, 1965, expressing his more moderate views, Malcolm X was assassinated. His killers, three members of the Nation of Islam who felt that he had betrayed the Black Muslims, were convicted of first-degree murder in 1966.

Asserting black power on campus

Because of the civil rights movement and the growing visibility of blacks in American society, many young African Americans discovered a new sense of racial awareness and pride. Although the Black Muslim movement appealed to poor blacks who were the most oppressed by white society, black college students experienced a new interest in their heritage and culture.

Establishing black student unions

In the 1960s, middle-class black students increasingly enrolled in mostly white universities. Despite the promise of academic freedom and the increasing liberalism in academia, many of these students soon realized that to fit in, they'd have to give up their black identities. Acknowledging that the only way to preserve their identity was to join with other black students, they formed black student unions on campuses across the country.

The objectives of the black student unions were to orient blacks into mainstream campus life and support them in preserving their heritage. Black student organizations worked to

✔ Encourage blacks in academic success

✔ Involve black students in mainstream campus activities

✔ Help incoming black students adjust to campus life

✔ Promote black concerns within the university

✔ Maintain communication and interaction between all black organizations on campus

Black student unions also made sure that the black voice was heard on campus, which they accomplished by bringing their issues to the student body and faculty and also by inviting speakers that would raise awareness of black concerns on campus. Black student unions are still active at colleges and universities today, and many of these organizations also include other minorities of color. Some even sponsor and fund scholarships for high school students.

Black is beautiful

As African Americans became more aware of and connected with their culture and history, they became more appreciative of their own unique traits and were less concerned with following the white standards of beauty. One of the most obvious signs of this new pride was letting their hair go free with Afros instead of straightening it with chemicals, sometimes styling it into *cornrows,* or rows of braids that lay flat to the scalp. They also came to accept their dark skin and stopped valuing light skin within their own community. To celebrate their roots, blacks began wearing *dashikis* (loose, brightly colored African garments) and other African fashions.

Whites also adopted black fashions. Especially among the counterculture, white students permed their hair into Afros and began wearing dashikis. Even today, white women occasionally get their hair done in cornrows.

Changing the curriculum

One of the main accomplishments of the black student unions was the campaign for black studies programs at universities throughout the country. In the late '60s and early '70s, black students wanted a curriculum that addressed black contribution to culture. Instead of studying only European history and culture, they wanted to learn about black literature, art, music, and government and wanted to know more about their African roots. These programs emphasize African history and African American history, social and political life, culture, arts, and religion.

San Francisco State University had the first Black Studies Department at a four-year college.

The focus of black studies departments is to increase self-awareness among blacks. Most departments include courses on black art, literature, and dance; the structure, life, and psychology of the black family and community; and economics and politics. Students can major or minor in Black Studies, but they can also take classes for self-enrichment and knowledge.

Fighting with the Black Panthers

Perhaps the most revolutionary group of the array of black associations during the 1960s was the Black Panther Party. Impatient with the progress of the fight for civil rights, Huey Newton, Bobby Seale, and David Hilliard founded the Panthers in 1966 in Oakland, California. (Stokely Carmichael, one of the most militant leaders of SNCC, also found a home in the Black Panther Party, eventually becoming its Prime Minister in 1968.) The Panthers were inspired by the concepts of black power, irritated by the passivity of nonviolent protest, outraged by police brutality, and opposed to the Vietnam War. Unlike the mainstream drive for integration and voting rights, the Panthers didn't much care about assimilating into white society — instead, their focus was black liberation and black power. They were largely dissatisfied with Martin Luther King Jr.'s belief in nonviolence and felt that more direct means would bring quicker results for the black community.

One of the Panthers' main principles was that blacks had the absolute right to defend themselves against violence, even if that violence was inflicted by police officers. They demonstrated for the right to be armed and oppose police brutality. One of their missions was to observe the police to make sure that they didn't harass or abuse African Americans. Black Panthers saw themselves as black urban revolutionaries.

Although the Panthers didn't have much impact on a national level, they implemented some effective local programs to improve education and housing and fight police violence against the blacks of Oakland. But some of their radical proclamations and violent protest gave them publicity that was out of proportion to their accomplishments in achieving equality for blacks.

Devising and implementing programs

The new party immediately created a ten-point program, designed to improve life in the community. Although the Panthers were able to improve conditions within the black community, many of the ten points were actually a list of far-reaching goals that weren't within their control:

1. Freedom to determine and pursue their own destiny

2. Full employment

3. Reparations for economic oppression by white America

4. Adequate, affordable housing

5. Decent education that emphasized black culture and exposed oppression by white society

6. Free healthcare

7. End to police brutality

8. End to American wars of aggression

9. Freedom for blacks and others unjustly imprisoned

10. The basic elements of human life, including land, bread, housing, education, clothing, justice, peace, and community control of modern technology

To help people in the black community, the Panthers formed *survival programs,* designed to provide necessary services to the poor. One of their first efforts was the Free Breakfast for Children Program, which began in Oakland in 1969 and was later expanded to every city where the Black Panthers had a chapter (they had chapters in 48 states). Later survival programs included free clinics, grocery giveaways, free shoes, school and education programs, senior transport and service programs, legal aid programs, and prisoner support.

However, the FBI saw these programs as Communism, and from there, they determined that the Black Panthers were subversives whose goal was to overthrow the government.

Another important issue for the Panthers was the large number of blacks fighting in Vietnam, in far greater proportion than their numbers in the population. This disproportionate number also struck a chord with the Berkeley student activists, who wanted to ally with the Panthers and fight against U.S. involvement in Vietnam (see Chapter 9 for more on the student movement in Berkeley).

To raise funds to buy guns and protest police violence, the Black Panthers resorted to grass-roots capitalism (although their party was definitely based on Marxist principles). They bought copies of Chairman Mao's *Little Red Book* at local bookstores and then sold them at a profit.

Resisting the law with violence

Public fear, as well as the FBI goal of exterminating the Panther party, prompted police and FBI surveillance and violence against Panther chapters across the country. In Chicago, after four raids on Panther headquarters, a shootout resulted in the slaying of Chicago party leader Fred Hampton and party member Mark Clark. Along with these direct attacks, the FBI used its counterintelligence program to conduct covert missions against the party.

In 1968, J. Edgar Hoover said that the Black Panther Party was "the greatest threat to the internal security of the U.S."

On October 28, 1967, Huey Newton, one of the leaders of the Black Panther Party, was arrested for killing a white police officer in an interchange that also left Newton injured. For the most part, the incident confirmed the whites' worst fears that the Panthers were truly dangerous, but for many blacks, the incident only reinforced their belief in police brutality, which, they were certain, started the gunfight. His arrest also confused some whites of the Left who didn't know quite how to react to the incident because they were still committed to nonviolent protest.

Newton was convicted of manslaughter for the death of Officer John Frey and was sentenced to 2 to 15 years in prison. Though Newton's conviction was overturned 22 months later, agitation and a "Free Huey" movement united and mobilized the Black Panthers and other militants, as well as their white supporters. The party leader became a symbol of oppression and police brutality, and "Free Huey" became the rallying cry of the militants (see Figure 7-1).

How and why the incident that landed Newton in jail even started is somewhat veiled in mystery — no one has a definitive answer. We do know that Frey stopped Newton's van and ordered him and his passenger out of the car. Another officer, Cliff Heanes, arrived as backup, and from there on, the only known fact was that a shootout ensued, killing Frey and wounding Heanes.

After he was released from prison, Newton had a dramatic shift in his ideas about the black power movement. He announced in 1971 that the party would embrace a nonviolent approach and focus on providing social services to the black community. In 1974 Newton was again accused of murder and fled to Cuba to live in exile for three years. When he returned and faced trial he was acquitted because two separate trials both resulted in hung juries.

Figure 7-1:
Black Panthers outside the Alameda County courthouse calling for the release of Huey Newton.

©Bettmann/CORBIS

Newton went on to earn a PhD in social philosophy at UC Santa Cruz in 1980 and continued to work within the black community and write about the oppression of blacks. In 1989 he was given a six-month jail term for misappropriating public funds, and in August of that year Newton was found shot to death on a street in Oakland.

Meanwhile, Eldridge Cleaver, a Black Panther living in exile in Algeria, proposed a radical, terrorist program in place of the ten-point program and was eventually ousted from the party. But Cleaver's ideas began a rift among the Black Panthers, whom Newton had been trying to shift to nonviolent methods. Soon afterward, the leadership fell apart, as many Black Panthers were exiled, expelled, imprisoned, or killed. By the close of the 1970s, the Black Panther Party was all but extinct.

Black Empowerment: The Legacy of the '60s

The lives of most African Americans have greatly improved since the days before the Montgomery Bus Boycott, but blacks have yet to achieve the full social, economic, and political equality for which they fought in the 1960s and subsequent decades. The reasons for this inequality are many and are hotly debated, even today. Some conservatives argue that the social programs begun in the '60s, such as welfare, aid to dependent children, and affirmative action, sapped the motivation of blacks to take advantage of their opportunities. However, many other people believe that racism is still a powerful force keeping blacks from full participation in American society, and that the growing gap between the rich and poor makes it more difficult to achieve the American dream.

Within the black community itself, however, the events of the '60s have had a profound affect. No longer are blacks content to "stay in their place" and defer to whites. Instead, when faced with injustices, they take it to the courts, to the media, and to the streets. They also work to honor their heritage with holidays such as Martin Luther King Jr. Day, a federal holiday; *Kwanzaa,* a December holiday established in 1966 that honors the African roots of African American culture; and *Juneteenth,* which celebrates the announcement of the end of slavery.

The civil rights movement also served as an inspiration for and changed the lives of many other minorities in America (see Chapter 13), as well as those of white Americans, who can now understand and appreciate the contributions of African Americans in society.

Part III
Fighting for Peace: Vietnam and the Antiwar Movement

The 5th Wave   By Rich Tennant

"Join the war, man."

In this part . . .

The Vietnam War was tragic not only for its loss of life on all sides, but also because it tore the United States apart, as perhaps no other event had ever done. Although U.S. history in the region went as far back as World War II, it wasn't until the 1960s that the United States became actively involved. Because of the cold war against Communism, the U.S. government wanted to stop Communism in Asia, and thus was committed to helping bolster the anti-Communist regime in South Vietnam. However, because of internal problems, the South Vietnamese required increasingly more assistance.

The United States first helped the South Vietnamese with arms and advisors, and by the middle of the decade, was actually sending troops to fight the war. For the first time since the Civil War, a large number of Americans vocally opposed the war effort. Students, angered at the draft, fired with indignation at an unjust war, and encouraged and empowered by successes in the civil rights movement, protested loudly and visibly, gathering numerous supporters. In the end, the Vietnam War so divided the country that it unseated a president. The war didn't end until 1973, after much agony, at home and abroad. In this part, we trace the war escalation through 1968 and the Tet Offensive, a major turning point, we examine the antiwar movement, and we detail Nixon's attempts at deescalating the conflict.

Chapter 8

Welcome to Vietnam

- -

In This Chapter

▶ Leaving Indochina: The defeat of the French and infighting in Vietnam

▶ Coming to Vietnam: Americans take a stand

▶ Escalating military involvement

▶ Experiencing defeat after the Tet Offensive

- -

*W*hen American ground forces entered Vietnam in large numbers in March 1965, few Americans knew much about this small Southeast Asian country or the reasons American troops were there. Throughout the 1960s, as the U.S. military increased its involvement, Vietnam became a central concern for many Americans, increasingly dividing them as a military and political issue. In this chapter, you see how cold war fears (see Chapter 2) led America into its longest, most divisive war to date.

Enter America: The Last Chapter of the Long Vietnamese Struggle

The Vietnamese struggle for independence stretches back over almost two millennia. What the Vietnamese refer to as the "American War" in the 1960s and '70s was just the last chapter in a long struggle for independence. Vietnam sought independence from its dominant neighbor China for almost 2,000 years; then the French colonized the country in the 20th century. Finally, with the decline and collapse of the French colonial empire in Indochina (French Indochina included Vietnam, Laos, and Cambodia) in the 1950s, the United States was the primary foreign nation involved in Vietnam until 1975, when the last U.S. troops were withdrawn.

Though most Americans think of U.S. involvement in Vietnam as beginning in the 1960s, U.S. military forces were first in the country during World War II to counter the presence of Japanese occupiers (who were allied with Nazi Germany). The U.S. formed the Office of Strategic Services (OSS) in 1941 as part of the war effort. You likely know the OSS better as the organization it later evolved into — the Central Intelligence Agency (CIA). In Vietnam, the

OSS forged informal alliances with the Viet Minh. The OSS supplied arms, ammunition, and radio equipment to the Viet Minh in exchange for intelligence on the Japanese and assistance in rescuing downed pilots.

The Viet Minh, led by Ho Chi Minh, was a coalition of nationalist and Communist groups formed in May 1941 during the Japanese occupation of Vietnam. This coalition came together to take advantage of the opportunity to organize and prepare to take over in the power vacuum expected after the Japanese withdrawal. See the "Ho Chi Minh: Historical nationalist or red star rising?" sidebar for more background on Ho.

By the end of World War II, the Viet Minh forces believed that the United States would support Vietnamese independence. President Franklin Delano Roosevelt (FDR) had often expressed strong anticolonial views. At the end of the war, when the cold war became America's greatest concern, U.S. policy changed to allow France back into Vietnam. The U.S. worked with the Communist Viet Minh during the war because they had the common goal of forcing the Japanese out of Vietnam. After that was accomplished, the desired goals began to diverge. The Viet Minh felt betrayed. They fought the French until they defeated them in 1954, and they would later fight their former allies, the United States, in the 1960s.

Ho Chi Minh: Historical nationalist or red star rising?

In the 1950s, Ho Chi Minh worked carefully to identify himself with the plight of the peasants, often appearing in peasants' clothing and calling himself "Uncle Ho." He had also worked for Socialist causes for many years, helping to found the Communist Party in France after World War I. During the 1920s and 1930s, he traveled to the Soviet Union and China searching for better models that could help free Vietnam from the French.

American policymakers often debated whether to view Ho Chi Minh as a Communist or a Nationalist. After China fell to the Communists in 1949, conventional cold war wisdom favored those who saw him first and foremost as a Communist. Fearing the falling dominos in the region, many policymakers believed that it would be a far worse mistake to see him as a Nationalist and overlook the possibility that he would work to turn Vietnam and all the rest of Southeast Asia into Communist nations.

These same policymakers overlooked the fact that after World War I, Ho tried to meet with President Woodrow Wilson to discuss national self-determination for all peoples. However, U.S. leaders didn't take him seriously and didn't allow him to meet with Wilson because France was still in control of Vietnam at the time, and he wasn't an official representative of Vietnam. After this event Ho turned to Communist ideology. Though he was an active Communist for almost all his adult life, his primary focus and motivation was always Vietnamese independence.

Continuing the colonial effort: The French in Indochina

Though the Viet Minh declared Vietnam's independence soon after the Japanese surrender in August 1945, the French wanted to hold on to their former colonial possession as a means to help rebuild France, which had been devastated by World War II.

Playing dominoes with cold war logic

Though FDR wanted to place Indochina under an international trusteeship as the first step to establishing Vietnamese autonomy, he was unable to do so before his death. When Vice President Harry Truman became president in April 1945, he inherited the complicated foreign policy goals of FDR, many of which he'd been left in the dark about — including the atom bomb project (the Manhattan Project). Faced with overwhelming complications in postwar Europe generated by the Soviet Union's aggressive foreign policies, Truman succumbed to pressure from French President Charles De Gaulle, who warned him that France faced economic collapse, which could lead to a political shift to the left and the election of Communists in the French government if France's colonies weren't restored.

The U.S. decision to support French aspirations in Vietnam was based upon the *domino theory,* which assumed that the fall of Vietnam — or any country in Southeast Asia — to Communism would act as the first domino in a line, building Communist momentum and causing subsequent countries to fall, until all of Southeast Asia was Communist. This theory was part of the larger *containment policy* that the United States had adopted to check the advance of Communism anywhere on the globe. The theory was based upon the belief that the Communist system contained flaws that would create its own demise; thus the U.S. strategy was to stop the spread of Communism and wait for it to implode of its own natural problems.

Truman believed that the people of Indochina should have independence, but it was more important to him that the French participate in the effort to counter the Soviet Army in Eastern Europe. In 1949, this same cooperative effort culminated in the creation of the North Atlantic Treaty Organization (NATO). Faced with the overwhelming political, economic, and social dislocations of World War II and concerns about worldwide Communist expansion, friendly relations with the Viet Minh seemed trivial. Truman withdrew the OSS and left the problems of Vietnam to the French, making the French Indochina War (1945 to 1954) inevitable. During these nine years the United States steadily gave more assistance to the French in Vietnam. Truman signed National Security Council Memorandum 64 in September 1950, establishing Vietnam as a strategic point in U.S. containment policy.

Witnessing defeat at Dien Bien Phu

Though the French enjoyed superior firepower and air superiority, they were unable to control the war, as the Viet Minh held indigenous support and could choose where and when to engage the French. As the French lost ground, they repeatedly asked the United States for more aid, and by 1954, the U.S. was funding 80 percent of the war effort.

In an attempt to reverse their fortunes in 1953, the French formulated a strategy to lure the Viet Minh into a decisive battle, where the superior French forces could finally break the back of the resistance. However, the French grossly underestimated the strength and determination of the Viet Minh, while overestimating their own strength and logistical abilities.

The French selected a village called Dien Bien Phu near the Laotian border and began setting up a trap. But, in 1954, in a move that the French didn't think possible, the Viet Minh hauled their artillery to the high ground and surrounded the village, encircling the French forces. From there, the Viet Minh slowly pounded the French garrison into submission, signaling the end of French rule in Vietnam. During the siege of Dien Bien Phu, President Dwight Eisenhower and his advisors discussed possible military intervention to save the French, but they recognized the difficulties of continuing the war by proxy and began moving toward a change of policy toward Vietnam.

Creating two Vietnams: The Geneva Conference

At the Geneva Conference of 1954, the French had to negotiate from a weakened position after their loss at Dien Bien Phu. Both sides accepted these provisions:

- ✔ Vietnam was divided at the 17th parallel to allow both sides to withdraw in an orderly manner.
- ✔ The French would leave Vietnam.
- ✔ The Vietnamese could organize elections to be held in 1956 to elect a new government and reunify the country.

Though the peace terms were unfavorable to U.S. cold war strategies (which didn't include a Communist victory), the Eisenhower administration could do little about the situation. The French and the Viet Minh, under the leadership of Ho Chi Minh, signed the agreement on July 20, 1954.

After the division of Vietnam, the northern half of the country formed the Democratic Republic of Vietnam (DRV), which emerged as a Communist government under the leadership of Ho Chi Minh. In the south, the Republic of Vietnam, under the leadership of Ngo Dinh Diem, ran its democratic government modeled after the United States. The plan for national elections in 1956 was designed to give the Vietnamese people a choice between the two governments. Figure 8-1 shows a map of the divided Vietnam and neighboring Laos and Cambodia.

Figure 8-1:
Vietnam
after the
Geneva
Conference.

Courtesy of the Vietnam Archive, Texas Tech University

Building a nation: The developing quagmire

Given the split between North and South Vietnam, the United States began to assume some control in South Vietnam where the Communists had less control. Fearful that an election would allow all of Vietnam to become Communist under the popular Ho Chi Minh, U.S. policy focused on perpetuating the north-south division. By supporting a strong anti-Communist government in the South, policymakers believed they could balance the Communist threat from the North and contain the spread of Communism worldwide.

The caustic leadership of Ngo Dinh Diem

Ngo Dinh Diem, the nationalist leader of South Vietnam, was educated in the West (see Figure 8-2). Diem was a shrewd politician who had maneuvered behind the scenes to earn his chance at power. Though concerned about Diem's lack of popular support (the Vietnamese associated him with French colonialism), U.S. officials saw him as the strongest possible leader based on his U.S. education, the years he spent living in the United States, and his solid credentials as an anti-Communist. But Diem was difficult to work with because he was inflexible, uncompromising, blindly loyal to his family, and paternalistic toward his people.

Figure 8-2:
Ngo Dinh Diem (center), paternalistic leader of South Vietnam.

Courtesy of the Vietnam Archive, Texas Tech University

Afraid of losing the national elections of 1956, Diem announced that because South Vietnam — as an independent country — hadn't signed the Geneva treaty, it wasn't bound by it. He also argued that the power of the Communist Viet Minh would undermine any idea of a free election. Though the North Vietnamese government protested this interpretation, the U.S. government supported Diem's strategy. With American support, Diem shifted his focus to building his economy and military, anticipating an invasion from the North.

Between 1954 and 1960, the U.S. spent $1.2 billion to assist South Vietnam, supplying 80 percent of Diem's military costs and about 50 percent of the nonmilitary expenses. Because the primary concern was the country's security, about three-fourths of the funds went to the Army of the Republic of Vietnam (ARVN).

For South Vietnamese President Diem, his success depended upon establishing a stable and viable nation with the help of the United States. Though initially Diem successfully eliminated rival factions, his elitist rule and nepotistic practices alienated him from the peasantry. The easy flow of U.S. dollars into South Vietnam fueled corruption and greed, further alienating the rich from the rest of the population. Even Diem's attempts to address the problems of corruption created further separation. He sent civic-action teams to peasant villages to hear their complaints and fears about corruption, taxation, and living conditions, but because the well-paid team members were often chosen for their political connections, villagers generally saw them as wealthy outsiders who couldn't be trusted.

The North Vietnamese strategy

In the North, Ho Chi Minh (see Figure 8-3) struggled with transforming the DRV from a colonial structure to a Socialist system. Following Diem's announcement that South Vietnam wouldn't participate in the 1956 national elections, DRV leaders recognized that they would have to either abandon the South or reunify Vietnam by force. Though some leaders favored a negotiated settlement, the hardliners won out, convincing Ho that they would have to take the struggle to the South.

Figure 8-3: Ho Chi Minh (third from right) was a Vietnamese leader for most of the 20th century.

Courtesy of the Vietnam Archive, Texas Tech University

Drawing the battle lines

North Vietnamese leaders kept a careful eye on the effects of corruption and the resulting alienation of the South Vietnamese peasants, capitalizing on the peasants' discontent as part of their strategy for victory. The Viet Minh conducted political assassinations against the more honest and successful government officials in the South, leaving the corrupt ones alone to further sow the seeds of discontent among the peasants. In the early 1960s, the North stepped up its assassinations of village chiefs in order to destabilize the South and ensure the cooperation of peasants against a government that seemed unwilling or unable to protect them.

In the aftermath of the war with the French, part of the treaty terms included allowing the French to withdraw south and the Viet Minh to pull back north to separate the combatants. The plan was that after national elections were held in 1956, the French would leave the country, and the Viet Minh soldiers who lived in the South but had withdrawn to the North could return to their land, families, and villages. When Diem refused to participate in the national elections (see the "The caustic leadership of Ngo Dinh Diem" section earlier in the chapter), the Viet Minh leaders saw that reunification would have to come by force. Many of these men began secretly returning to their villages in the South where they became the *Viet Cong,* fighting to destabilize the South Vietnamese government. Natives of the North would fight for the same goals as part of the *North Vietnamese Army* (NVA).

The Army of the Republic of Vietnam (ARVN) forces of South Vietnam fought back against these tactics by trying to deny the Viet Cong opportunity to control the countryside. As these two forces began to clash more openly, it was often the peasants who were caught in the middle. Both sides sought to punish villagers who collaborated with the enemy.

Facing a crisis of leadership in the South: The Coup of 1963

Following a failed assassination attempt in November 1960, Diem began to distrust his American advisors, believing that they had sanctioned the plot on his life. Distancing himself from the Americans, he turned instead to close relatives such as his younger brother, Ngo Dinh Nhu. Diem's inability to stop the insurgency in the South, his alienation from the U.S. advisors, and his failure to gain international acceptance for South Vietnam severely undermined his leadership. Tough U.S. advisors urged him to initiate reforms, but Diem refused, allowing himself to become further isolated. This development proved fatal for Diem in October 1963.

Rebelling Buddhists

The "Buddhist crisis" began in May 1963 as Vietnamese Buddhists prepared to celebrate the birth of Buddha in the old imperial city of Hue. When police enforced a previously ignored law prohibiting the display of religious flags without the South Vietnamese flag, the Buddhists protested. The Buddhists were disturbed by the fact that just one week before, Catholics in Hue flew the papal flags at their celebration without confrontation by the law.

The incident escalated when provincial troops opened fire on the protesters, killing one woman and eight children. This set off a series of Buddhist protests across South Vietnam. Because Diem believed that the Viet Minh encouraged these protests to further destabilize his government, he used the military to suppress them, escalating the crisis. The situation reached a peak on June 11, 1963, when Thich Quang Duc, an elderly Buddhist monk, calmly walked out into a busy Saigon intersection, sat down in prayer, doused himself in gas, and set himself on fire. His dying message to Diem and the world was a respectful plea, charity and compassion for all religions.

Warned ahead of time, Western journalists and the international media filmed the event, creating a powerful backlash against Diem. Over the next few months, other Buddhist monks followed Duc's example by immolating themselves before the cameras so that the world could watch in horror and begin to question why a man would voluntarily do such a thing (see Figure 8-4). The images had the desired effect of creating a great deal of condemnation of the Diem government from the international community.

Figure 8-4: A Buddhist monk commits ritual suicide in Saigon, protesting anti-Buddhist policies.

©Bettmann/CORBIS

Though U.S. advisors warned Diem to back off, he continued to press the Buddhists, prompting further public self-immolations. When Diem staged raids on Buddhist pagodas and arrested more than 1,400 monks, the situation was completely out of control.

President Diem's sister-in-law, Madame Nhu, furthered worldwide outrage by referring to the protests against the South Vietnamese government as "Buddhist barbecues" and stating, "Let them burn, and we shall clap our hands."

Overthrowing the government

Recognizing the growing crisis, two South Vietnamese generals secretly approached the United States through a CIA contact to suggest the ouster of Diem. After receiving reassurance that U.S. aid would continue after Diem and that the coup would have no repercussions, South Vietnamese troops captured and executed Diem and his brother on November 2, 1963. A 12-man military council took over the government, paving the way for deeper U.S. commitment.

Americanizing the War

Though the number of U.S. personnel in South Vietnam had grown to about 700 advisors during the Eisenhower administration, American commitment to South Vietnam grew exponentially under President John F. Kennedy, reaching more than 16,000 by late 1963. Further, the role of the American personnel shifted from advisement to direct military support of the South Vietnamese military.

Inheriting the conflict: JFK's legacy to LBJ

In 1960, Kennedy campaigned with the pledge to take a firm stand against the spread of Communism. In the first three years of his administration, he faced a variety of challenges regarding the worldwide advance of Communism, including the Bay of Pigs fiasco and the Cuban Missile Crisis (for more on these subjects, see Chapter 2). Kennedy based his Vietnam policy on his conviction that the United States must stand firm in the face of Communist aggression.

In 1961, South Vietnam President Ngo Dinh Diem requested a substantial increase in U.S. assistance. In response, Kennedy dispatched Army General Maxwell Taylor and national security expert Walt Whitman Rostow to South Vietnam to assess the situation. They reported that increasing American troops in South Vietnam would secure the country and prevent the dominos from falling. They called for 8,000 American troops to give the ARVN rapid response capability against enemy attacks. Kennedy's other cabinet members agreed, except for Undersecretary of State George Ball, who feared that troop escalation would only pull the U.S. further into a dangerous situation.

Kennedy's escalation emphasized using Special Forces, often called the *Green Berets*. Trained in guerilla warfare, these troops worked in small groups to train the Vietnamese to defend themselves. By living in close proximity to the people, the Special Forces troops built a solid relationship aimed at winning their hearts and minds. Though quite successful, particularly with the mountain people of Vietnam (called *Montagnards*), over time U.S. forces began to shift away from these tactics in favor of more conventional military tactics, which are much less effective for winning the hearts and minds of the people (see the "Committing U.S. Troops: Shifting from Advisors to Combatants" section later in this chapter).

When JFK was assassinated in November 1963, Vice President Lyndon Johnson (LBJ) inherited the presidency and Kennedy's foreign policy. Because LBJ made no significant changes in his cabinet, little would change.

Dealing with the conflict: The presidential campaign of 1964

Almost immediately after taking office, LBJ began campaigning for the 1964 elections, which were only a year away. The Republicans nominated Barry Goldwater, who campaigned as a "Hawk," calling for more troops and a bombing campaign against North Vietnam. Johnson campaigned as a "Dove," focusing on his domestic agenda designed to create the "Great Society" (see Chapter 3 for more details).

During his campaign, Johnson called for limited American commitment in Vietnam, stating that he had no intention of sending "American boys to fight a war that I think ought to be fought by the boys of Asia."

Though Johnson, running on a peace platform, won the election by a landslide, he couldn't keep his election promises, as the course in Vietnam had already been set in motion. Looking back at the fall of China to the Communists in 1950 and the severe political repercussions the loss created for Truman, Johnson couldn't afford to lose Vietnam to the Communists. As the war escalated, particularly after 1965, Johnson had little choice but to increase U.S. forces. Years later, as he lay dying, he blamed this pattern of escalation for undermining his dreams of the Great Society.

Wading in deep: The Tonkin Gulf incident

During his reelection campaign, Johnson also worked to bolster the U.S. position in Vietnam. Being a dove was good for getting reelected, but realities in Vietnam demanded that the United States strengthen its position or prepare to withdraw. In June 1964, he appointed General William C. Westmoreland as the new commander of the Military Assistance Command — Vietnam (MACV). Westmoreland firmly believed in American firepower and conventional military tactics.

As part of the preparations for a larger role in the war, the U.S. Navy began sending ships deep into the Tonkin Gulf to gather electronic intelligence (ELINT) and plot the coordinates of North Vietnamese radar installations, which would give the United States vital information needed to strike effectively against North Vietnam, if necessary. Called *DeSoto patrols,* these missions also placed U.S. destroyers in position to support South Vietnamese patrol boats during their attacks on Northern positions.

This buildup was part of a larger strategy created under Kennedy's administration, called Oplan 34A, in which the United States supplied the swiftboats, weapons, intelligence, and training for the Vietnamese Navy to bombard islands off the shores of North Vietnam. Through diplomatic channels, the North Vietnamese were warned that by supporting insurgency in the South, they were inviting retaliation in the form of direct attacks on North Vietnam. As the North Vietnamese sent their own patrol boats to defend against the attacks of Oplan 34A, the likelihood of contact with the U.S. ships on the DeSoto patrols increased.

A confrontation between American ships and North Vietnamese patrol boats in international waters could be — and eventually was — used to justify direct American intervention in the war against North Vietnam.

On July 30, as a part of the South Vietnamese efforts to agitate the North Vietnamese, South Vietnamese commandos raided two small islands off the North Vietnamese coast. The U.S. destroyer, the *Maddox,* cruised nearby to use its special ELINT equipment to monitor North Vietnamese radar positions and radio traffic during the raid. Over the next few days:

- **August 2:** The *Maddox* encountered three North Vietnamese patrol boats investigating its presence. According to reports, the patrol boats pursued and fired three torpedoes on the *Maddox.* Although the torpedoes scored no hits, jets were scrambled from the nearby aircraft carrier *Ticonderoga,* hitting three torpedo boats and sinking one.

  Although U.S. officials immediately sought details on the 20-minute encounter, the only physical evidence found was one bullet that had hit the *Maddox.* Johnson needed stronger evidence, so he ordered the *Maddox* to return to the area accompanied by a newer destroyer, the *C. Turner Joy.*

- **August 4:** The two warships reported that they were under attack by North Vietnamese torpedo boats. It was a dark night and the battle raged for more than two hours, with reports of 22 torpedoes fired. Yet there were no hits on either ship. The aircraft carriers *Ticonderoga* and *Constellation* sent jets to pound each target identified by the warships, and initial reports claimed that three North Vietnamese vessels had been sunk.

  Almost immediately after the attacks, Captain Herrick of the *Maddox* had second thoughts about the whole event. He quizzed his crew and searched the seas for evidence to prove the attacks, yet there was no physical evidence of sunken enemy ships, and his crew was now unsure about the whole attack. They speculated that the storm created phantom sonar signals, and they may have fired at nothing.

Johnson pressed the navy for positive verification of the attacks, but even before receiving proof, he told the American people about the attacks and unleashed a 64-plane retaliatory strike against North Vietnamese radar stations. He then asked Congress for the authority to react to what was described as unprovoked aggression by the North Vietnamese. Congressmen were told that U.S. destroyers had been conducting routine patrols and weren't told about Oplan 34A. The House of Representatives and Senate voted overwhelmingly in favor of the *Tonkin Gulf Resolution,* giving the president broad powers to respond to aggression with the force he deemed appropriate and necessary. Johnson now had all the authority he needed to significantly escalate the war. (See the "Consensus, dissent, and the concealed truth" sidebar for more on the sordid history of this resolution.)

Consensus, dissent, and the concealed truth

The reason Congress wasn't told about the South Vietnamese attacks was because Johnson's assistant secretary of state, William Bundy, had drafted the Tonkin Gulf Resolution many months before the incident, in anticipation of such an event. In other words, the situation was created and managed to justify and legitimize America's entrance into the war. Congress never officially declared the U.S. military actions in Vietnam a war. Thus, the Tonkin Gulf Resolution was the sole basis of legal presidential authority to engage in hostilities. Written in broad sweeping terms that left discretion to the president, Congress passed the resolution on its understanding that U.S. warships had been attacked. Later, as the war progressed, Johnson kept a copy of the Tonkin Gulf Resolution handy to show to anyone who questioned his authority to pursue the war.

"Overwhelming" may be an understatement in describing the Senate and House votes in favor of the resolution. The House voted 416 to 0 in favor, and the Senate passed it by a vote of 88 to 2. One of the two senators who voted against the Tonkin Gulf Resolution got a tip from someone in the military regarding the truthfulness of the account brought before Congress. Urged to raise questions about Oplan 34A and its relationship to the routine DeSoto patrols, Oregon Senator Wayne Morse questioned Secretary of State Dean Rusk and Secretary of Defense Robert McNamara when they testified before the Senate. Both men duplicitously denied any relationship or coordination between the South Vietnamese operations and the U.S. patrols.

The man who steered the resolution through the Senate was Senator J. William Fulbright, who pushed for the resolution's extensive powers based upon his personal trust of LBJ, never fearing it would be misused. Ironically, Fulbright eventually became Johnson's leading critic, as he became disillusioned by the continued escalation. After receiving insider information regarding the Tonkin Gulf incidents, he began a slow, painful investigation of the events.

Using evidence gathered from sailors involved in the cable traffic between Saigon, the navy, and the White House, investigators have now concluded that the first attack happened under very different circumstances than were apparent in 1964, and the second "attack" didn't happen at all. Congress repealed the Tonkin Gulf Resolution in May 1970.

Committing U.S. Troops: Shifting from Advisors to Combatants

In February 1965, Viet Cong forces overran a U.S. airbase in Pleiku in the central highlands, killing nine Americans and wounding 130. They also did extensive damage to U.S. aircraft. Johnson immediately ordered retaliatory strikes on targets in North Vietnam. These strikes evolved into a sustained bombing campaign named Operation Rolling Thunder.

With increased air activity, General Westmoreland requested combat troops to protect U.S. airbases, and Johnson immediately sent two battalions (more than 1,400 men) of Marines who landed at Danang on March 8, 1965. Within weeks, Westmoreland requested more troops to begin offensive operations. After a debate, many of the same advisors that Kennedy had relied on four years before favored escalation, claiming that they needed to act quickly to avoid a larger disaster. (See "Inheriting the conflict: JFK's legacy to LBJ" earlier in the chapter for more on the earlier debate.)

The lone voice of dissent was again George Ball. After deliberating, Johnson authorized the deployment of an additional 40,000 troops. As the U.S. combat role expanded, Westmoreland called for even greater numbers of troops, believing that he could control the situation with additional troops. Thus, the Pleiku incident was the beginning of major U.S. escalation.

By the end of 1965, the U.S. had some 200,000 troops in Vietnam. In 1966, the number would balloon to more than 360,000, hitting 475,000 in 1967. The United States hit the high point in the war in 1968 with more than 530,000 troops in Vietnam.

The U.S. was winning battles, yet failing at its mission to win people's hearts and minds. The massive forces sent to save South Vietnam were destroying the country militarily, environmentally, socially, and economically.

Relying on air superiority: Rolling Thunder 1

Operation Rolling Thunder was the Johnson administration's first major sustained bombing campaign. It began in March 1965 and continued intermittently until October 1968. It had three objectives:

- **Strategic:** Destroy North Vietnam's industrial capacity for war and disrupt its lines of communication with the South.
- **Coercive:** Intimidate the North Vietnamese.
- **Political:** Boost the morale of the ARVN forces by demonstrating American strength and resolve.

Introduced in phases, the bombing campaign was limited to targets approved by the administration. In the first phase, Johnson approved only military targets south of the 20th parallel, to avoid provoking the Chinese to the north. During the second phase, the U.S. expanded its operations yet prohibited targets within 30 miles of Hanoi (the capital of North Vietnam), 10 miles from Haiphong (the most important major port in North Vietnam), and anything close to the Chinese border. The third phase allowed previously prohibited targets, such as petroleum storage facilities, power plants, and infrastructure, including railroads, highways, and lines of communication.

Although the U.S. Air Force was allowed to select targets in North Vietnam from an authorized list, Johnson and his senior White House officials created this list. These men were primarily concerned about world perceptions of the bombing campaign and the possibility of reaction from the Soviet Union or China. Though successful in controlling the campaign, the system also created resentment among military planners who felt the Johnson administration was hampering the war effort by micromanaging it.

Bombing in the South in support of ground troops fighting the Viet Cong was much less restricted. Although much attention has been placed on the bombing of North Vietnam, more bombs were dropped on South Vietnam. Between 1965 and 1967, the U.S. and South Vietnamese Air Forces dropped more than 1 million tons of bombs in the South, more than twice the number dropped on the North in the same period.

Periodically, Johnson halted the bombing campaign to offer the North Vietnamese a chance to discuss peace, yet the Northern leaders often viewed this as a sign of weakening resolve and a chance to rebuild their facilities during the talks. When Johnson realized they were using the talks to stall for time, he resumed the bombing. Though the campaign in Vietnam dwarfed the tonnage used in World War II, there were definite limits to the use of air power in a country that had so few industrial targets of value.

Fighting a different kind of war

From the beginning, the war in Vietnam was different from previous wars. One problem faced by U.S. troops was that they couldn't easily distinguish their enemy from their allies. The enemy easily blended in with the population and struck at U.S. forces from within. Though the U.S. worked hard to define the enemy as an invading force trying to destabilize South Vietnam, this claim was only true of the NVA forces. The Viet Cong was the group who engaged U.S. forces most aggressively up until 1968, and these people can't be considered an invading force because they were originally from the area now known as South Vietnam (see the "Drawing the battle lines" section earlier in the chapter for a discussion on these two groups).

The Vietnam War was different in other respects as well. It had started as a war of independence from the French and had evolved into a civil war after the split between the North and South. In a conventional war, two sides struggle to advance their armies, but the war in Vietnam lacked that geographic goal. The U.S. Army wasn't trying to push the enemy from the field of battle except at the northern border. Instead, they were sent to quell a civil conflict by stabilizing the South.

As a result, the United States adopted a strategy of attrition and erosion. Recognizing its superior firepower and air dominance over South Vietnam, the U.S. used these strengths to find and kill VC and NVA soldiers in South

Vietnam. They employed superior firepower to produce much higher kill ratios, draining the North of both the men and the will to fight. The U.S. success was measured with the body count, "theirs" versus "ours." The erosion strategy tried to weaken North Vietnam's ability to wage war. By bombing military and industrial targets in the North, as well as supply lines along the Ho Chi Minh Trail, the U.S. strategy was to destroy the enemy's ability to supply its troops and inhibit the southern insurgents' ability to fight. Check out U.S. troops in the field in Figure 8-5.

Figure 8-5:
U.S. troops
wade
through a
stream in
Vietnam.

Courtesy of the Vietnam Archive, Texas Tech University

The Johnson administration believed that the bombing and attrition strategies would bring North Vietnam to its threshold of pain, forcing it to abandon its support of insurrection in the South. The plan was to increasingly apply these forces, looking for that point where the North would give in. Instead, this strategy forced the North Vietnamese to wage a protracted war, hoping to weaken the American will to sustain the conflict. Northern leaders prepared their people for a sustained struggle. Given the history of struggle against Chinese and French dominance, the Vietnamese were prepared for a struggle that could last for generations. Each bombing raid by U.S. forces served to reinforce rather than deplete the North's will to fight. In the South, the "hearts and minds" strategy was supposed to build nationalistic spirit, yet corruption in the South Vietnamese government and the shift to more conventional methods tended to undermine peasant support over time.

Relying on body counts

To see progress in the war, the U.S. military had to produce bodies. To do so, they used search-and-destroy missions designed to find enemies, then use America's superior firepower to annihilate them, tallying the number of dead bodies. One problem with this approach was that the NVA and VC could maintain initiative by deciding where and when to make a stand. Though U.S.

forces did catch some enemy troops by surprise, the sound of helicopters often signaled the arrival of U.S. troops, and the enemy could choose whether to fight or to melt into the jungles or hills.

The body counts went hand in hand with the *kill ratios* — the number of enemies killed compared to the loss of U.S. troops. Both were attempts to quantify the progress of the war and were routinely reported to the press at daily press conferences, often referred to as the "five o'clock follies."

Combat commanders recognized that their effectiveness was measured by body counts and kill ratios and that if they had aspirations to rise to higher ranks, they needed to have high numbers. Therefore, officers tended to inflate the figures to enhance performance ratings, sometimes by doubling the count based on body parts alone or by counting all dead bodies as enemy kills. Many field officers ignored age, sex, and whether the person had a weapon, instead simply noting that a dead Vietnamese person was a dead enemy. With these inaccuracies and inflation in the numbers, the statistical measure of progress was rendered almost meaningless.

Understanding the cold war concerns of maintaining a limited war

Throughout the Vietnam War, cold war struggle between the United States and the Soviet Union tended to define the conflict (see Chapter 2 for more on the cold war). The powerful belief in the domino theory was a driving force behind America's decision to make a stand in Vietnam.

Even while fighting in Vietnam, cold war fears shaped strategies and decisions. The United States feared that the struggle could escalate into a worldwide war with the Soviet Union or China. The lessons of pushing too far in the Korean War, where the Chinese sent one million troops into North Korea to push back U.S. forces when the U.S. ignored their warnings, were a constant brake on U.S. decisions to escalate. Although the U.S. knew that the Soviets and later the Chinese were supplying the North Vietnamese, it wanted to win in Vietnam without escalating into a war that could become a nuclear conflict.

The U.S. Rolling Thunder bombing campaign between March 1965 and October 1968 was designed to lessen the chances of such conflict:

- ✔ Targets close to the Chinese border were often off-limits due to Chinese threats. The North Vietnamese recognized this fact and used it to their advantage, stationing their few MiG fighters near the Chinese border.

- ✔ Dikes in the North weren't bombed, to avoid the appearance of trying to annihilate the North Vietnamese population through starvation.

- ✔ Attacking Haiphong Harbor was avoided for fear of hitting a Soviet or Chinese ship in the port.

Although many people even today complain that the United States was forced to fight the war "with one hand tied behind its back," the fear of escalation into worldwide nuclear war was a very real concern that required caution.

Failing to win hearts and minds

One major objective was for the U.S. to pacify and stabilize South Vietnam in order to claim victory. This goal had two components. The first was to find and defeat the enemy; the second was to gain support and cooperation from the people so that South Vietnam could become self-sustaining. The idea was to convince them that living under a capitalist republic was far superior to living under Communism. This has oftentimes been referred to as "winning their hearts and minds." Unfortunately, the U.S. military was far better at the first goal than they were at the second, and leaders like General Westmoreland believed that defeating the enemy was top priority and that they could worry about the rest after the enemy had been vanquished.

A nation of refugees

Though part of the U.S. program included building roads, bridges, schools, hospitals, and irrigation projects, the military mission undermined much of the goodwill created by these improvements. One major problem was that the massive firepower and the liberal use of chemical defoliants drove many peasants from their villages into the cities. American military operations created 4 million South Vietnamese refugees, representing a full 25 percent of the South Vietnamese population. These refugees were forced to live in squalid conditions, rife with disease. As they suffered, they became targets for Viet Cong recruitment.

Family life declined as children abandoned filial piety to pursue easy money and Western lifestyles. Bars and brothels clogged the streets of the cities, luring young people into servicing the soldiers and shattering traditional values and social structures. A young girl could make more money per week working as a prostitute for U.S. soldiers than her father could make in a year. Young Vietnamese boys were forced into the South Vietnamese army and separated from their families.

The vast influx of American dollars fueled inflation, causing further hardship on the already hard-pressed poor. Between 1965 and 1967, Vietnamese prices increased an average of 170 percent.

Ironically, then, as U.S. commitment deepened, relations between the American soldiers and the South Vietnamese became more strained. American soldiers distrusted the ARVN troops because they were reluctant to fight and because Americans feared the Viet Cong had infiltrated their ranks. The traditional Vietnamese family found the ideas of the VC more familiar and less ruinous to their values than the United States; thus, the villagers often cooperated with the VC. Many U.S. soldiers noted that villagers usually didn't step on the mines set for the U.S. soldiers, suggesting that they had cooperated or at least watched the VC plant them.

A lack of cultural understanding

Another problem that created alienation stemmed from the *Agroville* and *Strategic Hamlet* programs. Started under Diem's regime, these programs were designed to prevent the VC from gaining supplies from the rural villages. The South Vietnamese government recognized the VC's reliance on the peasants for recruits and supplies and instituted the strategic hamlets to prevent the VC from pressuring the villagers. To protect the villagers and deny the VC access to supplies, villagers were forced to move to South Vietnamese–established enclaves.

As the U.S. involvement deepened, these programs were expanded. The problem was that villagers were forced to build and live in the settlements. Americans ignored the deep multigenerational attachment of the rural folk to the land, their chief source of security. Even more importantly, the land held the ancestral shrines, tended and worshipped on a daily basis for generations. Finally, the Strategic Hamlets were fenced-in settlements with gates and razor wire, allowing American forces to confine the villagers, particularly at night when the VC were most active. Inhabitants viewed the camps more as prisons than villages, driving many into supporting the VC.

Designating "free-fire zones"

Another major problem was the designation of some areas under VC control as *free-fire zones,* where anything that moved was considered a target of opportunity. In free-fire zones, jets could unload unused ordnance to avoid the dangers of landing with live bombs aboard.

This indiscriminate killing further alienated the peasants. One example was the establishment of two Special Forces camps in the central highlands. After the camps were established, villagers were forced to live there, and the surrounding areas were declared free-fire zones. As a result, villagers were forced to either work in the Special Forces camps or go over to the VC.

Segregating the lines in combat

For every one combat troop on the front line, there were at least seven in the rear. Though the rear didn't offer complete safety, when compared to the risk faced by a combat grunt, it was a much safer place to be. This was the basis of many complaints about racism in the war, especially from civil rights leaders. Even Dr. Martin Luther King Jr. asserted that blacks represented a disproportionate number of draftees and combat troops.

Selective Service rules allowed deferments for college attendance and a variety of civilian occupations deemed essential. Deferments tended to favor white, middle- and upper-class groups. Also, blacks were underrepresented on the

Reaching poor youths with Project 100,000

Project 100,000 was a part of Johnson's Great Society Program. Aimed at generating an additional 100,000 recruits per year, it was launched in 1966, designed to enhance opportunities for underprivileged and poor youths in American inner-city neighborhoods by lowering the military entrance requirements, thereby allowing many who would have previously been unqualified for the military to serve. Of the 350,000 who enlisted under this program, 41 percent were black and 40 percent received combat assignments. Casualty rates among these soldiers were twice that of other categories of inductees, suggesting that they either received higher-risk positions or that the military hadn't trained them as well as other troops. Project 100,000 was a failure because few recruits received training that would aid in their rise in the military or in civilian life.

draft boards themselves. In 1966 blacks accounted for just about 1 percent of all draft board members, with seven states having no blacks at all.

Blacks did supply a disproportionate number of combat soldiers. Although they made up less than 10 percent of the U.S. armed services between 1961 and 1966, they accounted for just fewer than 20 percent of all combat-related deaths in the same period. In 1965 alone, blacks represented almost 20 percent of the army's forces killed in action. Military commanders worked to lessen these numbers, and by the end of the war, combat deaths of black soldiers amounted to about 12.5 percent. Yet U.S. census records for 1970 place their percent of the population at about 10.5 percent.

Black soldiers were aware of these disparities, yet the combat grunt could do little about it. The situation strengthened the feeling of community among blacks, who bonded together as "bloods." The North Vietnamese were aware of racial tensions within the U.S. military and worked hard to disseminate propaganda designed to increase these tensions.

The Tet Offensive of 1968

By 1967 the Vietnam War had hit a stalemate. Although the United States successfully kept the NVA and VC from toppling the South Vietnamese government, they were unable to stop the insurgency in the South. The drawn-out struggle benefited the North Vietnamese, whose leaders calculated that a major offensive might force Johnson to end the bombing and come to the negotiating table in a weakened position based upon growing U.S. public discontent with the war's costs and losses (see Chapter 9). Success in a major offensive might also demonstrate the limits of U.S. power and undermine

South Vietnamese confidence in U.S. power. This, in turn, could cause the people of South Vietnam to lose confidence in their own government, paving the way for overthrow or the possibility of a coalition government.

The *Tet Offensive* was a carefully planned series of simultaneous attacks by the North throughout South Vietnam. It was set for the end of January to take advantage of the lull in the action created by the annual Tet (lunar New Year) festivities. The assaults weren't aimed at perceived weak points in the U.S. and South Vietnamese defenses, but at the perceived strongholds.

As a precursor to the plan, the North Vietnamese took two important steps:

- ✔ As a conciliatory gesture, they offered to come to the negotiating table if the United States would stop the bombing campaign.

- ✔ They launched a series of diversionary attacks on U.S. posts along the Laos and Cambodian borders and near the demilitarized zone (DMZ) to draw U.S. strength to the area to allow for the real offensive in the cities of the South.

Diverting attention at Khe Sanh

An important part of the North Vietnamese Tet Offensive strategy was to make the American leaders think that they were trying to gain control of the northernmost part of South Vietnam. The initial assaults were followed by a buildup of North Vietnamese troops in the area of Khe Sanh, in the northwest corner of the country. To American leaders, the situation began to look much like the great siege of the French forces at Dien Bien Phu in 1954, which finally broke the French will to continue fighting (see the section "Enter America: The Last Chapter of the Long Vietnamese Struggle," earlier in this chapter). President Johnson, buying the North Vietnamese ruse, ordered General Westmoreland to hold Khe Sanh so the United States could avoid a repeat of the French debacle some 14 years before.

By the time the siege of Khe Sanh began on January 21, 1968, Westmoreland was prepared to hold his position by committing more than 50,000 U.S. troops. As the two-month battle ensued, the U.S. unleashed withering fire-power, including artillery, air strikes, and napalm on a scale previously unseen. Though the U.S. won the battle at Khe Sanh, this victory was all part of the North Vietnamese strategy of diversion from the main assault they were about to unleash on the cities of South Vietnam.

The U.S. Marines commander of Khe Sanh, Major General Lowell English, later called the position a "trap . . . to force you into the expenditure of an absolutely unreasonable amount of men and material to defend a piece of terrain that wasn't worth a damn."

Surprising the U.S. with the real attacks

While the preparations for the siege of Khe Sanh were going on in the North, the NVA and VC were quietly moving their troops and weapons into position in the South. Their journey carefully planned for the Tet holiday, most of the NVA and VC forces moved with the migration to the cities that always accompanied the Tet celebrations.

The attacks began just after midnight on January 31, 1968. The well-coordinated attacks by 84,000 NVA and VC troops hit six major cities, 36 of the 44 provinces, and more than 50 hamlets. Attacking from the DMZ all the way to the southern tip of the country, the assault was rapid and brutal, catching U.S. forces by surprise. The assaults in the capital of Saigon and the old imperial city of Hue were cleverly delayed by one day to create the illusion that the offensive wouldn't include these cities. As Tet celebrations continued the next day in the two cities, the U.S. forces, already reeling from the previous day's action, were surprised once again.

In Saigon the VC pulled off a daring raid on the brand new U.S. embassy compound. Twenty VC commandos drove through the city in a truck and a taxi, arriving at the embassy at 3 a.m. They quickly blew a hole in the outer wall and raced inside, killing five U.S. guards. Though reinforcements quickly arrived, the compound wasn't secured until the last commando was killed nearly four hours later. The commandos lost, but they accomplished one of the most important psychological objectives of the whole offensive — they had breached the walls of the very symbol of U.S. power, demonstrating American weakness.

The highly respected nightly newscaster Walter Cronkite reacted to the images of the overrun U.S. embassy, asking live on air, "What the hell is going on? I thought we were winning the war."

Across South Vietnam, battles raged in the cities and hamlets. The U.S. and ARVN forces had the advantage of mobility and firepower and, in most places, were able to repel the insurgents within days. A fierce battle developed in Hue as the NVA and VC forces uncharacteristically tried to hold the city. The Communist forces finally withdrew on February 23; the Tet Offensive was over, and the U.S. and ARVN forces had repelled the insurgents. Yet the city was in ruins, and thousands of officials, teachers, and perceived collaborators had been executed — but the impact of what had been accomplished was yet to be seen.

Assessing the aftermath: A military victory and a political defeat

The Tet Offensive stunned many Americans, even those who initially supported the war. The chaos and carnage created by the attacks were recorded by international news services and broadcast into the homes of millions of Americans. Vietnam was the nation's first televised war. For the first time, both the heroic and horrific images of the U.S. streamed into America's living rooms every night. No longer was war a something you read about or watched once a week in a newsreel at the movies before the feature film. And perhaps nothing demonstrated the power of television in Vietnam as forcefully as Tet.

Prior to Tet, LBJ had been cultivating a picture of steady, careful progress in Vietnam. General Westmoreland had repeatedly announced the fine progress of the war and told the American people just months before that the enemy was on the verge of defeat. The daily tally of body counts and kill ratios convinced many Americans that the U.S. military had the situation totally under control, and that it was merely a matter of time before the U.S. finished and brought the victorious boys home. The effects of seeing the attacks across the country and even in the U.S. Embassy were devastating. The president's claims came under steady fire after Tet, causing many to wonder what the truth really was.

The irony was that Tet really was a U.S. military victory. The U.S. and ARVN forces were successful in driving back the enemy in every province. Viet Cong losses were staggering. Tet had shattered the Viet Cong movement, shifting the burden of the fighting in the future to the NVA (see the "Facing the enemy: The North Vietnamese Army and the Viet Cong" section earlier in the chapter for background on these two groups). The administration persistently called Tet a military victory for the U.S., yet the fact that it could have happened at all raised serious doubts regarding the veracity of the government's claims.

Other televised scenes also shocked American viewers. Camera crews filmed Saigon's chief of police placing a gun to the head of a captured young Vietnamese man and pulling the trigger. The man slowly crumpled to his knees and fell backwards, blood spurting from his head. In another shocking image, you could clearly see the bodies in the streets and the gutted building in the background as the press interviewed General Westmoreland, who was trying to reassure Americans that the situation was well in hand.

The telling end to the siege of Khe Sanh

A few days after Johnson spoke to the American people about deescalating in Vietnam, the siege of Khe Sanh finally ended as a complete victory for the U.S. Marines. Having dropped more than 115,000 tons of bombs and napalm, the area around Khe Sanh looked like a lunar landscape, yet the North Vietnamese, having suffered heavy casualties, were forced to withdraw. The irony was that almost immediately after announcing the U.S. victory, the troops were ordered to abandon the place in order to pull back to a more secure position. To those who had fought and suffered, enduring the loss of friends and innocence to hold Khe Sanh at all costs, this move seemed almost incomprehensible. Yet in a war fought on the basis of body counts, such moves were common.

IN THEIR WORDS

"Four score and seven..."

A classic and disturbing war image was of an American military officer telling a reporter how his men had to destroy a village to prevent any sniper fire. In his words, "We had to destroy the town to save it." In many ways this statement has come to epitomize the U.S. role in Vietnam.

And while Westmoreland and LBJ proclaimed the Tet Offensive a U.S. victory, Walter Cronkite, who had just returned from Vietnam, told his TV audience that it seemed "more certain than ever that the bloody experience of Vietnam is to end in a stalemate." Tet dramatically increased U.S. discontent with the war, as public opinion polls showed a sharp increase in opposition.

In the aftermath of Tet, American momentum was severely depleted. As the U.S. entered a period of deescalation and negotiation, opposition to the war gathered momentum. What started as a small group of concerned individuals was now turning into a major movement. The soldiers themselves felt this shift as they began to think beyond the war. Gung-ho patriotism, while not totally gone from all the troops, was increasingly replaced by skepticism spawned by events such as the victory and abandonment of Khe Sanh. As troops learned more about the antiwar movement at home, they began to wonder what their own futures held beyond the war. The growing sense of stalemate and futility nurtured fears of being the last to die in a dying cause.

Chapter 9

Speaking Out against the War

● ●

In This Chapter

▶ Uniting for peace

▶ Rallying students to action

▶ Mobilizing against war

▶ Uniting the movement

▶ Ending the war for peace

● ●

Decades after the fact, a great deal of debate still swirls around the anti–Vietnam War movement in America, as do many myths about the movement's origins, goals, and its ultimate impact on the war itself. Although some people claim that the movement and protests helped bring an end to the quagmire by forcing U.S. government officials to deescalate the war, others insist that the protests gave support to the enemy and prolonged the war by encouraging the enemy with the idea that the United States would eventually leave. Some people define the movement as an activity of rich kids on college campuses who simply desired to avoid the draft, but statistics undermine this idea, showing that the antiwar movement grew as the war progressed to encompass a wide variety of people from all walks of life. Some people also call the antiwar protesters traitors to the American cause, while others claim that these same people represent the noblest traditions of dissent and free speech embedded in the rights of the U.S. Constitution.

Determining which view is right is difficult, because both views focus on the home front, but the real war was fought in Vietnam. The antiwar movement may have pleased both the Viet Cong and North Vietnamese leaders, but what won the war for them was their ability to hold the countryside and make insurgencies into the cities throughout South Vietnam. The antiwar movement, on the other hand, may have bothered the South Vietnamese Army of the Republic of Vietnam (ARVN), but the movement didn't create the corruption and self-serving methods that caused the ARVN to falter — their own greed and lack of national identity did. Ultimately, the antiwar movement may have affected the outcome of the war but didn't decide it.

No matter which idea you believe about the antiwar movement, we make one point clear in this chapter: In the early years of the war, the American people overwhelmingly supported U.S. government policy. But as the war progressed, the bodies came home, and victory seemed ever more elusive, public support began to decline, and the ranks of the war protesters swelled.

The Diversity of Dissent

One of the great difficulties in describing the antiwar movement comes from its diversity of ideas, methods, and efforts over the span of a couple of decades. The movement lacked a central leader or organizing agency. Though a few coalitions formed, they were often short-lived. Protesters employed a tremendous variety of tactics, ranging from peaceful civil disobedience and vigils to teach-ins and mass demonstrations. Some labored within the system, seeking change through lobbying efforts, letter-writing campaigns, and electoral politics, while others sought change from the outside through sabotage, bombings, and self-immolations (setting oneself on fire). The common factor among the protesters was that they all sought peace. However, the origins of the fierce antiwar movement can be traced along a few paths — the pre-1960s peace movements and the student movements that emerged in the early '60s.

Beginning with the peace movement

The origins of the antiwar movement lie in the opposition to the cold war in the 1950s, which is logical because the Vietnam War itself can be seen as a proxy war within the context of the larger cold war. During the 1950s, nuclear annihilation was a big concern. Well acquainted with the destruction at Hiroshima and Nagasaki in 1945, as well as the long-term effects of radiation, Americans feared the ongoing nuclear testing almost as much as they feared nuclear war. The *peace movement* was a movement of public advocacy aimed at avoiding war and drawing attention to nuclear testing and the dangers of a nuclear confrontation.

After the Nuclear Test Ban Treaty of 1963, which satisfied some of their concerns regarding nuclear proliferation (see Chapter 2), peace groups began to shift their focus. Though they started with different concerns and methods, with the escalation of the war in Vietnam throughout the decade, these groups began to concentrate on the growing war. Groups such as the Committee for a Sane Nuclear Policy (SANE), the Committee for Nonviolent Action (CNVA), the Women's Strike for Peace (WSP), and other peace organizations began to cooperate, allying their resources and networks. By 1967, many of these smaller groups began to merge with a common cause.

SANE

SANE was formed in 1957 based upon the "Call to Conscience" by renowned pastor, humanitarian, and scientist Dr. Albert Schweitzer. "Call to Conscience" was an article that moved many American citizens to action regarding the dangers of nuclear radiation. The committee's stated mission was to "develop public support for a boldly conceived and executed policy which will lead mankind away from war and toward peace and justice."

SANE became one of the leading voices for nuclear disarmament, attracting prominent spokespeople and supporters such as Dr. Schweitzer, Dr. Benjamin Spock (the baby doctor), Eleanor Roosevelt (former first lady), A. Philip Randolph (the founder of the Brotherhood of Sleeping Car Porters, a largely black labor union), Dr. Martin Luther King Jr., Coretta Scott King, Bertrand Russell (a prominent philosopher), Harry Belafonte (a singer and activist), and Walter Reuther (head of the United Automobile Workers). For SANE members, opposition to the war was a natural position to take, and SANE became an early leader in the antiwar movement.

CNVA

Founded in 1957, the CNVA was formed by a pacifist Quaker named Lawrence Scott. With branches in New York and San Francisco, this organization was the first of the peace groups to embrace civil disobedience as a means to protest nuclear proliferation.

- ✔ In 1957, their first action was a vigil held at an atomic weapons testing ground near Las Vegas, Nevada.

- ✔ In 1958, they used boats to enter the atomic testing zones in the South Pacific to interfere with planned detonations.

- ✔ In 1959, they began a protest against the production of Intercontinental Ballistic Missiles in Omaha, Nebraska.

- ✔ In 1960, they protested the Polaris nuclear missiles being placed aboard U.S. submarines in New London, Connecticut.

Each time, CNVA members were arrested and jailed. Yet according to their founding principles, they remained nonviolent, seeking instead to draw public attention to their protests in hopes that greater awareness would lead to a demand for a reduction in nuclear arms.

WSP

The WSP also arose in the late 1950s. Started in Washington, D.C., by children's book illustrator Dagmar Wilson, this group organized women to speak out for disarmament, a ban on nuclear testing, and a moratorium on the insults and name calling coming from both the pro- and anti-nuclear sides of the debate. Using the same networks as SANE and the CNVA, the WSP organized 25,000 women to voice their protest under the slogan, "End the Arms Race — Not the Human Race." WSP members believed that as women, they were fittingly appropriate to speak out in favor of the survival of the species. Figure 9-1 shows a WSP protest at the Pentagon.

Figure 9-1:
Members of
Women's
Strike for
Peace
protest the
Vietnam
War at the
Pentagon
in 1967.

©Bettmann/CORBIS

Participating in the student movement

The antiwar movement of the '60s was also anchored by two student groups — Students for a Democratic Society (SDS) and the free speech movement (FSM) — that together formed much of the *New Left,* a generation of young Americans who came of age in the 1960s and were motivated to action by the social injustices of the age. Leaders of the student movements began to consider ways to shape the growing peace sentiment into a broader political agenda, which was aimed at creating fundamental change with regard to issues such as peace and justice.

In the beginning, SDS was marked by idealistic ideas that were transformed into concrete action. The students were active in the civil rights movement on their own campuses, working to eliminate discrimination in fraternaties and sororities and improving conditions in urban ghettos. Many members of SDS traveled south to eliminate segregation and barriers to voting.

However, as the Vietnam War escalated and student deferrments were abolished, ending the war became the main focus of SDS. Along with the FSM in Berkeley, SDS developed chapters at campuses across the nation. To find out more about the history of the New Left student movement, its ideas, and its other activities, turn to Chapter 11.

The Emerging Antiwar Movement

Because the scope of U.S. involvement in Vietnam was limited in the late 1950s and early '60s, public opposition was also limited. Yet with the 1964 presidential elections, a large-scale antiwar movement began to take shape. Lyndon Johnson ran as a "Dove" or peace candidate, pledging to not send U.S. boys to Vietnam. By contrast, the Republican candidate, Barry Goldwater, ran as a "Hawk," or war candidate, to the point of even advocating the use of some tactical nuclear weapons in Vietnam.

The peace movement clearly supported Johnson, and the election was an easy victory for him. Ironically, though, the bombing of North Vietnam and the commitment of U.S. combat troops to Vietnam took place within months of Johnson's election (see Chapter 8). As a result of this increased role in Vietnam and the perception that Johnson had deceived voters, the antiwar movement emerged for the first time as a national phenomenon with a clear agenda and not just an outgrowth of presidential politics.

Spreading the word with teach-ins

A primary goal of the antiwar movement in its infancy was to educate national leaders and the American public. The tools to accomplish this education were *teach-ins,* which began in earnest in 1965. Believing that government policy was based upon ignorance and mistakes, intellectuals sought to educate the public to solve the problems.

Teach-ins were informal lectures and discussions given by professors and graduate students and open to anyone interested in the topic. The idea was that exposing people to the facts and raising questions could move people to action. After enough people were motivated, the government would be forced to listen as well. In a May 15–16 teach-in, for example, participants from Yale, Harvard, Columbia, the University of Chicago, and the State Department debated policy over a radio link connecting 122 colleges nationwide.

As college professors spoke out about the Vietnam War, President Johnson responded in a speech at Johns Hopkins University on April 7, 1965, stating that he was ready for negotiations regarding a free and independent South Vietnam, yet he wouldn't deal with the National Liberation Front (the political branch of the Viet Cong). Johnson's speech angered many antiwar groups and moved them to action. Throughout 1965, the teach-ins continued at campuses across the nation.

Holding early marches and demonstrations

On April 17, 1965, ten days after Johnson's Johns Hopkins speech (see the preceding section), SDS held its first march in Washington, D.C., to protest the war. A few thousand protesters were expected, yet some 25,000 people showed up, making it the largest antiwar protest in the city's history. Other large demonstrations soon followed:

✔ On October 15, 15,000 people marched in Berkeley, California, and another 20,000 marched in Manhattan, New York.

✔ On November 27, another demonstration in Washington drew 25,000 protesters.

Though these demonstrations were small compared to those of the late '60s, they were record setting for their day. Public demonstrations were the next logical step to take after the teach-ins, because the teach-ins seemed somewhat like preaching to the choir. Protesters were moving beyond words, reason, and education to place pressure on policymakers who seemed to be ignoring the will of the people, as expressed in the 1964 election.

Initiating civil disobedience

Many protesters who joined the emerging antiwar movement were veterans of the civil rights movement and understood the value of civil disobedience, particularly in the form of public moral sacrifice. In August 1965, Vietnam Day committee members (a group formed to coordinate antiwar activities in California) began to lie down on railroad tracks in northern California in order to block the movement of troops trains in the area. Another 350 protesters were arrested in Washington for civil disobedience for attempting to disrupt the government. Over the same summer, protesters began to burn their draft cards (see the "Resisting the draft" section, later in this chapter).

Following the lead of the Buddhist monks

In 1965, another form of protest emerged — that of public suicide to draw attention to the war. The first suicide occurred on a Detroit street corner on March 16, when Alice Herz, an 82-year-old pacifist, doused herself with cleaning fluid and ignited it. Herz left a note condemning President Johnson for trying to wipe out small nations and explaining that she was protesting in the same way that the Buddhist monks had in Vietnam in 1963 (see Chapter 8). Though this was the act of a single protester the media coverage shocked many into asking questions about the conduct and morality of the war.

On November 2, a 32-year-old Quaker made the ultimate sacrifice as an act of moral persuasion. Norman Morrison carried his infant daughter with him to the Pentagon, where he set her down and, standing in front of the office windows of Secretary of Defense Robert McNamara, doused himself with gasoline and set himself on fire. Like Herz, Morrison was consciously trying to emulate the monks. McNamara, one of the chief architects of U.S. policy in Vietnam (see Chapter 8), witnessed the suicide. He was shocked by the protest and in his memoirs referred to the incident as a personal tragedy.

One week later, a 22-year-old man named Roger La Porte killed himself in the same manner in front of the United Nations headquarters in New York. La Porte, like Herz and Morrison, sought to make a religious statement against the war in Vietnam.

Turning Up the Heat

In 1966, the antiwar protesters took a more aggressive stance, picketing President Johnson and his cabinet members at public engagements. In San Francisco in August, protesters found out that General Maxwell Taylor, former chairman of the Joint Chiefs of Staff and U.S. ambassador to South Vietnam, was staying in a downtown hotel. They picketed and called him a war criminal, forcing him at one point to take refuge in the manager's office as protesters banged on the door. Though the first family worried a great deal about whether the wedding of Johnson's daughter would be ruined by protest, that event in August went off with little problem.

Throughout 1966 and 1967, the antiwar movement gained momentum. In February, after the bombing campaign resumed following a short pause for negotiations, the antiwar movement began planning larger demonstrations. Though the antiwar groups worked continuously on the grass roots level, it was the big demonstrations that were designed to reach the general public. In April 1966, demonstrators put together the Vietnam Peace Parade on Fifth Avenue in New York. SANE and the Women's Strike for Peace assembled a peace rally at the White House in May. And the summer was spent rallying support for the midterm election of congressional doves.

Robert McNamara, who had been troubled over the suicide of Norman Morrison (see the preceding section), was further distressed by an incident at Harvard University on November 7, 1966, when a group of radical students surrounded his car and rocked it. Though unhurt in the incident, McNamara later described it as "a searing experience."

In 1967, antiwar leaders organized massive demonstrations on April 15, in New York and San Francisco. In the fall, the focus shifted to the activities of Oakland Draft Resistance week (see the "Instituting Stop the Draft Week" section later in the chapter).

Resisting the draft

Rather than just protesting, many young men began to defy the law and burn their draft cards as a public statement. The draft, which was reinstated in 1948 during a period of peace, became a focal point of protest for some groups. Drafts, or selective service, have always been a controversial subject in U.S. history dating back to the Civil War. The draft was used in World Wars I and II but was ended after each war. The 1948 Selective Service Act required all males between 18 and 26 to register for the draft, yet there was a list of exemptions one could claim to avoid serving. The draft was updated in 1951 and again in 1967, yet the loopholes that remained discriminated against working class and poor men who couldn't avoid the draft as easily as their richer counterparts.

On December 1, 1969, in the name of fairness, the Selective Service instituted a draft lottery. Each day of the year was printed on a piece of paper and placed in a jar. The dates were drawn randomly, and the first date picked was assigned number one, the second number two, and so on, until 365 (or 366 for leap year men). Draftees were then called in order of their draft number, lowest first, so those young men with a low number would be drafted first, and those with a high number were probably safe at home. Those with numbers below 195 were subject to being drafted while those above this mark were generally safe from the draft. If nothing else, the lottery gave draftees a sense of predictability in their lives.

One of the earliest antidraft groups was the May 2nd Movement in New York, issuing a pledge in 1964 to refuse to fight against the people of Vietnam. Other antidraft groups arose throughout the decade, seeking publicity and public support. By 1967 these groups had become a significant presence in the antiwar movement.

Reviewing the methods and consequences

On April 15, 1967, 150 young men in New York City burned their draft cards in public. In San Francisco, a group calling themselves "The Resistance" organized a national day for turning in draft cards on October 3, 1967, and burned 1,500 cards during the single-day event. By the time the war was over, close to 100,000 burned their draft cards (see Figure 9-2). In addition to destroying and returning draft cards, other methods of resistance included

> ✔ **Declaring conscientious objector status:** Throughout U.S. history, people have avoided military service by declaring *conscientious objector* status on the basis of membership in a religion that is categorically opposed to war, such as the Quakers or Jehovah's Witnesses, or personal religious

convictions. During the Vietnam War, men tried to be classified as conscientious objectors because they didn't oppose all wars, but only that particular war. However, they were denied this designation and were subject to the draft.

In 1970, the Supreme Court removed the religious requirement and allowed objection based on a deeply held moral conviction alone. In 1971, the Supreme Court refused to allow objection to a particular war, a decision affecting thousands of objectors to the Vietnam War. However, being a conscientious objector didn't necessary exempt someone from military service. Most frequently, they were assigned to noncombatant military service, such as being a medic or a cook. During the war, the Center on Conscience and War (CCW) estimates that 200,000 men registered as conscientious objectors.

✔ **Not registering for the draft:** Though all men between the ages of 18 and 26 were supposed to register with the Draft Board, approximately 250,000 never did.

✔ **Escaping to Canada:** Some 50,000 to 100,000 men are estimated to have left the United States to avoid being drafted. Most of them went to Canada, where the Vietnam War was unpopular and the door was open to immigration. During the war, the Canadian government allowed draft evaders and deserters to apply for landed immigrant status, which could be granted immediately at the Canadian border. In 1969, Pierre Trudeau, prime minister of Canada, instructed immigration authorities to not discriminate against applicants who may not have fulfilled their military obligations in other countries.

Figure 9-2:
Burning draft cards outside of the Pentagon in 1967.

©Bettmann/CORBIS

Any of these young men who were caught resisting the draft could be convicted and sent to prison. The U.S. Justice Department identified 570,000 men who violated draft laws. Of these, 206,775 were referred to the U.S. Attorneys for prosecution. Of these, 25,000 were indicted, more than 9,000 were convicted, and 3,250 were sent to prison for their resistance.

In 1977, when Jimmy Carter was elected president, he pardoned anyone who peacefully resisted the draft by leaving the country or failing to register for the draft. Amnesty wasn't granted, however, to military deserters.

Instituting Stop the Draft Week

The third week of October, the Resistance conducted an ongoing attempt to physically shut down the Oakland Induction Center in California, where people from West Coast states were inducted into the armed forces — this effort became known as Stop the Draft Week. Beginning on Monday, October 16, 1967, the Resistance held a nonviolent sit-in in an attempt to stop the flow of young men into the processing center. The demonstrators continued their efforts over the next five days, culminating in a five-hour battle between 10,000 demonstrators and 2,000 Oakland police officers. The Resistance used "mobile tactics" to control most of the streets of downtown Oakland, demonstrating their control and organization in a guerrilla style. They blocked buses full of inductees from the Induction Center with the use of barricades and with the crowds.

The men aboard the buses exchanged the "V" sign with the protesters, giving rise to the legend that the peace sign originated during Stop the Draft Week.

The draft resistance movement hit a milestone on October 20, 1967, when a delegation of prominent citizens, including Dr. Benjamin Spock and Reverend William Sloane Coffin, delivered a briefcase with more than 1,000 draft cards to the Justice Department.

As a coordinated effort in Stop the Draft Week, antiwar groups also organized a march on the Pentagon in Washington, D.C., on October 21 (see Figure 9-3). The protest groups estimated the crowd as being more than 100,000 strong, but Johnson administration officials estimated about 50,000 protesters. Nevertheless, the protest was huge. It started with speeches and music at the Lincoln Memorial, yet approximately 35,000 protesters were also gathered at the Pentagon, where they placed flowers in the guns of the Pentagon soldiers standing guard to secure the building.

Robert McNamara, Johnson's secretary of defense, who had already tendered his resignation and was ready to depart for his new position as head of the World Bank, feared that soldiers would have to shoot some of the protesters if the situation got out of hand. Though many Johnson administration officials downplayed the demonstration at the Pentagon, others, including McNamara and Press Secretary George Christian, saw the march as a major turning point for many in the administration as they came to terms with the fact that the peace movement wasn't fading away and was instead increasing in strength steadily.

Figure 9-3:
Protests
at the
Pentagon
during Stop
the Draft
Week in
1967.

Making diplomacy a personal mission

During the war, several prominent Americans went to North Vietnam on their own in order to give Americans the "view from the inside." Some of the men who conducted these missions of personal diplomacy were well-known Americans who traveled to Hanoi, North Vietnam, in 1965, '66, and '67. Their missions gave Americans new sources of information regarding the war, while exposing the inadequate and self-serving nature of the Johnson administration's assessments of the war. Reports from these missions served to bolster the antiwar movement at several critical points.

Three leftists . . .

Three leaders of the antiwar movement undertook the first mission to Hanoi in December 1965 to try to negotiate an end to the war. Staughton Lynd, a Quaker and Yale history professor; Herbert Aptheker, director of the American Institute for Marxist Studies; and Tom Hayden, cofounder of SDS, all agreed to accept an invitation from the North Vietnamese government to visit Hanoi and "to see firsthand the conditions and prospects for peace as the North Vietnamese saw them." Traveling through Communist bloc nations, the trio arrived in Hanoi on December 2.

During their 11-day stay, they visited factories, government buildings, and museums, where they met and questioned the North Vietnamese people. Though criticized for being led around and propagandized by the North Vietnamese, the men were less interested in uncovering facts than in putting a human face on the enemy. The book that Lynd and Hayden wrote upon their return to the U.S., *The Other Side,* emphasizes human suffering without debating the ideological foundations of the conflict. Their portrayal of human suffering raised the issue of the morality of U.S. actions.

Upon their return, Aptheker, Lynd, and Hayden spoke publicly about their experiences in Hanoi. Their work revealed the need for independent sources to ensure that the American public heard the truth. Johnson was furious with these private efforts, and the administration worked to counter the effects of this mission by calling the trio "leftist radicals" and branding them as unpatrotic. The number of people willing to listen to reports from Hanoi remained small in late 1965, due in large part to Lynd, Hayden, and Aptheker's political alignment with the far left. For the moment, the administration remained in control of the flow of information to the public. This situation would radically change in 1967, after Harrison Salisbury began publishing his stories on location.

. . . A Pulitzer Prize winner . . .

The next private mission to Hanoi was more difficult for the administration to handle. Before going to Hanoi in December 1966, Harrison Salisbury had already established himself as a trustworthy and powerful correspondent. He attained his position as assistant managing editor of the *New York Times* for his diligent reporting of events in Communist-aligned countries during the late '40s and '50s. He also won the Pulitzer Prize in 1955 for a series of articles on the Soviet Union. Thus, when Salisbury traveled to Hanoi, he was a credible voice, and the Johnson administration couldn't dismiss him as easily as they could Aptheker, Lynd, and Hayden.

Salisbury published a series of firsthand reports from Hanoi, beginning on Christmas Day 1966. Salisbury photographed and described bomb-damaged neighborhoods, putting a human face on the North Vietnamese for the first time in the mainstream American press. Further, his claims contradicted the administration's claims of conducting only carefully controlled, surgically precise bombing campaigns in North Vietnam. More importantly, Salisbury's observations led him to question the feasibility of American strategy in Vietnam and the morality of the American war effort itself. Though highly controversial at the time, Salisbury's reports raised issues that later visitors reiterated and that would remain controversial as long as the war continued.

. . . And a pair of journalists

As the Johnson administration struggled to manage the crisis created by Salisbury's articles, two more journalists arrived in Hanoi. Harry S. Ashmore of the Center for the Study of Democratic Institutions (and a Pulitzer Prize–winning reporter) and William C. Baggs of the *Miami News* arrived on the very same plane that was flying Salisbury out of Hanoi. Unlike Salisbury's mission, which had been completely independent of the U.S. government, Ashmore and Baggs had a semiofficial status, as they had coordinated with the State Department and were to make a number of inquiries on behalf of the U.S. government.

Upon arriving in Hanoi on January 6, 1967, Ashmore and Baggs began to assess the damage created by the air war. To prove their impartiality, they acknowledged the possibility of propaganda in their reports because they saw only the bomb damage that officials showed them, including damaged hospitals, schools, pagodas, and in one notable case, a leperarium (a home for the treatment of lepers). Though the two Americans attempted to remain neutral, the sheer number of bombed-out sites diminished the assumption that the North Vietnamese had carefully orchestrated everything they showed the men. Ashmore and Baggs visited many of the same areas that Salisbury had visited, and in their stories they substantiated Salisbury's reports.

As part of the official status of their mission, Ashmore and Baggs met with Ho Chi Minh for two hours to discuss the opening of a quiet channel for direct negotiations. Upon their return, they dodged eager reporters to deliver Ho's message directly to the State Department. Ho had expressed interest in negotiation, citing the friendship Vietnam had achieved with its former foe, the French.

Baggs delayed writing his articles in favor of advancing the peace initiatives that he and Ashmore believed they'd opened. They had been invited to testify before the Senate Foreign Relations Committee, but they declined at the request of the State Department. Though Ashmore and Baggs believed they had initiated negotiations that could possibly end the war, their hopes were dashed when negotiations with the State Department led only to continued debate over minute details such as whether negotiations "could" or "would" begin at the cessation of the bombing. The administration finally used this new channel to simply send the North Vietnamese yet another ultimatum.

Though the stakes were quite high, neither Johnson nor Secretary of State Dean Rusk met directly with Ashmore and Baggs. Ultimately, the two citizens felt that the administration had not only undermined their efforts, but also had successfully muzzled them. No longer fearing damage to the failed negotiations, Ashmore wrote a scathing, widely disseminated article accusing Johnson of duplicity in the peace overture. In 1968, Ashmore and Baggs published a book documenting all the details of the undermined peace initiative. The title itself explains their point of view: *Mission to Hanoi: A Chronicle of Double-Dealing In High Places*. And no, they weren't talking about the North Vietnamese.

Buying media coverage

Though media coverage and analysis of the Vietnam War got good air time in 1965, by 1966, coverage shrank. The networks did televise several documentaries on the war in late 1965 as well as the Fulbright hearings in February

1966, yet they ceased televising legislative events under pressure from the White House. Factual new stories were shown, but the media offered little analysis of the war after early 1966. The fascination with the war faded as the news seemed to be the same nearly every day.

The Fulbright hearings, led by Senator William Fulbright, were Senate Foreign Relations Committee hearings that debated issues concerning the war, including a huge appropriations bill requested by President Johnson. The hearings, which were televised, seemed to be a turning point in terms of increasing antiwar sentiment.

The antiwar movement began to shift to paid advertising to get its message out to the American people. On June 5, 1966, the *New York Times* ran an advertisement containing the names of 6,400 academics and professionals who opposed the war. The spread covering three pages of the Sunday *Times* cost more than $20,000 and reached a vast audience. The ads continued to increase in number and frequency through 1968.

Joining the fray: Civil rights and the antiwar movement

Following his receipt of the Nobel Peace Prize in 1964, Reverend Martin Luther King Jr. expressed concern over the growing war in Vietnam, yet he maintained a moderate stance that wouldn't alienate any factions within the civil rights movement. There were, however, a disproportionate number of African American soldiers fighting in Vietnam, and King saw this as another inequity to be addressed. Militant groups such as the Black Panther Party and the Student Nonviolent Coordinating Committee (SNCC) were openly denouncing U.S. policies as imperialism aimed at the nonwhite nation of Vietnam, while more conservative elements such as the NAACP and the Urban League sought to keep the civil rights movement from being lost within the antiwar movement.

Dr. King finally made his decision to take a strong stand against the war in April 1967. In Manhattan's Riverside Church, 3,000 people listened to King's speech, entitled, "Declaration of Independence from the war in Vietnam." The crowd rose to its feet and roared its approval, giving King a standing ovation.

Later that year, the National Advisory Commission on Civil Disorders, formed by President Johnson in July 1967, reported that the U.S. was increasingly becoming two separate societies — one white and one black. The report seemed to be underscored by the February 1968 massacre at South Carolina State College, where police and National Guard troops opened fire on unarmed black students, killing 3 and wounding 27 others. On April 4, 1968, Dr. Martin Luther King Jr. was assassinated in Memphis, setting off a whole new round of violence. In a week of violence in more than 125 U.S. cities, the government had to mobilize 55,000 troops to help the tens of thousands of local law enforcement officers trying to quell the unrest.

No sooner had order been restored after the King assassination than violence erupted on college campuses across the country. Police battled students at elite universities such as Stanford and Columbia. Increasingly, student demonstrators were linking their cause with that of the blacks and the poorer classes that bore the brunt of the military draft.

The Turning Point in 1968

In the late '60s, leaders of the antiwar movement recognized President Johnson's growing credibility problem and sought to exploit and publicize it at every opportunity. The straw that broke the camel's back was the Tet Offensive.

In January 1968, General Westmoreland gave a brilliantly optimistic report on the U.S. progress in Vietnam. However, within days, Westmoreland's report seemed ridiculous, as the Tet Offensive firmly placed the United States on the defensive throughout the Vietnamese countryside. The U.S. never regained the strategic offensive in the war. Within months, Westmoreland had been relieved of his command, the president had been compelled to withdraw from the election campaign, and antiwar candidates had swept the Democratic primaries (see Chapter 8).

In a single week, protests erupted. Even the world monetary system began to reel from the U.S. debt and the government's loss of credibility. When Johnson announced his withdrawal from the presidential race, he also announced that he'd begin to try to deescalate the war and seek peace with the North Vietnamese. The desire to win had shifted to a quest for a way out.

Confrontation in Chicago

The 1968 Democratic National Convention in Chicago had an inauspicious start. The convention center had burned to the ground, the favorite candidate (Robert Kennedy) had been assassinated (see Chapter 4), the antiwar movement was planning a huge protest, and Chicago Mayor Richard Daley, who supported the war and President Johnson's policies in Vietnam and hated hippies, was determined to thwart the protesters at every turn. He refused permits for marches and rallies and encouraged the use of force to subdue crowds, but the protests went on.

Witnessing "a police riot"

Thousands of people showed up in Chicago to protest the war, sure that their sheer numbers would win "hearts and minds." The Democratic National Convention was scheduled for Monday August 26 to Thursday August 29. There was a great deal of anticipation about the event with high expectations from the various protest groups, each of whom desired to make their own statement about the war. They began to gather in Chicago early in order to plan a variety of events. To add even more fuel to the already potentially explosive situation, the *yippies* (a highly theatrical youth protest group) arrived, not only to protest the war, but also to stage a "happening" of music, workshops, and a beach party including "folk-singing, barbecues, swimming, lovemaking." Needless to say, antiwar protests and yippie antics didn't exactly endear the "visitors" to the mayor and the citizens of Chicago.

Looking for media attention, the yippies generated their own publicity, such as threatening to put LSD in the Chicago water supply.

As protest and counterculture groups, many of the hippies, yippies, and other protesters had already had unfavorable confrontations with police, so when the authorities showed up at demonstrations or less serious events, they were greeted with shouts of "Pig!" Angered, and knowing that Mayor Daley never discouraged violence against protesters, the police pushed back the crowd and beat them with clubs. And this was before the convention even started. Though groups such as the yippies, the Mobe, and the Women's Strike for Peace applied for permits to peaceably assemble and protest, Mayor Daley had them all rejected, except for one rally in Grant Park.

On Friday, August 23, the yippies met in Civic Center Plaza and elected their candidate, Pigasus the Pig. The police weren't amused and after clashes with the yippies, seven protesters were arrested, and the pig was confiscated. That same day, some 6,000 National Guard troops were mobilized to begin practicing riot-control drills. On Sunday, August 25, the Mobe held a "Meet the Delegates" march near the Hilton Hotel, where most delegates stayed. The police established an 11 p.m. curfew and tried to enforce it with sweeps of baton-wielding officers. A crowd of about 2,000 people who were flushed out of Lincoln Park, were attacked by baton-wielding riot police in the Old Town section of Chicago. Police beat journalists, as well as protesters, during the riots.

On the morning when the convention opened, Tom Hayden, head of SDS, was among a group arrested as part of a 1,000-protester march on the police department. Though the march was detoured into Lincoln Park, the police assaulted the crowds and forced them to disperse.

On the first night of the convention, the police were a lot more forceful in trying to get the protesters out of Lincoln Park, which had been commandeered by the yippies and a series of protest bands to entertain the crowd. Police again imposed the 11 p.m. curfew, and at the designated hour, surrounded the park. The protesters built a barricade, and approximately 1,000 of them attempted to remain in the park. When a police cruiser began to push against the makeshift barricade, the protesters pelted the car with rocks and bottles. The police responded with tear gas and baton attacks. When the protesters started "oinking" at them, they began swinging their clubs at everyone and everything in sight until the park was cleared.

Rumor had it that when the park was emptied, the police attacked the parking lot, slashing the tires of cars with a McCarthy bumper sticker. (Eugene McCarthy was the most vocal antiwar candidate.)

Things only got worse after that. The police, tired, insulted, and encouraged by Mayor Daley, reacted to any opposition by the demonstrators. They arrested demonstrators, often dragging them off and clubbing anyone within reach, including innocent bystanders. The riots were broadcast live into American living rooms by photographers whose cameras weren't smashed in the melee (see Figure 9-4).

Figure 9-4: Police and protesters square off near the Conrad Hilton Hotel in Chicago during the 1968 Democratic National Convention.

©Bettmann/CORBIS

On Tuesday in Lincoln Park, 200 clergy and religious leaders joined the crowd of 2,000 protesters trying to stay in the park after curfew. Police again used tear gas and batons to clear the park. Though protesters kept trying to march to the Amphitheatre, the police and National Guard never let the marchers anywhere near the actual convention site.

The violence continued for the rest of the week, and the events at the Chicago convention became another one of those defining moments of the '60s. The demonstration and the police reaction polarized the country. People either believed that using force against an angry mob was justified, coming down on the side of law and order (usually equated with President Johnson and the Vietnam War) or sympathized with the protesters, viewing the actions in Chicago as police brutality and supporting the actions of the yippies, the hippies, and the rest of the antiwar movement.

There was actually a convention going on in the Chicago Amphitheater. Hubert Humphrey, Johnson's vice president, became the Democratic presidential nominee. But the party was too divided, and he was too closely associated with Johnson's stance on the war, so he lost the election to Richard Nixon (see Chapter 4).

During the week of the convention, 308 Americans were killed in Vietnam and another 1,144 were injured.

Trying the Chicago Eight

In an epilogue to the Chicago Riots, the organizers of the protests, Tom Hayden, Rennie Davis, David Dellinger, Abbie Hoffman, Jerry Rubin, Bobby Seale, John Froines, and Lee Weiner, were indicted for conspiring to cross state lines to incite a riot. They went to trial, and the trial became a bit of a circus, due to Hoffman and Rubin's antics. One day, Hoffman and Rubin showed up wearing judicial robes. On another day, Hoffman was sworn in as a witness with one hand on the Bible while the other was making an obscene gesture in the court.

Five of the original eight (Seale's trial was separated from the others, and Froines and Weiner were acquitted) were found guilty of intent to incite a riot across state lines, and all were acquitted on the conspiracy charge. The five were sentenced to a $5,000 and five years in prison, but in 1972, the convictions were overturned.

Winding Down the War

Lyndon Johnson's war soon became Richard Nixon's war. Though he had campaigned on the platform that he had a plan to end the war, Nixon had no better ideas than did Johnson, but Nixon had a brief "honeymoon period" — the antiwar movement temporarily slowed as the Nixon administration moved into the White House.

When it became clear that Nixon didn't have any clear and progressive plan to end the war, the antiwar movement began to push once again. In 1969, they planned two major events: Moratorium of 1969 and the November Mobilization (see the next section). When Americans became aware that Nixon was actually expanding the war in Cambodia, the movement again gained momentum.

The nationwide response to the Cambodian invasion (see Chapter 10) was the last major victory of the antiwar movement. Campus demonstrations and antiwar activity in general declined after the spring of 1970, though violent scenes such as Kent State massacre the Jackson State killings served to further the antiwar cause. When Nixon used ARVN troops to invade Laos in February 1971, the antiwar movement's reaction was smaller than expected. The fact that no U.S. troops were used, along with the steady withdrawal of U.S. forces from Vietnam, was slowly draining the will from the antiwar effort.

The Moratorium of October 1969 and the November Mobilization

Though many protest groups waited to see Nixon's plan unfold, the lack of progress by the spring of 1969 compelled the antiwar groups to gear up for a new round of protests and demonstrations. The major events planned for 1969 were the Moratorium of October and the Mobilization of November. The Moratorium was particularly worrisome for the Nixon administration because it was a nonviolent protest that threatened to disrupt business as an ongoing monthly protest. Millions of Americans took part in the October 15 Moratorium, while millions of others sympathized with the protest. There were more than 200 major demonstrations on that one day.

In November 1969, some 250,000 people converged on Washington to protest the continuing war. This protest was the largest to date. Nixon vowed not to bend to antiwar pressure. As a prelude to the main event, 40,000 demonstrators filed past the White House in a 36 hour March of Death, depositing in canisters the names of the 45,000 American soldiers killed in the war to date. The main event of the Mobilization was the Saturday morning rally on the Mall by the Washington Monument where a half million protesters gathered peacefully to call for a withdrawal from the war. The Moratorium and the Mobilization were the high water marks for the antiwar movement.

More than 14,000 people were arrested at the November Mobilization — as many as participated in many of the marches of 1965.

At the end of 1969, the antiwar movement and Nixon had reached a standoff. Nixon realized that he would not be able to force a breakthrough with an escalation of force and would have to settle for a strategy of Vietnamization. As long as Nixon continued the peace talks and continued to incrementally bring home the American soldiers, he could count on the public's support for his policies. By the spring of 1970, the antiwar movement lost momentum, and the protests began to be significantly smaller, because Nixon's Vietnamization seemed to be what the people wanted — a deescalation of the conflict and a steady flow of American boys back home.

Death on campus

On April 30, 1970, the previously secret bombing of Cambodia shifted into a ground-force invasion designed to stop the North Vietnamese supply lines. Nixon's announcement of the invasion and the *New York Times* revelation of the earlier secret bombing campaign prompted national antiwar leaders to organize a national student strike. As the strikes occurred at campuses across the nation, some turned into tragic events.

At Kent State University in Ohio, protesters focused their wrath on the campus R.O.T.C. building, prompting the governor to dispatch National Guard troops. On May 4, 1970, Guard troops confronting a hostile crowd fired on the students, killing four. Of the four killed, two had been a part of the protest, and the other two had been walking by on their way to class. The killing of unarmed protesters sparked further protests across the country. More than 400 universities and colleges shut down. One hundred thousand protesters marched in Washington, circling the Capitol and the White House. Nixon had campaigned on a promise to bring the troops home, yet after only a year and a half, the results were that the war had expanded.

Shortly after the Kent State Massacre, another group of National Guardsmen stormed a college dormitory on the Jackson State College campus. Two unarmed young black students were killed, and another 11 were wounded.

Over the next few months, hundreds of college campuses closed because of student strikes and demonstrations. Eighty percent of all college campuses reported some kind of protest in the wake of the massacres of unarmed students. A Gallup poll after the Kent State Massacre showed that campus unrest was one of the most important issues for many Americans.

Problems within the military

Though resistance to the draft was a serious problem for the military, it was far less serious than the problem of desertion. There were far more desertions than there were draft evaders. Many of these deserters embarrassed the government even more by forming active antiwar groups in Canada, England, France, Sweden, the Netherlands, and Germany. According to the Department of Defense there were 503,926 incidents of desertion between July 1, 1966, and December 31, 1973, but between 1963 and 1973 only 191,840 cases of men failed to respond to the draft.

The U.S. military faced even greater dangers from other internal problems such as morale, discipline, drugs, and racial conflict, which began to flare badly in the late 1960s and early 1970s. Soldiers challenged their leaders because they all knew that the United States was withdrawing under Nixon's Vietnamization program, and no one wanted to be the last to die in Vietnam. Soldiers lacked incentives to fight and began to rebel, oftentimes asking: "What are they going to do about it, send me to 'Nam?"

Drugs were a problem in Vietnam but it became even worse in the late years of the war. There was a steady, cheap supply of marijuana and heroin, and many soldiers used drugs as a way to cope with being in Vietnam. According to a 1971 congressional survey, drugs in Vietnam were more plentiful than cigarettes or chewing gum.

The path to advancement among officers was to have strong kill ratios, and as the war wound down, this became a source of direct conflict between officers and grunts (enlisted men). As officers sought to enhance their jackets, they pushed for aggressive action and engagement, but the typical grunt knew the United States was leaving and often tried to avoid any unnecessary contact with the enemy to increase his own chances of survival. Thus the search-and-destroy missions became search-and-evade missions instead. When gung-ho officers pushed the issue, the grunts began to "frag" their officers as a way to eliminate their problems. *Fragging* was the practice of tossing a grenade into the tent or foxhole of your commanding officer to wound or kill him — either way the grunts would be free of the officers who, they felt, placed them in danger. For obvious reasons, reliable statistics on fragging are difficult to obtain, yet some sources estimate the number to be more than 2,000.

Peace signs and the letters F.T.A. (F*%# the Army) became common symbols on combat helmets. Soldiers and sailors began to mutiny. As early as mid-1969, an entire company of soldiers in the 196th Light Infantry Brigade refused to go out of base camp on a patrol. Later in 1969, soldiers in the famed First Air Cavalry Division refused to go out on patrol right in front of a CBS television crew. Over the next 12 months the same division experienced 35 more refusals to engage.

Sabotage was another problem. On May 26, 1970, as the U.S.S. Anderson prepared to depart San Diego for Vietnam, it was discovered that someone had dropped nuts, bolts, and chain links into the main gear shaft, causing a major breakdown. Thousands of dollars of damage was done, and the departure was delayed several weeks. In a more serious case, the aircraft carrier, U.S.S. Ranger was also sabotaged as investigators found a paint scraper and two 12-inch bolts that had been dropped into the engine's reduction gears. This incident caused more than a $1 million in damages and delayed their departure by 3½ months. Sabotage of aircraft and helicopters cancelled missions, thereby rewarding those bold enough to commit such acts.

Overall, the military was coming apart at the seams. Each incident of insubordination inspired others to push further. The sheer numbers of the resistors kept the military from making mass arrests. As the war wound down, military planners recognized that the military would need to be rebuilt and revamped before it was ready for any new action.

The Winter Soldier Investigation

In February 1971 about 150 Vietnam veterans convened "The Winter Soldier Investigation" in Detroit to hold hearings on their experiences in the Vietnam War. These men were moved to tell their stories because the U.S. military had described the events of the My Lai Massacre as unique and unusual. They wanted to set the record straight, so 200 former soldiers testified about atrocities they had been involved in or had witnessed. The Winter Soldiers explained that incidents like the My Lai Massacre were the natural conclusion to the obsessive anti-Communist stance, the free-fire zones, and the body counts. The reports horrified the small number of Americans who dared to listen to them.

The VVAW

The Vietnam Veterans Against the War (VVAW) also protested the war, demanding an immediate end. Their former participation in the war gave them a unique perspective from which to criticize the conduct of the war.

The VVAW's participation in the antiwar movement made a stronger statement than protests from those who just wanted to avoid having to serve. Because the men of the VVAW *had* served, they were more respected, and thus they gathered a good deal of attention. In April 1971 the VVAW conducted what they called operation Dewey Canyon III — a protest in which thousands of veterans came to Washington, D.C., to demand an end to the war. Hundreds of veterans threw away the medals they had earned in combat as a powerful demonstration of their frustration and shame for their role in the war.

In the 2004 presidential campaign, Democratic candidate John Kerry was either praised or condemned (depending on your point of view) for participating in the VVAW.

Chapter 10

Shifting the Burden: Leaving Vietnam

•••

In This Chapter

▶ Analyzing the repercussions of the Tet Offensive

▶ Changing of the guard: The Nixon leadership

▶ Building South Vietnam while getting U.S. troops out

▶ Providing fodder for antiwar protests

▶ Going beyond the Vietnamese borders

▶ Enduring the final months until the arrival of peace

•••

*T*he Tet Offensive in early 1968 and its aftermath affected the antiwar movement and shifted the U.S. position in Vietnam as government officials began to recognize that they were losing the battle at home. It also widened a rift between President Lyndon Johnson and members of his own Democratic Party over his war policies. Realizing that he couldn't win a second term, Johnson announced that he wouldn't run again. Division in the Democratic Party had been slowly building since the Tonkin Gulf Resolution passed in 1964. Questions about U.S. goals in Vietnam had pushed Robert Kennedy to challenge Johnson even though a challenge from within the party of incumbent president is rare. The Tet Offensive, the assassination of Bobby Kennedy, and the riots at the convention in Chicago all but assured the election of a new commander in chief.

After Republican candidate Richard Nixon triumphed in the election of 1968, he recognized that he needed to shift the U.S. strategy. Not only was the country not winning the war, but the administration's policies were also losing the war at home — more and more Americans opposed the war. Nixon knew that something had to be done. *Vietnamization,* a term Nixon coined for placing more responsibility for the war on the Vietnamese, was his answer, designed to appease all sides of the debate. Implementing this plan, however, turned out to be full of difficulties.

The Aftermath of Tet

As a consequence of the Tet Offensive, during which the Viet Cong launched a surprising challenge to U.S. and ARVN troops (see Chapter 8), the Johnson administration began to rethink its Vietnam policies. Though General William Westmoreland, the U.S. military commander in Vietnam, requested an additional 206,000 troops in February 1968, Johnson denied the request because they had no evidence that the additional troops would change the situation, except to further inflame the protests at home. Johnson's strategy of using force to compel the North Vietnamese to accept U.S. terms hadn't worked. The North Vietnamese were willing to accept the costs of defying the U.S. military strength and continue to press for reunification of Vietnam.

With little prospect for victory in the near future and the growing pressures at home, Johnson saw that he needed to change his strategy in Vietnam. With no clear way to use military force to make the North Vietnamese accept U.S. terms, the question became how to withdraw U.S. troops to ease the problems on the home front while still pursuing the important objectives of the war. Johnson concluded that a negotiated settlement was his best option.

On March 31, 1968, Johnson addressed the nation on television. He announced an immediate end to all bombing above the 20th parallel and a willingness to begin peace negotiations at any time and place. In the most shocking statement of the speech, Johnson announced that he wouldn't seek another term as president. He had taken the first steps to deescalate the war.

Seeking negotiations with North Vietnam

Johnson's offer to begin formal peace negotiations opened a new set of talks set in Paris. After he dropped out of the presidential race, Johnson continued the bombing campaign in the South against the insurgents and pressed the North Vietnamese for a negotiated settlement in Paris. Though the Johnson administration had been trying to negotiate since the early stages of the war, they accomplished little because both sides followed the same strategy of talking while fighting. Each side tried to gain an advantage on the battlefield that could be used to compel concessions at the bargaining table. Thus the talks in Paris weren't making much progress until Hubert Humphrey, the Democratic presidential candidate and the current vice president, broke with Johnson and began to advocate a total cessation of the bombing.

Sensing the shift in the U.S. position, the North Vietnamese suddenly dropped their resistance to including the South Vietnamese government in the negotiations, in exchange for including the National Liberation Front (NLF), also known as the Viet Cong, and halting the bombing campaign entirely. North Vietnam's offer was designed to boost Hubert Humphrey's campaign because they believed that Nixon, who had built a career as an anti-Communist, would be more difficult to deal with than Humphrey.

Johnson, not wanting to appear as though he'd turned down a chance for peace, was forced to end the bombing campaign on October 31, 1968, in a televised address to the nation. Having gained an important concession in the cessation of bombing, the North Vietnamese went back to the strategy of talking while fighting. The Paris talks stalled again for another five years.

Electing a new president in 1968

By March 1968, when LBJ announced that he wouldn't run for reelection, the Vietnam War had driven a wedge in the Democratic Party. Since Tet, public opinion polls showed a sharp increase in opposition to Johnson's conduct of the war (see Chapter 8 for more on the public's reaction to Tet). Johnson, the great consensus builder of Congress, had lost the consensus among his own cabinet. Secretary of Defense Robert McNamara's resignation in early 1968 reflected the struggles within the administration. Sometime during the fall of 1966, McNamara concluded that the war couldn't be won using the current strategy. Though he continued to try to influence Johnson, he began to feel like an outsider within the administration. Finally, in June 1967, without the knowledge or consent of the president, McNamara commissioned a massive study of the roots of U.S. involvement in Vietnam — this study became known as the Pentagon Papers, which were leaked to the press in 1971, shedding important light on the subject and fueling the antiwar movement.

Originally, the primary race for the Democratic presidential nomination was simple; the sitting president seemed the shoe-in for the party nomination. Eugene McCarthy joined the race as an antiwar candidate and quickly received the support of thousands of young idealistic college students and antiwar protesters. After McCarthy did well in the first primary race in New Hampshire on March 12, 1968, it began to look like a challenger may have a chance after all. Four days later, Robert F. Kennedy joined the race. It looked like a three-way race between Johnson, McCarthy, and Kennedy. Kennedy's entrance in the primary race put further pressure on the president.

Surprised by McCarthy's strong showing in New Hampshire and facing fears of a loss to McCarthy in the upcoming Wisconsin primary, Johnson withdrew on March 31, leaving Kennedy and McCarthy along with Hubert Humphrey, Johnson's vice president who joined the race after Johnson withdrew, as the democratic hopefuls. On June 4, Kennedy won the pivotally important California primary but was assassinated that evening as he left a celebration of his victory. Johnson's withdrawal and Kennedy's assassination made Humphrey and McCarthy the Democratic candidates. Yet many Americans weren't ready to accept anything less than a victory, and at a turbulent Democratic National Convention, Humphrey squeaked by McCarthy while Richard Nixon secured the Republican nomination.

Without a doubt, the most important issue of the 1968 election was the Vietnam War. Johnson's decision not to run for reelection reinforced the idea that the situation abroad was out of control. In efforts to ease broiling tensions and win American hearts, Nixon campaigned on his promise to bring "peace with honor." Nixon's plan was intentionally vague, yet as good rhetoric, it played well with the American people. Humphrey preferred to end the bombing campaign and pursue a negotiated settlement. However, as vice president, he faced severe pressure from Johnson to support the policy of continued bombing. Johnson felt that without any concessions from the North Vietnamese, ending the bombing would simply give the North Vietnamese a reprieve that they would use to resupply and press on in their attacks in order to gain an advantage. To preserve solidarity within the Democratic Party, Humphrey gave in to Johnson's pressures at the Democratic National Convention and toned down the antiwar elements of his speech.

Humphrey starting singing a different tune, though, by September, when he broke with Johnson and condemned the bombing — but by then it was too late. Nixon was already gaining ground, based on the rumor that he had a secret plan to end the war (which, as it turns out, wasn't really the case — see the next section). Many Democrats were disillusioned and sat out the 1968 election, believing that Humphrey was only a different face on the Johnson policy. At the polls, Nixon squeaked by with 43.4 percent of the vote, compared with Humphrey's 42.7 percent.

Playing the Cold War Card

Once elected, Nixon recognized that Johnson's policy of escalation did nothing to bring U.S. forces closer to victory. Johnson's attempts to reach a negotiated settlement with the North Vietnamese were also failures, although he'd tried both force and concessions.

Many believed that Nixon had a secret plan to end the war (an idea that was partially responsible for his election), but the reality was that he had only some general ideas about how to begin manipulating the situation. Unlike Johnson, who perceived himself as the great domestic reformer, Nixon's interests were much more focused on international affairs. Accordingly, he saw the potential solution to the problem of Vietnam in the larger concerns of the cold war.

Kissinger, a man of the world

Henry Kissinger, a German Jew who immigrated to the United States in 1938, was secretary of state under presidents Richard Nixon and Gerald Ford from 1973 to 1977. He also served as assistant to the president for national security affairs from 1969 until 1975. Kissinger was educated at Harvard, earning his PhD in political science in 1954. Before his government service, he was a member of the Harvard faculty.

As a liberal Republican, Kissinger supported Governor Nelson Rockefeller for the Republican nomination for president in 1960, 1964, and 1968. However, ever the pragmatist, Kissinger switched his support to Nixon when it became inevitable that he'd receive the Republican nod in 1968. Though not always agreeing with Nixon, Kissinger not only supported but also greatly influenced policy throughout the president's administration. Some of his greatest achievements were the *détente* (a lessening of tensions) with the Soviet Union and the opening of diplomatic relations with China in 1972. He also negotiated the Strategic Arms Limitation Talks (culminating in a treaty, SALT I) and the Anti-Ballistic Missile Treaty. In 1973, Kissinger was awarded the Nobel Peace Prize along with Le Duc Tho of Vietnam for their work on the Vietnam peace accords.

Although he certainly wasn't good-looking, Kissinger was sophisticated and dated some of the more attractive Hollywood talents, such as Jill St. John, Shirley MacLaine, and Candice Bergen. When asked how he attracted such beautiful women, Kissinger replied, "Power is the ultimate aphrodisiac."

As Nixon assembled his top advisors, he clearly had foreign policy in mind, choosing either men who held similar views to his own regarding cold war strategy or those who would follow him without question. Nixon's greatest ally was Henry Kissinger, who, as national security advisor, dominated the foreign policy ideas of Nixon's top advisors.

Nixon's approach to Vietnam was based on a larger global strategy in which the superpowers would work together to uphold world stability. To achieve this consensus, Nixon and Kissinger began to work at improving U.S. relations with the Soviet Union. They also sought to create diplomatic relations with the People's Republic of China, which would end the 20 years of animosity that had existed since China's Communist revolution (see Chapter 4 for more on Nixon's dealings with the Soviet Union and China).

The main goal of this strategy was that after Nixon and Kissinger achieved these diplomatic objectives, they could persuade the Soviets and Chinese to influence the North Vietnamese into accepting a compromise settlement. As it turns out, the two men were masters of this type of *triangular diplomacy*, in which they used a third party to manipulate concessions from their primary opponent.

Taking Initial Steps Toward Vietnamization

Nixon's global cold war strategy took some time to establish. In the meantime, he was still facing major pressures at home. In his first few months in office the protests had subsided a bit as moderate antiwar protesters waited to see what Nixon would do, yet it was clear that most Americans expected some action. Nixon had to begin withdrawing U.S. troops and deescalating the war effort, yet he had to do so without encouraging the North Vietnamese to press on toward a military victory.

Nixon found his solution to this difficult problem in Vietnamization, which was designed to shift the burden of the war onto the South Vietnamese by bolstering their ability to fight. The challenge here was that withdrawing U.S. troops tended to demoralize the South Vietnam forces (also referred to as the Army of the Republic of Vietnam, or ARVN) if it was done too rapidly. However, if American forces were withdrawn too slowly, Americans would perceive it as a stalling tactic and would likely reinvigorate the antiwar movement.

Reassuring South Vietnam

Central to Vietnamization was the effort to reassure the South Vietnamese government that the United States wasn't abandoning their cause. Several steps were focused on proving to the South Vietnam government that the U.S. was still committed to its struggle:

- The U.S. began equipping the ARVN with the latest military hardware, providing more than 1 million of the newer M-16 rifles in addition to 40,000 M-79 rocket launchers and 12,000 M-60 machine guns.

- Training programs were intensified to ensure that the ARVN could defend the nation.

- Though some of the responsibility of the U.S. Air Force was transferred to the South Vietnamese Air Force, the United States remained deeply committed to providing U.S. air support for South Vietnamese troops.

Withdrawing U.S. troops

In June 1969, Nixon announced the first troop withdrawals with a return of 25,000 soldiers, thereby effectively undermining renewed antiwar criticism at home. The removal of the troops began to shift combat strategies on the ground in Vietnam. With fewer troops, the massive sweeps in which large numbers of combat troops moved through an area destroying any enemy they encountered had to be abandoned in favor of smaller unit action, which reduced the number of troops and the amount of area they could clear. The result was a decrease in U.S. casualties after 1969, yet the ARVN casualty rates remained high.

As the U.S. contingent shrank, the ARVN increased in size. The South Vietnamese forces accomplished this growth by lowering their draft age to 18, something the United States had done three years before.

By the end of 1969, the total count of U.S. troops in Vietnam had been reduced from 550,000 to 475,000. By the end of 1970, U.S. troops numbered 335,000.

Negotiating with the North

While building international relations with the Soviet Union and China and bolstering the ARVN forces, Nixon continued the talks with the North Vietnamese. The North continued to talk and fight, biding its time and trying to rebuild its forces in the South, which had been severely damaged by its defeat in the Tet Offensive. The North Vietnamese were well aware of the U.S. antiwar movement and the fact that time was on their side. The United States followed the same strategy of talking while fighting. Both sides hoped to gain some advantage in the process.

Sensing the stalemate, Nixon chose to borrow a page from President Eisenhower's history and sought to coerce the North Vietnamese into negotiations by making them fear he was willing to go much further than Johnson had in order to win. He tried to pressure the North Vietnamese into compromise by creating fear that he was willing to annihilate the North Vietnamese people in order to win. Though Johnson had been careful not to target population centers, Nixon began to approve them as appropriate targets. Nixon called this his "madman theory."

In July 1969, Nixon sent a private message to Ho Chi Minh, the leader of North Vietnam, through a French neutral party, threatening that unless he saw a diplomatic breakthrough by November 1, he'd resort "to measures of great consequence and force." Ho's answer, which arrived in Washington on August 30, rebuffed Nixon's threat by simply reiterating the standard Communist stance regarding the reunification of all of Vietnam. Though Nixon interpreted this as a "cold rebuff," and began to plot his first massive bombing campaign, the response likely wasn't written by Ho himself because he'd been suffering heart failure since early 1969 and died on September 2 at the age of 79.

Ho's last exhortation to his people was to carry on the fight all the way to victory. Though the antiwar movement was slowly undermining the U.S. war effort, the North Vietnamese showed great support for the war, and Ho's death only strengthened their resolve.

Feeding the Protest Fires

As Nixon sought to refine his strategy, he implemented several new tactics. Though he did his best to keep his new programs under wraps, such changes always leaked to the public at some point. Each time the leaders of the antiwar movement caught wind of anything that seemed to be an expansion of the conflict, it breathed new life into the protests, which limited Nixon's ability to make new policy.

Eliminating Communists: The Phoenix Program

The Nixon administration instituted a variety of programs ranging from those focused on controlling corruption in the South Vietnamese government to those seeking to undermine the Viet Cong efforts to rebuild following Tet. As part of the Vietnamization strategy, Nixon's programs had mixed results; the most controversial was the Phoenix Program, aimed at destroying the Communists' political structure. The CIA created this program with the cooperation of South Vietnamese officials, with the primary goal of identifying Communist agents and supporters working in the South and then assassinating them to render them useless as an effective fighting and recruitment force. The Phoenix Program also focused on confiscating weapons and supplies to further undermine the enemy. The program was highly effective at eliminating people, yet the question of how many were really Communists is a troubling one (see Chapter 8 for a discussion on distinguishing Communists from nationalists).

To eliminate the leadership of the Viet Cong, South Vietnamese agents infiltrated the Communist cells and identified Communists and Communist supporters, who were then either imprisoned or killed. Although the CIA described these efforts with the soft term "neutralizing," many reports of the Phoenix were troubling. One problem was that village chiefs were often given quotas to fulfill and thus killed just to satisfy the requirements, identifying all the victims as Communists, regardless of whether they actually were. Often, a mere suggestion from a jealous neighbor could lead to the neutralization of an individual or family. Pervasive corruption within the South Vietnamese government was another problem. Some estimates claim that 70 percent of the true Communists were able to bribe the ARVN troops to gain their freedom. At home in the United States, many critics saw this program as little more than organized murder, particularly after journalists began noting that the numbers killed were significantly higher than the number of weapons confiscated. The CIA claimed that in the first year of the Phoenix Program, they neutralized almost 20,000 Communists. By the end of the program in 1975, they cited 60,000.

After the war, North Vietnamese officials admitted that the Phoenix Program had crippled their recruiting efforts and had disrupted many of their cells. Although they stated that they didn't fear a division of soldiers, the infiltration of their own ranks was tremendously destructive.

Hitting the press: The My Lai Massacre

Another challenge that Nixon faced in his first year in office occurred when the story of the My Lai Massacre hit the press in November 1969. Although this event occurred on March 16, 1968, before Nixon took office, it created a strong antiwar backlash when the news came to the American public's attention. The massacre of old men, women, and children happened as CIA and military leaders ordered U.S. soldiers in Charlie Company, a unit of the 11th Light Infantry, to sweep the South Vietnamese village of My Lai. At the briefing before the operation, the men were told to expect heavy resistance from the Viet Cong, yet when they entered the village, all they found were older men, women, and children. The lieutenant, 24-year-old William Calley, had his men gather up and kill more than 500 villagers.

Though some soldiers refused to kill unarmed civilians, others fired their weapons at point-blank range into the crowd of frightened and huddled villagers. Some were forced into a large ditch, where Calley and his men shot them all. At one point in the midst of the carnage, a helicopter pilot, Hugh Thompson, sickened by what he saw going on below him, set his chopper down and began rescuing any villager he could. At one point he even ordered his door gunner to open fire on any U.S. soldier he saw who was still executing the villagers. Thompson radioed details of the ongoing massacre to his command, and Charlie Company was pulled back. The U.S. military immediately began a coverup of the atrocity, calling it a great victory against the Viet Cong and mentioning that about 20 civilians had been accidentally killed in the battle. Even General Westmoreland himself sent his congratulations to Charlie Company.

The story may have ended there had a discharged soldier by the name of Ronald Ridenhour not sent letters describing the massacre to U.S. congressman Morris Udall and 30 other prominent politicians, including President Nixon. Two separate investigations began after the letters in March 1969, and 26 U.S. soldiers were put on trial, yet only Calley was found guilty of murder. At their trials, the others insisted that they were either following Calley's orders or, in the case of higher-ranking officers, that they hadn't given Calley orders to kill noncombatants.

The rest of the story of the tragedy in My Lai

Though William Calley was sentenced to life in prison at hard labor, many Americans felt that his conviction was wrong. Some people excused Calley's actions believing that they were understandable and merely the natural result of war. Others, however, felt that though Calley should be punished, the real responsibility lay with the U.S. Army itself and that Calley had simply become their scapegoat.

In early 1971, under pressure from both supporters and critics of Calley, Nixon announced that he'd review Calley's case, and three days after the trial, he ordered that Calley be held under house arrest in a comfortable apartment on a stateside army base. On November 9, 1974, after serving a mere 3½ years, Calley was paroled.

As the four-month trial of Calley unfolded in the U.S. press, the antiwar movement was reinvigorated. Many Americans were shocked to hear the testimony of soldiers who admitted firing clip after clip of ammunition into the villagers. The facts that only three weapons were found in the village and that many of the dead were women and children, even babies, horrified the American public. The massacre also deeply hurt the reputation of the U.S. Army. Even strong supporters of the war who truly disliked the peaceniks found that they couldn't explain or defend the massacre. Though this incident happened while Johnson was still president, the fallout was on Nixon.

Widening the War

Although part of the Vietnamization campaign involved withdrawing U.S. troops and replacing them with South Vietnamese forces, the other part of Nixon's strategy included the measured use of American military power that went beyond Johnson's strategy regarding acceptable targets in the bombing campaign and a willingness to expand the war into other Southeast Asian countries. Nixon referred to this strategy as his "big-play tactic," which consisted of three objectives:

- To weaken the ability of the North Vietnamese to wage war in South Vietnam
- To bolster ARVN forces by reassuring them of continued U.S. support
- To intimidate the North Vietnamese into accepting U.S. terms for peace

Moving into Cambodia

Nixon's first application of his big-play tactic was the expansion of the war into Cambodia. The goal was to take the war to the enemy, hitting him in the places where he believed he had sanctuary. Though the Cambodian government had proclaimed neutrality regarding the Vietnam War, the North Vietnamese were using the country as staging and supply points for their movement of troops and supplies to the South along the Ho Chi Minh Trail.

The Cambodian government, under Prince Norodom Sihanouk, had allowed the North Vietnamese to violate their territorial integrity in exchange for North Vietnam's promise to not support the antigovernment Cambodian Communists, called the Khmer Rouge. The Johnson administration had been reluctant to go after North Vietnamese bases in Cambodia because of fears of expanding the war. However, Nixon decided that the benefits of bombing the bases there outweighed the risks of widening the conflict. Nixon began his attacks on the Vietnamese bases in March 1969 with Operation Menu. Operation Menu lasted 14 months and included 3,600 B-52 bombing raids over Cambodia, dropping a total of more than 100,000 tons of bombs on Cambodia (Figure 10-1 shows a B-52 on a bombing mission).

Figure 10-1: B-52 bombers brought the fight to Cambodia.

Courtesy of the Vietnam Archive, Texas Tech University

Cognizant that recognition of the extension of the war would generate criticism from the antiwar movement, Nixon worked hard to keep this operation a secret. Government officials didn't tell Americans of the bombing campaign, yet when the news inevitably broke it created a tremendous backlash against Nixon for expanding the war.

In April 1970, a month before the bombing ended, Nixon allowed U.S. and ARVN forces to clearly cross into Cambodia for the first time in the war to destroy the Vietnamese bases. The Cambodians cooperated with the U.S. incursion and provided the U.S. military with intelligence regarding the location of North Vietnamese camps. The campaign was a military success, as the U.S. and South Vietnamese troops destroyed 800 bunkers and captured large amounts of weapons and supplies. The extension of the war into Cambodia had three primary positive effects:

- ✔ It proved to be an important test of the ARVN forces, which was maturing into a strong standing army.

- ✔ It disrupted the flow of supplies and men from North Vietnam to the South and disrupted North Vietnamese military plans.

- ✔ It bought time to allow the Vietnamization campaign of shifting the burden of fighting to the ARVN forces to begin to work.

Though the incursion and subsequent destruction of their bases and weapons created a setback for the North Vietnamese, it didn't produce the decisive victory over the Communists that the Nixon administration had hoped for. In fact, the widening of the war had a number of negative consequences for the Nixon administration.

Gaining another dependent

Politically, the results of Operation Menu were less satisfying. Though the North's war strategy was disrupted, the U.S. and ARVN offensive hadn't intimidated them into making any concessions at the bargaining table. The new problem created by the widening of the war was that the previously "neutral" state of Cambodia had shifted toward the U.S. position, effectively pushing the North Vietnamese into closer cooperation with the Khmer Rouge (see the "Beware your friends — from Lon Nol to Pol Pot" sidebar). The Cambodian government removed Prince Sihanouk as head of state and placed Prime Minister Lon Nol in charge of the new government. The U.S. invasion created greater political instability in the country, forcing the United States to accept Cambodia as yet another dependent nation requiring U.S. support.

Facing a backlash: The antiwar movement

The most devastating effect of Nixon's widening of the war was that it touched off some of the most vigorous and tragic antiwar protests at home. In response Nixon asserted that the invasion of Cambodia was hastening the end of the war, yet many Americans interpreted this move as a betrayal of the effort to wind it all down. Instead, they saw this operation as a widening of the conflict into a previously neutral nation.

This massive objection created a credibility gap for Nixon similar to the problems that had plagued Johnson from 1966 to 1968. Anger over this perceived

Beware your friends — from Lon Nol to Pol Pot

As was often the case of U.S. policy in the region, the expansion of the war had some unintended consequences as it promoted the rise of the Communist regime of the Khmer Rouge under the control of the brutal leader Pol Pot. U.S. leaders thought they'd found a perfect ally in Prime Minister Lon Nol — he was anti-Communist and even helped the United States depose Prince Sihanouk for supporting the North Vietnamese Viet Cong. In protest, Sihanouk threw his support to Pol Pot. Because of Sihanouk's popularity and the resistance against the U.S. invasion of Cambodia, Pol Pot's popularity grew, and Lon Nol's support waned.

When the United States left Vietnam in 1974, the Viet Cong left Cambodia, and within two years,

Lon Nol's government collapsed and he fled to the United States. Sihanouk was returned to power in 1975, but he didn't remain in power for long. The Khmer Rouge dismantled the government, Cambodia became a Communist republic, and in May 1976, Pol Pot became prime minister of Cambodia. His regime was extremely harsh on political dissent — opposing the government meant arrest, possible brainwashing, and often a painful death. During his 3-½-year rule from 1975 to 1978 the Pol Pot regime practiced genocide on their own people, killing nearly two million people while the economy, particularly in cities like Phnom Penh, was almost utterly destroyed.

betrayal led to violent confrontations. At the news of the Cambodian invasion, previously unfocused resistance at college campuses across the nation suddenly got a clear focus. See Chapter 9 for more in-depth information about the antiwar protests.

Having a fallout with Congress

The Cambodian invasion rekindled the passions of the antiwar protestors, but more importantly, it began to create a backlash among politicians attuned to the war's growing unpopularity. Public sentiment wasn't in favor of any widening of the war, and Congress began to act on this sentiment.

In May 1970, after lengthy investigations revealed that the Tonkin Gulf Resolution (which stated that the president had the authority to use whatever force necessary to stop South Vietnam from falling) had been passed based upon some false statements by Secretary of Defense Robert McNamara and Secretary of State Dean Rusk, the Senate repealed the resolution. The men had claimed that both attacks in August 1964 had occurred, when they knew that the second attack hadn't happened and that there were serious doubts about the first one. Further both men claimed to have no knowledge of the relationship between the South Vietnamese attacks on the isles of Hon Me and Hon Nu and the U.S. Desoto patrols although they were well aware of the coordination of the two missions.

The dogged pursuit of the truth by Senators Wayne Morse, Earnest Gruening, and J. William Fulbright led to inconclusive debate in congressional hearings in 1968, yet these hearings laid the groundwork for others to finally prove that the resolution had been passed based upon false information. The fact is that Congress never declared war on North Vietnam, and the sole justification for Johnson and Nixon to pursue the war had been based on this fraudulently obtained document. Senator Morse, one of only two senators who had voted against the resolution in 1964, had stated, at the time, that its supporters "will live to regret it." In May 1970, Morse was finally vindicated.

On December 22, 1970, as a means to further restrict Nixon's ability to widen the conflict, Congress passed the Cooper-Church Amendment to the Defense Appropriations Bill. This amendment prohibited the use of any U.S. *ground forces* for operations in Cambodia. Though Nixon wasn't restricted in his use of air power, this amendment definitely foreclosed the opportunity for further operations like the Cambodian incursion.

Relying on the ARVN in Laos

Nixon had no choice but to continue withdrawing U.S. troops in 1970 and 1971. The process of Vietnamization continued as U.S. advisors trained and supplied the growing ARVN force. Though the administration experienced a violent backlash against the invasion of Cambodia, Nixon boldly decided to try a similar operation in Laos in 1971. Again, the goal was to disrupt and destroy the North Vietnamese supply lines and buy more time for the South to strengthen itself. The difference in Laos was that Nixon had to limit the use of American personnel and rely primarily on ARVN troops. If successful, he'd have a real sign that South Vietnam was ready to defend itself.

The invasion focused on the town of Tchepone, which lay about 20 miles inside the Laos-Vietnam border. (The assault was named Operation Lam Som 719, after a Vietnamese village that withstood an invasion by the Chinese in 1427.) Nixon hoped that the use of an all-ARVN invasion force would mute protest from the home front, although the ARVN troops were given U.S. air support for the operation. This attack was another bold thrust by Nixon, yet it wasn't the first U.S. action in Laos. Since 1964, the CIA had been conducting covert operations in the country, and the U.S. had been heavily bombing Vietnamese positions there. Unlike the Cambodian invasion, which attacked isolated North Vietnamese sanctuaries, the assault into Laos was taking on a much larger and more entrenched enemy, including North Vietnamese tank and artillery regiments.

While U.S. air power pounded the North Vietnamese divisions, the invasion force of more than 21,000 ARVN troops captured the town of Tchepone on March 6, 1971, which had largely been reduced to rubble under heavy U.S. bombing raids. Having succeeded in their original objective, the South Vietnamese forces began their withdrawal, although intelligence indicated that the North Vietnamese had rushed troops and artillery to the area and that a counterattack was imminent.

As the ARVN forces withdrew, the North Vietnamese ordered their troops to make massive assaults on the South Vietnamese forces, hoping that a decisive victory against the ARVN would prove that the U.S. strategy of Vietnamization was a failure. Under pressure from the North Vietnamese, the orderly withdrawal of ARVN forces fell apart, as even the elite airborne and marine units panicked and fled, leaving behind tanks, artillery, and equipment. Only the heavy use of U.S. air power kept the situation from being a total rout of the South Vietnamese forces.

Although the mission had succeeded in disrupting the North Vietnamese preparations for a major invasion of the South, it also revealed the weakness of the ARVN forces and the failure of Vietnamization. For many U.S. military planners, the fiasco of the ARVN retreat raised questions about whether Vietnamization could ever work. To the North Vietnamese, the retreat signaled that they could defeat the ARVN even though it had been substantially improved by the U.S. training and equipment.

Coming to a Head: The Easter Offensive

For President Nixon, the backlash over the Cambodian and Laotian invasions, including the congressional limitations on his power to wage war, emphasized that time was running out on the American ability to keep fighting in Vietnam. Well aware of Nixon's domestic dilemma, the North Vietnamese decided to turn up the heat in the war with a new offensive in 1972. Their strategy was to take advantage of the political pressure created by the upcoming U.S. presidential elections.

Knowing that Nixon could ill afford to send any more troops, the North Vietnamese felt that the U.S. inability to respond to a new push on the battlefield may put enough pressure on the ARVN forces to collapse the South Vietnamese regime. They were also driven by the changes occurring on the diplomatic front. Because of improved U.S. relations with both China and the Soviet Union, the North Vietnamese feared a future reduction in Soviet and Chinese aid and felt compelled to push for a victory before this could happen. Therefore, both the United States and the North Vietnamese had powerful incentives to negotiate and felt that the time to end the war was rapidly approaching.

The North Vietnamese offensive was called "Operation Nguyen Hue," named after the famous Vietnamese nationalist leader who stopped Siamese expansion into Vietnam in 1785. The operation involved more than 200,000 men. The battle plan called for three separate thrusts into South Vietnam. For the North, the best possible result was that their offensive would cause the collapse of the

South Vietnamese government and the withdrawal of U.S. forces. The worst-case scenario was that the offensive would further damage morale in the South and continue to undermine the success of Vietnamization. In any event, operation Nguyen Hue would give the North a better position at the political bargaining table.

The Easter Offensive took American military leaders by surprise. In the weeks just before the attack, U.S. secretary of defense Melvin Laird stated that a large-scale enemy invasion was "not a serious possibility." The North Vietnamese invasion shook the U.S. and South Vietnamese forces on three fronts, which ranged from the Demilitarized Zone in the North, through the central highlands in the middle of South Vietnam, and a thrust toward Saigon in the South.

Bombing Hanoi and Haiphong: The U.S. response

Though U.S. troop levels in Vietnam had been reduced to about 70,000, America still had tremendous air power to call upon. Responding to the attacks, Nixon ordered a renewed air campaign against the North called "Operation Linebacker." Nixon removed almost all the restrictions on the bombing campaign that had been in place throughout the war, including the bombing of population centers and military bases near the Chinese border. He also ordered the bombing of the North Vietnamese capital, Hanoi, and Haiphong, the most important port in North Vietnam. Nixon also ordered the mining of North Vietnamese harbors including Haiphong.

The round-the-clock bombing raids targeted North Vietnamese fuel and ammunition supplies. In addition to the sustained air assault on the North, the United States also employed large-scale bombing missions in the South to support the ARVN forces.

In the southern attack, amidst heavy fighting, the ARVN forces held the city of An Loc but only with the aid of heavy bombing by U.S. aircraft. ARVN forces also held the city of Kontum in the central highlands, yet again the crucial element was U.S. air support and heavy bombing. The heaviest fighting was the northern invasion in Quang Tri, where it took the ARVN ten weeks to finally dislodge the North Vietnamese forces from the city. Here, too, the use of U.S. air and naval support was key. Each day an average of 25,000 rounds of artillery shells were fired, and U.S. bombers flew some 40 missions per day as well.

Dissecting the North Vietnamese miscalculation

The Easter Offensive was a disaster for the North Vietnamese. They sustained tremendous damage from the American bombing in the North and had lost more than 100,000 men in the assault. They had seriously miscalculated both the fighting ability of the ARVN forces and the power and will of the U.S. forces still in Vietnam.

Although the Soviet Union and China protested the bombing campaign, their objections were fairly muted, clearly seeking to maintain the relations that they'd been developing with the United States. The North, fearing they'd lost vital support from the Communist superpowers, recognized the need to reach an agreement before the 1972 U.S. presidential elections, when Nixon, who was likely to win reelection, would no longer face the pressures and restrictions of an election year.

Though pleased at their own ability to repel the northern invasion, the South Vietnamese leaders recognized that American air power had been crucial in their victory. As the U.S. forces continued to withdraw, the South Vietnamese would no longer be able to count on that air power. Thus, for both the North Vietnamese and the South Vietnamese, the Easter Offensive underscored the need to end the bloodbath that the war had become.

Clearing the Last Hurdles to Peace

Both the U.S. and North Vietnamese leaders came to the same conclusion following the Easter Offensive: Military strength hadn't led to victory, and political considerations called for compromise. Talks between U.S. National Security Advisor Henry Kissinger and North Vietnamese politburo representative Le Duc Tho resumed in July 1972. On October 8, they concluded an agreement that called for the withdrawal of U.S. forces from Vietnam within 60 days, as well as the exchange of prisoners of war, and democratic elections in the South, which would include the National Liberation Front (NLF) Viet Cong. The plan also called for peaceful reunification of North and South Vietnam into one nation with national elections, and an American contribution to rebuilding the country.

Nixon and Kissinger were pleased that the North Vietnamese had dropped their demands of the removal of the Thieu government in the South. But President Thieu rejected the agreement, calling it a plan for a coalition government — something that the South Vietnamese government had consistently rejected. The plan began to unravel. The North Vietnamese leadership, believing that Thieu's rejection of the agreement was a U.S. trick because they thought Thieu would never defy his powerful American allies, accused the United States of purposely undermining the agreement. Kissinger scrambled to get the negotiations back on track before the U.S. presidential election, proclaiming on October 31 that "peace is at hand."

Following Nixon's landslide election in 1972, Kissinger turned his attention to convincing the South Vietnamese that the United States wasn't abandoning them to their fate. He initiated a massive airlift of war materiel to the South Vietnamese, transferring hundreds of aircraft (giving the South Vietnamese the fourth largest air force in the world) as well as tanks, trucks, artillery, and munitions. Nixon promised Thieu that he would seek to renegotiate the peace turns and promised that "we will respond with full force should the settlement be violated by North Vietnam."

On December 13, Le Duc Tho, feeling that Kissinger was trying to renegotiate some of the issues that had already been agreed upon, suspended the dead-locked negotiations and returned to Hanoi for consultation. Nixon responded to the delay by initiating a renewed bombing campaign, Linebacker II, often-times referred to as "the Christmas bombing."

Beginning on December 18 and lasting for 11 days, Linebacker II was the most devastating bombing campaign of the war. U.S. B-52s and other aircraft dropped 40,000 tons of bombs focused on the Hanoi-Haiphong corridor. Though the bombing severely weakened the North Vietnamese foreign supply lines, it also created international criticism for the United States. The Chinese and Soviets protested the bombing, as did many of the U.S. allies in Europe. The antiwar protest in the U.S. also briefly flared, and polls showed Nixon's approval ratings drop to 39 percent.

The North Vietnamese returned to the negotiating table in January 1973, though it's unclear whether they felt compelled by the bombing campaign. On January 27, the United States, South Vietnam, and North Vietnam finally reached an agreement for peace. The agreement was essentially the same as the draft agreement created the previous July, specifying the U.S withdrawal from Vietnam, the exchange of prisoners of war, and democratic elections in the South, which would include the NLF (Viet Cong). Finally, the plan called for peaceful reunification of North and South Vietnam and an American con-tribution to rebuilding Vietnam. Using the phrase on which he'd campaigned, Nixon proclaimed that they'd reached peace with honor. By June, the U.S. Congress passed the Case-Church Amendment, which cut off U.S. aid to South Vietnam after August 15, 1973. The U.S. war in Vietnam was over, yet for those with a clear understanding of the realities of the situation, the fall of South Vietnam seemed inevitable.

Epilogue: The fall of Saigon

After watching the ARVN strength decline in late 1973 and 1974, the North Vietnamese resumed their efforts to attain a military victory over the South Vietnamese government. Though President Nixon had promised to return if the peace efforts broke down, the Watergate scandal had already forced him to resign. His successor, Gerald Ford, called on Congress to support the South Vietnamese government, yet the years of war and protest had eroded the desire to continue U.S. involvement in Vietnam. The ARVN forces collapsed under the North Vietnamese assault, and the provinces fell one after another, until the South Vietnamese capital of Saigon fell on April 30, 1975.

Scarcely one day after Saigon fell, the city was renamed Ho Chi Minh City, and the Republic of Vietnam was effectively ended. If nothing else, the new name of the South Vietnamese capital was a symbol of the failure of U.S. policy in Vietnam. The American involvement in Vietnam was over.

Part IV

Starting a Revolution: Social Upheaval and Angst

The 5th Wave   By Rich Tennant

"Hey man, I thought you paid the power bill!"

In this part . . .

The 1960s were a decade of upheaval. After the relative conformity of the 1950s, many young people began to question almost everything about their lives, their government, and their parents' morality and lifestyles. Some of the questioning came from this discontent, while others came from the sense of youthful empowerment created under Kennedy's New Frontier platform. University students challenged the administration's authority, especially concerning issues such as civil rights, freedom of expression, and most of all, the Vietnam War.

Women began to question their roles as wives and mothers and worked to gain equal employment opportunities as well as change men's perception of them as sex objects. The civil rights movement inspired other groups to fight for recognition and equal treatment under the law. Led by Cesar Chavez, Hispanics used nonviolent methods, such as demonstrations and boycotts, to improve working conditions, and American Indians worked to reclaim their rights and full participation in American society. And as the decade closed, gays and lesbians began their public battle against discrimination and prejudice. But not everyone agreed that the changes they were seeing was the proper direction for American society. These folks made their voices heard as well. In this part, we cover the efforts of all these groups to remake the fabric of the nation and assert their place in it.

Chapter 11

Leaning to the Left

• •

In This Chapter

▶ Looking at the liberal past

▶ Starting a new movement

▶ Speaking freely in Berkeley

▶ Uniting American students

• •

American college campuses were a focal point and a launching pad of efforts to institute change during the 1960s. However, the '60s weren't the beginning of *left-wing* politics (those embracing Socialist or liberal principles) in 20th-century America. Beginning with the struggle for decent wages and working conditions, labor unions were among the pioneers using direct action, such as strikes, to achieve their aims. People and organizations were also working for peace and integration before the '60s.

However, prompted by recognition of social injustices, support for the civil rights struggle, and the struggle against the Vietnam War, students throughout the United States organized in the 1960s to further their causes. The two core organizations of the New Left were the free speech movement (FSM) in Berkeley and the Students for a Democratic Society (SDS), which had chapters all over the country. This chapter looks at the ideas, goals, tactics, and battlegrounds of this left-wing movement.

Left Wing of the American Eagle: Liberal and Socialist Politics before the 1960s

Socialist and progressive tendencies have played a significant role in American society. As far back as the 19th century, communities such as the Shakers and labor organizations such as the National Labor Union (NLU) and the International Workers of the World (IWW), also known as the Wobblies, have believed in working toward the common good in society. At the end of the 19th century, however, these principles became even more widely accepted. This Gilded Age, as Mark Twain dubbed it, fostered the creation of huge monopolies that exploited their workers and employed unscrupulous tactics in pursuit of profit. In response, workers demanded safer working conditions and a more humane standard of living.

During the early 20th century, in an era called the Progressive Age, workers formed organizations to curb the growing power of big business. Although the progressive movement sought to reform exploitive business practices, others still held onto the ideas of truly remaking the capitalist system. Men such as Eugene Debs, who formed the American Railway Union, tried to curb the excesses of the capitalist giants but failed because business interests had already secured government support. After losing his battle in the famous Pullman strike of 1893, Debs was jailed for obstruction (in this instance, blocking interstate commerce). While in prison, Debs became a Socialist.

After being released from prison, Debs organized the Socialist Party of America. He ran for president in 1900 and received more than 4,000 votes. In 1904 he received 400,000 votes, and in 1908 he received 900,000 votes. In the election of 1912, Debs garnered 6 percent of the popular vote.

Though many people involved in the early labor movements tended toward leftist politics, especially among immigrants who were exposed to Socialist ideas in Europe, eventually the labor movement itself became less radical, except for those such as Debs who followed Socialist ideas in their attempts to improve the lives of workers.

Throughout the 20th century, many members of American society and politicians in power distrusted the left end of the political spectrum. American culture was marked by individualism and *capitalism,* the ability of anyone to create wealth and power for him or herself. Socialist and Communist ideals, which held that capitalism exploited workers and advocated that workers press for their rights, opposed this concept.

The Palmer Raids

Though Socialists and labor unions both enjoyed a period of growth during World War I, in late 1919 and early 1920 the American Socialist movement was dealt a severe blow with the Palmer Raids. Instituted by U.S. Attorney General Mitchell Palmer, the raids were meant to root out subversive elements in American society by arresting, imprisoning, and deporting suspected Socialists and anarchists. These efforts chilled the Socialist movement for a time. However, the impulse for Socialist principles continued to simmer below the surface.

Pinks and reds in the 1930s and '40s

During the Great Depression (1929–39), in which many Americans suffered severe economic decline, many political moderates began to embrace Socialist or Communist ideas. Though many would regret this shift later in the repressive climate of the '50s, during the Depression it made sense. As the leading capitalist nations all suffered real decline, the Communist Soviet Union was experiencing tremendous growth led by Joseph Stalin's aggressive five-year plans for development.

Leftist politics lost some of their appeal, however, after Franklin Roosevelt's election in 1932, and the government agencies he created began to relieve some of the hardship. When the Soviet Union supported Adolf Hitler in the late '30s, some Communists became disillusioned with the movement.

With the end of World War II, the struggle between the Soviet Union and the United States solidified into the cold war (see Chapter 2 for more details about the cold war). To respond to this "red menace" of Communism, the U.S. government introduced a loyalty oath program in 1947, requiring many state, local, and federal employees, including schoolteachers, to sign loyalty oaths stating that they didn't seek to overthrow the U.S. government, in order to keep their jobs. Fearful of being painted with the "pink" paintbrush (Communist sympathizers were often referred to as "pinkos" — a lighter shade of red), several labor unions began to purge their openly Communist members and distance themselves from anyone that seemed to have Communist sympathies. The House Un-American Activities Committee (HUAC; see Chapter 4), founded in 1938, and Senator Joseph McCarthy (see the next section) were at the forefront of the drive to root out Communism.

J. Edgar Hoover explained in his testimony before HUAC in 1947 why he opposed Communism:

> As such, it stands for the destruction of our American form of government; it stands for the destruction of American democracy; it stands for the destruction of free enterprise; and it stands for the creation of a "Soviet of the United States" and ultimate world revolution.

McCarthyism and the Communist hysteria

After the Soviets exploded an atomic bomb in 1949, and Communist leadership gained power in China in 1949 under Mao Tse Tung, U.S. officials became even more afraid of Socialist or Communist sympathizers. Senator Joseph McCarthy took advantage of this threat by promoting his anti-Communist agenda and threatening to expel Communists in all walks of American life. He spearheaded Senate hearings to expose Communists, during which committee members asked witnesses if they'd ever been Communists and if they knew the names of others who may have been Communists at any time. Many of these witnesses refused to cooperate and, as a result, were blacklisted. In Hollywood, the film industry blacklisted several actors and screenwriters; many never worked again.

In the beginning, playing on people's fears, McCarthy was successful and had popular support, and he believed he could do anything and point the finger at anyone. He accused people in government and the military of Communism, although these charges were overwhelmingly unfounded. In the end, some of McCarthy's accusations were so outlandish that Americans began not only to disbelieve him, but they also realized the harm that his fanaticism created. The Senate eventually censured McCarthy on November 9, 1954, for abuse of power, and the Red Scare was over. Years of hard drinking took its toll, and McCarthy died in 1957. McCarthy's methods created such a backlash that ironically he created a unifying effect among liberals and many moderates.

Another incident that united left-of-center citizens was the conviction and execution of Julius and Ethel Rosenberg. After being found guilty of spying for the Soviet Union, the Rosenbergs were executed for treason. Some people believed that the Rosenbergs were innocent and that their conviction was just another example of the anti-Communist hysteria of the times.

Birthing the New Left

The New Left was a politically radical youth movement centered on college campuses that sought to correct social injustice in the United States. Although they were largely white and middle class, the students eagerly joined the civil rights movement, calling attention to the injustices of segregation and the plight of blacks and the poor. They also opposed the power of the *military-industrial complex* (the cooperation of corporate and military interests) in the United States, but eventually the movement's main focus became the end of the Vietnam War.

Getting clean for Gene

The New Left adopted some of the more traditional methods of forwarding their agenda in 1968 and 1972, when Eugene McCarthy was vying for the Democratic nomination for president. To promote their antiwar candidate, many antiwar protesters cut their hair and rid their preppy duds of mothballs to "Get Clean for Gene." However, McCarthy was too liberal for most traditional Democrats and never received the nomination.

Red-diaper babies, who were children of progressive, politically active parents in the '40s and '50s, became some of the leaders of the New Left in the '60s.

Although many New Left activists had liberal parents, their methods still created a generation gap. Parents were more in favor of traditional methods of changing unjust laws (and worried about their kids' safety, as well as their futures). What made the New Left "new" was that they weren't allied with the traditional labor movements as a means of creating change within society. Instead, they saw social activism as the agent of transformation of society. Though still leftists, liberals, and even radicals, they were less theory driven than the earlier liberals. Further, they avoided traditional methods of political persuasion, such as lobbying and petitioning congressional members, in favor of more active protests. However, they did actively campaign for candidates that backed their causes, both locally and nationally.

Also, the New Left embraced several points of view. Though some were alienated and cynical, others believed that American society was worth transforming and were willing to risk their education, their future careers, and even their personal freedom, in some cases going to jail to work for peace and justice.

Besides being inspired by the civil rights movement and its nonviolent protests, student radicals were inspired by books and films that criticized conventional, middle-class life. More politically astute students were attracted to works of social criticism by people such as leftist writers Herbert Marcuse, Michael Harrington, and C. Wright Mills, who worked to expose economic and social injustices in the United States.

What were they fighting for?

Throughout the '60s, New Left causes became larger and more intense. They ranged from the personal to the political, from the local to the national, and eventually, to the global concern for world peace.

Student issues

At first, student protests focused on issues that directly impacted their lives on campus. They demonstrated against and objected to a wide variety of issues, including

- Dress codes
- *In loco parentis* (in place of the parent) rules that imposed curfews
- Limited dorm visits by the opposite sex (mainly in girls' dorms)

> ✔ Religious and racial discrimination in sororities and fraternities
>
> ✔ Required courses that they considered irrelevant to real life
>
> ✔ The rigid grading system
>
> ✔ Same-sex dormitories

Battling the military-industrial complex

Some of the more politically aware students also protested against university involvement with the military, especially as the Vietnam War escalated. Many campuses had large-scale demonstrations against military recruitment on campus and the presence of the Reserve Officers Training Corps (ROTC). Across the country, New Left students also fought against university involvement in research that benefited the military-industrial complex and furthered the tensions in the cold war. Though the student protest was aimed at the military, it created a rift between students and university administrators who looked favorably upon such research because it brought funding to the university.

Civil rights

At many northern, largely white campuses, many liberal students joined in the struggle for civil rights in the South. They went south to participate in voter registration drives, desegregation protests, and sit-ins at lunch counters (see Chapter 6). They were arrested and beaten, and some were killed. They marched on Washington, D.C., with Martin Luther King Jr. to show solidarity with blacks. In the segregated South, they witnessed poverty, discrimination, and violence firsthand for the first time.

And end to the War

The Vietnam War was also a personal issue for many of the student protesters. Besides being appalled at the undeclared war waged by their country, most young men in college were of draft age. Although many avoided recruitment with student *deferments* (which delayed military service while a person was a full-time student) and enlistment in the National Guard (and in some cases alleged medical problems), they were aware of and sometimes embarrassed by the fact that poor and minority groups were often bearing more than their proportionate share of the war burden. However, when the Johnson administration ended student deferments in 1966, opposition to the war and the draft became even more personal, and student anger over the war's escalation intensified. See Chapter 9 for more on the New Left's central role in the antiwar movement.

Protesting with direct action

The New Left wasn't subtle. Using overt, public displays, they attracted press coverage, which made people aware of their concerns. Because New Left students believed that the establishment was corrupt, for the most part they ignored indirect actions, such as lobbying and working to elect favorable candidates. Instead, protesters during the '60s used direct action, which not only demanded immediate remedies for the problems they saw but also had the advantage of calling attention to their cause. Protest by direct action started with the labor movement in the late 19th century, but throughout the 20th century, activists promoting various causes used direct action to advance women's suffrage, protest the treatment of veterans, and promote environmental issues.

Protest marches

One of the most visible methods of demanding change was by using massive protest marches. Marchers shouted, sang, carried signs, and talked to the crowd to convert others to their cause (and ideally get them to march along with them). The length of the march wasn't important — sometimes the protesters walked only a few blocks. However, as soon as they reached their destination, they usually had a huge rally, complete with speeches and music.

Sit-ins

During *sit-ins,* protesters occupied a building or public area to protest an injustice or demand change, holding their ground until they were either forced out or their demands were met. During the civil rights movement, protesters often sat in at segregated, southern lunch counters and refused to leave (see Chapter 6 for a discussion of the lunch counter sit-ins). Because sit-ins were nonviolent, they usually drew public support, especially if the police tried to forceably remove the protesters. One of the largest student sit-ins was in Sproul Hall, the administration building of the University of California at Berkeley (see the section "The sit-in at Sproul," later in this chapter). In a *lie-in* (a variation of a sit-in), demonstrators blocked public access by lying prone across a road or doorway.

Civil disobedience

Civil disobedience took protest up a notch, because protesters usually broke laws (normally those laws that didn't threaten life and limb) in order to form a blockade or occupy a business or agency. Usually, the protesters were asked to leave and were arrested if they refused, for example. As such, before a civil disobedience event, many protesters figured out how to react to arrest and resist attack.

Protest through the new millennium

The popular protest methods of the '60s have been used to promote various causes throughout the rest of the 20th century and into the new millennium. Almost every group — gays and lesbians, feminists, the religious right, pro-choice and pro-life activists, environmentalists, vegetarians, animal activists, and antiwar activists — has staged demonstrations at some time or another; they've all marched, rallied, sang, and spoke.

One of the largest '60s-style demonstrations was the protest against the World Trade Organization (WTO) in Seattle, Washington, in late 1999. The protesters came from all over the world and represented a variety of causes and were successful in disrupting the WTO meetings despite the Seattle rain and the police crackdowns.

Although the protests were largely peaceful, a violent minority caused the Seattle police and National Guard to declare a state of emergency, which led to curfews, arrests, and tear gas. The news media coverage was disproportionately attracted to the violent minority (because such depictions sell more papers and raise viewer ratings) and portrayed the protesters as unkempt weirdos, although most of them were simply concerned citizens wanting to make sure that environmental concerns and human rights weren't lost in the rush toward a worldwide economy.

Fighting for Free Speech

At first glance, in 1960, the University of California at Berkeley seemed an unlikely place for protest. Students were not only some of the best and the brightest but also the epitome of middle-class California. A look at campus photographs at the beginning of the decade shows crew cuts, ponytails (only on the girls), oxford shirts, and penny loafers. Though this image shifted radically by the end of the '60s, the Vietnam War wasn't what started the fire — it was an orderly protest against HUAC, one of the most invasive government organizations of the era.

Although Berkeley has the reputation of being a haven for student radicals in the '60s, most of their early protests were orderly and peaceful. The free speech movement (FSM) arose as a reaction against Berkeley officials, who were pressured by some government and business leaders to stop students from actively working for civil rights and protesting the involvement of the military-industrial complex on campus.

Perhaps if the officials hadn't reacted so strongly to relatively mild student resistance, the massive demonstrations, sit-ins, and the occupation of the university administration building never would've happened.

Berkeley activism before '63 — HUAC

In May 1960, several student organizations banded together to protest the House Un-American Activities Committee (HUAC) hearings in San Francisco. As we cover in Chapter 4, the goal of HUAC was to root out Communism in the U.S. This issue was very relevant because it heavily involved the academic community (more than 25 percent of the witnesses subpoenaed were teachers). The protesters felt that HUAC encouraged a climate of fear, where people were willing to rat on their friends, neighbors, and colleagues to avoid being called Communists.

Protesters attempted to get in the hearings, but only people with HUAC-issued passes could enter. Unfortunately, the police responded aggressively, even turning fire hoses on the demonstrators. However, the police brutality had just the opposite effect — in the days that followed, San Francisco newspapers printed indignant editorials against the police's excessive force, and the number of demonstrators increased. The protests didn't stop the hearings, but in response, HUAC produced a film condemning the demonstrations and labeling the students as Communist dupes. This film, *Operation Abolition*, was shown throughout the country but had an ironic effect — when the movie was shown at a Harvard ROTC meeting, the promoters found that the student officers actually supported the San Francisco protest.

The university administration tried to appear neutral, but a year later, they showed their bias. They changed the status of SLATE (a campus political party that supported the HUAC protest) from on-campus to off-campus, which limited its ability to organize, distribute materials, and raise funds on campus. The fight between the students and the administration had begun.

Striking for civil rights

Despite their privileged backgrounds, Berkeley students were extremely sympathetic to the civil rights movement. They were concerned not only with integration in the South (and many of them had, in fact, gone south to support the fight for equal rights) but also with economic opportunities right in their own backyard.

In 1963, students banded together with black activists to form a committee to protest hiring discrimination in the San Francisco hotel industry, where blacks were rarely employed as anything other than maids or janitors. The action's objective was to create an intolerable situation for the hotels, forcing them to respond. Mario Savio, later one of the leaders of the FSM, was arrested in a sit-in at San Francisco's Palace Hotel (see the sidebar "Mario Savio — An unlikely radical," later in this chapter).

HISTORIC TRIVIA

Willie Brown, who later became mayor of San Francisco from 1996 to 2004, was the lawyer for protesters who were arrested during the sit-in.

The demonstrations were successful — the protests resulted in an agreement guaranteeing greater opportunities for blacks. The success of this action created a feeling of euphoria among the protesters, spurring them on to further political activity. They believed that by banding together for a just cause they could accomplish anything.

Exercising freedom of speech

After the HUAC protests and the strikes in San Francisco, the Berkeley administration decided to curtail any political activity that might threaten the business community or jeopardize research money from the military-industrial complex. The hotbed of political activity at Berkeley was Bancroft and Telegraph avenues, where activist groups set up tables and booths to distribute political literature and raise funds. On September 16, 1964, the university banned these tables to stop the messages that it didn't like.

However, the ban backfired. Students realized that the right to make their political views known wasn't only a left-wing issue; it was also in accord with their First Amendment rights. Diverse student groups rallied to protest the ban, and even some conservative students joined in the fight. Throughout most of the month, students unsuccessfully tried to negotiate with the administration, but by September 29, students decided to take direct action.

The first mode of attack was civil disobedience. Students continued to set up the tables and distribute literature. When the police ordered the students who were working the tables to leave, other students replaced them. Eventually, on October 1, the university suspended the demonstration leaders and had them arrested. These suspensions and arrests infuriated the students, who surrounded the police cars and began demonstrations at Sproul Hall. One student sat in an immobilized police car for 32 hours — and Mario Savio stood on this car to make his famous speech (see Figure 11-1 and refer to the sidebar "Mario Savio — An unlikely radical" in this chapter).

On October 5, the continuing protests were seriously impairing the university, so they agreed to appoint a committee of students, faculty, and administrators to deal with the issues. As a result, the students agreed to stop demonstrating, and the administration appointed a committee to re-examine the rules. However, when the committee recommended reinstatement for the suspended students, the administration refused, and the students again demonstrated at Sproul.

No matter what the administration agreed to, its main goal was to break up the student coalition. The administration decided that students could have their tables back but couldn't advocate unlawful activity. Sounds reasonable, right? The catch was the contention that because the civil rights advocates and other left-wing groups encouraged civil disobedience, they were promoting unlawful activity.

The sit-in at Sproul

The administration at Berkeley refused to reconsider its position on the student suspensions (see the preceding section) or on political activity, so once again led by Mario Savio, the students had a massive sit-in in and around Sproul Hall, the university's administrative center, on December 2, 1964. Students made themselves comfortable in the hall — it was almost like a dormitory, with people playing music, dancing, studying, or just talking. Chancellor Edward Strong ordered the students to leave the building at 3 a.m., threatening police action if they refused. However, all that happened was that police surrounded the building and allowed people to leave, but they didn't let anyone enter. People who wanted in were so determined that they climbed up ropes to get in through the windows.

Governor Pat Brown ordered the students to withdraw, and on December 3, 600 campus and Berkeley police officers, deputy sheriffs, and highway patrolmen started clearing the hall, carrying students out. Many refused to leave, and leaders of the sit-in began to demonstrate how to resist by making their bodies go limp when the police tried to drag them out. Ultimately, the police arrested and carried out 814 students to end the sit-in. However, the protests continued as Savio called for a general strike, which virtually disabled the campus (see Figure 11-1).

Figure 11-1: Mario Savio rouses the free speech demonstrators.

©Bettmann/CORBIS

Joan Baez — The voice of free speech

Joan Baez loved to sing and write folk songs (see Chapter 15), but she was equally committed to social change. Since the beginning of her career, her music reflected her concern with civil rights, equality for workers, freedom of speech and expression, and opposition to an unjust war. In 1964, she withheld 60 percent of her income tax from the Internal Revenue Service to protest military spending. Baez participated in the birth of the free speech movement at UC Berkeley and sang at several of the protests, including Stop the Draft Week in Oakland, where she was arrested (see Chapter 9 for more about Stop the Draft Week).

Today, Sproul Hall and the surrounding plaza are locations for protests, marches, and literature distribution of any political position. The steps leading to Sproul Hall are called the "Mario Savio Steps," and anyone can reserve them for a speech or rally.

After the arrests, the administration had a meeting to explain its position, but the meeting only made matters worse. Savio asked to speak at the meeting, but the administration refused. Savio shouted out anyway, turning the meeting into a complete free-for-all. In the end, the students considered their FSM a victory when, on December 8, the *Academic Senate* (a body consisting of members of the administration and faculty responsible for managing faculty, curriculum, and admissions issues) passed a resolution that reversed student suspensions and limited the administration's power over political activity on campus. Yet the student protests at Berkeley were far from over as new issues gathered students' attentions — by this time Vietnam began to occupy student thoughts and efforts.

One way the establishment tried to deal with the FSM was with ridicule. The conservative media asserted that the movement attracted a bunch of "weirdos" from all over who saw the sit-in as a giant sexual political party. Some referred to the demonstrations as a "civil rights panty raid," and this assertion was partly true — although the students were serious and committed to their cause, they also had fun. Then-governor of California, Ronald Reagan used movie analogies to express his contempt for student protesters. "A hippie," he said, "is someone who looks like Tarzan, walks like Jane, and smells like Cheetah."

Part of Reagan's gubernatorial campaign in 1966 was attacking the "mess at Berkeley." Referring to the FSM protests in 1964, he said that the "ringleaders should have been thrown out of the university." He thought the radicals were immoral, and he gave an example of a dance sponsored by the Vietnam Day Committee (VDC), with huge crowds, multiple rock bands, and psychedelic movies that suggested nudity and sex. When faculty members supported the student protests, Reagan scolded them like an angry parent, telling them that they were old enough to know better.

Mario Savio — An unlikely radical

Mario Savio was one of the most recognizable leaders of the student protest movement. He was, in a way, an unlikely radical, a young Catholic altar boy from a working-class family in Queens, New York. Savio's activism began during the summer of 1964, when he joined the Student Nonviolent Coordinating Committee (SNCC) to register black voters in Mississippi. However, later that year, on the Berkeley campus, he became a true activist leader, inspiring students and faculty to join the free speech movement (FSM). He became a media darling when his picture, standing on top of a police car and addressing thousands of students, hit the newspapers and the small screen.

Savio wasn't only charismatic, he was poetic. In his speech before the takeover of Sproul Hall (check out "The sit-in at Sproul" in this chapter for more), he said, "There is a time when the operation of the machine becomes so odious, makes you so sick at heart that you can't take part, you can't even tacitly take part, and you've got to put your bodies upon the gears, and upon the wheels, upon the levers, upon all the apparatus. And you've got to make it stop." These were certainly Savio's most famous words and were a rallying cry for the FSM and for activism as a whole.

Savio risked his academic career, as well as his personal freedom, to participate in the marches, sit-ins, and other demonstrations — he spent four months in jail for supporting free speech and the right to demonstrate and protest. After the FSM ran its course, Savio led a quiet life and limited his activism to working against Proposition 187 in 1994, which cut off some health and social services and access to public education to illegal aliens and their children, and Proposition 209 in 1996, which was designed to undermine affirmative action on state campuses.

Berkeley meets the Haight

While Berkeley students were true political activists, the counterculture was alive and well on the other side of the bay, in San Francisco's Haight-Ashbury neighborhood. Although they were against the Vietnam War and for civil rights, hippies were more interested in free love and drugs and a life free of materialism and middle-class values (for more about the hippies, see Chapter 14).

The hippies were against the war, but they disagreed with the Berkeley students about how to stop the war. They believed that music, love, "flower power," and a little bit of weed would stop the war, while the Berkeley protesters believed in strikes, sit-ins, and demonstrations. However, as the '60s progressed, the groups drew closer together — the end was more important than the means, and the hippies joined with antiwar groups from all over the country to protest at the 1968 Democratic National Convention in Chicago (see Chapter 9).

. . . and Oakland

Just as with the San Francisco strikes to end hiring discrimination, the students' concerns went beyond the Berkeley city limits. The Vietnam War brought the protesters into Oakland. In May 1965, antiwar protesters formed the Vietnam Day Committee (VDC) to bring attention to what the United States was doing in Vietnam. Protesters decided to march to the Oakland army terminal to stop the trains taking soldiers on the first leg of their journey to Vietnam. The city of Oakland refused to give them a permit, but the VDC decided to hold the march anyway.

In October 1967, Berkeley again met Oakland during Stop the Draft Week, a nationwide effort to protest the continuing war in Vietnam (see Chapter 9). On October 16, Stop the Draft Week organizers led 3,000 protesters to the Oakland Induction Center to try to prevent new recruits from entering the building. Police formed a human barricade to enable inductees to pass and then arrested the demonstrators. However, the results were mostly symbolic. Protesters didn't stop one inductee from going to Vietnam.

At this point, the FSM went from protest to active resistance, because their protests hadn't had much effect — the war just kept escalating. Because the protesters had become more alienated from society as a whole, they were willing to be more militant. One of their objectives was to raise the cost of the war on the home front by creating civil unrest. Their position was that if the war continued, they would cause chaos in the streets at home.

People's Park

Despite the long-standing conflict between the administration and students at UC Berkeley, a dirt parking lot at Telegraph Avenue and Haste Street finally created an all-out war.

Turning a parking lot into paradise

Originally, People's Park was a piece of property that the university bought in 1968 in order to build new dorms. The university demolished some dilapidated houses that were there, but the dorms were never built. By sheer coincidence (accidentally on purpose?) the old wood houses were home to student radicals that were thorns in the administration's side.

By 1969, the Berkeley community, including UC Berkeley students, decided to make the old parking lot into a community park. Building the park was truly a joint effort by students, hippies, street people, activists, and ordinary citizens.

No walk in the park

People's Park remained a controversial and embattled site throughout the years. The fence stayed up until May 1972, when demonstrators, protesting Nixon's proposed bombing of North Vietnamese ports (see Chapters 3 and 8 for more information about the Vietnam War), ripped it down. In September, the Berkeley City Council voted to lease the site, and People's Park actually came to be used as it was originally intended — a park for all the people of Berkeley.

However, the fragile armistice didn't last. In 1991, UC Berkeley was ready to take People's Park back to build volleyball courts. It seemed like déjà vu — negotiations failed, UC sent in the bulldozers, and the students and residents protested. Although the university won and built their volleyball courts, they were plagued by constant vandalism. In 1997, the university dismantled the courts, and today, community groups and the university manage People's Park.

They laid sod, planted trees, and built a playground. It was an ideal example of people working together to create something that could benefit everyone in the community.

Unfortunately, the park didn't please everyone. The university decided that because it legally owned the land, only it could decide what to do with the land. For about three weeks after the park was finished, the builders negotiated with the university, hopeful that they could reach a settlement that would please everyone. However, the administration abruptly stopped negotiations, sent in the police, and built a fence. Those who built People's Park were furious. They wondered why the authorities waited until all the hard work was finished before telling them they couldn't have their park. The battle was on.

Calling out the troops — tragedy strikes

On May 15, Berkeley students quickly organized a rally at Sproul Plaza (in front of Sproul Hall, the university administration building) on the Berkeley campus to protest the fence. When a student leader said, "Let's go down and take the park," police turned off the sound system. Then, 6,000 people marched down Telegraph Avenue toward the park, but the police were waiting, armed with rifles and tear gas. Fire hydrants were opened, rocks were thrown, and the day descended into chaos and violence. When sheriffs' deputies fired into the crowd, about 120 people were hospitalized, and a bystander, James Rector, died of gunshot wounds.

Eventually, supporters of People's Park were the losers. The day after the shootings, Governor Reagan called out the National Guard and was reported to have said, "If there has to be a bloodbath, then let's get it over with."

Helicopters sprayed tear gas on the protesters, and the Guard barricaded and occupied the city for several weeks, imposing a curfew and a ban on public assembly at the park. But mass demonstrations continued. Two weeks after the fence went up, a peaceful group of 30,000 marched to the park, but to no avail — the fence stayed up, and for the moment, active rebellion ended.

Participating in Student Society

The Students for a Democratic Society (SDS) was an organization of student activists founded in 1959, but it was actually an association that evolved out of many older, student political organizations, starting as far back as the early 20th century. When SDS met at a United Auto Workers Conference Center in Ann Arbor, Michigan, in 1962, it adopted the *Port Huron Statement* as its mission statement. SDS was focused on correcting social injustices within the United States and working for world peace. They advocated nonviolent civil disobedience and focused on peaceful efforts to promote the civil rights movement, but in time, as with many other student groups around the country, opposition to the Vietnam War became its primary focus. Although mainstream SDS still opposed violence, they became more confrontational with their nonviolent protests.

The Port Huron Statement condemned "the permeating and victimizing fact of human degradation, symbolized by the Southern struggle against racial bigotry," and "the enclosing fact of the Cold War, symbolized by the presence of the Bomb."

The main author of the Port Huron Statement was Tom Hayden, a former editor of the student newspaper at the University of Michigan. Like Mario Savio, he was born in a working-class Catholic environment. Hayden spent the greater part of 1961 protesting segregation in the South. Later, inspired by Jack Kerouac's beat novel *On the Road,* he hitchhiked across the country and got a firsthand look at was going on at Berkeley.

Hayden, one of the leaders of the New Left, was actively involved in antiwar protests. In 1968, he flew to North Vietnam to protest against the war, and later that year, he was one of the prime movers of the demonstrations at the 1968 Democratic National Convention (see Chapter 9).

In 1973, Hayden married Jane Fonda, the actress and antiwar activist who was known as Hanoi Jane for her 1972 visit to Hanoi. He was one of the few New Lefters who eventually worked within the system. Hayden became a progressive politician, active in California state politics.

Participatory democracy and direct action

One goal of the Port Huron Statement was to change American politics by sweeping away its hierarchical structure and bureaucracy. It called for *participatory democracy* — direct involvement of individuals in the decisions that affected their lives. They believed that with participatory democracy, all the people, rather than just those in power, would control social policy. This idea became a guiding principle of the New Left.

SDS grew dramatically, from fewer than a thousand members in 1962 to at least 50,000 in 1968, due mostly to student opposition to the Vietnam War (which involved many people who previously didn't care about politics). Its largest growth occurred after 1965, when SDS spearheaded an antiwar march on Washington, which attracted more than 15,000. Over the next three years, thousands joined SDS.

SDS's most popular slogan, "Make Love — Not War!" became the rallying cry of the movement.

In 1968, about 40,000 students on nearly a hundred campuses across the country demonstrated against the Vietnam War and against racism. Protest against one cause often morphed into protest against the other. At Columbia University, an antiracist demonstration developed into a huge protest against the war and military research at the university. Students occupied and barricaded the administration building and other campus buildings and set up "revolutionary communes" behind the barricades. (See Chapter 9 for a detailed look at the antiwar movement.) Again, as happened in Berkeley, official overreaction caused a far greater problem. When the police stormed the buildings and brutalized the occupying students, even the moderate majority of students at Columbia joined a boycott of classes, and eventually shut down the university.

Knowing which way the wind blows — the Weathermen

Ultimately, SDS proved that participatory democracy didn't work, even in its own democratic society. The radicals, feeling that a moderate approach didn't accomplish anything, broke away from SDS. The most well-known SDS splinter group was the Weathermen. Led by Mark Rudd and Bernadette Dohrn, they rejected nonviolence in favor of urban terrorism to call attention to their demands. The Weathermen agreed with more moderate protesters that the Vietnam War was unjust and evil, but they also believed that demonstrations and protest marches did absolutely nothing to change the status quo. However, the war wasn't their only concern. They were militantly anti-imperialist, anti-nuclear, and anticapitalist and believed that they were at the forefront of a worldwide revolution.

The Weathermen chose their name from the verse "You don't need a weatherman to know which way the wind blows" from the Bob Dylan song "Subterranean Homesick Blues."

One of their first major actions was the Days of Rage demonstration in Chicago in October 1969, designed to tear the "pig city" apart. The Weathermen hoped that tens of thousands of people would wage guerilla war in the streets, but fewer than 300 showed up. The demonstrators not only vandalized banks and corporations but also destroyed the property of ordinary working people.

After the Days of Rage, the Weathermen lost any sympathy they had from moderates. They knew that they were acting alone, and that made them even more determined and violent. Although most of them were from comfortable middle-class backgrounds with no knowledge of weapons or violence, they plotted to bomb buildings in major cities and mentally convinced themselves that they could murder in the name of revolution.

Two events transformed the already radical Weathermen into revolutionaries. On December 4, 1969, Chicago police shot to death two Black Panthers, Fred Hampton and Mark Clark. Because the FBI had publicly declared its intention to wipe out the Panthers by the end of the decade, the Weathermen considered that this was the opening act of a war between the government and people of America. These two murders confirmed the Weathermen's belief that violence was necessary to revolutionize society, and they planned bombings against government targets. In March 1970, a bomb that they were building exploded in a townhouse in New York's Greenwich Village.

After the explosion, the Weathermen went underground, creating false identities and moving around the country to avoid detection. Although they continued bombing corporate and military targets, the Weathermen did everything possible to avoid death or injury as a result of their bombings by phoning in warnings to evacuate the targeted buildings.

At the height of the Weather Underground, members were determined to abandon all the bourgeoisie standards and comforts. They lived communally, often in old or condemned buildings, opposed monogamy, and experimented with drugs and casual sex.

The Weather Underground was fairly successful at avoiding arrest, but by the late '70s, the group began dissolving. With the exception of Kathy Boudin (who spent more than 20 years in prison for participating in the 1981 Brinks robbery, during which an employee was killed), most Weathermen who were caught or surrendered rarely served long prison sentences.

Chapter 12

I Am Woman: From the Frying Pan into the Fire

In This Chapter

▶ Bringing women's rights to Capitol Hill

▶ Drawing out the woman within

▶ Joining voices to create a chorus of protest

▶ Resorting to more militant measures

▶ Having sex without the stress

▶ Facing the reaction

When the 1960s began, a woman's place was in the home, or so it seemed. Middle-class women appeared happy tending to their suburban homes, raising their children, coddling their husbands, and creating mouth-watering casseroles. They were convinced that they had fulfilled their greatest dreams, or at least the goals that their families — and society as a whole — had for them. Younger women went to college to earn their coveted MRS or PHT (putting hubby through) degrees (and a major in education "just in case").

However, as the '60s progressed, women's lives began to change, and by the end of the decade, feminism was a powerful movement. The publication of a landmark work, *The Feminine Mystique* by Betty Friedan; the participation of young women in the civil rights and antiwar movements; and the introduction of a new birth control method, "the Pill," combined with other factors made women question their place in this land of the free.

The push for gender equality that began in the '60s wasn't the first women's movement. In the late 19th and early 20th centuries, women fought for the right to vote. Their long struggle culminated with the ratification of the 19th Amendment to the Constitution in 1920, which extended the vote to women. With the right to vote, women felt empowered and became more independent — they entered the work force, opted for more comfortable and revealing fashions, and adopted some of the more questionable rights of men — such as smoking and drinking in public.

In the beginning, this "second wave" of feminism, as it has become known, began in earnest in the mid-'60s with the establishment of the National Organization for Women (NOW), which tried to accomplish its goals through conventional legislative means. By the end of the decade, however, more radical feminists brought the methods of protest that they learned in the civil rights and antiwar movements to the fight for women's rights — they marched, they held sit-ins, they challenged conventional ideas about their roles in society, and they adopted a view that personal choices can be political statements.

Although many of the efforts, events, and results that were associated with the women's movement and substantially changed gender relations in the United States occurred in later decades, the far-reaching effects wouldn't have been possible had women not taken the first steps in the 1960s.

Exposing the Feminine Mystique

Although the beginning of the '60s showcased women in frilly white aprons, spatula in hand and crying child on hip, females hadn't been in such a role forever. During World War II (1941–45), women left the sphere of house and home and adopted what had been considered male roles in society. They worked in factories and kept America running as the country's young men headed off to war. The famous image of Rosie the Riveter comes from this period. Other women joined the armed forces, and although they didn't have combat roles, they made great contributions to the war effort as nurses, motor mechanics, weather forecasters, air traffic controllers, and radio/telephone operators. However, when the war ended and the GIs returned home, many women were forced to leave their jobs to make room for the returning soldiers.

Fast forward a few years to the 1950s, when the World War II veterans, many of whom had been to college on the GI Bill, were earning good salaries. To accommodate these upwardly mobile families, suburban housing developments were springing up to provide safe and affordable housing. Middle-class white women, lured by white picket fences, new laborsaving appliances, advertising and marketing messages, and the ideals presented on television adopted the roles of mother, helpmate, and homemaker to the exclusion of almost everything else. In fact, this view of the proper role of middle-class women in society became so pervasive that a woman choosing to remain single or to successfully pursue a career was looked on as either a pathetic spinster or a cold dragon lady.

The idyllic script for women's roles in society, of course, didn't apply to all women. Working-class and poor women of all races did just what they always did — they worked to survive and provide their families with the necessities. Often the work was backbreaking, demeaning, or mundane, and the pay was much less than a man would receive for the same job. At times, working conditions were brutal and unsafe. Their work was often treated as less than professional, thereby justifying the employers' desire to pay low wages and offer few benefits. For example, in the 1950s, black women often worked as cleaning ladies for more well-to-do families. Though the work was difficult and demanding, the families they worked for didn't even have to provide social security contributions for them.

Early in the '60s, suburban white middle-class women supposedly had it all. They didn't have to work, had lovely homes, beautiful children, attentive husbands, new cars, and an increasingly prosperous lifestyle. But even though life seemed heavenly, underneath it all, many of these women had vague feelings of uneasiness and boredom. They couldn't quite put their finger on it, but they had a sense that life must have more to offer than marriage, babies, and a well-ordered house. Many of these women were also well educated and somehow felt vaguely guilty that they'd abandoned their ideals and wasted their educations pursuing a life that would reach no further than the kitchen or the laundry room. They became resentful of the mind-numbing boredom of their daily routines. But how could they complain? They had everything they ever wanted.

In 1963 Betty Friedan put those unspoken feelings in print with the publication of her book *The Feminine Mystique,* bringing to light the dark side of the domestic dream. After the book hit shelves nationwide, nothing was ever the same. According to Friedan, the *feminine mystique* was the mistaken theory that marriage, homemaking, and childbearing were the ways that women could fulfill themselves. She contended that the media and advertising were the creators and purveyors of that vision as a way of maintaining demand for consumer goods. (Check out the sidebar "The mother of the movement" in this chapter for more on Friedan's background and how she decided to write about this issue.)

In preparation for her revitalizing work, Friedan interviewed thousands of women, giving them the opportunity to say what they really felt about their lives. They reported that although they were happy with their families and felt that they'd achieved everything they ever wanted, something was missing. After talking to those women and hearing the same feelings expressed over and over again, Friedan had a title for the book's first chapter: "The Problem that Has No Name."

After the book was published, millions of other women recognized themselves in its pages. They remembered who they were in college and in their short-lived careers and wondered where their bright, stimulated, and interesting selves had gone. *The Feminine Mystique* led women to examine their lives, and the results changed American society. When women reconnected with their less domesticated selves and demanded gender equality in the family, workplace, and government, they instigated social changes that continued into the next millennium.

The mother of the movement

Betty Friedan graduated in 1942 from Smith College with a degree in psychology and did graduate work at the University of California at Berkeley. She worked as a journalist for several years and married in 1947. After her children were born, she worked as a freelance writer for a number of magazines while living the typical life of a suburban wife and mother. Although her life was "ideal," she was somewhat bored and dissatisfied and wondered whether other women felt the same. In 1957, she sent a questionnaire to her Smith classmates to see what their lives had been like since graduation.

Friedan was no stranger to opposing conventional views. While at Smith and Berkeley, she was active in Socialist and Communist organizations. After graduation, while working as a journalist, she mainly wrote for left-wing publications, promoting labor unions and denouncing poor working conditions for women.

The results of her survey showed that many of her classmates felt the same say she did. Friedan became so interested in women's lives that she developed more detailed questionnaires, conducted personal interviews, and discussed her results with psychologists and other professionals. When she submitted her work to three separate women's magazines, they all turned her down because her ideas contradicted conventional thinking about the roles of women (and probably would've angered their advertisers as well). Over the next five years, Friedan organized, compiled, and expanded her research, and in 1963, she published *The Feminine Mystique*. The book quickly became a bestseller with more than a million copies sold and sparked a nationwide debate over the role of women in society.

However, the concerns of working-class and African American women were largely absent from Friedan's work. Idle women, bored in their suburban homes, didn't often fit the reality that these women experienced.

Looking to the Government with Mixed Results

In the early '60s, the federal government took steps to evaluate and eliminate sexual discrimination, particularly in the areas of employment. However, in spite of commissions and legislation, women's employment opportunities and pay lagged behind that of men.

Establishing a commission and legislating equal pay

Even at the beginning of the 1960s, before the second wave of feminism began, the wheels were already in motion to eliminate gender inequality. In 1961, Esther Peterson, the highest-ranking woman in President John F. Kennedy's government as the assistant secretary of labor for women's affairs, recommended that the president create a commission to study discrimination against women and ways to eliminate it. That same year, Kennedy established the President's Commission on the Status of Women.

The commission's 26 members were politically and professionally diverse and included educators, writers, leaders of women's organizations, union leaders, cabinet secretaries, and members of Congress. Under Kennedy's orders, federal departments and agencies provided the commission with the information it needed.

Eleanor Roosevelt, the former first lady, chaired the bipartisan President's Commission on the Status of Women.

The commission's main focus was recommending ways to eliminate discrimination and suggesting legislation and services that would help women to achieve equality. The group achieved some important objectives:

- ✔ An executive order requiring equal employment opportunities for women in companies working under federal contracts

- ✔ Recommendations for changes in state laws that excluded women from

    - Jury duty

    - Owning property or a business

    - Legal control of their earnings

In the early 1960s, a married woman's status was largely determined by what state she lived in. In some states, women could own property, start and run a business, and have complete power to manage their finances. But in other states, married women couldn't make contracts, buy or sell property, manage their money, or make wills without approval from their husbands.

- ✔ A commission on the status of women in every state in the union

- ✔ Recommendations on issues concerning the availability of affordable day care, access to education, and wages

But by far the most important of these changes was the Equal Pay Act that President Kennedy signed in 1963. This legislation made it illegal to pay women less than men based on sex and put enforcement under the supervision of the Equal Employment Opportunity Commission (EEOC). Although the Equal Pay Act made it illegal for employers to pay less for the same work based on gender, they could still pay different wages based on experience, seniority, education, or merit. These differences, though valid for determining pay, also provided loopholes that made proving gender discrimination difficult.

The job interview

Even after the president's commission dissolved in 1963, job discrimination continued. In the mid-'60s, as young college graduates entered the professional job market, employers had a not-so-subtle way to avoid hiring them.

One woman, married for two years, was looking for a job in the computer industry, then in its infancy. Either directly or indirectly, she was often asked about her plans for children. Of course, the young woman knew that if they asked the question, they already had their own answer. Eventually, she was hired by a company with a huge turnover problem, so it didn't matter if she left after six months. But she stayed for six years. To manage the problem of employers questioning their personal lives, many engaged and married women left their wedding and engagement rings at home.

At the time Kennedy signed the Equal Pay Act in 1963, women's average income was far lower than men's, even for the same work. Management justified this discrepancy because historically, most women worked for a few years and then left their jobs to raise children. Therefore, employers were unwilling to invest time in training and developing women for high-level careers. They preferred to employ women in lower paying occupations and usually didn't want to promote them out of the secretarial pool. The conventional wisdom was that women didn't "need" the money — some day, they'd have a man to take care of them. So as the rationalization went, when a woman held a high-paying job, she was taking the position away from a man who needed the money to support his family.

Even today, women earn less than men in the same jobs. Sadly, in 2003 women earned only 75.5 cents to every dollar that men earned.

Including women in the Civil Rights Act of 1964

The Civil Rights Act of 1964 was mainly enacted to address the issues of racial inequality that were raised by the civil rights movement (see Chapter 6). Some of its provisions, however, affected women in that they protected the voting rights of all citizens and prohibited discrimination in education, public facilities, and federally assisted programs. The Civil Rights Act also provided for equal employment opportunities regardless of race, color, religion, sex, or national origin.

Coming Together to Build a Movement

Commissions not withstanding, women were on the move, but they soon realized that they couldn't do it alone. As women left the home and entered the outside world, they became more aware that the legal and social structure worked against them. They were confronted with discrimination in the workplace, education, government, and the military. A number of factors came together and lit the spark for women's movement in the mid-1960s:

- **More women encountering workplace obstacles:** Through the fifties and sixties, more women were entering the workplace. Therefore, more women were exposed to related discrimination and restrictions. In 1950, about 31 percent of women were in the workforce; in 1960, about 35 percent were working; but by 1970, 42 percent of women worked outside the home.

- **Expanding minds in college:** By the early 1960s, there were already large numbers of women in college, and the numbers were growing. Throughout the decade, then, more women were exposed to both higher education and the accompanying professional expectations. Also, more women gained exposure to the civil rights and student movements of the time (see the "Getting Radical" section later in the chapter).

Organizing to take a stand — NOW

By 1966, frustrated that laws didn't change minds, women became more politically active. Some women decided that they needed to take their destinies into their own hands, so they formed the National Organization for Women (NOW) in order to take action on issues that were important to women. The organization was largely made up of educated, professional women who knew how to work inside the system in order to create change. Friedan, author of *The Feminine Mystique*, was one of the 30 original co-founders of NOW and was its first president. In the beginning, the organization's main focus was ending discrimination and unequal pay in the workplace. However, their original statement of purpose also included other issues that were (and still are) important to women, such as

- Full civil rights for women

- Increased role in government

- Equal educational opportunities

- Society's recognition of the value of homemaking and childcare

- Improving popular images of women in the media

In the here and NOW

Over the years, NOW has become one of the most important forces of change for women in the United States, taking advantage of establishment methods such as lawsuits, lobbying, and political action committees (PACs). Although NOW still prefers these traditional methods today, it doesn't shy away from more confrontational ways to get its message across. Although some members of NOW said that protest marches, rallies, pickets, and nonviolent civil disobedience were very '60s and passé, NOW doesn't hesitate to support, and in some cases even organize, huge (and widely attended) demonstrations. NOW organized the following protests:

✔ **1978:** A march on Washington to support the Equal Rights Amendment.

✔ **1986, 1989, and 1992:** March for Women's Lives in Washington, D.C., to support reproductive rights.

✔ **1995:** Mass demonstration in Washington, D.C., to fight violence against women.

✔ **1996:** A March to Fight the Right in San Francisco, focused on affirmative action.

✔ **2004:** A March for Women's Lives at the National Mall in Washington, D.C., was the largest demonstration (more than 1.15 million) supporting reproductive rights in U.S. history.

At the time of this writing, NOW has 500,000 contributing members in 550 chapters in all 50 states and the District of Columbia.

Reflecting the professional status of its members, who were accustomed to working in corporations and functioning in committees, NOW was organized along traditional lines. It had elected, salaried officers, established local dues-paying chapters, and held national conferences. To create change, NOW lobbied legislatures, signed petitions, and filed discrimination lawsuits.

The women's movement during the '60s was largely white — black women were divided on which was more harmful for them, racism or sexism, and many felt that equality for black men was more important than women's rights.

Making waves for working women

As the women's movement grew, the needs of working women became a priority for NOW. Because many mothers had to work, the availability of subsidized day care and early childhood education was important.

Although NOW was focused on equal employment opportunities for women, they also recognized that workers in traditionally female occupations, such as secretaries, waitresses, domestic workers, hospital workers, and flight attendants, needed to take action for fair working conditions. Another key focus was helping women enter traditionally male occupations, such as construction and law enforcement. The fact that certain jobs were considered men's jobs and others were considered women's work was reflected in employment want ads, which, in the early 1960s, were often divided into "Help Wanted Male" and "Help Wanted Female."

Change didn't happen overnight. Slowly, women acknowledged their feelings and began to think about how to improve their lives, which wasn't easy at first. They faced enormous resistance from husbands and children, who resented having their full-time wives and mothers busy with other pursuits. In fact, as late as 1969, a woman wanting to continue her career after having children, unless she absolutely needed the money to survive, was often looked on as a bad mother and a selfish woman who shouldn't have had children in the first place. Women also fought enormous feelings of guilt, as "experts" blamed working mothers for everything from their childrens' poor grades to unhappy husbands and juvenile delinquents. But many women persisted and resisted, going back to school and entering the workplace.

Determined to enhance their lives, many middle-class women went to law school or medical school or earned MBAs. They became social activists, working for peace, racial equality, and better schools for their children. They fought for equal pay with men and for new opportunities for their daughters in academics and sports.

A brief history of the Equal Rights Amendment

Though many people believe that the Equal Rights Amendment (ERA), prohibiting sex discrimination, was a recent development, Alice Paul introduced the constitutional amendment, named the "Lucretia Mott Amendment" in 1923, stipulating that men and women should be treated equally. At that time, opposition to the amendment was mainly based on labor laws that were designed to protect women and children.

The women's movement of the 1960s revived interest in the ERA, which was supported by organized labor and other mainstream groups. In 1972, Congress passed the amendment, but only 35 states ratified the ERA (38 were required to pass the amendment.) As the 1979 deadline for ratification approached, NOW lobbied for a three-year extension, which Congress granted, but the amendment still didn't pass. The Equal Rights Amendment was reintroduced in Congress in 1982 and has been introduced in every session of Congress since then.

Getting Radical

As the women's movement progressed, some women felt that changes weren't happening fast enough. NOW seemed too slow and conservative for some. Much of their dissatisfaction arose during the late '60s as an outgrowth of women's participation in the civil rights, free speech, and antiwar movements. While working with the associated groups, women came to distrust working within the "establishment" (through courts or legislation) and also learned methods of nonviolent protest and gained experience organizing rallies. This experience would serve them well through the 1960s and beyond when fighting for economic equality and reproductive rights.

In spite of their contributions, however, women who participated in these social and political movements realized that although they were on the front lines, often being arrested and sometimes beaten along with the men, they were still regarded as peripheral and were disregarded when important decisions were being made. They felt that they were still treated as second-class citizens by their male comrades-in-arms, often relegated to fetching coffee and making copies while men did the "important" work. It was obvious that the men of the New Left and sectors of the civil rights movement believed, quite literally, in the proclamation, "All *men* are created equal."

As much as women contributed to the civil rights and antiwar movements, a flippant remark by Stokely Carmichael, chairman of the Student Nonviolent Coordinating Committee (SNCC), expressed some of the rampant sexism of the times. When asked about the role of women in the SNCC, he said, "The position of women in SNCC is prone."

One concept that women took away from their years in the civil rights movement was that "the personal is political," which means that their personal lives reflected not only their own decisions but were highly influenced by society and the political climate. As a result of this realization, radical feminists worked toward overthrowing some of the institutions that they felt were oppressive, forgoing NOW's view that women could achieve equality by bringing lawsuits, and lobbying for legislation.

In their approach to protesting existing political and social structures, radical feminists tended to be more outspoken than the conventional activists relying on petitions and lawsuits. They staged sit-ins and poetry readings, sang songs, and performed street theater to publicize their concerns. These women also publicly spoke about their private lives, revealing information about their sexual preferences and activities. Some even went public about their illegal abortions. Although such actions turned off many traditionalists, they effectively brought feminism to the front of public consciousness.

HISTORIC TRIVIA

The roots of PC vocabulary

Although promoting gender-neutral language wasn't one of the top priorities of the women's movement, their emphasis on workplace equality eventually gave rise to new terms in the decades that followed, such as

✔ Flight attendants instead of stewardesses

✔ Ms. instead of Miss or Mrs.

✔ Police officer instead of policeman

✔ Chair instead of chairman

✔ Mail carrier instead of postman

REMEMBER

Radical feminism also changed the common language, bringing new terms such as "sexism," "Ms.," and "male chauvinist" (with or without pig) into common usage. However, these candid tactics also created a vocal anti-feminist backlash (see the "Facing a Backlash: Men and Women Fight Back" section later in this chapter). Radical feminists criticized the ideals of femininity that were portrayed in the media, believing that they were degrading to women, and also protested that women were regarded for their looks alone, rather than for their accomplishments. They were suspicious of marriage, believing that it was just a form of involuntary servitude, and some envisioned a society almost completely without men. As part of this feminist ideal, they felt that lesbianism was just as valid as a heterosexual partnership.

Bringing the movement to the national stage: Miss America 1968

In the late '60s, some feminists began to publicly question the standards of beauty and femininity, the widely held view that women were the weaker sex, and women's own views of themselves. One of the more radical feminist views during the '60s was that society treated women like objects. They thought that beauty pageants, such as the Miss America Pageant, were a glorification of physical beauty as defined and idealized by men. With this idea in mind, many feminists organized protest demonstrations to get their message across. In 1968, a group of feminists picketed the Miss America Pageant to protest its emphasis on physical beauty as the most important feminine quality — Figure 12-1 shows the demonstration.

As part of the protest, women threw girdles, cosmetics, high-heeled shoes, and bras into a trashcan to point out the artificial standards of beauty. They also mocked the pageant itself by crowning a goat with a tiara, and some of them would speak only to female reporters. The press, however, decided to enhance the drama. Using photos of bras hurled into a trashcan, they established a myth that women stripped to the waist and tossed their bras into a bonfire. Although the burning bra was a manufactured image, the idea behind the myth had some truth to it. Radical feminists rejected the common standards of beauty by going braless, refusing to shave their legs and underarms, giving up makeup, and not wearing provocative or uncomfortable clothing, such as high-heeled shoes. For these women, the bra, as well as the tiara, were symbols of the "old regime." And quite quickly, the burning bra became the public symbol of radical feminism.

Figure 12-1: Feminists rise up against the 1968 Miss America Pageant.

One of the most important results of this demonstration — nationwide awareness — came about thanks to the media coverage. Although much of it was negative and played on the most outrageous aspects of the demonstration (also featuring women that the press considered unattractive), it made people aware of women's lib.

HISTORIC TRIVIA

The term *women's liberation* was first used in March 1968 in a feminist newsletter; it was later abbreviated to women's lib.

The idea that women weren't sex objects had some far-reaching effects. As women became more common and powerful in the workplace, they refused to be pressured for sexual favors, sometimes at the expense of their jobs. Eventually, sexual harassment legislation was passed in almost every state, making it illegal to make unwanted sexual advances toward women.

Raising consciousness

To help women become more aware of their own feelings and enhance their relationship to other women, consciousness-raising groups sprang up all over the United States. At first, they were mostly a vehicle for exploring "the problem that has no name." Meeting and talking with other women made women realize that they weren't quite so alone in feeling isolated and overwhelmed.

However, as consciousness raising began to spread beyond the middle-class suburbs, other issues emerged, such as the uneasy feelings that women experienced when men made rude remarks on the street, either critiquing their bodies or making unwanted sexual advances. They began to examine their feelings about their bodies and their sexuality. By talking together, women also began to realize that they weren't valued for their minds or abilities. Further, beautiful women were presumed to be stupid, and intelligent women were found unattractive.

Women on the small screen

As the 1960s began, viewers were still watching the ideal American family on TV — mom, dad, a couple of kids, probably a dog, and a house with a white picket fence. Sitcoms reflected the "typical" white, middle-class American family.

Some of these shows are actually regarded as '50s icons — *Ozzie and Harriet*, *Leave It to Beaver*, and *Father Knows Best* are often nostalgically considered great examples of "the good old days," when mom was waiting at home with milk and cookies for the kids and a martini for her husband. In fact, Donna Reed was held up as the perfect example of American womanhood (although she never mopped her floors in high heels and pearls — this was just an urban legend). Even *Bewitched,* a sitcom infused with magic, showed a happy housewife willing to largely ignore her gifts to please her successful wage-earning husband.

With the women's movement in the works, could new roles for women be far behind? On *The Dick Van Dyke Show* (1961 to 1966), Rob Petrie was actually shown fixing a meal. Even though Laura, played by the up-and-coming Mary Tyler Moore, was a stay-at-home mom, she clearly had a mind of her own and mostly wore Capri pants (a refreshing change from the mid-calf-length skirts of days past). Sally, Rob's co-worker, was a single career woman (although part of the shtick was that she was always on the lookout for an eligible man).

Julia, starring Diahann Carroll, which ran from 1968 to 1971, was a groundbreaking show on two fronts. She was not only a single professional mom (albeit one who lost her husband in Vietnam) but also an African American in a leading role. *That Girl,* starring Marlo Thomas, was another first. In the show, which ran from 1966 to 1971, she was a single woman, building a career and loving her life. These shows definitely led the way for the shows of the '70s and beyond, showing career women who lived full lives without husbands and babies.

Perhaps the most influential drama of the '60s was *Star Trek,* which debuted in 1966 and ran until 1969. The show featured men and women of all races and nationalities working together (of course, the captain was a man, but hey — it was still only 1966!). In fact, the crew of the Enterprise spaceship worked in such harmony that Captain Kirk and Lieutenant Uhura had the first interracial kiss on prime-time TV. Although *Star Trek* broke some important boundaries, it reinforced others — all the women aboard the Enterprise wore sexy, tight-fitting, and extremely short dresses.

In the consciousness-raising groups of the '60s, women explored issues that made them reevaluate their lives, asking themselves questions such as

✔ How do you feel about housework and childcare?

✔ Do you like sex? Do you think it's dirty?

✔ Is your work (either inside or outside the home) important?

✔ How do you feel about men? About other women?

✔ Do you like being a wife? A mother?

✔ What do you want to do with your life?

Another outgrowth of these groups was the realization that women could take action in order to fix some of their problems. They began to see that instead of competing with each other, they could unite to solve problems, such as establishing day-care centers, exploring job possibilities, or planning the best strategy for getting their husbands to help with the housework.

In consciousness-raising groups, women also began to study their own history and realized that they had a far larger role in the progress of this country and the world than they had previously believed, in areas of labor, education, literature, and other fields. By the mid-'70s, in response to demands to make curriculum more reflective of society and therefore more relevant, many campuses instituted women's studies programs that not only explored women's issues but also studied and celebrated women's contributions to the arts, the sciences, and government. Even at the elementary and high-school levels, textbooks were rewritten to include a more balanced view of the role of women. Women's studies were part of the same drive that created black studies programs — an effort to recognize the contribution of minorities to American history and culture.

Using the "L" words: Liberation, love, and lesbianism

In looking at the problems of women in society, many feminists determined that Western patriarchal society was the cause of most social problems, such as violence, discrimination, and oppression against women. Some radical feminists came to the conclusion that men weren't just a necessary evil but were, in fact, completely unnecessary.

A popular saying attributed to Gloria Steinem, writer, feminist, and founder of *Ms. Magazine,* goes, "A woman without a man is like a fish without a bicycle."

Another concept that grew out of '60s feminism was free love (actually, this idea wasn't new at all, but feminists rejected the double standard and claimed the same sexual rights that men had). Due to the idea that women could enjoy sex without fearing unwanted pregnancy (see the "Getting It On: The Power of the Pill" section, later in the chapter), there was no reason, other than patriarchal principles, why women couldn't love whomever, whenever, and wherever they pleased.

Along with sleeping with men, women also claimed the right to love other women. In time, the movement's acceptance of lesbianism fed the new gay liberation movement that began at the end of the '60s and is still active today (see Chapter 13). Some radical feminists, however, not only accepted the lesbian lifestyle but also embraced it as a political statement. They felt that any relationship with a man was "sleeping with the enemy" and consciously made the choice to have only lesbian relationships.

In NOW's early years, some leaders were afraid that backing lesbian rights would lose support for feminism, so lesbians were asked to stay in the closet. However, by 1968, Ti-Grace Atkinson, head of the New York City chapter, left the organization to protest its stand on lesbianism, and within a year, others followed. By 1971, NOW changed its position to support lesbian rights and after 1975, made it one of their main priorities to eliminate discrimination against gays and lesbians — currently NOW supports same-sex marriage.

Getting It On: The Power of the Pill

Historically, no matter how educated, hardworking, rich, or poor women were, pregnancy defined their lives. Unplanned pregnancies could interrupt educations, stall careers, and throw economically marginal families into poverty.

A pregnant belly was a visible sign of sex, and in the early '60s, no one talked about "nice" women and sex. Even married women were forced to leave their teaching positions as soon as they began to show, because the clear evidence that they had taken a roll in the hay wasn't considered a good role model for children. For unmarried women, pregnancy meant a shotgun marriage, a back-alley abortion, or a visit to a home for unwed mothers, followed by a hastily arranged adoption. Obviously, then, the greatest deterrent to sex was pregnancy.

As of May 9, 1960, the times began to change. On that date, the U.S. Food and Drug Administration (FDA) approved the use of a female oral contraceptive — called the *Pill*. Taken every day for three weeks followed by a one-week hiatus, the Pill completely stopped ovulation while a woman took it, which eliminated unplanned pregnancies. For the first time, preventing pregnancy was completely under a woman's control.

BC (birth control) BP (before the Pill)

Throughout history, women used a variety of herbs and other substances, some even as potentially lethal as mercury or arsenic, to prevent pregnancy. However, as well as being dangerous, these methods resulted in lots of babies, since choosing the right herb was largely a matter of trial and error. Barrier methods, including various types of condoms, were also widely used throughout history, with varying effectiveness. Although diaphragms were common in the 1950s and early '60s, they were tricky to use, so society saw a lot of "diaphragm babies" in those days.

In the 1920s, birth control became an open topic of conversation (and some heated debate) due to the work of Margaret Sanger, who founded the American birth control movement and, later, Planned Parenthood. She believed that every woman has the right to control her own body, every child has the right to be wanted, and every woman is entitled to sexual pleasure. Through her efforts, many laws that prohibited distribution of birth control information were repealed.

Embracing planned pregnancy

When the Pill was first introduced, it didn't have much of an effect on single women because many doctors refused to prescribe it for them. But eventually it became more accessible, and women realized that if they took the Pill, they could decide to have sex without worrying about an unpleasant surprise a month later — they were free to enjoy their own sexuality.

After the Pill was approved in 1960, women quickly accepted it. In 1963, about 2.3 million American women were on the Pill, Fast-forward to 1967, and 12.5 million women around the world were using it.

With the government approval of the Pill, many women felt that they finally had control of their own bodies. For married women, the decision of whether to use contraception was no longer up to their husbands or subject to error. Single women no longer had to fear becoming pregnant out of wedlock. Suddenly, women — married and single — had the opportunity to plan their own futures. They were able to pursue their careers without worrying about unpleasant surprises. This freedom made them resentful that employers, university admissions, and others discriminated against them because "they'd only get pregnant anyway." Resentment by itself changed nothing, but women used their anger to work for economic equality.

Unleashing female sexuality

In one fell swoop, the Pill separated the physical aspects of birth control from lovemaking. Though both men and women felt the effects, the Pill psychologically helped women enjoy sex more when they could be sure that they wouldn't have unwanted pregnancies.

Many foresaw the "side effect" of the Pill and worried that without the fear of pregnancy, unmarried women would be more promiscuous — and in many ways, they were right. As more women took advantage of the freedom that effective contraception gave them, even respectable unmarried women were open about having sex, and in time, female sexuality lost the negative connotation it once had. Eventually, this new freedom gave rise to unmarried couples living together, later marriages, no-fault divorce, and single parenthood by choice, concepts that are quite commonplace today but were virtually unknown in 1960.

Sexuality was so under the covers in the late '50s and early '60s that TV characters, such as Ricky and Lucy Ricardo of *I Love Lucy* and Rob and Laura Petrie of *The Dick Van Dyke Show,* slept in separate beds.

The Pill helped usher in the sexual revolution, a significant change in sexual morality and behavior. Before then, some commonly held views included:

- ✔ Sex shouldn't be talked about openly.
- ✔ Women didn't enjoy sex as much as men.
- ✔ Premarital sex was okay for men but not for women.

Although the sexual revolution wasn't in full swing until the '70s, women's awareness of their sexuality, the availability of effective contraceptives, and the notions of personal freedom embraced by the hippies and the New Left encouraged people to explore new lifestyles. Also, censorship against sexually explicit material in books, films, and magazines was gradually easing (see Chapter 16). This revolution, which continued into the next millennium, was as much a willingness to flout convention and be open about sex as it was about having more premarital sex.

In all actuality, the Pill was simply the proverbial straw that broke the camel's back of the old view of women's sexuality. In 1953, Alfred Kinsey published his book *Sexual Behavior in the Human Female,* which scandalized America and made news all over the world. By interviewing thousands of women, Kinsey learned that one in four wives commit adultery and that half of all women have premarital sex. But the most shocking thing about the Kinsey Report wasn't just what women said but what they implied — that women could, and in many cases did, enjoy sex as much as men. In 1966, *Human Sexual Response* by William Masters and Virginia Johnson was published, which talked about sexual arousal, orgasm, and masturbation. This book confirmed what Kinsey had said — sexual pleasure was possible and important for both men and women.

Fighting to extend women's rights to abortion

Abortion didn't become a federally protected right for women until 1973, with the *Roe v. Wade* decision. In the 1960s, the procedure was still illegal in many parts of the country, although in some states women could get abortions if the mother's life was in jeopardy. If a woman had the right connections (and enough money), she might even get a sympathetic doctor to certify that she was indeed in danger.

Another option was to travel abroad or to one of the 17 states where abortion was legal. The problem was that these options were only open to wealthy or middle-class women; the poor either had their unwanted babies or attempted back-alley abortions, sometimes with lethal results. For many women, the right to abortion was a life-and-death issue. Before abortion was legalized, estimates were that 500 to 1,000 women a year died from back-alley abortions.

NOW and other feminists of the 1960s supported legal abortion as another viable method of birth control. From 1969 to 1970, women mounted massive demonstrations to demand the end to anti-abortion laws.

Banning birth control: The Catholic Church weighs in

Even before the Pill, the Catholic Church opposed any artificial birth control, endorsing the rhythm method as the only acceptable way to practice pregnancy prevention. In fact, one often-told joke had some accidental babies being named "Rhythm." During the '60s, the Pill gained widespread acceptance as a reliable method of contraception, even among Catholics. To stem this rebellion, in 1968, Pope Paul VI issued an encyclical entitled *Humanae Vitae* (Of Human Life), which reaffirmed the church's stance on artificial birth control, calling it a mortal sin. This ruling divided the church, causing many Catholics to use their own conscience instead of church dogma on the issue of family planning. By 1970, two-thirds of Catholic women were using contraceptives, and 28 percent of them were on the Pill.

Although issued by the pope, the *Humanae Vitae* encyclical ignored the recommendations of the Papal Commission on Birth Control. In 1966, the commission issued its report, which advocated that sexuality was part of marriage itself and not necessarily tied to procreation. They also recommended that a husband and wife should be able to choose any suitable method of family planning except abortion.

Nothing expressed the conflict within the church as much as the fact that Dr. John Rock, the Pill's codeveloper, was a devout Catholic and a father of four. In his view, the Pill was an acceptable and natural method of birth control because it didn't use a physical preventative, such as a condom or diaphragm.

Facing a Backlash: Men and Women Fight Back

Any movement as far-reaching as women's liberation was sure to create a backlash. Many men were threatened by more independent wives at home and more competition in the workplace. They became particularly vocal when the movement became more radical by embracing lesbianism and the idea that traditional marriage was really an example of indentured servitude.

The more radical aspects of the movement also engendered some mean-spirited mockery and focused on women's opposition to being treated as sex objects. This outspokenness was often interpreted as ugly women's jealousy of pretty ones and of the fact that the best opportunities for upward mobility (such as rich men) often went to beautiful women. Opponents of feminism glorified the fact that real women, feminine women, delighted in dressing and acting to attract and please men. Regarding the wolf whistles and catcalls, these conservatives said women should appreciate that men found them attractive.

Many women agreed with these views, and in time, a women's antiliberation movement arose, which advised women to be subservient to men and dress in sexy lingerie when their husbands came home from work (obviously, these women didn't work outside the home). Many women were also threatened by the feminist movement, fearing that their husbands would no longer have to support their families and that they would be forced into the workplace. Later, they fought against the Equal Rights Amendment, fearing that it would place women on the front lines of the military and result in unisex bathrooms — their worst fears were realized. And up until the current day, one of the largest issues of contention is abortion and reproductive rights.

Some of the backlash was also aimed at what traditionalists claimed was feminists' hatred of men, stressing that men were the real victims, ridiculed in the comics and on TV as stupid and ineffective, while they bore the brunt of supporting the family, being bound to jobs for the majority of their adult lives.

Another cause for resentment was what many felt was the erosion of the family. The counteraction was widely embraced by religious fundamentalists, who strongly believed in rigid biblical gender roles and opposed sex outside of marriage. Along with political conservatives, they fought birth control and abortion and worked to defeat federal and state funding for sex education and other progressive programs.

Leaving a Legacy

Many results of the women's movement of the 1960s, including federal guidelines against coercive sterilization and laws that encourage more women to report rape, domestic violence, and child abuse, weren't realized until several years later. Other results cropped up later as well, including

- ✔ **The legalization of abortion:** One of the most hotly debated issues during the late '60s was the legalization of abortion — the *Roe v. Wade* decision of 1973, which protected abortion as an outgrowth of the right of every citizen to privacy, is still a political hot potato today.

- ✔ **The crackdown on discrimination:** Although the Equal Rights Amendment, which addressed equal civil rights for women, failed to pass Congress in 1982, many of the provisions of that amendment have become law. The government enacted affirmative action programs to correct gender and race discrimination, and although unequal pay for equal work is still a problem, it's no longer legal.

- ✔ **The rise in educational opportunities:** Because of feminist activism, society has seen great changes in education to promote equal opportunities for girls. As a result, today great numbers of women are active in the medical, legal, business, and academic arenas.

- ✔ **The support for women's sports:** Even sports were affected by the women's movement. In 1972, Title IX mandated equal funding for girls' sports programs in any school receiving federal funds.

- ✔ **More balanced parental roles:** Today, men are much more involved in family life (although nowhere near being *equal* partners in the daily work of homemaking and childcare). In 2005, you can see fathers changing diapers, preparing meals, and (gasp!) even driving carpools to soccer practice.

Although the women's movement spawned many positive changes for women and society, it also caused a spike in the divorce rate. As soon as women were no longer economically dependent on their husbands, they were freer to leave unsatisfactory marriages. This financial independence also meant that divorced women didn't feel compelled to remarry just to support themselves and their children. Eventually, alimony laws changed as well, because the courts determined that not all women needed their ex-husbands' support, and men even began receiving alimony in some situations.

Chapter 13

Protesting for Equality and Pushing for Change

In This Chapter

▶ Striking for the farmworkers: Latinos on the march

▶ Reclaiming Native American soil

▶ Showing gay pride

▶ Balancing the political scale: The conservatives react

Although the civil rights and antiwar movements were at the forefront of the fight for economic, social, and political change during the 1960s, other individuals and groups mobilized against the status quo, pressing for more rights and freedom on their terms. Buoyed by the efforts and successes of other groups, Latinos, Native Americans, and homosexuals refused to be ignored by the rest of America. Although these movements didn't reach their heights until the 1970s, their roots are firmly planted in the fertile soil of the 1960s and the powerful prevailing mood that encouraged people across the United States to believe that change was possible.

Of course, those who longed for the good-old days couldn't understand and refused to tolerate the revolution all around them. They united as well; the conservatives and the *silent majority* (Americans who, even during a tumultuous time, didn't protest and largely thought things were okay the way they were) also had their say during the '60s.

¡Sí, Se Puede! Cesar Chavez and Latino Activism

During the 1960s, under the leadership and inspiration of Mexican American labor activist and leader of the United Farm Workers, Cesar Chavez (see Figure 13-1), Latinos united to claim the right to equality and dignity. *Si, se puede* — yes, you can — became the catchphrase for the times.

Figure 13-1:
Cesar
Chavez, one
of the most
influential
Latino
leaders in
the U.S.

©Jason Laure/The Image Works

Although Latinos represented a substantial segment of the American population, especially in the western states, they often occupied the lowest rungs of society. They were maids, dishwashers, nannies, and gardeners, but most often they were migrant field workers, traveling from one place to another planting and harvesting the fruits and vegetables that fed America. They were paid substandard wages and were often exploited by their bosses, but they felt powerless to change their lot. However, inspired by the successes of the civil rights movement and led by Chavez, Latinos found their voice and began to demand fair treatment.

Moving from the fields to the picket line

Cesar Chavez, one of the most important Latino leaders in U.S. history, grew up knowing injustice. Born in 1927 near Yuma, Arizona, Chavez and his family were swindled out of their home by unscrupulous Anglos. In 1938, they moved to California, where the entire family worked the fields of the state before settling in the *Sal Si Puedes* (Get Out if You Can) barrio in San Jose, California. As a child, Chavez disliked school, because his English was poor and he was forbidden to speak Spanish in class. He also didn't see how a formal education related to the life of a migrant worker, so he left school after the eighth grade.

Despite his early educational experience, Chavez believed later in life that education provided a way for Latinos to get out of the fields and into mainstream American life. He educated himself by becoming an avid reader of everything from biography to philosophy and believed in using education to further the cause of humanity. One of Chavez's most famous quotes was, "The end of all education should surely be service to others."

After serving in the U.S. Navy during World War II from 1944–45, Chavez married Helen Fabela and settled in San Jose, California, in 1948 to raise his family. Both Cesar and Helen were interested in bettering the lives of farmworkers. Believing that Mexicans would be more willing to fight for their rights if they became American citizens, they taught the farmworkers how to read and write.

Influenced by Father Donald McDonnell and Fred Ross, community activists and organizers, Chavez learned about organizing strikes and nonviolent protests and realized that he could use this new knowledge to help his people. In 1952, Chavez joined the Community Service Organization (CSO), a Latino civil rights group that worked to register Mexican Americans to vote and also to fight discrimination. Eventually, he became the national director of the CSO and remained with the organization until 1962. Although he had successes in registering voters, getting farmworkers to stand up for their rights was a tough task — they were always afraid of losing their jobs.

Before they unionized, agricultural workers barely earned a subsistence wage. Perhaps even worse, their working and living conditions were deplorable. Many of the farmworkers were migrant workers, who moved to follow the crops — after they harvested the crop in one location, they moved somewhere else to work another crop. Usually, migrants lived in camps with primitive living conditions — a lack of clean facilities, poor (if any) schools for their children, and no medical care. Although some migrants were illegal aliens, many were citizens. But regardless of their status, it was difficult to organize migrant workers in protest, first because they were on the move, but just as importantly because no matter how rough their lives got, migrants were unwilling to rock the boat and possibly lose the only jobs they had.

Brandishing the boycott

In 1962, Chavez founded the National Farm Workers Association (NFWA), the first farmworkers' union in the United States. At first, the union struggled to stay alive, because most migrant workers could barely put food on the table, much less pay union dues. However, Chavez persevered, organizing the farmworkers to fight for better working conditions and a living wage as well as bringing the problems of farmworkers to the public.

In 1965, the NFWA supported the Agricultural Workers Organizing Committee (AWOC), a Filipino farmworkers union, in a strike against grape growers. In March 1966, together with Dolores Huerta, another labor organizer, Chavez planned and led a march from Delano, California, to Sacramento to press for state laws allowing farmworkers to unionize and engage in collective bargaining. By the time they arrived in Sacramento, Schenley, one of the largest growers, signed an agreement allowing farmworkers to engage in collective bargaining. On August 22, 1966, the NFWA and AWOC merged to become the United Farm Workers (UFW), with the support of the American Federation of Labor–Congress of Industrial Organizations (AFL-CIO).

One target of the UFW was the grape industry because labor conditions were particularly bad for workers in the vineyards and because grapes were a popular consumer product. The first grape boycott, which started in 1967 and lasted until 1971, encouraged people not to buy table grapes. The boycott gained the support of prominent labor leaders and unions, such as the United Auto Workers. In 1970, the UFW signed its first contract with a major grape grower.

Throughout the sixties, the farmworkers continued pressing for fair treatment, using nonviolent methods including boycotts, pickets, and strikes. Chavez was greatly influenced by Mahatma Gandhi's strategy of passive resistance. Among many other things, Gandhi is famous for his long March to the Sea, which protested the British laws that prevented Indians from producing salt. Although the march didn't result in an immediate repeal of the laws, it was a model for civil rights marches, as well as the farmworkers' march from Delano to Sacramento. Like Gandhi, Chavez also went on hunger strikes, bringing attention to the harsh lives of the farmworkers and showing his people that they didn't need to resort to violence to achieve their goals. In 1968, he went on his first hunger strike, living on only water for 25 days.

Senator Bobby Kennedy was sympathetic to the farmworkers' cause and called for fair treatment for Hispanic agricultural workers. In 1968, Kennedy joined Chavez at a mass that ended his hunger strike, calling Chavez "one of the heroic figures of our time."

For the rest of his life, Chavez worked to improve the lives of farmworkers, insisting that growers live up to and improve agreements with the union. Chavez and the UFW organized strikes and boycotts against grape and lettuce growers whenever contracts were violated and continually pressed for better wages and working conditions for farmworkers. Chavez died on April 23, 1993, and almost 40,000 mourners marched behind the casket.

By using nonviolent methods of protest, Chavez and the UFW were able to organize tens of thousands of farmworkers and negotiate contracts giving them higher pay, family health coverage, pensions, and union hiring halls, which effectively ended discrimination in hiring. Amidst the turmoil of the sixties and the numerous civil rights and antiwar protests that had mixed results, Chavez and the farmworkers' unions had some impressive victories — due in part to the economic hardships that the boycotts and strikes imposed on the growers as well as the awareness and moral outrage that the peaceful protests aroused in ordinary citizens.

Grape grievances and successes after the sixties

In 1973, the UFW began a second grape boycott, which received even more support than the original 1967 action. At the peak of the boycott, 17 million Americans refused to buy grapes. Two years later, this second boycott ended when the Agricultural Labor Relations Act was passed, allowing farmworkers to organize and engage in collective bargaining. In 1984, Chavez organized another boycott to protest the spraying of pesticides in the vineyards. This action lasted 16 years, and in the end, growers stopped using the most toxic chemicals.

Up through the present, the UFW has won important benefits for farmworkers. Growers now must provide rest periods, clean drinking water, hand-washing facilities, and regulations protecting workers from pesticides. Farmworkers are guaranteed seniority rights and job security. Union health benefits were established for farmworkers and their families. And a pension plan and a credit union were created for retired farmworkers.

Leaving the Reservation

Another minority group inspired by the civil rights movement was that of American Indians. More than any other group, they believed that they had history on their side. These people weren't dragged to the United States as slaves nor did they immigrate, fleeing persecution or looking for a better life. They were on North American soil first, and the European conquerors stole their land and destroyed their way of life.

In 1969, the occupation of Alcatraz by American Indians pushed the history — and plight — of the group squarely in front of the rest of the American public. As a result, the move for American Indian self-determination gained wider support. And perhaps most importantly, the occupation of Alcatraz was the beginning of a political movement that is still going strong today.

Breaking into Alcatraz

Alcatraz was famous in American society as a prison for the worst of the worst. The last stop for such career criminals as Scarface Al Capone, Machine Gun Kelly, and Robert Stroud, the Birdman of Alcatraz, the small island was the last place that anyone wanted to call home. The greatest Alcatraz legends are about inmates who tried to escape from "the rock" and brave the currents of San Francisco Bay to swim to freedom. Officially, none of them ever succeeded (but some were never heard of again, so who knows if they ever made it across the bay).

After the prison was closed in 1963, American Indians returned to Alcatraz to symbolically reclaim the island for the native people. In the first occupation in March 1964, five Sioux demanded to use the island as a cultural and educational center. The initial justification for this occupation was the 1868 Treaty of Fort Laramie, which promised to return surplus federal land to the American Indians who originally occupied it. The occupation lasted only a few hours, however, and United States marshals escorted them off the island.

The next occupation began on November 9, 1969, when a group of American Indians chartered a boat and returned to Alcatraz. Because many different tribes were represented in the occupation, they named themselves "Indians of All Tribes," claiming the island for all American Indians. Although this initial group left the island the same evening, they realized that they had begun a movement. During the next two weeks, Richard Oakes, the leader of the occupation, visited the University of California in Los Angeles and recruited approximately 100 American Indian students and others to join the Indians of All Tribes. On November 20, they returned to Alcatraz, where they stayed for more than 18 months. Richard Oakes, an articulate leader, was often identified as the chief of the Indians of All Tribes and was sometimes called the mayor of Alcatraz.

The protest became much more than a giant sit-in. The occupation forces actually established a viable community on the island. They elected a council to govern themselves, although all decisions were made by consensus (another case of participatory democracy, as described in Chapter 11). The council ran their community effectively, administering security, sanitation, day care, school, and housing. Figure 13-2 shows the American Indian occupation of Alcatraz.

A place of punishment — then and now

Although most information about Alcatraz before the whites is based on oral history, some of the legends are most interesting — especially the one saying that American Indians who violated tribal laws were often ostracized by being sent to the island. Legend also says that American Indians went to Alcatraz to gather food, especially bird eggs and sea life. After the Spanish arrived in 1542, some American Indians fled to Alcatraz to escape the California Mission system, which coerced their tribes into church-run communities to learn to farm, read and write, speak Spanish, and become Christians.

In 1847, the army took over Alcatraz and used it as a fortress and a military prison until 1933.

Among those incarcerated, ironically, were many American Indians. In 1873, Modoc Indians were confined to the island prison after they were convicted of murdering a general, and in 1895, Hopis were incarcerated in Alcatraz for resisting government regulations that would eradicate their way of life.

In 1934 Alcatraz became a federal penitentiary, housing some of America's most hardened criminals. But because the prison was old and expensive to operate, and the philosophy of long-term incarceration was contrary to the newer theory of rehabilitation of prisoners, Alcatraz was closed in 1963.

Of course, the federal government had no intention of ceding the island to the "invaders" and insisted that the American Indians leave, but the tribes weren't ready to give up. Although the U.S. government agreed to formal negotiations, they felt that the tribes' demands were intolerable — the American Indians wanted the deed to the island and planned to establish a university, cultural center, and museum on the site.

At the beginning, the American Indian society on the island was almost Utopian. When federal officials tried to blockade the island, sympathizers managed to get supplies to the protesters. However, by early 1970 the organization began to fall apart. Students left to return to school, and Indians from reservations and urban areas arrived to take their place. Attracted by the communal nature of life on the island, the hippies also arrived, bringing alcohol and drugs to Alcatraz. Then, when Oakes finally left the island after the death of his stepdaughter, the tribes had no effective leadership. The community on Alcatraz began to reflect all the problems of society everywhere, and although the settlement lasted for another year and a half, it never recaptured its earlier idealism. During this period, the population was fluid — people came and stayed for several months, and others simply visited for a few days.

Figure 13-2: American Indians take back Alcatraz.

©Bettmann/CORBIS

The government decided to play a waiting game. Fearing violence, they didn't take any overt action to oust the American Indians. However, they did try to make life a little more intolerable — at one point, the government shut off all electrical power and removed the barge that supplied fresh water to the island. In January 1971, two oil tankers collided at the entrance to the San

Gambling on the future

Although the demonstrations and occupations were important in increasing awareness of American Indian life, perhaps nothing has changed the lives of American Indians more than the Indian Gaming Regulatory Act (IGRA), passed by Congress in 1988. Just a year earlier, the U.S. Supreme Court recognized that American Indian tribes were sovereign political entities and could operate gaming facilities free of state regulation. However, none of this recognition may have come about without the earlier activists, who made people realize that the American Indians were, in fact, sovereign nations entitled to govern themselves on their own lands. For many tribes, gaming has provided the funds for economic development.

Francisco Bay. Though everyone knew that the occupation of Alcatraz played no part in the collision, the crash gave the federal government an excuse (however lame) to act. On June 10, armed federal marshals, FBI agents, and Special Forces removed the five women, four children, and six unarmed American Indian men who were still on the island. The occupation was over.

Taking AIM into the 1970s and beyond

Russell Means, born into the Lakota nation, became an American Indian activist in the late 1960s. After the Alcatraz occupation was over, Means became active in the American Indian Movement (AIM), an Indian rights organization founded in 1968. In 1973, he led AIM members and Lakota to the former Wounded Knee camp in South Dakota, attempting to take back the land that was promised to the Oglala Sioux in the Fort Laramie Treaty of 1868. As with many other protests, the FBI and the National Guard became involved, resulting in a 71-day siege. By the time the siege ended, 2 people were dead, 12 were wounded, including 2 marshals, and nearly 1,200 were arrested. From that point on, the federal authorities hounded Means and AIM members.

Although Means wasn't the only American Indian activist, he was one of the most visible, even appearing in films (*Last of the Mohicans* and *Natural Born Killers*). (Another notable leader was Wilma Mankiller, the tribal leader of the Cherokee nation, who worked to improve life for her tribe in areas of economic and educational opportunities, adult literacy, and healthcare.) Despite the fact that he was often jailed, Means remained committed to the cause of justice for American Indians. At the time of this writing, he's active in the Colorado chapter of AIM. He actively works to prevent strip mining and the dumping of radioactive waste on native lands. He also works to keep American Indian families together and improve education on the reservations. But first and foremost, Means tries to preserve American Indian culture and promote their pride, living up to his name Oyate Wacinyapi (Works for the People).

Since the 1960s, AIM has fought to force the United States government to honor American Indian treaties, including the restoration of native lands and increased funding for schools on reservations. Working to repeal state authority over native lands, tribes have been able to become economically independent by establishing gambling casinos, as discussed in the "Gambling on the future" sidebar.

Opening the Closet Door

Gays and lesbians have also had an unhappy history of persecution in Western society. At best, homosexuals were tolerated, as long as they didn't overtly show that they were gay. The 1960s witnessed an increased drive to publicly assert their sexual identity, and events at the end of the decade helped forge a full-fledged movement.

Coming out

As a result of the women's movement and the increasing overt nature of sexuality in the country, as well as the high visibility of the civil rights and antiwar movements, gays and lesbians began to feel more comfortable about asserting who they were and demanding the right to be treated equally with other Americans. When women began exploring and enjoying their sexuality, they fostered a freer atmosphere for others to explore individual sexuality as well. And when gays saw that other groups could press their agendas, they began to believe that they, too, could advocate for their rights. They were tired of being "in the closet," pretending to be heterosexual in order to keep their jobs, families, and friends.

Americans began publicly discussing homosexuality after the 1948 publication of Alfred Kinsey's book, *Sexual Behavior in the Human Male,* which said that approximately 10 percent of males have a homosexual experience in their lives.

The most visible sign of gay activism during the '50s and early '60s was an increased willingness for gays and lesbians to come out of the closet and identify themselves as homosexuals, even to a straight society. They began to congregate in gay communities in large cities and in gay bars, which were long considered a hotbed of immorality.

Gays became less willing to be considered social outcasts, and by the late '60s they began to demand equal treatment with heterosexuals. At that time, the main focus was on ending discrimination, decriminalizing sodomy and repealing other repressive laws, and changing the public view that homosexuality is a sin. Today, however, the scope of gay activism has expanded to include freedom from hate crimes against homosexuals, equal employment and housing opportunity, the right to serve in the military, and official recognition of domestic partnerships and, most recently, gay marriage.

Rioting at the Stonewall bar

Before 1965, raids on gay bars were fairly routine. However, that year a politically involved gay activist — Dick Leitsch of the Mattachine society, a gay rights organization dedicated to improving homosexuals' lives and working for equality — challenged the New York State Liquor Authority (SLA), which had a policy of taking away the liquor license of any bar serving three or more homosexuals at one time.

In 1966, after alerting the media, Leitsch held a "sip-in," intending to have a drink with two other gay men at a bar. When the bartender turned them away, they complained to the city's human rights commission. Embarrassed by press coverage of the event and its aftermath, the chairman of the SLA denied that the department prohibited selling liquor to homosexuals. The following year, the courts determined that the SLA couldn't revoke a liquor license without evidence of violations (which didn't include serving gays).

However, on June 27, 1969, police thought they had a good reason to raid the Stonewall Inn, a gay bar in Greenwich Village. The bar didn't have a valid liquor license, had ties with organized crime, offered scantily clad boys as entertainment, and brought an unruly element to Sheridan Square. So that night, after 1 a.m., police raided the bar. Although many patrons escaped arrest, the cops nailed anyone without an ID or anyone who was cross-dressed.

The patrons were incensed, and the riot was on. Competing accounts of the chaotic event make it difficult to determine whether the riot was started by a drag queen clubbed by a policeman or a lesbian crowded into a squad car, but whatever the cause, the anger was contagious, and the crowd moved to overtake the police. The police tried to retreat into the bar, but when they grabbed and beat an innocent bystander, the violence escalated. Some rioters set the bar on fire, and others ripped parking meters from the sidewalk to use as weapons. Soon, not only were the patrons of the Stonewall lashing out — the entire neighborhood got involved in the melee. Even a tactical force sent in to quell the riot was unable to control the angry mob, who protested throughout the night.

The crowd returned for the next few nights. Although the violence lessened as the nights wore on, the protesters, chanting "Gay power!", were no less outraged at the way police had treated gays for years. After the Stonewall Riots were over, the gay community decided to turn their anger to positive change. By the end of July, the Gay Liberation Front (GLF) was formed in New York. The Stonewall Riots mobilized the gay community — homosexuals, who were no longer content to hide at the margins of American society, started newspapers, formed community organizations, and became politically active.

The battle over gay rights today

By the end of the 20th century, most states had repealed their sodomy laws, and the remaining states declared these laws unconstitutional in 2003. Today, many companies and local governments prohibit hiring or housing discrimination based on sexual orientation and ban sexual harassment. Several states have passed domestic partners legislation, which extends health benenfits to unmarried partners and protects their rights in case of illness or death. Another important piece of legislation enacted by several states categorizes gay bashing as a hate crime, which is a violation against human rights (however, federal hate-crime legislation doesn't yet include sexual orientation).

Despite the progress of gays, the fight is far from over. Today shows more widespread acceptance of gay rights, but they're still opposed by a number of religious and politically conservative groups who believe that the Bible considers homosexuality a sin and that marriage should only be between a man and a woman. Conservative state governments and the administration of President George W. Bush at the beginning of the 21st century fought back, opposing calls for the legalization of gay marriage and proposing a constitutional amendment banning it.

By 1970, the GLF had chapters across the country. In June, they held a march to commemorate the Stonewall Riots. Between 5,000 and 10,000 men and women marched from Greenwich Village to Central Park, which inaugurated the tradition of the gay pride celebration. Today, in many American cities, gay pride parades are normally held on the last weekend in June to honor the Stonewall Riots and celebrate the gay lifestyle. Although most major legislation wasn't passed until the 1970s and later, the progress of gay rights started in the '60s.

Preserving the Status Quo: The Conservatives

Not everyone supported civil rights or protested the Vietnam War during the 1960s. Several vocal groups were actively anti-Communist, fought racial integration, opposed government social programs, and believed that the Vietnam War was protecting democracy. Although the '60s conservatives didn't all adopt each of these mind-sets, a key underlying factor was that most of them strongly objected to the protests that they felt were unpatriotic and to the protesters, whom they saw as dirty, lazy, immoral, and unprincipled.

During the early 1960s, the most prominent and respected conservative was Barry Goldwater, one of the founders of the American conservative movement. He ran against Lyndon Johnson for the presidency in 1964 but was so out of step with the majority of voters that Johnson won by a landslide. Many people feared that Goldwater would undo much of the progress made over the past years, especially in social programs (see Chapter 3).

Goldwater's conservatism (and that of most of the 1960s conservatives) was focused mainly on a strong anti-Communist stance as well as the least amount of interference by the federal government. He opposed federal regulation of business as well as federal laws that infringed on states' rights, which made many people believe that he agreed with racial segregation. He believed in personal freedom and responsibility and didn't think that people need government interference in their private lives.

Among some of Goldwater's greatest supporters were the Young Americans for Freedom (YAF). Founded in September 1960 at the estate of William F. Buckley Jr., the founder and editor of conservative magazine *The National Review,* the YAF became the most powerful right-wing youth group in the country. Later in the decade, YAF actively clashed with radical groups such as Students for a Democratic Society (see Chapter 11) and continues to support conservative causes today.

In spite of his loss, Goldwater and his followers turned the Republican Party toward the right, and just 16 years later, Ronald Reagan, who agreed with Goldwater's position on most issues, won the presidency. Late in his life, Goldwater disagreed with many of the views promoted by conservative Republicans, including their opposition to gay rights, believing that the conservative movement shouldn't promote a religious and social agenda. In fact, today he'd probably be a *Libertarian* (someone who believes in the absolute minimum amount of government regulation and interference) rather than a Republican.

Fighting the Communist conspiracy: The John Birch Society

In 1958, the John Birch Society was established in Indianapolis, Indiana, by Robert Welch Jr., a conservative businessman from Massachusetts, to fight liberal tendencies in American politics and stop alleged Communist infiltration and control within American society. (He chose the name in reference to a Baptist missionary who had been killed by Communists in China in 1945.) Welch believed that social programs, welfare, and unions were all moving the country toward socialism. The society used grass-roots efforts, organizing local chapters, mounting letter-writing campaigns, and making the views known in the community. Started with only 11 members, this group's ranks swelled in the early 1960s to have somewhere from 60,000 to 100,000 members and an annual income of $5 million.

The society received much of its support from wealthy businessmen who had a vested interest in fearing Communist ideology. Believing that men such as Joseph McCarthy (see Chapter 11) were right in fearing that Communists had heavily infiltrated the U.S. government, the John Birch Society accused some of the most prominent men of the era of being part of a grand Communist conspiracy. Ironically, many of the people they accused were strong conservatives, such as President Dwight D. Eisenhower, CIA Chief Allen Dulles, and U.S. Supreme Court Chief Justice Earl Warren. Although they a powerful, well-funded group (and backed Barry Goldwater for president), the John Birch Society never seized control of the Republican Party, yet they did their best to pull the Republican agenda further to the right.

The society still exists today and still promotes extreme right-wing views. Their Web site identifies their current political campaigns as trying to withdraw the U.S. from the United Nations, reclaiming the Panama Canal, and stopping the Free Trade Agreement of the Americas.

Stumping for segregation

Though many southern governors actively opposed racial integration and made headlines by blocking school doors and loudly stating their views, George Wallace of Alabama was perhaps the most outspoken (or at least got the most press). Early in his career, Wallace was actually a liberal compared to many of his southern colleagues, although he was a strong supporter of states' rights and against any federal program that stepped on the states' toes. This resistance meant he was opposed to any federal civil rights program, such as school integration, because education was a matter reserved for the states in the Constitution.

In 1962, Wallace ran for governor on a pro-segregation, pro-states'-rights platform. On June 11, 1963, he reaffirmed his anti-integration stance by barring the schoolhouse door at the University of Alabama to prevent two black students from enrolling, although he eventually stepped aside when federal marshals showed up. Figure 13-3 shows Wallace at the university, probably his most famous photograph.

In 1964, Wallace ran for the Democratic nomination for president, and in 1968, he established the American Independent Party and ran as its first presidential candidate. He ran on a platform of states' rights, segregation, law and order, and support for the war in Vietnam (as well as his hatred for hippies and condemnation of protesters as traitors). Although he did gather support, he was too extreme for many voters.

Speaking to the silent majority

Although the late '60s were marked by vocal protests and left-wing sentiment, when Nixon ran for president on a Republican platform in 1968, he was able to take advantage of the confusion and disarray in the Democratic Party (see Chapter 11 for information about the 1968 Democratic National Convention)

as well as a *silent majority* of Americans — large parts of the white working and middle classes who felt that the nation had become caught up in anarchy and narrow self-interests, to the detriment of the greater interests of the majority (see Chapter 4).

Figure 13-3:
Alabama National Guard general tells Governor Wallace (left) that the Guard will enforce federal law to admit African American students to the University of Alabama.

©Bettmann/CORBIS

In his campaign, Nixon promised "peace with honor" as a way to resolve the Vietnam War. Although he gave no details on how he'd end the conflict, many supported him because they believed that the Democrats would only continue escalating the war, which, so far, had produced rather dismal results.

HISTORIC TRIVIA

Nixon's clown prince

Like him or hate him, most people agreed that Richard Nixon was intense, serious, and came across as basically humorless. However, his running mate, Spiro Agnew, openly expressed Nixon's (and the silent majority's) scorn and distaste for the hippies, antiwar activists, what he called the intellectual elite, and liberals in general. What made Agnew more than a political rabble-rouser were his interesting turns of phrase,

such as "nattering nabobs of negativism," which were a source of great amusement to the press, which he in turn called the "effete corps of impudent snobs." Agnew's history foreshadowed his boss's eventual downfall — in 1973, he was forced to resign from office when he pleaded no contest to charges of extortion, bribery, and tax evasion while he was governor of Maryland.

Part V
Tuning In, Turning On, and Dropping Out: Transforming American Culture

In this part . . .

The 1960s were a time of experimenting with different lifestyles. The hippies adopted a nonmaterialistic lifestyle, accepted premarital sex, and used marijuana and other drugs. They dressed unconventionally, tried living communally, and believed that love was the answer, for everything. The '60s were also a time for experimenting with new styles of music, while looking back to some of the older forms. Folk, soul, blues, the surf sound, and acid rock were all popular, and all types of music were played at festivals, such as Woodstock. Creativity was rampant everywhere — fashions ranged from the scant and provocative miniskirts to the thrown-together hippie style, and art was op, pop, and psychedelic. Comics were not only funny, but they also made people laugh at the absurdity of their lives. And TV reflected life during the decade and brought the events of the day into Americans' living rooms as it had never before done.

Chapter 14

Far Out: The Counterculture

In This Chapter

▶ Following the trail of bohemians and beats

▶ Finding freedom from the establishment

▶ Experiencing the transcendental through the use of drugs

▶ Revisiting the center of the counterculture in its heyday

*I*n the 1960s, many young people discovered the joys of personal liberation and self-expression in lieu of following their parents' scripts. They didn't feel the need to spend their lives striving for financial success and a house with a white picket fence; rather, they wanted to live freely, joyously, and peacefully. Many of these people, who became known as *hippies* to the rest of society, saw hypocrisy in their parents' lifestyles — dad hated his job but wanted junior to follow in his footsteps; the folks didn't seem happy together, but mom couldn't wait for her daughter to get married — and wanted to pave a new path for life.

Although you don't see many hippies walking down the street these days, their legacy is still evident. Today, people either are nostalgic for the '60s or condemn the decade as the source of all society's evils. Liberals view that tumultuous period as a time of hope and social change, considering the hippies to be examples of a freer, more just world. Conservatives, on the other hand, blame the counterculture for the breakdown of the family, permissive child raising, pornography, and drugs.

In a sense, both sides are right about the long-term effects of the '60s counterculture. Americans today are more open to exploring other religions, questioning authority, expressing their political views, and living different lifestyles. Having a nuclear family is no longer the only way to live or raise children. Unmarried couples live together and raise families. More people live communally — this situation has become particularly effective for older people, who find that pooling their resources is financially, socially, and economically valuable. People are less willing to stay in jobs or marriages that are unsatisfying and are more willing to make radical changes to find happiness. Would this change of living situations have happened if hippies never existed? Perhaps, but it probably would've taken a lot longer.

Contrary to popular belief (or perhaps wishful thinking), the hippie lifestyle didn't completely die out by the '70s. Throughout the world, you can find small communities still living hippie lifestyles. These people also have annual gatherings, such as the Rainbow Gatherings Peace Fest, which celebrates a bohemian lifestyle and works for peace, and the Burning Man festival, held in the desert of Nevada. In this chapter we chronicle the evolution of the '60s counterculture and the hippies.

Defying Convention: Alternate Lifestyles before the Hippies

Unconventional lifestyles didn't start with hippies in the 1960s; people have always lived outside the mainstream and flouted convention. Throughout the 20th century, creative types, sexual adventurers, political protesters, and religious groups have lived differently than the middle class. However, by the '60s, overt political involvement and intense media coverage brought alternative lifestyles right out in the open. The groups most often thought of as precursors to the hippies include the following:

- ✔ **Bohemians:** In the late 19th and early 20th centuries, bohemians were artists, writers, musicians, and others who hadn't found their nitch in conventional society. Usually, they congregated in cheap, seedy neighborhoods, where they could live as they pleased. Because bohemians lived in their own little enclaves, the middle class didn't see too much of these avant-garde types, but those they did know, they didn't like. The middle class looked down on bohemians as lazy and immoral — and the dislike was mutual. The poets and painters considered the bourgeoisie uncultured and, for the most part, didn't care who approved of their lifestyle.

- ✔ **Beats:** In 1948, novelist John Clellon Holmes and poet Jack Kerouac came up with the term "beat generation" to distinguish themselves from the Lost Generation of the 1920s, which was responsible for many great artists, writers, and poets. The phrase became famous, however, when the *New York Times Magazine* published an article by Holmes entitled, "This Is the Beat Generation."

Like all bohemians before them, the beats (or *beatniks,* as they became commonly called) were a small group of struggling writers, artists, musicians, and malcontents. Though few of them made an indelible mark on history, the beats began a trend that would evolve into the hippies of the '60s and beyond. They were famous not only for their controversial work but also for their lifestyles; they were promiscuous and were quite willing to experiment with drugs. More than anything else, they offended middle-class values because they seemed to live happily without the stresses of day jobs.

From beat to hippie: Allen Ginsberg

Allen Ginsberg was a famous beat poet (and hippie) who wrote throughout the '50s and '60s. During those two decades, Ginsberg, with his openness and tolerance for many different viewpoints, was loved by many different arms of the counterculture. One of his main inspirations was jazz and the hip jazz culture, part of which was drugs. He loved the freedom of the jazz life and saw it as a way to free himself, and society, of what he saw as the boring, middle-class life of the '50s.

Ginsberg used marijuana, peyote, and LSD to expand his consciousness, looking for inspiration for his poetry. Because he used drugs, explored Eastern religions, and questioned authority and conventional morality, he appealed to young people throughout the '60s and into the '70s. He not only worked for liberated lifestyles but also was politically active, fighting for civil rights and against the Vietnam War.

Ginsberg's most famous poem is "Howl," which was published in 1956, uses foul language, and talks about things that were still taboo at the time of publication — drugs and homosexuality. (Lawrence Ferlinghetti, the poet and owner of the City Lights, the San Francisco bookstore that published "Howl," was arrested for obscenity but later acquitted of the charges.) Throughout his life, Ginsberg not only continued to write, but actively supported causes that he believed in, such as freedom of speech, gay rights (he was openly gay before it was accepted), and supporting struggling artists and writers. Ginsberg died of cancer in 1997.

One of most well-known beat writers was Jack Kerouac. He spent most of his adult life traveling around the United States and abroad, writing about the places he saw, the people he met, and his thoughts and feelings about what he encountered along the way. His most famous novel was *On the Road,* published in 1957. Because he garnered so much attention for writing about a free, nomadic, unconventional life, Kerouac is sometimes considered the father of the hippies.

Being In and Loving In

Enter the hippies, heirs to the bohemians and beats, who embraced the counterculture of the 1960s (see Figure 14-1). Like the nonconformists that came before them, they rejected middle-class, materialistic values and adopted a communal, nomadic, sexually liberated lifestyle. Much of the hippie movement was hedonistic, but it also had a spiritual basis that incorporated aspects of Buddhism, Hinduism, and American Indian belief systems. Mostly, hippies congregated in New York's East Village and San Francisco's Haight-Ashbury, but they could be found all over, especially as they started to form communes (see the "Living cooperatively" section later in this chapter).

Figure 14-1:
A 1967
"love-in"
in Los
Angeles.

Although hippies usually lived a nonmaterialistic lifestyle, most were white, middle-class youngsters who never wanted for anything. But they saw American society as dull, dehumanizing, commercialized, competitive, conformist, and hypocritical. Though the hippies didn't always know what they wanted, they knew what they didn't want: their parents' lives and the worries and responsibilities that came with them. They wanted to be young and free. The hippies did what all young people have always done — be outrageous and shock their parents. And the conventional world of parents, teachers, government, and law was definitely uncomfortable with them. It was hard for parents to watch their kids rejecting all their advantages, "wasting" their education, and rejecting the ethics of hard work, duty, and responsibility. The '60s generation gap was different from all the others to date, though, because it had a more far-reaching effect — the 1960s counterculture influences the way people live today, some 40 years later.

Journalists actually coined the term *hippie,* and hippies rarely used it to describe themselves. They usually called themselves "heads" or "freaks."

Though the hippies evolved from the beats, they didn't hit their stride (or cause that much of a stir) until the late '60s. It was obvious that they were a force to be reckoned with when the cover story of *Time* magazine on July 7, 1969, was "The Hippies: The Philosophy of a Subculture."

Showing hippie style

Although the beatniks tended to be a bit sloppy and preferred wearing black, the hippies were immediately recognizable to the *establishment* (the hippies' term for anyone who embraced traditional middle-class values). They dressed in bright colors, adopted psychedelic patterns, including batik and tie-dye, sometimes hit the thrift stores for interesting clothing, and often wore mismatched clothes (see Chapter 16 for more about hippie fashion). One of their most obvious and disturbing characteristics — especially for the men — was their long hair. Unlike the Beatles and their cute mop-tops (see Chapter 15), hippie men often wore their hair longer than women did, which made conservative, older people uncomfortable. Even without the long, flowing locks, hair was a big issue all around — men grew beards, and blacks let their hair go natural in a style called the Afro.

Although hippies had a reputation for being dirty, many of them were quite clean and were especially diligent about washing their long hair. (Most of them, after all, grew up in middle-class homes.)

By the end of the '60s, the hippie style had entered the mainstream. You could easily buy bell-bottoms or a tie-dyed T-shirt at your local retailer. Because of the hippies, even mainstream people adopted a much more relaxed view of hairstyles and fashion, which continues today.

Quitting your day job and hitting the road

For the most part, hippies rejected the values and ethics of the American consumer society. They didn't work except in their own communes (see "Living cooperatively"). Although many of the hippies were from middle-class families, a lot of them had little or no money, mainly because their families were reluctant to support their lifestyle.

Interestingly, though, many of the young people who worked at steady jobs and lived conventional lives during the week dressed up (or down) as hippies and invaded the Haight-Ashbury in San Francisco or the East Village in New York on Friday nights to become weekend hippies.

Adopting the experience of Jack Kerouac, which the author fictionalized in his novel *On the Road* (see the "Defying Convention: Alternate Lifestyles before the Hippies" section, earlier in this chapter), many hippies were nomadic, taking road trips across the country looking for adventure and mind-expanding experiences, often in painted Volkswagen camper buses or the full-size variety (see Figure 14-2). Perhaps the most famous road-trippers were Ken Kesey, author of *One Flew Over the Cuckoo's Nest,* and his band of Merry Pranksters. See the "Day-tripping with LSD" section for more information on Kesey and his Pranksters.

Living cooperatively

Many conservatives saw the hippies as mere pleasure seekers who wanted to avoid all responsibility, but when hippies created communes where they could live together away from the pressures of mainstream America, they worked hard to build homes, either grow or collectively buy food, and pursue their interests, especially in the arts. Urban legend said that the hippies were moving to communes in order to escape urban crime, police interference, and mainstream culture. Some examples of hippie communes are "Drop City," an artists, and writers, colony that was established in May 1965, and "Tolstoy Farm," which began two years earlier and was centered on the community-oriented ideas of Tolstoy and Gandhi.

Figure 14-2:
Taking the bus to Woodstock.

©Henry Diltz/CORBIS

Although many communes adopted rural lifestyles, hippies also lived communally in the cities. In both the Haight and in New York's East Village, groups of hippies banded together and lived as a family, sharing cooking, cleaning, and childcare (and decorating their homes with psychedelic art). On many communes, children were expected to contribute by doing basic chores.

City hippie

Whether in the city or the country, people in hippie communes and other back-to-the-landers wanted to know and work with their neighbors. One way to do so was to be involved in community projects and cooperative businesses (in *co-ops,* everyone contributed their money and labor to the enterprise and shared the profits).

The late '60s saw the rise of consumer co-ops. Many of these co-ops were stores, some of which sold only organic, whole, unrefined, and bulk foods (some of today's natural food stores started as co-ops). Although some co-ops used the business methods of the establishment — they had regular business hours and had paid staff and store managers — others worked on a more spontaneous basis, were run by volunteers, and opened at limited times or whenever the workers felt like opening them. Most co-ops welcomed anyone as customers, but members sometimes received year-end dividends or got discounts on their purchases.

Country mouse

Although many of the hippies moving to rural communes had never grown a vegetable or seen a cow's rear end, they eagerly embraced what they thought was a less artificial way of life. Influenced by earlier writers such as Henry David Thoreau and turned off by the consumerism, pollution, and stress of urban life, they wanted to reconnect with nature and enjoy the satisfaction of physical work. As amateur farmers, the people on rural communes wanted to be as self-sufficient as possible.

For both economic and ecological reasons, many of the people who went back to the land tried to use natural energy sources, such as solar energy, wood fuel, or well pumps. They also tried to grow their crops and feed their livestock without the use of chemicals, believing that organic food is inherently healthier. To support their efforts, they read publicationss such as *The Whole Earth Catalog,* an ecologically conscious almanac, both to educate themselves and to find where to get the tools they needed.

Many succeeded and stayed on the land, but great numbers returned to the cities when they realized that life on the land was physically exhausting, financially draining, and isolated. People who "returned" to the land they'd never been on idealistically believed that they could earn what they needed by selling their produce and other homemade items — they didn't count on the expenses involved, such as machinery, feed, seeds, and other supplies. Those who made it were in stable relationships, had outside sources of income (sometimes from creative work and sometimes from their families), and knew a thing or two about country life before going whole hog.

Making love (not war)

Two middle-class standards that the hippies considered extremely restrictive were marriage and monogamy. Especially for the younger rebels, college and postgraduate education caused them to postpone marriage (and, in theory, sex) until their mid-20s, and they needed a way to deal with their hormones.

After young people started to question their parents' values, politics, and traditions, it wasn't surprising that they also questioned conventional sexual morality. Those with more Marxist leanings viewed marriage as an economic arrangement. Women, armed with the Pill, discovered their sexuality and saw no reason to observe the old double standard, which made premarital sex okay for men but not for women (see Chapter 12 for more on the women's movement).

As a result, many young people, though not necessarily condemning marriage, didn't want to wait for it or rush to the altar just to have sex. In addition, they certainly saw no reason to restrict themselves to one partner. Sexual jealousy and possessiveness were obsolete after the issue of multiple partners became acceptable — although that idea was more accepted in theory than in practice.

Although the sexual revolution didn't reach full flower until the 1970s, it was perhaps the most enduring legacy of the 1960s counterculture. Casual sex became more acceptable, even as the need to protect against sexually transmitted diseases became more important. Women demanded satisfying sex and no longer viewed it as a necessary evil. Gay and lesbian lifestyles also became more socially acceptable, and many homosexuals felt free to come out of the closet. The bottom line is that after the sexual liberation of the '60s, sexual pleasure was viewed as something that definitely contributed to one's pursuit of happiness, although it may not have been exactly what Thomas Jefferson had in mind (or, on second thought, maybe it was). And although conservatives and the religious right regularly condemn the on-going sexual revolution, there's probably no going back — the counterculture has redefined sexuality in America.

Letting the spirit move them

With their rejection of conventional rules, hippies naturally rejected their parents' religion. For them, it was filled with too many "thou shalt nots," and they believed that mainstream religions, such as Christianity and Judaism, were hypocritical. They couldn't quite buy into a faith that preached peace but supported war or that said God loved everyone but turned a blind eye toward racism. Instead, many embraced religions that promoted individual responsibility for virtue and a "oneness" with nature:

- ✔ **Eastern religions:** The Eastern religions, such as Zen Buddhism and Hinduism, were appealing to the hippies because they emphasize that individuals can work toward goodness without a church telling them how. Also, the Zen concept on expanded states of consciousness fit perfectly with the use of psychedelics — the hippies wanted enlightenment, and they wanted it immediately (see the section on drugs and the counterculture later in this chapter). They also embraced the Hindu idea of passive resistance, which was promoted by Gandhi, who inspired the nonviolent aspects of the civil rights movement.

- ✔ **American Indian religions:** The counterculture also embraced American Indian religion, which emphasized peoples' oneness with the universe. American Indians believe that the spirits control the forces of nature and are an integral part of a person's life and the life of the community. Native people also believe that humans exist as part of the natural environment rather than as its masters.

An important result of the counterculture is that Americans are now open to a wider variety of religious experiences. The interest in Eastern religions didn't fade with the 1960s — people today are still interested in the principles of Buddhism and Hinduism, and practicing yoga is commonplace. Also, many mainstream religions are changing to appeal to young people who are more apt to question the "old-time religion." Today, some Catholic masses incorporate guitar music, synagogues hold "rocking Shabbats," and clergy give sermons that emphasize personal growth, responsibility, and ethics along with faith and adherence to dogma. Evangelical churches today have embraced Christian rock, rap, and blues.

Getting political: Peace and equal rights

Originally, the hippies weren't particularly political, although they rebelled against establishment values. Their main focus was on creating alternate lifestyles that reflected their values. However, hippies did get involved in the civil rights marches and the anti–Vietnam War demonstrations.

As we discuss in Chapter 11, although they were against the war, many hippies disagreed with student antiwar demonstrations and protests, believing that peace, love, and flower power could change people's hearts and minds. However, by 1968, the hippies began to feel the need to become more active in opposing the Vietnam War. Many joined with a loose coalition of different groups called the "Mobes" (for mobilization), which included Students for a Democratic Society (SDS), the Quakers, the Socialist Labor Party, a variety of liberal and pacifist organizations, and other antiwar organizations. Mobes, along with hippies, yippies (a free-thinking, fun-loving counterculture group) and other individuals opposed to the war, made their presence known at the 1968 Democratic National Convention in Chicago (see Chapter 9 for more information about the Chicago protests).

Rebelling through writing: The underground press

Considering their rebellion against school, parents, corporate America, and the government, is it any surprise that the hippies (and other counterculture types) disbelieved the news as presented in the traditional press and on TV? Although they welcomed coverage in the establishment media to promote themselves, they created their own mouthpieces to express their views.

Some of the earliest underground newspapers were the *Los Angeles Free Press* and the *East Village Other* in New York, but in almost every major city and college campus, an underground newspaper or magazine sprang up. By 1969, about 400 underground papers were being published, speaking to anyone who was opposed to the Vietnam War and embracing alternative lifestyles. Unlike conventional media, underground newspapers never claimed to be objective. And they didn't just report the news; at times, they *created* news by staging events they wanted to write about.

The underground press fulfilled a number of functions:

- ✔ **It supported the protests.** The most important function of the underground press was to mobilize the counterculture to rally around causes that they considered important. For example, months before the 1968 Democratic National Convention in Chicago, the underground press announced the upcoming antiwar protests, although some debated whether it was wise or ethical to bring thousands of flower children to a protest that could turn violent.

  "Don't come to Chicago if you expect a festival of peace," warned the *Chicago Seed,* which heavily promoted the protests.

- ✔ **It covered the culture.** The underground journalists wrote about music and advertised (and staged) rock concerts. They let the hippie community know where to find free or cheap food, clothing, medical care, and the best *head shops* (places to buy pipes, rolling papers, and other drug paraphernalia). They also wrote about sex, drugs, and religion.

As the '60s came to a close, the underground press became more specialized, branching out with gay newspapers and feminist newspapers. Although many of the original hippie publications folded, they made some lasting contributions to pop culture — for example, the *East Village Other* was one of the first papers to feature underground comics. The free newspapers and magazines in most large cities are more mainstream but still appeal to the young — they're guides to the best movies, music, and parties (see the "Almost underground: *Ramparts* and the *Village Voice"* sidebar).

Almost underground: *Ramparts* and the *Village Voice*

Ramparts was a slick political and literary magazine from 1962 through 1975; it strongly opposed the Vietnam War and also published one of the first conspiracy theories about the Kennedy assassination, as well as many controversial works, such as Che Guevara's diaries with an introduction by Fidel Castro (see Chapter 2 for more on Cuba) and the prison diaries of Eldridge Cleaver (see Chapter 7).

The *Village Voice,* founded in 1955 in New York City and still going strong, is an alternative publication that embraces liberal politics and lifestyles, does investigative reporting, and also reviews and analyzes arts and culture. Over the years, the newspaper magazine has published many famous writers such as Henry Miller, Lorraine Hansbury, Allen Ginsberg, and Ezra Pound. In spite of its political views and artistic slant, the *Village Voice* has gone establishment — it owns several alternative weeklies around the country.

In 1970, women staffers of the New York underground newspaper *Rat* protested the sexist advertisements in the newspaper by kicking out the male editors and starting their own paper, *Women's LibeRATion*. In their first issue, Robin Morgan expressed women's anger at sexism in the New Left organizations, such as SDS, and the Berkeley free speech movement. See Chapter 12 for information about radical feminism.

Flying with Lucy in the Sky with Diamonds: Drugs and the Counterculture

Since the beginning of the hippie movement, the counterculture has often been linked with and defined by psychedelic drug use. The rebellious circle had many more defining characteristics, of course, but the drugs made good press — long hair and outlandish clothes weren't enough to sell a good story. As it so happens, though, the hippies used a lot of recreational drugs, especially marijuana and LSD and sometimes peyote and mushrooms, all in an effort to have mind-altering experiences.

Getting high isn't a new phenomenon — it's been a part of the human condition since the dawn of time. In the United States, drugs have always occupied a place just below the surface of mainstream society. It was an open secret that many jazz musicians smoked pot (and sometimes dabbled in harder drugs). During the '50s and early '60s, the beats used marijuana and sometimes more intense hallucinogens, such as peyote, mushrooms, and LSD.

Students going through the questioning period of late adolescence, who read the beats (or studied under professors who read the beats), were attracted to drugs as a way to explore new ways of living. Also, learning that marijuana wasn't highly addictive and wouldn't lead one to heroin addiction not only reinforced the idea that the older generation were hypocrites but also made trying it a lot more attractive. Finally, LSD, which promised visions of a higher consciousness, was popular because it was relatively available until it was banned in the United States in 1967.

Day-tripping with LSD

Along with marijuana, LSD (lysergic acid diethylamide, commonly referred to as "acid") is the drug most often associated with the 1960s. Hippies used it for recreational purposes and as a means for increasing spiritual awareness, because it caused them to have visions and see the world in a new way.

Being a synthetic hallucinogenic drug, LSD intensifies a person's senses, feelings, memories, and awareness, sometimes for up to 12 hours. Someone on an "acid trip" usually imagines unusual and visual effects and brilliant colors. Objects (real or imagined) often move in different patterns, and images can "shape shift." People on acid trips usually see the world in a different way, may have illusions, daydreams, and fantasies, and have distorted views of time and space. Some of these visions can be wonderfully magical and beautiful, but they can also be terrifying — the kind of trip someone has depends on the tripper's mood before setting out.

Until 1966 no laws prohibited using, producing, or selling LSD. However, as feelings turned against the hippies for their rebelliousness and promiscuity, the government began to look at LSD use. In 1967, the U.S. government banned LSD.

Turning on with Timothy Leary

In 1938, a Swiss chemist named Albert Hofmann created LSD. During the '50s, LSD was used recreationally by mental health professionals, who later gave it to friends and colleagues. It eventually found its way into the hands of the beats. The U.S. Army and the CIA conducted some chilling trials with the drug, administering it to unsuspecting subjects. Experiments to determine the drug's physical and psychological effects continued until the early '60s, when the American public first heard about it.

Timothy Leary was the man who brought LSD to the forefront of American consciousness. An academic psychologist at Harvard, Leary became fascinated with hallucinogens after taking psilocybin mushrooms while in Cuernavaca, Mexico, in 1960. When he returned to Harvard, he obtained pure *psilocybin* (a psychedelic found in some mushrooms that causes hallucinations) and began his own research and experimentation, using a variety of subjects such as colleagues, friends, graduate students, inmates of a state prison, and, of course, himself.

Becoming Ram Dass

Richard Alpert, who conducted experiments with LSD at Harvard along with Timothy Leary (see "Turning on with Timothy Leary" in this chapter), took a different path than Leary after leaving Harvard. In 1967, he traveled to India and met his spiritual mentor, Neem Karoli Baba, also known as Maharaji. His teacher gave him the name Ram Dass, which means "servant of God." Since 1968, he has explored different spiritual practices based on Buddhism, Hinduism, yoga, meditation, Sufism, and Judaism. Ram Dass has written a number of books and has worked to bring spiritual practices to different communities, such as prisoners and the business community.

In 1961 a Harvard colleague, Richard Alpert, joined Leary in his experiments. In 1962, Leary tried LSD for the time and began experimenting with it instead. Together, Leary and Alpert conducted their experiments, which some said were more like wild parties than serious experiments. Their research drew media coverage and national attention (especially with the credibility that the Harvard connection gave them). However, this publicity wasn't the kind that Harvard craved, and in 1965, Leary and Alpert were dismissed from the faculty. However, the two moved to a mansion in Millbrook, New York, where they continued their LSD experiments.

Taking the acid test

Starting in 1964, the Merry Pranksters, the author Ken Kesey and his friends, traveled across the country in a psychedelic painted school bus, making music, partying, and using lots of pot and LSD. In their travels, they introduced LSD to many of the people they met along the way. They held many impromptu festivals called *acid tests* (for the question they posed, "Can you pass the acid test?"). For a $1 admission, people got a cup of Kool-Aid laced with LSD and could spend the evening among psychedelic art, light shows, and sometimes music by the psychedelic band the Grateful Dead, the court jesters (er, musicians) for the Merry Pranksters. By the way, those who got through the night in one piece passed the acid test.

Tom Wolfe immortalized Ken Kesey, the Merry Pranksters, and their acid tests in his 1968 novel *The Electric Kool-Aid Acid Test*.

The Pranksters and their acid tests were mainly responsible for the spread of psychedelic style. Psychedelic art, designed to reflect the vision of an acid trip, had swirling patterns and lettering, vibrant colors, and a feeling of floating in a fantasy. Day-Glo paint and black lights further expressed what it was like to go on a trip (without even going anywhere).

Burning grass

Despite its many names (pot, grass, herb, pakalolo, Mary Jane, and so on), the drug known as marijuana is really a plant called *cannabis sativa*. Throughout history, people have smoked, eaten, drank, and sniffed marijuana and also used the fibers for clothing and rope. Until 1937, marijuana was legal in most of the United States. At that point, a concerted effort to ban the drug resulted in criminalization of its sale and use.

Beginning in the '60s, marijuana use became more widespread. Just as their elders used alcohol, young people used the drug recreationally for the simple reason that it made them feel good — it heightens the five senses and at the same time, makes people feel mellow and relaxed. Marijuana makes people more aware of their bodies, thoughts, emotions, and surroundings.

Young people of the '60s found music more meaningful when marijuana was involved, and they thrived on the heightened senses of motion and color. During a revival of Walt Disney's *Fantasia,* with its abstract color patterns vibrating to music, the smell of marijuana often pervaded theaters. And in 1968, you could probably get high just by walking into a showing of *2001: A Space Odyssey.*

Flower Power: Haight-Ashbury and the Summer of Love

If you go to the Haight-Ashbury (known as "the Haight" or "Hashbury") section of San Francisco today, you'll be able to tell that this area was the epicenter of the hippie counterculture in the late 1960s. However, along with the tie-dye and head shops, chain stores such as the Gap have opened their doors since then. The scenario in the summer of 1967, the Summer of Love, was quite different. You could smell the pot and *patchouli* (incense designed to camouflage the smell of marijuana) in the air, and the longhaired hippies held flowers and greeted each other with the peace sign. Psychedelic designs were painted on buildings, and coffeehouses were more numerous than bars. Some of the cultural icons of the '60s, such as the Grateful Dead, Janis Joplin, and the Jefferson Airplane, spent time in the Haight.

In June 1967, the First Annual Monterey International Pop Music Festival inaugurated the Summer of Love (see Chapter 15 for more on this festival and others). Upon hearing that the Haight was the place to be, young people came to San Francisco from all over the United States to enjoy music and poetry, expand their minds, and of course, to make love, not war. But, although the Summer of Love started out well, by the end of the summer, crime and drug abuse was on the rise, and the atmosphere of peace and love slowly disappeared.

Because many of the hippies had little or no money, they were always looking for "freebies." Fortunately, there were people such as the Diggers who fed the people of the Haight for free, with a stew made from donated vegetables, or whole-wheat Digger Bread, which they baked in coffee cans. They also ran the Diggers Free Stores, nicknamed "a trip without a ticket" where people could get everything from clothes to rolling papers.

The Diggers published *The Digger Papers* and *The Realist,* where they coined the famous '60s phrases, "Do your own thing" and "Today is the first day of the rest of your life."

Youth culture in the Haight didn't start in the '60s. During the '50s, students from San Francisco State College and beats from North Beach were drawn to the low-rent apartments in large, run-down Victorian homes. By the summer of 1967, due to the Summer of Love, San Francisco and the Haight in particular became the hippie capital of the world. The Summer of Love was more than a season; it empowered people with a feeling of freedom, and middle-class kids from all over the country came to enjoy the sex, drugs, and rock 'n' roll.

The Summer of Love actually began in the winter. In January 1967, the Human Be-In ("just humans being together," in the words of one of the organizers) took place in San Francisco's Golden Gate Park. More than 20,000 people joined the festival, including hippies, antiwar protesters, and some of the greatest counterculture celebrities, including Timothy Leary, Allen Ginsberg (see the "From beat to hippie: Allen Ginsberg" sidebar, earlier in this chapter), and Jefferson Airplane.

Later in 1967, the Haight became a tourist mecca. Tour buses passed through the area, and visitors, many of whom had never seen a hippie "in the flesh," stopped to take pictures. Turned off by the commercialism, disillusioned flower children held the "Death of Hippie" event in October of that year, featuring a mock funeral for their way of life.

Blood on the Flowers: The Manson Murders

Perhaps no one did more to end the hippie era of peace, love, and happiness than Charles Manson and his family of misfit murderers. He was antisocial and spent most of his life in jail, but he had a unique talent for attracting alienated, unhappy young people (especially women) who were drawn to his charismatic personality and eagerly joined his "family," living in a commune on the outskirts of Los Angeles.

Although Manson appeared to be sympathetic, he made it clear that he was the leader and that he expected complete obedience from family members. Charlie didn't need to do much to keep his followers in line — controlled with sex and drugs, they were completely subservient to him and followed him almost blindly. With the sex, drugs, and his charismatic personality, Manson convinced his family that he was both Jesus and the devil.

Manson idolized the Beatles, and in his twisted mind, he believed that they were speaking to him through codes embedded in their music. Inspired by his misinterpretation of the song "Helter Skelter" on the White Album (actually titled *The Beatles*), Manson was convinced that a worldwide race war was on the horizon, which he then tried to instigate by committing heinous murders and blaming it on the blacks. On August 9, 1969, at Manson's instigation, members of his family invaded the home of Sharon Tate, a beautiful, young movie star, and murdered her along with three others, including Abigail Folger, heir to the the Folger Coffee fortune. The next night, the family also killed Leno and Rosemary Lo Bianca, ordinary folks who lived in another section of Los Angeles. At both crime scenes, the words *pig* and *helter skelter* were written in blood all over the walls and mirrors.

The murders shocked people, even more intensely because Tate was eight months pregnant. As much as they were horrified by the gruesome manner of the crimes, people were even more distressed by the family's lack of remorse and the Manson girls' antics and lack of repentance during their trials.

People considered the Manson murders to be the dark side of the counterculture, although it was more like the dark side of humanity. But because the Manson family lived a communal lifestyle, practiced free love, took drugs, and looked like hippies, many people no longer considered hippies to be harmless, peace-loving eccentrics. The decade of the counterculture was over.

Chapter 15

A Long, Strange Trip:
Music in the 1960s

In This Chapter

▶ Moving forward into a new decade

▶ Exploring the sounds of America

▶ Forming an Anglo-American music alliance

▶ Singing for a cause

▶ Becoming a roadie: The festivals

Emerging from 1950s rock 'n' roll, folk music, jazz, and the blues, the British invasion and American rock icons (think Janis Joplin, Jimi Hendrix, and Jim Morrison) took popular music to a new level. The '60s also saw the emergence of soul and the Motown sound, as well as the *music of revolution,* songs that supported the civil rights movement and the antiwar protests. This chapter explores the various chords (and faces) that made up the '60s music scene. (If you'd like to get a year-by-year glimpse of exactly which songs and artists were topping the charts, see Chapter 17.)

This Ain't Your '50s Rock 'n' Roll

Popular rock 'n' roll was born in the spring of 1954 with the release of "Rock around the Clock" by Bill Haley and the Comets and its subsequent promotion by Alan Freed, a popular disk jockey. However, the roots of rock 'n' roll went further back, owing a lot to jazz, blues, and ragtime, with a touch of *rockabilly* (a fusion of the blues and country music).

What is rock 'n' roll? It depends on whom you talk to. Some people believe that it was an effort to "whitewash" what was essentially "black" music and clean up its sexual overtones. Other people think that rock 'n' roll was a genre to market to teenagers, who were bored with their parents' music, such as that of Mitch Miller. Early rock 'n' roll was fairly tame compared to the music of the late '60s. Its early stars were the likes of Little Richard, Chuck Berry, the Everly Brothers, and, of course, the King — Elvis Presley.

But rock 'n' roll wasn't the only music that dominated the charts as America turned the corner from the late 1950s to the early 1960s. *Doo-wop,* an upbeat vocal style featuring nonsense syllables (which gave the style its name), and a capella groups were popular in the late '50s and early '60s. Crooners such as Frank Sinatra, Perry Como, Dean Martin, and Tony Bennett were also popular and remained so well into the '70s and beyond (if only to those "over-30" folks).

Rhythm and Blues (R & B) and soul music were big sellers, but largely in the black community. However, unknown to many, soul music and R & B influenced not only Elvis, but even white-bread performers such as Pat Boone. The biggest influence of R & B and soul, however, was on the other side of the pond, with groups such as the Beatles and the Rolling Stones.

The rockabilly stars of the previous decade (such as the Everly Brothers and Elvis Presley) were still popular in the '60s, but a whole new generation was gradually taking over. However, the times definitely were changing — folk music and the surf sound were also finding their niche in the pop music scene. Before long, the British sound, Motown, and psychedelic rock would revolutionize the music scene until the late '60s, and the rock 'n' roll of the latter part of the decade bore almost no resemblance to the music of the '50s.

The World before the Beatles

Contrary to popular belief, new sounds didn't start with the Beatles. In the United States, innovative, uniquely American sounds such as surf music created a loyal following, and Motown brought distinctively black sounds to white America, while other musicians introduced a different kind of music by going back to the past and resurrecting folk songs.

Goin' surfin'

Surf music was a little bit rockabilly yet was fast, casual, and evoked the sand, surf, sun, and tanned, long-legged, blonde California girls. The best-known surf group was the Beach Boys, who introduced vocals to the sound. Although surf music was at its peak during a short time and in a specific place, namely Southern California in the early '60s, it had a huge influence on rock 'n' roll by bringing the electric guitar to the forefront of popular music.

Surf music was invented mostly by musicians who didn't surf, such as Dick Dale, the Bel Airs, and the Atlantics. Dennis Wilson was the only Beach Boy who actually surfed, and Jan and Dean got into surf music only after being inspired by the Beach Boys.

Although many other groups struggled to be heard during the years of the surf fad, only Jan and Dean achieved success with the sound, adapting it to the other California craze: hot cars (namely cruising and drag racing). By 1964, the Beach Boys got tired of surf and expanded their horizons, tackling more challenging themes than cars, the surf, and girls (see the "Watching through a purple haze: Psychedelic rock" section).

Getting down in Motown

Soul music was around way before the 1960s, but it wasn't well known outside the black community except to jazz and blues aficionados. On January 12, 1959, Berry Gordy Jr. tore down the walls by starting his now immortal Motown label on a borrowed shoestring. Motown featured black performers with a distinctive sound made up of jazz, blues, soul, and a touch of gospel. Many of Motown's most popular artists, such as Marvin Gaye, Stevie Wonder, and Smokey Robinson, not only wrote their own music but wrote songs for other Motown artists as well.

Although Detroit's traditional nickname was Motor City, Motor Town (Motown) was the nickname for Detroit's Ford Motor plant, where Berry spent some time working on the assembly line.

During the '60s, Motown was a huge presence on the charts with hits such as "ABC" by the Jackson 5, "You Keep Me Hangin' On" by the Supremes (who sizzled onstage with their sexy gowns and fabulous hairstyles, as well as their singing style — see Figure 15-1), "How Sweet It Is (To Be Loved by You)" by Marvin Gaye, "It's the Same Old Song" by the Four Tops, and "My Girl" by the Temptations.

Motown acts weren't just singing groups — they were complete packages, with glamorous costumes, chic hairstyles, and smooth moves that conveyed the mood of the music. This slick image was designed not only to create a spectacular impression onstage, but also to give a sophisticated, upscale impression of black musicians and artists. This effort was socially as well as financially conscious — Gordy wanted to make sure that the artists and their music appealed to white as well as black audiences, and he achieved that goal. For the first time, a black company produced the music of the black community and successfully marketed to white audiences. Because of the Motown sound (as well as other artists such as James Brown and Aretha Franklin, as we cover in the "Saying it loud — with respect" sidebar), black music became part of the mainstream, where it remains firmly in place today.

Saying it loud — with respect

Not all black music in the '60s came through Motown. James Brown, otherwise known as the godfather of soul, was one of the moving forces in merging gospel and R & B into a new form: soul and funk. His music has, in turn, gone on to influence recent genres, including rap and hip-hop. He also used a unique performing style, with energetic movements and screams that punctuated his music. Perhaps his greatest contribution, however, was to promote black pride, with songs such as "Say It Loud (I'm Black and I'm Proud)" and "I Don't Want Nobody to Give Me Nothing (Open Up the Door, I'll Get It Myself)."

Not only did soul have a godfather, but it also had a first lady — Aretha Franklin. Her style isn't like Brown's, because her music is more influenced by gospel, the music she sang as a child. The black community widely celebrated "Lady Soul" not only for her powerful voice but also as a symbol of the increasing confidence and pride of African Americans — perhaps it was all about R-E-S-P-E-C-T.

Figure 15-1:
The Supremes in 1965 (from left to right, Florence Ballard, Diana Ross, and Mary Wilson).

©Bettmann/CORBIS

Although the Motown sound was popular among white audiences (at least partially, due to the active civil rights movement), it never left its roots. Motown was black, urban, poor, and troubled, but it was also sensuous, humorous, and elegant. Gordy was cautious about backing political or social causes that could affect Motown's success, but at the same time, he allowed Motown music to express black views and concerns. However, political meaning was imposed on some songs, regardless of the lyrics' intent. For example, although "Dancing in the Street" by Martha and the Vandellas was meant to be a party song, it was seen in some quarters as a call to take to the streets in political protest and was often associated with the Watts Riots of 1965 (see Chapter 7 for information about the Watts Riots).

Though Motown as an organization tried to stay away from some of the controversial issues of the '60s, some of the individual artists associated with it rebelled. In 1970, Marvin Gaye wrote and performed songs that addressed issues such as the Vietnam War and racial tensions.

Reliving history with folk music

By the late 1950s, interest in *folk* music, usually older music that was mostly unwritten and played by ear, had increased. The music was appealing not only for its tunes but also because it was nostalgic, with lyrics describing what people felt was a simpler time. As does almost every other musical genre, folk music dealt with love (and lust) and loss, but it also sang of the pain of poverty and the toil of working in the mines, on the railroad, and on the chain gang. Most folk songs were played on acoustic guitar, with one or more singers.

The popularity of folk music rose and fell throughout the 20th century. During the 1930s, Woody Guthrie and Pete Seeger not only sang original folk songs but also adapted folk tunes to reflect life during the era of the Great Depression.

The Kingston Trio was perhaps the leader of the folk revival, bringing to the table songs such as "Tom Dooley" and "MTA." During those years, the group played in clubs and college campuses all over the country.

The trend took hold on the campuses and in large cities, places that were definitely ahead of the curve as far as adopting new trends was concerned. As interest grew, performers and music historians began researching folk tunes by going into rural areas and recording songs from both the United States and other nations. Musicians began performing these authentic folk tunes at clubs, coffeehouses, festivals, and concerts.

Popular folk groups during this era were the Chad Mitchell Trio and Peter, Paul, and Mary. Solo performers such as Bob Dylan, Joan Baez (check out Dylan and Baez in Figure 15-2), Odetta, Harry Belafonte, Phil Ochs, Pete Seeger, and Arlo Guthrie were also popular during this period. As the music became more popular, amateur musicians began to play folk tunes, and well-known performers began to write and perform their own music. The popularity of folk music extended beyond the United States; Mariam Makeba, the famed South African singer, appeared in the United States with many American artists. We talk about some of these artists later in this chapter, in the section "Singing with the Revolution."

Figure 15-2:
Bob Dylan
and Joan
Baez in
1965.

Hootin' and hollerin' at a Hootenanny

When folk singers performed, their concerts were often *hootenannies,* where the repertoire was at least partially impromptu, and the audience usually joined in. Here's the story behind that strange term: A young cowboy star, Hoot Gibson, and his wife, Annie, used to throw some great parties. These parties often turned into jam sessions that went on forever, and everyone wanted to be there. When anyone asked, "Where's the party?" the answer was, "At Hoot 'n' Annie's."

In 1963, TV decided to cash in on the folk music craze and bring Hootenannies to the small screen with a show called (would you believe) *Hootenanny.* The show was taped on college campuses and featured popular folk acts, such as Theodore Bikel and the Irish group the Clancy Brothers. However, considering that many of the folk singers were also political activists, it was only a matter of time before *Hootenanny* had some issues of its own. Reacting to the pressures of McCarthyism (see Chapter 11), the show, in a display of anti-Communism, blacklisted Pete Seeger, which caused the most popular folk singers, including Bob Dylan; Joan Baez; Peter, Paul, and Mary; and the Kingston Trio to boycott the show.

Hootenanny couldn't avoid all controversy, however. The Chad Mitchell Trio sang several protest songs, including "John Birch Society" (see Chapter 13 to find out more about the John Birch Society), which had been banned from many radio stations. The show also presented prime time's first interracial group, the Tarriers.

In the early 1960s, Harry Belafonte popularized *calypso,* Afro-Caribbean music that originated in the West Indies, into his own folk music niche, which caught on with the public. His songs "Jamaica Farewell" and the "Banana Boat Song (Day-O!)" were chart-toppers. However, social causes were as important to him as his music. Belafonte was (and still remains) active on behalf of civil rights and economic equality. Over the years he has fought against social injustices, from nuclear proliferation and the Vietnam War to opposition to the war in Iraq.

Although the folk revival had followers all over the country, some of the most popular venues were the Berkeley Folk Festival in California and the Newport Folk Festival in Rhode Island. Folk musicians often performed in clubs, such as Gerde's Folk City, the Gaslight, and the Bitter End in New York's Greenwich Village (an area with many little clubs where aspiring entertainers worked for little or no money, hoping to be discovered).

Ultimately, folk and rock had a fusion of sorts, called, you guessed it — folk rock. Folk rock adopted the electric guitars, amps, and other accoutrements of the rock scene. Introduced to the world by Bob Dylan at the 1965 Newport Folk Festival (see the section "Coming Together and Falling Apart: The Music Festivals," later in this chapter), folk rock combined American folk music with rock 'n' roll, jazz, and a touch of the blues. On July 25, Dylan took the stage and launched into plugged-in versions of his song "Maggie's Farm." The crowd, comprising folk music purists, heartily booed him for using an electric guitar, thinking that he was selling out to the rock music establishment. But as the decade progressed, folk rock (also with Dylan's influence) became more socially relevant at the same time as it became more popular.

The British Invasion

On February 7, 1964, the Beatles landed in New York. Within a week, they appeared on the *Ed Sullivan Show* (see Figure 15-3). After that, rock music was never the same. They may have failed in 1812, but in 1964, the British invaded and won, armed only with guitars, drums, and four mop-top haircuts.

The *Ed Sullivan Show* was a popular, long-running variety show (called "a really big shew" for Sullivan's accent) that featured singers, musicians, actors, dancers, comedians, circus acts, plate spinners, and acrobats. Mostly, the show was pretty tame stuff, but beginning with Elvis, Sullivan started booking rock 'n' roll acts as well.

Figure 15-3:
The Beatles and Ed Sullivan the day before the Beatles made their U.S. debut.

©Bettmann/CORBIS

Ladies and gentlemen, the Beatles

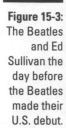

The band that shook the music world rose from humble beginnings. The Beatles, four lads who just liked to make music, came from working-class families in Liverpool, in England. Formed from several earlier bands, they became the Beatles in 1960, and the original four were John Lennon, George Harrison, Stuart Sutcliffe, and Pete Best — no kidding. Sutcliffe decided to leave and make Hamburg, Germany, his home — Paul McCartney took his spot. In 1962, for reasons that are still unknown, the other Beatles asked Best to leave the band and replaced him with Ringo Starr.

In the beginning, the Beatles were famous for their boyish antics and light-hearted, playful tunes, such as, "Help!", "I Want to Hold Your Hand" (teenage girls not only wanted to hold their hands, but bought tons of their records), and "A Hard Day's Night." The Beatles took their zany, humorous style into the movies, too, and, if possible, became even more popular with their foray onto the silver screen with *A Hard Day's Night*. The four lads from Liverpool also won the female adulation that in earlier years had gone to Frank Sinatra and Elvis Presley.

Some debate exists about which song was the Beatles' first hit single in the United Kingdom, but the contenders are "From Me to You" (May 1963), "She Loves You" (September 1963), and "I Want to Hold Your Hand" (December 1963).

The Beatles were so popular that they almost single-handedly overshadowed almost all the existing rock 'n' roll groups — only the Beach Boys, the Four Seasons, and the Motown sound held their own against them. At one point, they had the top five records on Billboard's Hot 100 list.

The American Invasion

The fertilization of American rock by the British was part of a movement across the pond that actually went both ways. The Beatles and other British rock groups were influenced by American rock 'n' roll, R & B, jazz, and the blues. In fact, the Brits were probably more influenced by black American music than American musicians were.

The Beatles' new sound influenced almost every pop and rock group after them. American musicians imitated English accents and adopted foppish costumes and longer hair. Beatles imitators arose almost overnight, with groups such as the Knickerbockers, Beau Brummels, the Buckinghams, Sir Douglas Quintet, and the Turtles. Even those musicians who didn't directly imitate the Beatles adapted their musical styles. Bob Dylan started performing with an electric guitar, and when the Byrds recorded "Mr. Tambourine Man," they incorporated a touch of the British sound in their folk music.

But the Beatles didn't meet with widespread adulation everywhere. In those early years, they were criticized by the older generation for their long hair and the different nature of their music. Toward the end of the decade, however, with their musical innovations, nontraditional clothing, long hair, and experimentation with drugs, which was reflected in their songs (see Chapter 14 for more information about the '60s counterculture), adults ironically longed for the mop-topped Fab Four of 1964.

By 1967, the Beatles began experimenting with drugs, and their music became more psychedelic and revolutionary. Getting by "With a Little Help from My Friends" was very obviously "getting high with a little help from my friends," and it didn't take a brain surgeon to figure out the acronym for the famous "Lucy in the Sky with Diamonds." Both of these suggestive songs found their place on the landmark *Sergeant Pepper's Lonely Hearts Club Band* album, along with other hits such as "When I'm Sixty-Four" and, of course, the album's title track. That same year, Sergeant Pepper became the anthem for the Summer of Love (see the "Flower power in Monterey" section, later in this chapter, and Chapter 14 for more information about that summer of celebration).

The Beatles also became interested in Indian mysticism, and in 1968 they spent time in Rishikesh, India, at the Maharishi Mahesh Yogi's retreat to study transcendental meditation. Gradually, they became disillusioned, concerned that the Maharishi was using them to promote himself, so they returned home.

Even before the trip to India, George Harrison was interested in Indian sounds and instruments. In 1965, he used an Indian sitar on "Norwegian Wood," and he continued collaborating with Ravi Shankar on songs such as "Within You, Without You" (1967) and "The Inner Light" (1968). The other Beatles also had their unique styles, and devoted fans could often figure out who wrote what. John Lennon's songs owed a lot to rockabilly and folk tunes until he became fascinated with psychedelic music. Paul McCartney was known for the group's romantic ballads, such as "Yesterday." Ringo, the endearing clown prince of the Beatles, didn't write.

Unfortunately, the good times didn't last. By the time they recorded *The Beatles* (more commonly known as the White Album) in 1968, the band members had already started going their separate ways, and some of the songs on that album were recorded individually. By 1970, the band had split. Some said that Lennon's marriage to Yoko Ono was the straw that broke the camel's back and finished the breakup that had already begun.

Although *Let It Be* was the last Beatles album released (1970), it was a compilation of earlier songs. *Abbey Road* (1969) was the last album that the Beatles produced together.

Even after they split up, the Beatles countinued influencing popular music and appealing to audiences, and their music remains forever current. Today their music is classic in more ways than one — some symphony orchestras even tune up their guitars during their summer pops seasons.

Like the Rolling Stones

In the wake of Beatlemania, other British bands headed to the United States. The Animals, the Yardbirds, the Who, and the Kinks were some of the edgier groups who took advantage of America's passion for British rock, but the most popular band was the Rolling Stones (called "the Stones" for short). They didn't adopt the Beatles' initial cute, clean-cut image and were the first band to wear whatever they wanted onstage, from T-shirts and jeans to flashy mod costumes (see Chapter 16 to find out all about the mods). Hairstyles were wilder, too, and these changes were definitely shocking to audiences that were used to impeccable, classically turned out musical groups. Figure 15-4 shows the Stones in action.

Although the Stones' first albums (three appeared in January 1964 — *The Rolling Stones, 12 x 5,* and *England's Newest Hit Makers*) featured remakes of classic R & B tunes, lead guitar player Keith Richards and lead singer Mick Jagger soon began writing their own songs, but even these tracks were heavily influenced by the American blues.

Figure 15-4:
The Rolling
Stones in a
London
park, 1967.

©Topham/The Image Works

By 1967, the Stones were synonymous with the '60s philosophy of sex, drugs, and rock 'n' roll. Their music reflected a hedonistic lifestyle (check out "Satisfaction," "Let's Spend the Night Together," and "Honky Tonk Woman") and glorified the drug culture — in large part because the musicians were personally involved. Police regularly searched them for drugs and usually found what they were looking for. All over the world, the press regularly reported (and probably exaggerated) their escapades, and the Stones seemed to enjoy and actually cultivate their reputation for debauchery. Their album *Beggar's Banquet* showed their attraction to the dark side — or at least their desire to get conservatives' britches in a wad — with the song "Sympathy for the Devil."

The other '60s music

Even rock music went mainstream and appealed to the under-13 and over-30 sets. Well-known but more mainstream artists from the 1960s were singers Neil Diamond and Barbra Streisand, groups such as Herb Alpert and the Tijuana Brass, and the music of Bert Bacharach. Also, the Rat Pack crowd, including Frank Sinatra, Sammy Davis Jr., and Dean Martin, remained popular, as did Elvis Presley, through all his ups and downs.

However, even the more traditional singers became caught up in the changes of the '60s. Bobby Darin was a nightclub performer, whose lifelong ambition was to be bigger than Frank Sinatra. Although he never quite achieved that acclaim, he was extremely successful, but in the late '60s, personal crises, as well as the assassination of Bobby Kennedy, made him reevaluate his life. He took a year off and came back to produce two folk-rock protest albums.

The Rolling Stones remained hugely popular through the 1970s and into the new millenium. They're still on the concert circuit, and many music critics, as well as the public, take great pleasure in looking at pictures of the Stones of the 1960s who are now in their 60s, wrinkles and all. In an ironic twist, the Stones, like many performers of their generation, have become a marketing and money-making machine. They cemented their ties to "the establishment" when their song "Start Me Up" was, for a while, a theme song for Microsoft.

Singing with the Revolution

Most people think of 1960s revolutionary music being about the Vietnam War, and to a large extent, they're right. But the music also reflected some of the huge social changes that were taking place. In the beginning of the decade, songs such as "We Shall Overcome" became symbolic of the civil rights struggle. A lot of music took on the themes of social justice, and yet other groups, such as the Beatles and the Rolling Stones (see the preceding section) celebrated the wild, exuberant youth culture, characterized by unconventional clothing, lots of sex, and drug experimentation.

The lyrics to the song "We Shall Overcome" were derived from Charles Tindley's gospel song "I'll Overcome Some Day" (1900) and the opening and closing melody from the 19th-century spiritual "No More Auction Block for Me" (a pre–Civil War song).

Watching through a purple haze: Psychedelic rock

Making music (or even listening to it, for that matter) while stoned or on an LSD trip (see Chapter 14 to find out about how the '60s went psychedelic) resulted in a whole different kind of music — *psychedelic* (or *acid*) *rock,* which featured melodies that interpreted the musicians' drug-induced visions. American psychedelic music was created and popularized on the West Coast in the mid-'60s with bands such as the Grateful Dead (see the "And the music never stopped" sidebar), Jefferson Airplane, Jimi Hendrix, and the Doors (see the "Living large and dying young" sidebar). In England, beginning with the *Sergeant Pepper's Lonely Hearts Club Band* album, the Beatles were at the forefront of psychedelic music, but the Who, Pink Floyd, and Cream (featuring Eric Clapton) also recorded psychedelic hits.

The influence of psychedelic rock, though, extended far beyond those most closely associated with the sound. By the mid-'60s, the Beach Boys got tired of the surf sound (see the section "Goin' surfin'"), and their music became more psychedelic and experimental. After Brian Wilson stopped touring with the group, he wrote and recorded the music for the 1966 album *Pet Sounds*.

The songs feature vocal harmonies as well as unusual instruments (such as harpsichords) and sound effects (from barking dogs to rattling soda cans). Although not a top seller, *Pet Sounds* influenced other musicians, such as the Beatles on their Sergeant Pepper album. The psychedelic movement even inspired Motown — the Temptations and the Supremes tried psychedelic music before deciding that they were more successful with their own sound.

Marching to the music: Rock protests

Political protest music actually began with the musicians and singers of the folk revival and the early days of folk rock, including Bob Dylan and Phil Ochs. Other politically active folk musicians were Joan Baez, Buffy St. Marie, Tom Paxton, Paul Simon, and Tom Lehrer. Protest music had many different faces — from anger to sorrow to outright ridicule. However, protest music didn't start with the Vietnam War — many of the early protest songs were folk songs dealing with the plight of workers, and though Pete Seeger's "Where Have all the Flowers Gone?" was written during the '50s, it remained relevant through the Vietnam War era.

People all over the world have called Bob Dylan a poet and a sermonizer, and many of his early songs, such as "Blowin' in the Wind" and "The Times They Are A-Changin'," talk about the changes that many young people wanted in their society — peace and justice. One of the most popular singers of the era was Joan Baez, who was a staunch supporter of the free speech movement and antiwar protests at Berkeley (see Chapter 11). To this day, Baez uses her talent to support issues such as migrant workers' rights. Another woman who wrote and performed politically active material was Buffy St. Marie, who brought American Indian issues (see Chapter 13) into her repertoire.

And the music never stopped

The Grateful Dead, who formed in 1965, wrote and performed unique music that was a potpourri of rock, folk, bluegrass, blues, country, jazz, and a liberal dose of psychedelia. Their lead guitarist (and de facto leader) was Jerry Garcia. Although they recorded albums, they were best known as a touring band — during the 1960s, the Dead played just about every rock concert and festival.

Even into the 1990s, the band had a devoted group of fans, called Dead Heads, who were the band's camp followers. They had reason for such devotion — the Dead not only allowed but also encouraged fans to tape (and share) their shows — as long as it wasn't for profit. After Garcia's death in 1995, the remaining members formally decided to retire the name "Grateful Dead," although they continued touring under various names. In 2003, they renamed themselves "the Dead."

Living large and dying young

One of the more tragic aspects of the music scene in the 1960s was the drug culture. Instead of occasionally smoking pot, like many of their fans, three of the most influential and innovative musicians of the decade burned the candle at both ends, ruined their careers, and ultimately paid with their lives.

Jimi Hendrix was a wildly creative (and just plain wild) musician and performer, who managed to coax highly original sounds from his electric guitar. Hendrix definitely cultivated his rebellious image, which made him hugely popular but also brought a lot of criticism. Critics considered him lewd and indecent — however, one of his most famous antics was neither — he often broke or burned his guitar on stage, and one of these relics was recently sold at an auction. However, his conduct offstage is what led to his ultimate downfall — drinking and drugs led to erratic performances, arrests, and, ultimately, his death in 1970 of an overdose of sleeping pills.

Jim Morrison of the Doors (named for the Aldous Huxley book *The Doors of Perception*) wrote socially and politically conscious lyrics to go with the group's distinctive sound. Their music, as well as their performances, was provocative and rebellious. Morrison wanted people to start thinking when they heard the Doors' music. He said, "I like any reaction I can get with my music. Just anything to get people to think. I mean if you can get a whole room full of drunk, stoned people to actually wake up and think, you're doing something." Before appearing on live TV, ABC insisted that they change the line "Girl, we couldn't get much higher" to "Girl, we couldn't get much better" in their hit song "Light My Fire," but onstage, Morrison sang the original line instead. In concert, Morrison often was outrageous and unrestrained — once, he allegedly exposed himself and was charged with both a felony (which he beat) and a misdemeanour (which he didn't). Although he used drugs regularly, Morrison didn't die of an overdose (as far as anyone knows). He died mysteriously in Paris in 1971, and some fans actually believe that he faked his death to get out of the spotlight.

Janis Joplin was one of a kind — she didn't quite fit into any particular genre. As a member of Big Brother and the Holding Company and later a solo artist, she was definitely a free spirit, singing with complete abandon. Rarely seen on stage without her bottle of Southern Comfort, Janis sang tunes that were based on folk songs as well as beatnik poems, but she was most memorable for singing about the pain of life and love in her powerful, gravelly voice. Unfortunately, like many other musicians of the '60s, she got caught up in drugs, and in 1970, died from a heroin overdose at age 27.

These innovative performers have definitely influenced the way music is heard and staged today. The concerts that feature wild antics, creative costuming (which sometimes features little or no clothing), outspoken lyrics, and elaborate staging have emerged from the likes of these three icons, who broke guitars on stage, performed nude, and cried, wailed, and cursed at their audiences.

The Vietnam War brought about many songs protesting the war. The "I-Feel-Like-I'm-Fixin'-to-Die-Rag" by Country Joe and the Fish expressed the way many people felt about going to Vietnam, as did "Fortunate Son," made famous by Creedence Clearwater Revival. At Woodstock, Richie Havens made his feelings known by singing "Handsome Johnny," a song about generations of Americans going off to war.

The Weird Al of the '60s

Tom Lehrer was a musician whose music tackled some of the issues of the day with a satirical bite and a sense of the ridiculous. Even his titles convey his zany approach to war, racism, education, and life in general, with songs such as "World War III Rag," "Pollution," "Vatican Rag," "National Brotherhood Week," "Poisoning the Pigeons in the Park," "New Math," and "Masochism Tango." After Lehrer retired from music, his songs remained popular for a long time on shows such as radio's *Dr. Demento*.

One song that brought many of the themes of the '60s together was "Alice's Restaurant" by Arlo Guthrie. The long song is really a story about a man who gets arrested for littering. When he shows up at his draft board with ratty clothes and long hair after smoking a joint or two, he's rejected; because of his littering conviction, he's not considered morally fit to go and kill people. The song manages to talk about all the things that were important to young people of the '60s and poke fun at the bureaucratic establishment.

Coming Together and Falling Apart: The Music Festivals

In the early years of the decade, the largest music festivals were the Newport Jazz and Folk festivals in Rhode Island. Began in 1959, the Newport Festival served as one of the largest venues for both new and established folk artists (see the section on folk music for some information about Bob Dylan at Newport). In the late 1960s, the Newport Folk Festival had a hard time getting an audience as many people had drifted toward rock musicians, who had taken over the protest music. (However, the festival weathered the changing times and continues today as one of the major folk festivals in the United States.) In the late 1960s rock was king, and several huge festivals celebrated not only the new music but also the socially liberated lifestyles of the times.

Flower power at Monterey

In June 1967, the First Annual Monterey International Pop Music Festival (subtitled "An Aquarian Exposition") inaugurated the famous Summer of Love. Flower power was at its peak, and more than 200,000 young people met at the county fairgrounds in Monterey, California, for a three-day celebration of music, peace, and love. (Check out Chapter 14 for more on flower power.)

The music was phenomenal. Most performers appeared for free. Some of the most popular groups took the stage, including the Mamas and the Papas, Big Brother and the Holding Company with Janis Joplin, Jefferson Airplane, the Jimi Hendrix Experience, the Who, Country Joe and the Fish, Otis Redding, Lou Rawls, the Byrds, Simon & Garfunkel, Ravi Shankar, and the Grateful Dead.

Money from the festival funded the Monterey Pop Foundation, which helps community-based causes such as the Haight Ashbury Free Clinic (see Chapter 14).

The big one: Woodstock

Although Woodstock wasn't the first or only rock event of the 1960s, it was the most famous. What began as a typical three-day music festival on August 15, 1969, turned into the largest single gathering of people to listen to live music. The concert's promoters originally anticipated around 50,000 people, but between 500,000 and 1 million (taking an accurate tally was impossible) came to Woodstock for three days of peace and good tunes (check out a small slice of the crowd scene in Figure 15-5).

Promoters originally planned the festival for Woodstock, New York, but it really took place in nearby Bethel, New York.

Figure 15-5:
Lounging at Woodstock with a half million of your closest friends.

©Henry Diltz/CORBIS

Just putting on the concert was a feat. It took about nine months to organize it, including getting the musicians, finding and preparing the site, and working with city politicians. Most residents of Bethel, who were either farmers or played host to families escaping New York City for the summer, weren't terribly enthusiastic about the coming event. Not only were they concerned about the crowds and the traffic, but they also had concerns about the type of people who would be coming in for three days of rock 'n' roll. They'd seen more than enough of the longhaired, strangely dressed hippies on TV and preferred that the shady characters stayed away.

But the hippies came — and came. They walked and they rode, arriving on everything from horses to motorcycles, cars, vans, and school busses. Traffic was far worse than people had anticipated — cars were lined up for miles to get into the concert venue, and eventually, the New York State thruway leading to Bethel was closed. Some residents felt that an army of freaks was invading their town. However, they were resigned to the fact that they'd have to deal with the situation and felt that it would be okay as long as the visitors behaved themselves. By the time the festival was in full swing, its population made Bethel the second largest city in New York. Amazingly, there were no police and no trouble.

Even the promoters were overwhelmed by the sheer numbers. Because of the massive crowd and the fact that the promoters had problems with their ticket booths, sometime during the first day, they announced that admission was free. At the end of the festival, the facilitators said that they took a financial bath but that the event wasn't about the money. It was beautiful — you couldn't buy the experience for anything. They realized what was really important: People can live together peacefully without fear.

Much of Woodstock was about the music. Looking back, many people think it was all about protest music and psychedelic rock (and to a large extent, it was). But with a diversity of musicians including Richie Havens; Joan Baez; the Who; the Grateful Dead; Sha-Na-Na; Joe Cocker; Country Joe and the Fish; Arlo Guthrie; Crosby, Stills, and Nash; Santana; Sly and the Family Stone; Jefferson Airplane; Janis Joplin; and Jimi Hendrix (to name just a few), the air was filled with everything from folk to traditional rock 'n' roll to country to Latin rhythms and, of course, protest songs and psychedelic rock.

Why did this music communicate so well with young people? Because it was about what was going on at the time and it affected their lives — many of them were of draft age and actively protested the Vietnam War, and most were experimenting with new lifestyles, such as communal living, free love, and recreational drugs. One of the more memorable musical moments at Woodstock was Jimi Hendrix's long, acid, atonal version of the "Star Spangled Banner." He created effects on his guitar that simulated the horrors of war — machine guns, bombs, and screams. The rendition was highly debated — some people hailed it as symbolic of the unrest in the United States, and others reviled it as anti-American mockery. Figure 15-6 shows Hendrix at Woodstock, perhaps at the moment when he was singing the U.S. national anthem.

Figure 15-6:
Jimi
Hendrix at
Woodstock.

Amazingly, the ambiance of those three days almost eclipsed the music. The festival was plagued with problems, but somehow they were all overcome. Because the roads were blocked, many of the artists had to be flown in (and the helicopter noise made it difficult to hear some of the music). Toilets, food, shelter, and medical supplies were scarce, but pot was never in short supply, so everyone stayed mellow. A spirit of sharing and caring was in their midst. Even the U.S. Army pitched in, airlifting food and medical supplies. Despite the antiwar feelings of most of the partipants, they recognized and appreciated the help. "They're with us, not against us" was the common sentiment.

And then it rained. As the organizers scurried to cover up the equipment and urged people away from the towers, the fields turned to mud. Fortunately, the weather was warm — many people took the occasion to get naked. They took shelter together in tents, under plastic, and in sleeping bags. Until the music came back on, people made their own music and danced and played in the mud. Woodstock was about people getting together peacefully to create a great experience. Participants felt it was a beginning and looked at it as an example of how the new generation could pull together and live in a new way. Even some of the residents agreed.

Years later, promoters tried to capitalize on the festival's fame by staging a Woodstock 1999, but it was nothing like the original, put on solely for commercial gain and lacking the spirit of the '60s. If you want to experience the real Woodstock for yourself, check out the film *Woodstock: 3 Days of Peace and Music.*

A day of violence and music: Altamont

After Woodstock, people wanted the feeling to continue, and the Altamont concert was born. The concert was going to be free and was originally supposed to take place in San Francisco. However, organizers quickly realized that the crowd would be too large for the city, so they moved the concert to an auto racetrack in Altamont, California. It was a good thing they did — they expected about 100,000 people, but almost 300,000 showed up.

The Rolling Stones were the headliners and sponsors of the one-day event on December 6, 1969, which also featured Santana; the Grateful Dead; Jefferson Airplane; and Crosby, Stills, Nash, and Young. Everyone hoped for the peace and love of Woodstock, yet the Stones, upon the advice of the Grateful Dead, hired the Hell's Angels motorcycle gang for security. The Stones certainly didn't intend to promote violence — the English branch of the Angels was quite tame compared to their American counterparts.

Throughout the day, several incidences of violence occurred, which were fueled by the Angels' overreaction to even the most minor incidents. However, the worst tragedy occurred during the Rolling Stones' set when Meredith Hunter, an 18-year-old black man, was attacked and killed when Hell's Angels found that he was carrying a gun. Several times, Mick Jagger begged the crowd to quiet down, stay calm, and stop fighting, but each time he started a song, violence began again. Three others died (of other causes) at the Altamont concert, and four babies were born.

Just about everything related to Altamont was a disaster. Poorly organized and conceived, it was the complete opposite of Woodstock. After that, rock festivals were never quite the same. People thought that Woodstock was a fluke and, only a couple of months after the infamous event at Altamont, no longer believed that young people could come together in peace and love. The love-in of the '60s was over.

Some believe that the lyrics "the day the music died" in Don McLean's "American Pie" refer to Altamont.

Chapter 16

Exploring Pop Culture

. . . .

In This Chapter

▶ Changing fashion

▶ Entertaining and educating: Arts and culture

▶ Sporting life

▶ Learning the lingo

. . . .

In addition to all the political and social change going on in the 1960s, the decade saw the birth of new trends in fashion, the arts, popular entertainment, and even slang. To get a feel for the decade as a whole, you can't overlook '60s pop culture — where teens and adults alike left their drab knee-length skirts, suits, ties, and Beaver Cleaver haircuts back in the '50s and let their bodies (and hair) run free and wild. In this chapter, we show you how to "dig" the '60s and highlight the greatest in theatrical entertainment, the arts, sports, and more.

However, more important than the individual changes in fashion, the arts, and the language was the overall effect of the '60s — the feeling that a person could look differently, think "outside the box," speak one's mind (even on subjects like sex, politics, and religion) and march to his or her own drummer. Some folks felt that all this individuality wasn't a good thing and gave rise to a selfish "me generation," but after the '60s, people were certainly committed to expressing themselves.

Stylin' in the '60s

Every decade has fads and fashions, but the 1960s seemed to usher in another fad every other week. Some were classic styles and others were merely cute and fun, but many reflected the social upheavals and gave the youth of the decade a way to create a culture all their own and shock their elders.

In 1960, women's clothes were still classic and conservative, reflected by First Lady Mamie Eisenhower, who wore tailored suits, medium heels, and pearls. The well-dressed man wore suits and ties, along with hats (picture Eliot Ness in *The Untouchables*). By the middle to the end of the '60s, however, new fashion trends, from miniskirts to space-age fabrics and styles, seemed to emerge almost every other week. The trendiest women's clothes were revealing (more sheer and skimpier), and men made bold statements with bright color palettes, velvet jackets, and special touches such as ruffles.

However, not everyone showed their colors and exposed flesh. Many people still wore classic preppie styles and conservative office wear (three decades passed before casual Fridays became a standard). But if '60s fashion had any lasting legacy, it was that people now feel freer to express their individuality and wear clothes that reflect their personalities and lifestyles.

Reinventing women's wear, from Jackie to Twiggy

When Jackie Kennedy came to the White House following her husband's 1960 election, *haute couture* (high fashion) became the catchword. Women everywhere imitated her bouffant hairdo, pillbox hats, and elegant style. Jackie was also one of the first ladies to be photographed in casual attire; in Hyannisport (the Kennedy's vacation home) she was often seen in T-shirts and capri pants. Jackie's style was popular not only with the American public but also throughout the world.

On a diplomatic trip abroad, President Kennedy referred to himself as "the man who brought Jackie to Paris."

Although Jackie didn't wear miniskirts (this trend didn't make the scene until 1963), she did raise her hemlines to the knee, and her sleeveless, A-line dresses looked equally good when cut off at midcalf. Throughout the '60s and beyond, Jackie's style was popular, although by the middle of the decade, it was no longer trendy.

The '60s saw London emerging as a new fashion capital, not necessarily competing with Paris but existing in a kind of parallel universe. Instead of appealing to wealthy, middle-aged women (like the name brands Dior and Chanel), British fashion was designed and priced for the young. Carnaby Street in London was the hub of the London fashion explosion.

Mary Quant, a Carnaby Street designer, brought out the miniskirt, which went great with André Courrèges' *go-go boots* (white midcalf boots with flat heels). Along with go-go boots, knee high boots, popularized by Nancy Sinatra's song "These Boots Are Made for Walking," were trendy during the '60s. At first, the style was simply laughable — real women dressing like cheerleaders. Twiggy, who was Quant's most famous model, looked like a teenager herself — she was thin, somewhat androgynous, and looked perfect in the designer's clothes. In fact, she became the standard for fashion models — even today, the "almost anorexic" look is the hallmark of fashion models.

Although Carnaby Street style started in London, Americans adopted it as enthusiastically as they embraced the Beatles. TV helped the latest fashions and fads not only cross the ocean but also travel quickly across the United States, as performers wore the latest styles.

Speaking of androgynous, the '60s saw the rise of the pants suit for women. Ironically, the same people who objected to bare legs (and more) shown off by the micromini also objected to pants on women — they didn't want women dressing like men. Although pants for women were becoming more acceptable throughout the '60s, it was the introduction of the *midi* (mid-calf) and *maxi* (floor-length) skirts in 1968 (which many young women hated) that led to the real popularity of pants as an alternative. Feminism (see Chapter 12) also contributed to pants as a fashion option — women didn't see why they shouldn't be as comfortable and free to move around as men.

As the decade went on, skirts got shorter, blouses became more see-through, and the public got used to skin. Bikinis, which were seen only in Europe until the mid-'60s, became common sights on American beaches (encouraged by the teenage beach movies with Annette Funicello and Frankie Avalon).

Saying goodbye to plain and white: The men and the mods

Men's fashions changed during the 1960s as well. Packing away the staid white and pastel shirts and striped ties of the '50s, even businessmen of the '60s began dressing in bright colors and sporting wide ties (with the exception of IBM, which kept their white-shirt rule into the '70s).

Off the job, men became more flamboyant. Evolved from the English *Teddy Boy* style — which adopted some Edwardian styles — velvet coats, ruffled shirts, and bows made a dramatic statement. In the '60s, men's leisure wear emulated rock stars instead of golfers.

Those who couldn't quite go for ruffles adopted a more casual style. Thinking that sports jackets and ties were still too much like office wear, they adopted turtlenecks as after-hours wear. For men (as well as women), bell-bottom pants were the fashion of the day for off-the-job attire.

Hanging loose, hippie style

By the mid '60s, along with protests and flower power, students rejected high fashion and adopted a completely casual style. The young conformed to the cult of nonconformity — although they dressed differently from their parents, they had a kind of uniform (though with many variations). Both men and women wore faded, ripped jeans; tie-dyed shirts; and army surplus, often decorated with peace signs. Both sexes also adopted peasant and Indian fabrics and fashions. Copying John Lennon's style, granny glasses were popular, and most hippies sported love beads. Of course, to dress like a hippie, you have to wear sandals or go barefoot, put a flower in your hair, and wear a headband.

As with so much of the hippie culture, the exact origin of the counterculture fashion defies description, because it had so many influences. The anti-materialistic lifestyle led many hippies (or at least those who really didn't have money) to haunt thrift shops and army surplus stores. Their interest in other cultures (especially Indian, both American and Asian) inspired them to wear ethnic clothing. The most general statement you can make about hippie fashion is that it was anti-fashion.

Whiskers, sideburns, and the long and short of hair

For women, hair in the 1960s started with the Jackie bouffant — somehow, though, the style just didn't go with miniskirts, jeans, or peasant skirts. So what happened? Hairstyles were either very short, as in the geometric Vidal Sassoon cut, or long and straight (which was often achieved by rolling hair around small juice cans — kudos to the person who invented the straightening iron).

The '60s also saw the birth of unisex hairstyles, as women adopted the mop-top Beatles style. But the mop-top was short-lived — as the Rolling Stones grew their locks, so did their fans. By the late '60s, men's hair (for anyone who didn't have to show up at an office) was long, either worn loose or tied back. Facial hair was in, too, from beards to moustaches to long sideburns, often all at once. If you were a hippie, you made sure that your facial hair was scruffy, even if you had to work at it; even the suit-and-tie crowd sported sideburns if they wanted to be "in."

Bringing Society to the Big Screen

Until the 1960s, the *studio system* (where a few major studios controlled the production and distribution of movies), along with the *Hays Code,* which defined what was morally acceptable in films (see the "Confronting social and political issues" section), determined the kinds of films that the American public could see. But by the sixties, court rulings had broken up the studio system (on antitrust grounds), and moviemakers were increasingly ignoring the restraints of the voluntary Hays Code. These combined forces meant that the movie-going public would see grittier, more realistic films that reflected the changing times. But the public experienced no shortage of the usual fare of musicals, romantic comedies, and historical epics.

In the '60s, a lot of young directors, who would dominate films for the rest of the century, began their careers — including Woody Allen, Robert Altman, Peter Bogdanovich, Sidney Lumet, and Roman Polanski.

We cover a lot of movies in this section. If you want a more visual look at the 1960s, take this chapter with you to the video store. And check out Chapter 18, where we suggest ten great films to rent that feature many of the people and events that we cover throughout this book.

Revisiting popular themes and characters

During the 1950s, musicals, historical epics, comedies, and dramas dominated films, and this trend continued through the '60s, with films such as *Lawrence of Arabia, The Sound of Music, Cleopatra, West Side Story, The Miracle Worker,* and *Some Like It Hot.*

Fighting the cold war

Before Vietnam came to the forefront of American consciousness (see Chapter 9), Communism, the cold war, and the threat of nuclear annihilation were on people's minds, and the movies reflected those thoughts and fears. Espionage films lit up the big screen, including *The Spy Who Came in from the Cold*, and movies embraced comic portrayals of the enemy, such as in *The Russians Are Coming, the Russians Are Coming.* Some chilling satires also entertained audiences, including *Dr. Strangelove, or How I Learned to Stop Worrying and Love the Bomb.*

Preaching principles

As the '50s ended, new revelations about the Holocaust, concerns about nuclear war, and the emerging civil rights movement all served to raise social consciousness. Even though World War II was 20 years in the past, films such as *Judgment at Nuremberg,* which showed the horror of the concentration camps, and *Ship of Fools* and *The Pawnbroker,* which depicted the more subtle effects of the Nazi regime, drew audiences.

Other films depicting past events, such as *Inherit the Wind,* which dealt with the conflict over evolution, and *On the Beach,* which speculated on life after nuclear war, were also popular. One of the most popular, well-acted films of the decade was *To Kill a Mockingbird,* which talked about the problems of blacks in the South.

Imagining a different world

Science fiction was a popular genre since the advent of silent movies, and the '60s were no exception. *Fantastic Voyage* took viewers on a trip through their arteries and veins, and *Planet of the Apes* (another evolutionary tale) provided an interesting "what if?" scenario. But by far the best example of 1960s sci-fi was *2001: A Space Odyssey.* This film reflected the public's fascination with space but inadvertently appealed to the counterculture — theaters where *2001* was showing often reeked of marijuana smoke.

Being best buddies

Buddy films are as old as movies — remember Laurel and Hardy, Abbott and Costello, and Martin and Lewis? In the late 1960s, however, two very different buddy films became famous. *Easy Rider* was not only a buddy film but also the ultimate road-trip movie, featuring two drugged-out bikers — played by Dennis Hopper and Peter Fonda — trying to escape the bonds of conformity. In the course of their wild ride across America, they meet George (played by Jack Nicholson, who was also a cowriter of the script), a good-old Southern boy who also happens to be a lawyer for the American Civil Liberties Union and whom the bikers convert from booze to pot.

Butch Cassidy and the Sundance Kid was an outlaw movie of the buddy type, but one where the audience actually roots for the bad guys. Butch (Paul Newman) and Sundance (Robert Redford) are personable, funny, optimistic (no matter what difficulties they encounter), damned good-looking, and above all, human.

Driving fast cars and scoring hot babes

Bond . . . James Bond. Witty, urbane, and handsome, this man always gets the bad guy and the girl (excuse us, the girls!), and he's been doing it for more than four decades. Adapted from the popular spy novels by Ian Fleming, 007 movies, full of action, romance, fast cars, dry martinis, and gadgetry, were some of the most popular movies of the '60s. From *Dr. No,* which was released in the United States in 1963, until the 1969 film *On Her Majesty's Secret Service,* Americans enjoyed *From Russia With Love, Goldfinger, Thunderball,* and *You Only Live Twice.*

HISTORIC TRIVIA

All the film that's fit to see

The Hays Code was named for Will Hays, the president of the Motion Picture Producers and Distributors of America from 1922 through 1945. He regulated how sex and violence could be presented in films. Neither could be shown explicitly, and the "evildoers" in the film could never be sympathetic and must always get their just desserts. Among other things, bad language was a no-no, reverends (of all denominations) had to be depicted with reverence, and interracial relationships were forbidden. The film-rating system that replaced the Hays Code didn't seek to restrict or censor films in any way. Instead, the intent was to let people know what was in the films, according to the following ratings:

✔ **G:** General audiences, including children.

✔ **M:** Mature audiences — parental guidance was suggested, but all ages were admitted.

✔ **R:** Restricted — children under 16 weren't admitted without a parent or adult guardian.

✔ **X:** No one under 17 was admitted.

Over the years, the rating system has changed to further refine the categories and adapt to changing public perceptions. For example, some of the movies that were X-rated during the '60s would receive an R rating today.

Confronting social and political issues

In addition to the adventurous, scientific, and nostalgic films of the '60s, some of the memorable films of the decade did reflect the changing times and emerging social and political issues — such as sex, drugs, and race — that were banned from movies since the Hays Code of the '30s (see the "All the film that's fit to see" sidebar). Compliance with the code was entirely voluntary and self-regulated, but the studios abided by it to avoid government censorship. In the '50s, filmmakers began pushing the envelope of what was acceptable, and by the mid-'60s, the Hays Code was virtually ignored. People wanted more explicit films, yet they wanted to control the films that children could see. Therefore, in 1966, the movie rating system went into effect, indicating whether films were suitable for children. This, as well as the more free-spirited times, effectively ended movie censorship.

Crossing the color line

From the days of silent movies, when blacks appeared on-screen, they were cast in stereotyped roles. The only positive images in films aimed at the general public were those that featured musical greats such as Duke Ellington. During the 1920s through the '40s, black producers made a number of *race films,* which were low-budget movies made for black audiences. However, during the late '40s and '50s, things began to change as actors like Sidney Poitier, Dorothy Dandridge, and Harry Belafonte appeared in roles that showed blacks in a positive light.

John Wayne in the Vietnam era

John Wayne, one of the most beloved movie actors of the century, appeared in many macho roles in westerns and war films, to the point that people saw him as the roles that he played rather than the man that he was. Although he never served in the military, he made so many war films and was so openly patriotic that this stereotype worked for him — until the Vietnam War.

Wayne loudly supported the Vietnam War and played in the only Vietnam War movie produced and played while the war was on — *The Green Berets*. This role, along with his cooperation with Senator McCarthy's Communist witch hunts (see Chapter 11) and anti-integration statements, cost him fans among some segments of the population as the country became more polarized during the late '60s.

Perhaps more than anyone else, Sidney Poitier was responsible for creating meaningful roles for blacks in American movies. *A Raisin in the Sun, Lilies of the Field,* and *In the Heat of the Night* were some of his most famous films, but *Guess Who's Coming to Dinner?*, which featured an engaged interracial couple, was definitely a first for 1960s films.

Reflecting a youth explosion

Just as the youth of the '60s were exercising their independence and searching for new meaning in life, teens and young adults on-screen explored their freedom. One film that definitely presents a young person trying to find himself is *The Graduate,* which shows a young man questioning his parents' values and ambitions for him (and also exploring a typical young man's fantasy — hooking up with Mrs. Robinson, an older woman).

However, not all '60s youth films were especially introspective. Between 1963 and 1965, Frankie Avalon and Annette Funicello starred in a series of beach movies, which were ripe with bikinis, surfboards, and surf music (see Chapter 15). Gidget films, which were all about a girl who wanted to surf, were also popular in the early '60s.

Getting an X rating

Even before the sexual revolution was in full flower, sex found its place in '60s movies. In *The Apartment,* an office worker loans his apartment to his bosses for liaisons in order to curry favor. *Splendor in the Grass* portrays teen pregnancy, *Some Like It Hot* shows audiences the joys of cross-dressing, and *Tom Jones* demonstrates that it's possible to get physical while eating a lobster dinner.

By the middle of the decade, American audiences could view full frontal nudity in films such as *I Am Curious Yellow, Blow Up,* and *Medium Cool.* These movies created the call for a rating system — although many people had no use for censorship, they weren't quite ready for their children to watch sex on the screen.

One film that illustrates just how far the sexual revolution had gone was *Bob and Carol and Ted and Alice* in 1969. Not only did this film show wife-swapping, but it also involved people other than the "crazy, long-haired hippies" — two normal suburban couples exploring their sexuality.

A Hair-Raising Experience: The '60s Make It to Broadway

Like the movies, theater and the Broadway stage, for a good part of the 1960s, followed tried-and-true formulas: historical dramas and elaborate musicals. Some of the top dramas of the decade were *Becket, A Man for All Seasons,* and *The Great White Hope.* The blockbuster musical comedies were *The Sound of Music, Camelot, How to Succeed in Business Without Really Trying, Mame, Man of La Mancha, Cabaret,* and *Hello, Dolly!*

But in 1968, a brand new musical, *Hair — The American Tribal Love-Rock Musical* made the geographically short (but very long) journey from off-Broadway to the "Great White Way," paving the way for a whole new format for the musical theater. Inspired by the hippies of New York's East Village, James Rado and Jerome Ragni, two out-of-work actors, created *Hair* in 1966, hoping it would find a home on Broadway.

The play was rejected many times by Broadway producers, but the writers' luck changed when the head of the New York Shakespeare Festival Public Theater offered them a limited run in 1967. In time-honored show business tradition, an "angel" (a financial backer) saw the show, fell in love with it, and made it his mission to bring it to Broadway. But the musical's first uptown venue wasn't on Broadway; rather, it was in a working disco, where the show was the opening act for the late-night dance crowd.

Eventually, pressed for funds, *Hair* closed, but everyone still had Broadway on the brain. Rado and Ragni revised the show, rehearsed in the East Village, and eventually opened in Broadway's Biltmore Theater on April 29, 1968. The message of this musical was to have fun, live free, and do your own thing (but don't hurt anyone else). Unbound by conventional morality, the show glorified sex, drugs, rock 'n' roll, racial equality, peace, and love. As a social commentary, *Hair* provides insight into the philosophy of the flower children of the 1960s. As the first and most successful of the rock musicals, it paved the way for later musicals such as *Jesus Christ Superstar, Godspell,* and *Tommy.*

Reflecting Life on the Small Screen

Television, which became available (and loved) in so many American homes during the 1950s, really came into its own in the '60s. It entertained people, made them laugh, absorbed them, and showed them the news as it happened. But as the decade progressed, TV also reflected the changes that were taking place in society.

Late-night talk shows

Although the TV talk show was started in 1954 by Renaissance man Steve Allen, it became quite popular in the '60s, bringing stand-up comedy, satire, and celebrities into America's living rooms, up close and personal. Because it was shown late at night, talk-show material could be slightly more risqué than prime-time fare, although Jack Paar, Allen's successor, was bleeped more times than he thought he deserved. In 1962, Johnny Carson took over and became a late-night institution, hosting the *Tonight Show* until 1992. However, this show wasn't the only game in town — Dick Cavett had a talk show from 1969 to 1972, which was considered the "thinking man's" show because he featured more controversial, edgier guests.

A new kind of variety show

Comedy and variety shows also tackled some of the tough issues. *Rowan & Martin's Laugh-In* was probably the most popular. This fast-moving show featured music, running skits, and an ensemble cast of characters that turned up every week. Cast members wore some of the outrageous and skimpy clothing and fads of the '60s (such as body painting) and managed to be suggestive without using any off-color words, opting instead for such expressions as "very interesting," "ring my chimes," "look that up in your Funk and Wagnalls," and "sock it to me" — you just had to be there! In the opening monologue, both Rowan and Martin managed to make their political opinions known. Figure 16-1 shows *Laugh-In*'s cast.

Some famous stars, such as Goldie Hawn and Lily Tomlin, got their big break on *Laugh-In*.

The *Smothers Brothers Comedy Hour,* however, was more outspoken. Although they featured famous, well-respected comedians and singers, the brothers pushed the envelope to see how much they could satirize and criticize the government and the Vietnam War without being censored (and they were

often censored). They waged their greatest battle, however,
cancelled in 1973. They sued, claiming that their First Amendm
were violated, and eventually won a financial and moral victory.

Figure 16-1:
The *Rowan & Martin's Laugh-In* ensemble.

©Bettmann/CORBIS

The vast wasteland: '60s sitcoms

From the earliest days, comedy has been a staple of TV. Uncle Miltie and
Your Show of Shows with Sid Caesar and Imogene Coca kept people laughing
throughout the '50s, when often a whole neighborhood gathered around an
old black-and-white TV set. Situation comedies (otherwise known as *sitcoms*),
starting in the '50s with *I Love Lucy, Ozzie and Harriet, Leave it to Beaver,* and
Father Knows Best, are often nostalgically regarded as great examples of the
good-old days. The public's love affair with the sitcom continued throughout
the '60s and into the 21st century, although *The Donna Reed Show* is a far cry
from *Sex in the City*.

Perhaps it was a yearning for more innocent times, but in a decade of cold
war, assassinations, protests, hot war, and social change, the country bump-
kin show became popular. *Petticoat Junction, Hee Haw,* and *Green Acres* were
guilty pleasures for many so-called sophisticates and intellectuals (much like
today's tabloids). However, slapstick and somewhat childish comedy wasn't
limited to country. Who could possibly take *My Mother the Car, Mr. Ed,* or
Gilligan's Island seriously? Sitcoms also got into the magic and fantastic in
such 1960s classics as *The Munsters, Bewitched,* and *I Dream of Jeannie*. But
just as with westerns and cop shows, TV liked to make fun of itself — for
example, the classic spy spoof, *Get Smart*, which was popular in the last half
of the decade.

ook at the news

...l amused, it also educated. The American public
...current events as never before. They watched
...y and Nixon in 1960 and then the assassination of
...er 2). They also saw the horrors of Vietnam, the
...e Chapter 6), and the brutality of the 1968 Chicago
...graphically than newspapers or the radio could
...celebrated when Neil Armstrong took his first
...oter 4). In addition, the great news stories of the
...t TV newscasters, such as Walter Cronkite, Chet
...d Edward R. Murrow.

Poking Serious Fun: The New Comedians

Comedians are as old as recorded history — people throughout time have needed someone to make them laugh and forget life's problems. In the 1950s and early '60s, comedians such as Bob Hope, Red Skelton, Jackie Gleason, and Milton Berle helped people laugh out loud, not only at jokes and slapstick routines, but also at humanity, with its public and private missteps. But in the more open atmosphere of the late '60s, a new breed of comedian became popular — one who, with humor, looked at people's hypocrisy as well as the problems of society.

In 1962, the album of a comedian named Vaughn Meader, *The First Family*, rose to the top with his right-on imitation of President Kennedy. His career, like the Kennedy presidency, was brief — after the assassination, Meader pledged to never again do his Kennedy voice as a comedy act.

When asked how he felt about Meader's impression of him, Kennedy retorted, "I've heard Mr. Meader's album. I thought he sounded more like Teddy."

However, most of the comedians of the '60s were far more biting and critical. Here are a few:

- **Mort Sahl:** In the late '50s, Sahl brought a new style to the stage with his casual clothes and improvisational and conversational delivery, instead of the standard joke-telling that was common at the time. His patter was about anything and everything — relationships, current events, politics, you name it. His *iconoclastic* style (debunking traditionally accepted ideas) remained popular through the '60s and influenced many later comics and comedy writers.

Mort Sahl ended his routines with the line, offended?"

- **Lenny Bruce:** Sahl's comic style inspired Lenny act from doing impressions to telling stories and pe more natural style. He also brought profane and contr into his act and didn't avoid using four-letter words. Thi brought him dedicated audiences but also unwanted atten law — he was arrested for obscenity several times. Eventuall was convicted of obscenity after a six-month-long trial but neve his four-month sentence. He used his encounters with the police a courts as material for his routine, which put him under even closer scrutiny. Blackballed in many cities in the United States and overseas, Bruce's last stand was at the Fillmore in San Francisco. On August 3, 1966, he died from a drug overdose.

- **Dick Gregory:** One of the first black comics to become popular with all audiences was Dick Gregory, who was not only a comedian but also a social activist, working for civil rights both on- and offstage. During the '60s, Dick Gregory joked about the conditions of blacks in the South. He became involved in causes such as social justice, anti–Vietnam War activism, economic reform, antidrug issues, alternate history (conspiracy theories), and others. To support his views, he went on several hunger strikes. In 1968, he ran for president of the United States as a write-in candidate, and later he wrote the book *Write Me In* about that political campaign.

Hitting the Books

Even with the popularity of movies and TV, people were still reading a lot of books in the '60s. Popular fiction as well as nonfiction including diet books, cookbooks, and astrology topped the *New York Times* bestseller list. However, among the counterculture, older books often inspired and supported their quest for a new way of seeing the world. And with the launch of the sexual revolution, magazines featuring light pornography began to have their heyday.

Topping the charts

The bestseller lists of the 1960s were heavily weighted in favor of historical fiction, political novels, and suspense by popular authors such as Irving Wallace, Allen Drury, Irving Stone, and James Michener. Steamy potboilers, such as *Valley of the Dolls* and *The Love Machine* by Jacqueline Susann, and books by Harold Robbins also flew off the shelves.

"Is there any group I haven't

Bruce, who changed his
performing skits in a
oversial material
edginess
ion from the
Bruce
served
nd the

ntrospective also hit the top of the
The Confessions of Nat Turner by
ok, and *Couples* by John Updike
e Godfather by Mario Puzo rose to
gain fame as the subject of two

d their niche during the decade.
Conscience of a Conservative by
esident 1968 by Joe McGinniss
n with politics and politicians.

only influential books of the
nd *Civil Disobedience* by Henry
se, *The Little Red Book* by Mao Tse
t Heinlein, *Brave New World* and *The*
d *1984* and *Animal Farm* by George
encouraged the alternate lifestyles

Embracing the Playboy philosophy

A lot of what people call the hedonism and rampant sexuality of the 1960s was embodied in *Playboy* magazine, which glorifies the good life — clothes, cars, music, sports, and, of course, sex. Founded in 1953, Playboy was definitely ahead of the curve (pun absolutely intended).

Hefner also strove to undermine his critics in the "thought police" by giving his magazine an intellectual side. Each issue of *Playboy* featured an interview with a famous personality, such as Muhammad Ali, George Wallace, and Martin Luther King Jr., and often featured fiction and articles by top-name authors. But what *Playboy* is most known for is its nude centerfolds (although many people claim to read it "just for the articles").

In 1965, *Playboy* began losing its grip on the market, as other magazines copied its format. *Penthouse,* a sensational version of the original, hit the streets, featuring more explicit photos and content.

Changing Perspective: Pop, Op, and Psychedelic Art

Pop art was a popular 1960s movement that featured objects from popular culture. Consumer products, movie stars, and comics were common pop art subjects. One of the first artists to create such art was Roy Lichtenstein, who drew comic-like paintings featuring dots (as you'd see in a comic book) and speech bubbles, which express the subject of the paintings. One of Lichtenstein's most famous paintings is *Whaam!* (a large cartoonlike painting of a plane hitting a target, with the word "Whaam" at the point of impact), painted in 1963. Another famous pop artist was Andy Warhol, whose paintings and prints featured repeated images of a person or a thing. Warhol is most famous for his painting of Campbell's soup cans and also for his *Marilyn green, pink, red, and gold,* depicting Marilyn Monroe.

Op art, an abbreviation for optical art, emphasized optical illusions by using spirals, wavy patterns, and the repeated representation of simple geometric forms, often in different proportions. Op art patterns were not only shown in paintings and posters, but by the mid-'60s were also featured in advertising and on clothing. Two of the main op artists were Victor Vasarely and Bridget Riley.

Psychedelic art, inspired by drug-induced hallucinations, wasn't a huge feature of art galleries and museums. Instead, it decorated album covers and posters. Psychedelic art often depicted objects seen through a kaleidoscope and used contrasting colors and detailed images, which often morphed into each other. Some famous examples of psychedelic art are Peter Max posters, which display a combination of art deco swirls and psychedelic patterns. He often used *Day-Glo* paints (specially designed to glow under black lights) and bright, contrasting colors. Although his work reflected the freewheeling youth culture, it was used to market everything from linens to tea bags.

Playing the Game

Before multimillion-dollar contracts, steroid scandals, killer athletes, and drug-addicted players, Americans had a love affair with sports, supported the home teams, win or lose, and idolized their star players.

The dynasties

In the both baseball and football, the 1960s saw sports *dynasties,* teams that, for a few years, seemed absolutely unbeatable.

The pinstriped New York Yankees of the early '60s seemed to be a sports monopoly. Of course, it had happened before — the team of Babe Ruth and Lou Gehrig also dominated the sport in the late 1920s. Armed with power players such as Mickey Mantle and Roger Maris, the "Bronx Bombers" seemed unstoppable and won the World Series from 1960 through 1964. In fact, Maris was the first player to break Babe Ruth's single-season home record, hitting 61 balls out of the park in 1961. Mantle was considered to be one of the greatest of all time — he was a great outfielder and base runner, as well as a power hitter.

When Detroit Tigers player Al Kaline was heckled by a kid who said, "You're not half as good as Mickey Mantle," he replied, "Son, nobody is half as good as Mickey Mantle."

Before the 1960s, professional football wasn't particularly popular — most football fans were devoted to their favorite college team. However, three things changed the place of football in the American consciousness: televising the game, the Super Bowl, and the most powerful team of the decade, the Green Bay Packers. Coached by the great Vince Lombardi, the Packers went from being a losing team in a small city to the major force in the sport.

The first Super Bowl, played in 1967, was organized to pit the championship American Football League (AFL) team against the first-place National Football League (NFL) team. The two leagues merged in 1970, with each league becoming a conference within the NFL. From then on, the Super Bowl was a game between the AFC and the NFC.

The underdogs

America loves an underdog and celebrates when a dismal loser rises to the top. In New York City, 1969 was the year of the underdog as two last-place teams moved to the head of the line.

After the New York Giants and Brooklyn Dodgers left New York for California, the city wanted a new National League team, so the New York Mets were born in 1962. They were a disaster. Not only did they seem to have permanent possession of last place, but they also "achieved" the worst record (40 wins and 120 losses) of any 20th-century baseball team. They made every mistake in the book, even running the wrong way around the bases. But in 1969, they surprised everybody when they won not only the National League pennant, but also the World Series. The celebration in the city was legendary.

The New York Jets, founded in 1959 as one of the teams in the new American Football League (which later merged with the NFL), had one of the most talked about quarterbacks in the league. Unlike the typical jock, Joe Namath was a bit of a rebel, with his long hair, mustache, and white shoes on the football field (which, incidentally, became the standard for years afterward). However, the public would forgive "Broadway Joe" anything, as long as he kept on throwing his deadly accurate passes.

Namath was also cocky — he guaranteed a win for his team in Super Bowl III, even though odds-makers listed the Jets as a 17½-point underdog to the powerful Baltimore Colts. But he had the stuff to back it up and went on to lead his team to victory. Broadway Joe was probably the first and last football star who was as popular as a rock star — he was a major party animal who stayed out all night and usually dated beautiful women, and his fans, both men and women, loved it. In fact, Namath was so popular that he was able to get away with appearing in a TV commercial wearing a pair of pantyhose, with no loss to his reputation.

International politics at the Olympics

Although the Olympic games were pure sport, designed to foster international competition and cooperation, they were never free of politics. The 1964 Olympics saw a nation barred from the games for their domestic policies — South Africa was banned from participating because of their policy of apartheid.

The 1968 games, however, saw the most overt political statements by athletes. When U.S. runners Tommie Smith and John Carlos stood on the victory platform to receive their medals, they each raised a black-gloved fist in a black power salute as the *Star Spangled Banner* played, protesting racial inequality in the United States. Because the International Olympic Committee (IOC) decided that this gesture went against the spirit and ideals of the Olympics, Smith and Carlos were expelled.

In expelling the runners, the IOC stated, "The basic principle of the Olympic games is that politics play no part whatsoever in them. U.S. athletes violated this universally accepted principle . . . to advertise domestic political views."

The Greatest: Muhammad Ali

People either loved him or they hated him, but very few people felt neutral about Muhammad Ali. Learning to box at age 12, Cassius Marcellus Clay had big dreams — to be the heavyweight champion of the world. Before his 18th birthday, he won six state Golden Gloves championships and two national Golden Gloves championships, and shortly after he turned 18, he won a gold medal at the 1960 Olympics.

Clay was an unorthodox fighter, using moves that were rarely seen in the ring. He danced around his opponents and adopted the catchphrase "Float like a butterfly, sting like a bee" to describe his fighting style. He also used what he later called the "Ali Shuffle," where he would quickly shuffle his feet and, whenever possible, deliver a blow while dancing.

Besides his moves in the ring, Clay moved his mouth — a lot. Instead of letting his managers be his mouthpiece, he talked to the press, both to promote himself and to intimidate his opponents, with patter such as, "To prove I'm great, he will fall in eight!"

In 1964, while training for his title bout against Sonny Liston, then heavyweight champion of the world, where he was a heavy underdog in spite of his confidence, Clay met Malcolm X and became a member of the *Nation of Islam* (a black organization that embraced the principles of Islam and advocated self-reliance, as we discuss in Chapter 7). The day after he beat Liston in a huge upset (see Figure 16-2), Clay announced his conversion and his new name, Cassius X. Later that year, Elijah Muhammad, founder of the Nation of Islam, gave him the name Muhammad Ali.

Figure 16-2: Cassius Clay taunts then-champion Sonny Liston during their 1964 title fight.

©Topham/The Image Works

In 1967, Ali was drafted into the military but refused to be inducted on religious grounds as a practicing Muslim minister. After that, almost every state and city cancelled his boxing licenses. In spite of the growing antiwar sentiment, he was stripped of his title and faced a five-year prison term (in 1970, the Supreme Court reversed his conviction and upheld his conscientious objector claim, and he won back his boxing licenses).

Muhammad Ali's refusal to serve in Vietnam led to his statement, "I ain't got no quarrel with them Viet Cong. . . ."

In 1970, Ali began his comeback but wasn't up to his former form, and he lost the 1971 fight against heavyweight champ Joe Frazier. However, this minor setback was just a prelude to the 1974 "Rumble in the Jungle," where he fought George Foreman, the world heavyweight champion, in Zaire. Again, Ali was the underdog. Realizing that he couldn't do his usual dance because of the heat, he developed the "rope-a-dope" strategy, where he stood with his back to the ropes, slipping punches and absorbing punishment until Foreman tired, making it easier for Ali to knock him out. Afterward, a series of wins and losses ensued until he ended his boxing career in 1981 with 56 wins (37 by knockout) and 5 defeats.

As a boxer, a man of principle, and someone who always captured the public interest, Muhammed Ali was an outstanding sports star of the 1960s and the late 20th century.

Walking the Talk

Every generation has a language all its own, designed for youngsters to bond with their friends and keep adults out of their lives. But in the tumultuous '60s, a whole new slang evolved, some of which is still used — although now the slang is part of everyday language, and (ugh) even parents use it. Here are just a few hip words and phrases:

- **Bag:** Thing, usually used in the negative to describe something you're just not into, as in "Math just isn't my bag."

- **Bread:** Money — enough said!

- **Cool:** This word was popular way before the '60s and is still popular today.

- **Crash:** Hit the hay, get some winks — you get the idea (in case you don't, it means to sleep).

- **Dig it:** Understand.

- **Do your own thing:** Do whatever you want, without worrying about pleasing someone else.

- **Downer:** Something that puts you in a bad or sad mood, as in "The ending of Romeo and Juliet is a real downer."

- **Far out:** Fabulous, great, the best. "That band is far out!"

- **Freaked out:** Uneasy, scared, or distressed — generally a really bad feeling. This started with having a bad *trip* but can relate to anything: "She was really freaked out when she got the speeding ticket."

- **Go with the flow:** Don't try too hard or resist what's happening.

- **Grass:** Marijuana.

- **Hang-up:** An emotional problem or an obsession with something. "She's got a hang-up about her looks."

- **Karma:** The new age version of "what goes around comes around."

- **Lay it on me:** Tell me or give it to me. If someone says, "I've got good news and bad news," you might say, "Lay it on me."

- **Make love, not war:** The catchphrase of the antiwar movement.

- **Man:** A way of addressing another person, as in "Hey man, what's happening?" People sometimes use it to address women, too.

- **Mind blowing:** Astounding or awesome, as in "Those fireworks were mind blowing."

- **Outta sight!** See *far out*.

- **Pad:** A place to sleep. Decorated in whatever was available, this place could hardly be called a home. A hippie, who wasn't really into ownership and possessions, often allowed anyone to *crash* at his or her pad.

- **Pot:** See *grass*.

- **Rip-off:** A con or swindle.

- **Spaced out:** Another term that originated with drugs, describing someone who's not thinking clearly. However, people now use it to describe anyone who's not quite "with it" (regardless of why).

- **Split:** Leave, as in "I gotta split, man!"

- **Square:** Hopelessly "out of touch." Parents, teachers, cops, or anyone in authority was considered square.

- **Stoned:** Under the influence of marijuana.

- **Tell it like it is:** Tell the truth.

- **Trip:** What you go on after dropping acid (LSD).

- **Uptight:** Frigid, conventional, tense, or rigid. Someone who didn't like sex, drugs, rock 'n' roll, and long hair would be considered uptight.

- **Vibe:** An intuition or a feeling that you get from something or someone. "I got really good vibes hanging out in the Haight."

Part VI
The Part of Tens

"Gayle and I met in the era of free love.
So far, that free love has cost me nearly
$60,000 in college tuitions."

In this part . . .

The Part of Tens is a *For Dummies* institution, and although the 1960s were all about fighting the powers that be, this is one institution we think that you'll agree is great. In this part, we take a year-by-year look at the decade, revisiting some of the great hits and misses in the world of popular music. Then we move on to ten great movies that really give you a feel for the decade. Finally, we list ten items that you could buy for a buck during the decade.

Chapter 17

Ten Years of Hit Songs

In This Chapter

▶ Starting off with the King and other '50s folk

▶ Enjoying the sounds of the surf

▶ Crossing the waters: Britain comes to the U.S.

▶ Groovin' in Motown

The 1960s were a decade of amazing creativity in music. The '60s also saw some of the huge music festivals such as Newport, which showcased folk music, and Woodstock, the most famous (though not the only) rock festival (see Chapter 15 for more on the music and the festivals). In this chapter, we've assembled a brief tour through some of the chart-topping artists and hits of the decade. This sampling of number-one songs provides a pretty good snapshot of the pop charts throughout the '60s. So whether you're ready to remember some of your old favorites or you're looking to discover some great music that's new to you, you can't go wrong with any of these tunes.

1960

The year was 1960, and Elvis was still the King. Though America had officially entered the 1960s, the pop charts sounded a lot like the '50s.

✔ **Ray Charles:** "Georgia on My Mind"

✔ **Chubby Checker:** "The Twist"

✔ **The Drifters:** "Save the Last Dance for Me"

✔ **Connie Francis:** "Everybody's Somebody's Fool," "My Heart Has a Mind of Its Own"

✔ **Brian Hyland:** "Itsy Bitsy Teenie Weenie Yellow Polka-Dot Bikini"

✔ **Brenda Lee:** "I'm Sorry," "I Want to Be Wanted"

✔ **Elvis Presley:** "Are You Lonesome Tonight," "It's Now or Never," "Stuck on You"

1961

The year 1961 saw a number of acts hit the top of the charts. Many of them were guys singing about their girls and groups of girls singing about their guys.

- **Dion:** "Runaround Sue"
- **The Marvelettes:** "Please Mr. Postman"
- **Ricky Nelson:** "Travelin' Man"
- **Del Shannon:** "Runaway"
- **The Shirelles:** "Will You Love Me Tomorrow?"
- **The Tokens:** "The Lion Sleeps Tonight"
- **Bobby Vee:** "Take Good Care of My Baby"

1962

More about guys and gals getting together and breaking up, but America was getting ready to dance, with hits like "Loco-Motion."

- **The Crystals:** "He's a Rebel"
- **Shelley Fabares:** "Johnny Angel"
- **The Four Seasons:** "Big Girls Don't Cry," "Sherry"
- **Little Eva:** "Loco-Motion"
- **Neil Sedaka:** "Breaking Up Is Hard to Do"
- **The Shirelles:** "Soldier Boy"
- **Bobby Vinton:** "Roses Are Red (My Love)"

1963

The surf sound hit the top of the charts for the first time in '63.

- **The Angels:** "My Boyfriend's Back"
- **The Chiffons:** "He's So Fine"
- **The Essex:** "Easier Said than Done"

✔ **Lesley Gore:** "It's My Party"

✔ **Jan and Dean:** "Surf City"

✔ **Bobby Vinton:** "Blue Velvet," "There! I've Said It Again"

1964

And then there were the Beatles. Not to be lost in the shuffle, the Supremes also started a run of hits in 1964 that would last throughout the decade.

✔ **The Animals:** "House of the Rising Sun"

✔ **The Beach Boys:** "I Get Around"

✔ **The Beatles:** "Can't Buy Me Love," "A Hard Day's Night," "I Feel Fine," "I Want to Hold Your Hand," "Love Me Do," "She Loves You"

✔ **The Dixie Cups:** "Chapel of Love"

✔ **Martha and the Vandellas:** "Dancing in the Street"

✔ **The Righteous Brothers:** "You've Lost that Lovin' Feelin'"

✔ **The Supremes:** "Baby Love," "Come See About Me," "Where Did Our Love Go"

1965

In 1965, the surf sound continued, the Byrds scored hits with their pop-friendly take on folk, and the Rolling Stones hit the charts, looking for some satisfaction.

✔ **The Beach Boys:** "Help Me, Rhonda"

✔ **The Beatles:** "Eight Days a Week," "Help!" "Ticket to Ride," "Yesterday"

✔ **The Byrds:** "Mr. Tambourine Man," "Turn! Turn! Turn! (To Everything There Is a Season)"

✔ **The McCoys:** "Hang On Sloopy"

✔ **The Rolling Stones:** "Get Off of My Cloud," "(I Can't Get No) Satisfaction"

✔ **Sonny and Cher:** "I Got You Babe"

✔ **The Supremes:** "Back in My Arms Again," "I Hear a Symphony," "Stop! In the Name of Love"

1966

In 1966, the Beatles, Supremes, and Rolling Stones continued to score hits. But take a look at some of the other chart-toppers, including a father/daughter combination and a made-for-TV foursome (the Monkees).

- ✔ **Four Tops:** "Reach Out (I'll Be There)"
- ✔ **Tommy James and the Shondells:** "Hanky Panky"
- ✔ **The Mamas and the Papas:** "Monday, Monday"
- ✔ **The Monkees:** "I'm a Believer," "Last Train to Clarksville"
- ✔ **Frank Sinatra:** "Strangers in the Night"
- ✔ **Nancy Sinatra:** "These Boots Are Made for Walkin'"
- ✔ **Percy Sledge:** "When a Man Loves a Woman"
- ✔ **The Young Rascals:** "Good Lovin'"

1967

After their solo chart-topping efforts in 1966, Nancy and Frank Sinatra decided to team up. And you didn't think we could go two years without putting the Beatles, Stones, and Supremes on our list, did you?

- ✔ **The Beatles:** "All You Need Is Love," "Hello Goodbye," "Penny Lane"
- ✔ **The Doors:** "Light My Fire"
- ✔ **Aretha Franklin:** "Respect"
- ✔ **Bobbie Gentry:** "Ode to Billie Joe"
- ✔ **Lulu:** "To Sir with Love"
- ✔ **The Rolling Stones:** "Ruby Tuesday"
- ✔ **Nancy and Frank Sinatra:** "Somethin' Stupid"
- ✔ **The Supremes:** "The Happening," "Love Is Here and Now You're Gone"

1968

In 1968, more Motown stars hit the top with Marvin and Otis, and Paul Simon and Art Garfunkel had their first number one from the hit movie *The Graduate* (see Chapter 18 for a complete rundown on this recommended Friday-night rental).

- **The Beatles:** "Hey Jude"
- **The Doors:** "Hello, I Love You"
- **Marvin Gaye:** "I Heard It through the Grapevine"
- **Tommy James and the Shondells:** "Crimson and Clover"
- **The Rascals:** "People Got to Be Free"
- **Otis Redding:** "(Sittin' on) the Dock of the Bay"
- **Simon and Garfunkel:** "Mrs. Robinson"
- **Sly and the Family Stone:** "Everyday People"

1969

Elvis was back in '69 to close out the decade. And a young kid named Michael Jackson, along with his brothers, shot to the top.

- **The Beatles:** "Come Together," "Get Back"
- **The 5th Dimension:** "Aquarius/Let the Sunshine In," "In Wedding Bell Blues"
- **The Jackson 5:** "I Want You Back"
- **Peter, Paul, and Mary:** "Leaving on a Jet Plane"
- **Elvis Presley:** "Suspicious Minds"
- **The Rolling Stones:** "Honky Tonk Woman"
- **The Temptations:** "I Can't Get Next to You"

Chapter 18

Ten Movies to Take You Back in Time

In This Chapter

▶ Fighting for their rights

▶ Viewing Vietnam

▶ Dancing to the music

*I*f you're nostalgic for the '60s, or you wanna know what it was like to live during those ten terrific and terrible years, you don't have to look any further than your video-rental store. A number of great movies made during the 1960s, as well as those produced in later years that feature a look back, give a glimpse of what life was like back then. We cover a little bit of everything with the selections in this chapter, including civil rights, the cold war, Vietnam, adolescence, and the counterculture, along with the hope, dismay, alienation, controversy, and good-old sense of fun in the '60s.

So go grab some popcorn and a soda, find a comfy couch, and take a trip back in time with one of these films.

Malcolm X

This 1992 film, produced by Spike Lee, of *Do the Right Thing* and *Jungle Fever* fame, traces the life of the Black Muslim leader, based on the biography by Alex Haley. It follows Malcolm's path from an impoverished childhood and a life of petty crime to his eventual prison conversion and subsequent work within the Nation of Islam. Naturally charismatic, Malcolm X (played by Denzel Washington) attracted many followers who believed his message of black self-reliance and pride but also alienated many whites who supported the civil rights movement. He disagreed with integration and the passive resistance of Martin Luther King Jr., but as he became disillusioned with his former mentor, Elijah Muhammad, and more enmeshed in the principles of Islam, he softened his position on black separatism before his eventual assassination. Check out Chapter 7 for more on Malcolm X.

Ali

This 2001 film depicts the life of Olympic gold medalist and heavyweight champion of the world Muhammad Ali (played by Will Smith). Through his friendship with Malcolm X, Ali became a Black Muslim, but during the split in the Nation of Islam, he shifted his alliance to Elijah Muhammad. The film portrays Ali as brash and loud but principled as he refuses induction into the army on religious grounds, refusing to fight in Vietnam. We cover Ali in detail in Chapter 16.

Dr. Strangelove, or: How I Learned to Stop Worrying and Love the Bomb

During the early years of the '60s, the cold war with the Soviet Union and the threat of nuclear annihilation was a huge concern. American movies mirrored those concerns, often in a dramatic fashion. But one film from the era falls squarely in the satire column.

Dr. Strangelove (1964) was meant as a satire of nuclear war and the men who promoted it as a solution to the world's problems. The film was embraced by antinuclear activists, who used it to point to the inherent madness of those with the power to destroy the world. The movie stars Peter Sellers in three roles: as the American president, a British diplomat, and Dr. Strangelove. However, the most chilling portrayals are the men who make the decisions, with their fingers on the button. The film lambastes those who believe that building more missiles will maintain a balance of power in order to avoid war, and it features an unforgettable image of the bomber pilot straddling the bomb as it falls to earth, cheering as he rides all the way to his doom.

Thirteen Days

Unlike Dr. Strangelove, *Thirteen Days* (2000) is a dramatization of the 13 days of the Cuban Missile Crisis. Shown through the eyes of Kenny O'Donnell, special assistant to President John F. Kennedy, and played by Kevin Costner, the film shows the nerve-racking, nail-biting tension of those days when the president had to decide how to meet the Soviet threat and prevent a nuclear war. At times, the conflict was as much between Kennedy and his aides as between Kennedy and Soviet Premier Nikita Khruschev, as the president tried to balance the need to face down the Soviets with the need to save the future of the world.

The Green Berets

In 1968, John Wayne, the Hollywood he-man dedicated to fighting Communism, directed and starred in his hawkish action flick. In *The Green Berets,* the special elite force is shown as patriotic, clean living, upstanding, and compassionate defenders of democracy, and the only horrors of war that are shown are committed by the Viet Cong. The movie, the only film that was released during the war, was loved by the hawks and condemned by the doves, who contended that it was mere propaganda. We cover the Vietnam War and the related protests in Part III.

Hamburger Hill

This film, released in 1987, depicts a fictitious army squad in one of the worst battles of the war in Vietnam, which was called Hamburger Hill because of the physical condition of the killed and wounded after the battle. It depicts not only the filth, the fear, and the friendship but also the racism and cynicism that the soldiers faced. The movie doesn't glorify the war — in fact, it hints that the effort was futile — but it does glorify the loyalty and strength of the men who fought it.

Platoon

Like *Hamburger Hill, Platoon* (1986) shows the effects of the Vietnam War on an individual soldier, an idealistic, educated college student (played by Charlie Sheen) who could've easily gotten a deferment but instead chooses to fight for his country. However, he soon loses his idealism as he sees the horrors of war, including friendly fire and the killing of innocent civilians. He also faces two very different sergeants (Willem Dafoe and Tom Berenger), one who's gung-ho and enjoys killing and one who tries to support his men as much as possible, gradually embracing the counterculture. Ultimately, *Platoon* is about how war changed one man, and by implication, how the Vietnam War changed the nation.

Good Morning, Vietnam

Although this 1987 film introduced humor into the story of the Vietnam War (and how could it not, starring Robin Williams), it also depicted its absurdity.

It's the story of Adrian Cronauer, a real-life disc jockey deployed to Vietnam. His broadcasts were irreverent and controversial, and his superiors definitely weren't amused. But the takeaway from the film is the humanity of all involved — from the American grunt on the frontlines to the Vietnamese villagers.

American Graffiti

The sixties weren't all hippies and drugs, but there was sex and rock 'n' roll, even in the early years. *American Graffiti* (1973) takes a look at the great American car culture in the years before the Vietnam War changed everything. This film is all about cruising, making out, and picking up chicks before four pals head off to college. The movie also features a soundtrack that made many people of the '60s remember (or wish they did) a more innocent time, when teens and young adults weren't trying to find themselves — they were trying to find a girl in a white T-bird.

The Graduate

The Graduate (1967), often compared to the coming-of-age novel *The Catcher in the Rye* by J.D. Salinger, is about a young college graduate, Benjamin Braddock (portrayed by a young Dustin Hoffman), who questions his parent's middle-class values and is trying to find himself, a search that many young people undertook during the '60s. Although he wants to reject the middle-class lifestyle, he literally embraces it when Mrs. Robinson (Anne Bancroft), the wife of his dad's business partner, seduces him into a physically passionate but emotionally sterile affair. Eventually, he meets the love of his life, Elaine, the only person that understands him, but the problem is that she's Mrs. Robinson's daughter. How Benjamin resolves his dilemmas (at least for the moment) is what *The Graduate* is all about.

Easy Rider

If anything epitomizes the "up the establishment" attitude of the '60s, it's *Easy Rider* (1969), the story of a road trip across America. After making some major bucks on a drug sale, two free-spirited bikers, Wyatt and Billy, played by Dennis Hopper and Peter Fonda, head from Los Angeles to New Orleans for Mardi Gras, throwing away their watches as a symbol of their newfound freedom. On the way, they meet rednecks, hippies, prostitutes, and hitchhikers —

in other words, a cross-section of American society. The film reflects both the hope of change as well as the evidence of a society that's bent on resisting change. This film was a breakthrough performance for Jack Nicholson, who was also a writer for it. In it, he plays an alcoholic southern ACLU lawyer whom Wyatt and Billy convert from alcohol to pot and who joins them on their wild ride. And if you're looking for a great movie soundtrack that screams late-sixties rock, you can't get much better than this one.

Woodstock: 3 Days of Peace & Music

If anything represented the hope of the '60s, it was Woodstock — the music festival that embodied the peace and love that were the highest ideals of America's youth. The crowds were huge, the weather was dismal, food was scarce, and bad drugs were prevalent. But during those three days, life happened — skinny-dipping, lovemaking, childbirth, and loved ones lost and found. And don't forget the great music, from the Grateful Dead to Sha-Na-Na, and Arlo Guthrie to Jimi Hendrix. The film, released in 1970, is the next best thing to being there. Check out Chapter 15 for more on Woodstock and the music of the '60s.

Chapter 19

Ten Things You Could Get for $1

In This Chapter

▶ Eating well

▶ Filling the tank

▶ Getting gorgeous

▶ Buying some odds and ends

▶ Toasting the '60s

A dollar really went far in the 1960s — much farther than it does today. The lists in this chapter may have you really pining for the good-old days. But before you get too nostalgic, remember that the median household income in 1967 was $7,143, and the minimum wage was $1.40 per hour. Of course, on the other hand, that same year, an average American home cost $24,600, and a Love Bug (a Volkswagen Beetle) could be had for a mere $1,500.

Three Gallons of Gas

Back in the '60s, people pulled up to the gas pump and actually said to the attendant, "Gimme a dollar's worth." In 1965, this amount could get you quite far, because gas was only 31 cents a gallon (it was up to 35 cents by 1969). To make sure your car would always start, you could get jumper cables for a buck, and if you wanted to keep your ride looking great, you could buy car wax for a mere 99 cents.

20 First-Class Postage Stamps

In 1963, you could send letters to 20 friends for $1, or if you didn't have a whole lot to say, you could send 25 postcards. But by 1968, prices went up — it cost 5 cents to send a postcard and 6 cents to send a letter.

The post office instituted zip codes in 1963.

A Hamburger with Fries, Salad, and Dessert

Actually, in 1965 you could score a meal with a *double-decker* burger for a buck! If you wanted to go out to dinner, you could eat at Oscar's (a family restaurant chain in California), and for $1 you'd get a double-decker hamburger with French fries, salad, and ice cream for dessert. For only 30 cents more, you could get a complete fried chicken or shrimp dinner (also with fries and salad). Pie was only 35 cents a slice, an ice-cream sundae was 40 cents, and coffee or a soft drink cost 10 cents. By the way, if you wanted to grab a quick bite at a lunch counter, you could get a hot dog and a coke for 49 cents.

A Gallon of Milk (And Other Groceries)

In 1965 you could get a few food items for close to $1, but for the most part, the things you'd need to buy cost quite a bit less. So fill your vintage shopping cart with these items:

- **Gallon of milk:** 95 cents
- **One regular size bottle of Heinz ketchup:** 22 cents
- **One dozen eggs:** 53 cents
- **One-ounce Hershey bar:** 5 cents (Although the price remained the same, the size of the bar shrunk to ⅞ ounce in 1966 and ¾ ounce in 1968.)
- **Pillsbury cake mix:** 25 cents
- **Pound of pork chops:** $1.03
- **Pound of sirloin steak:** 85 cents
- **Six-pack of Pepsi:** 59 cents

Ten Razor Blades (And Other Toiletries)

Then as now, Americans wanted to look their best. Here's what you'd have to part with to do just that in 1965:

- **Package of ten Gillette razor blades:** 99 cents
- **Can of shaving cream:** 59 cents
- **Tube of toothpaste:** 55 cents

- ✔ **Can of hair spray:** 47 cents
- ✔ **Revlon lipstick:** $1.25
- ✔ **Revlon nail enamel:** 75 cents for crème and 90 cents for frosted

Enough Aspirin for 50 Headaches (And Other Meds)

Got a headache? In 1965, you could get 100 aspirin for only $1. You could also stock your medicine cabinet on the cheap with these other meds:

- ✔ **Generic cold relief capsules:** 60 cents for two packages of 12
- ✔ **Cough drops:** 23 cents for three packages
- ✔ **Cough syrup:** 59 cents for a bottle
- ✔ **Contact decongestant tablets:** 77 cents for a package of ten

Numerous Copies of Your Favorite Magazine or Newspaper

In 1965, if you wanted a good dose of the printed news, you could get the *New York Times* for 10 cents from Monday through Saturday, but you'd need to spend 30 cents for the Sunday edition. If you were into the local news, you'd spend a bit less: *The Daily Record*, a newspaper in Morristown, New Jersey, sold for 7 cents. For another view of the world, you could get a copy of *Life* magazine, *Time* magazine, *or Sports Illustrated* for 35 cents.

A Paper Dress (For You, Not a Doll)

The mid-'60s gave rise to a new fad for a disposable society — paper clothing. As a promotion, in 1966 the Scott Paper Company sold paper dresses for only $1.25, and they sold like hotcakes! Just think — if the dress was too long, you could have a minidress just by using a pair of scissors. However, these dresses were just as expensive to produce as regular dresses, which sold for quite a bit more, so the fad quickly died out.

A Home Decoration or Two

Most home decor items cost more than $1, but you might like to know what it cost to do a little redecorating in 1965. You could buy a sheet for $1.76, two bedspreads for $5, a lamp for $1 (or you could spend up to $5 if you wanted to splurge), and Oneida dinnerware for $3.98–5.40 per place setting.

A Six-Pack of Beer

The best news of all . . . you could get a six-pack of your average American beer for just 99 cents!

Appendix

Taking a Trip through Time

● ●

Keeping ten years' worth of events and dates straight can be difficult. So here we include a timeline of the major events of the 1960s that we discuss in this book, along with a few other interesting and informative happenings.

1960

Feb 1: First lunch counter sit-in, Greensboro, North Carolina.
Apr 14–17: Student Nonviolent Coordinating Committee (SNCC) formed.
May 1: U.S. U-2 spy plane piloted by Francis Gary Powers shot down over the Soviet Union.
May 9: U.S. Food and Drug Administration approves birth control pill.
Sept 26: First televised presidential debate between Richard Nixon and John F. Kennedy.
Oct 19: Martin Luther King Jr. jailed in Atlanta during a sit-in at a restaurant.
Nov 8: John F. Kennedy elected president, defeating Richard Nixon.

1961

Mar 1: President Kennedy signs an executive order creating the Peace Corps.
Mar 13: President Kennedy creates the Alliance for Progress to aid Latin American countries.
Apr 12: Cosmonaut Yuri Gagarin (U.S.S.R.) becomes the first man in space.
Apr 17: Bay of Pigs invasion starts.
May 4: First freedom ride begins.
May 5: Alan Shepard becomes the first American in space.
Aug 13: Construction on the Berlin Wall begins.
Nov: 16,000 advisors sent to Vietnam.
Dec: President Kennedy creates the President's Commission on the Status of Women.

1962

Feb 7: President Kennedy expands U.S. embargo on all goods to and from Cuba except for food and medicines.
Feb 20: John Glenn becomes the first American to orbit Earth.
Apr 11: President Kennedy orders steel price rollbacks.

June 11–15: Students for a Democratic Society (SDS) write and adopt the Port Huron Statement.

Oct 1: James Meredith, the first black student admitted to University of Mississippi, attends his first class.

Oct 15–28: Cuban Missile Crisis.

1963

Jan 14: President Kennedy proposes a $10 billion tax cut.

May: Civil rights protests in Birmingham, Alabama.

May: President Ngo Dinh Diem begins moving South Vietnamese people into strategic hamlets.

June 11: Governor George Wallace blocks the door to prevent the integration of University of Alabama.

June 13: NAACP field officer Medgar Evers murdered in Mississippi.

June 16: Soviet Union sends first woman, Valentina Tereshkova, into space.

Aug 5: The U.S. and Soviet Union sign the Limited Test Ban Treaty.

Aug 28: March for Jobs and Freedom in Washington, D.C.; Martin Luther King Jr. delivers his "I have a dream" speech.

Sept 15: Four little girls killed in Birmingham, Alabama, church bombing.

Nov 2: South Vietnam president Diem assassinated.

Nov 22: President Kennedy assassinated. Lyndon Johnson sworn in as president.

Nov 24: President Kennedy assassin Lee Harvey Oswald killed by Jack Ruby.

Nov 29: Warren Commission appointed to investigate President Kennedy assassination.

1964

Feb 7: The Beatles arrive in the U.S. for the first time for their February 9 appearance on *The Ed Sullivan Show*.

Summer: Freedom Summer organized to register black voters in Mississippi.

July 2: President Johnson signs the Civil Rights Act into law.

Aug 6: Bodies of three civil rights workers found in Mississippi.

Aug 7: Tonkin Gulf Resolution passed.

Oct 1: Berkeley protesters defy ban on political activity at Bancroft and Telegraph avenues.

Oct 14: Martin Luther King Jr. receives the Nobel Peace Prize.

Oct 15: Nikita Khruschev deposed; Leonid Brezhnev takes power in the Soviet Union.

Oct 16: China explodes its first atomic bomb.

Nov 3: President Johnson defeats Barry Goldwater to win the presidential election. Robert Kennedy elected as a senator from New York.

Dec 2: Student sit-in at Sproul Hall on University of California–Berkeley campus.

1965

Feb 21: Malcolm X assassinated.

Mar: Operation Rolling Thunder begins.

Mar 7–21: Selma to Montgomery marches.

Apr 17: SDS holds its first march in Washington, D.C., to protest the Vietnam War. .

Apr 21: President Johnson authorizes the dispatch of 40,000 combat troops to Vietnam.

June: Search-and-destroy missions start in Vietnam.

June 3: Supreme Court overturns law prohibiting birth control.

June 3: General William Westmoreland requests troop increases up to 180,000 men, with another 100,000 for 1966.

July 28: Congress passes Medicare law.

Aug 6: President Johnson signs Voting Rights Act into law.

Aug 11–17: Watts Riots in Los Angeles.

Sept 8: Cesar Chavez begins his long battle with vineyard owners, which lasts five years.

Sept 24: President Johnson issues executive order creating affirmative action.

1966

Oct: Mao Tse Tung begins the Cultural Revolution in China.

June 6: James Meredith shot during his solo civil rights march from Memphis, Tennessee, to Jackson, Mississippi.

June 13: Supreme Court hands down Miranda decision.

June 30: National Organization of Women (NOW) founded.

Oct: Black Panthers formed.

1967

Jan 3: Jack Ruby dies.

Jan 14: Human Be-In held in Golden Gate Park.

Apr: General Westmoreland predicts that the 475,000 troops by the end of the year will only be enough to hold Vietnam and that 100,000 to 200,000 more will be needed to shorten the conflict.

Apr 19: Stokely Carmichael coins the phrase "black power."

Apr 28: Muhammad Ali refuses induction into army on religious grounds.

June 12: In *Loving v. Virginia,* Supreme Court overturns laws banning inter-racial marriage.

June 16–18: Monterey Pop Festival rings in the Summer of Love.

July: Riots in Detroit and Newark.

Oct 2: Thurgood Marshall becomes the first African American Supreme Court justice.

Oct 16: Stop the Draft Week begins. Antiwar protesters march to Oakland Induction Center.
Oct 21: Antiwar protesters march on the Pentagon.
Oct 28: Black Panther leader Huey Newton arrested for killing police officer.

1968

Jan 31: Tet Offensive begins.
Mar 16: My Lai Massacre.
Mar 31: Johnson withdraws from presidential race.
Apr 4: Martin Luther King Jr. assassinated.
Apr 11: President Johnson signs Civil Rights Act of 1968, prohibiting discrimination in housing.
Apr 23: Columbia students begin antiwar protest.
June 5: Robert Kennedy assassinated in Los Angeles.
July 28: Pope Paul VI issues the *Humanae Vitae* encyclical, reaffirming the Catholic Church's stance against birth control.
Aug 26–29: Democratic National Convention held in Chicago and meets with protests.
Sept 7: Women's rights advocates protest the Miss America Pageant.
Oct: Tommie Smith and John Carlos lose medals for black power salute at the Mexico City Olympics.
Oct 31: President Johnson ends bombing campaign in Vietnam.
Nov 6: Richard Nixon elected president over Hubert Humphrey.

1969

Mar: President Nixon announces his Vietnamization plan.
Mar 20: Chicago Eight indicted for conspiracy.
Apr: Berkley community creates People's Park.
June: President Nixon announces first troop withdrawals from Vietnam.
June 27: Stonewall Riots begin.
July 20: Neil Armstrong becomes the first man to walk on the moon.
Aug 9: Charles Manson and his "family" murder four people in Los Angeles, California.
Aug 15–17: Woodstock.
Sept 2: North Vietnam leader Ho Chi Minh dies.
Oct 15: Moratorium antiwar protest in Washington, D.C., and other cities.
Nov 9: Indians of All Tribes occupy Alcatraz.
Nov 15: November Mobilization antiwar protest in Washington, D.C.
Dec 1: Selective Service institutes a draft lottery.
Dec 6: Altamont music festival.

Index

• A •

Abernathy, Ralph (civil rights leader), 111, 116, 134
abortion, 240, 248, 250
Academic Senate, Berkeley, 224
acid (LSD), 277–279
Addison's disease, 23
advertising, 55
Afghanistan, 1980s proxy war in, 33
African Americans. See blacks
Agency for International Development, 31
Agnew, Spiro (vice president), 18, 75, 264
Agricultural Labor Relations Act, 255
Agricultural Workers Organizing Committee (AWOC), 253
AIM (American Indian Movement), 17, 258–259
Alabama. See also Birmingham, AL
  "Bloody Sunday" violence, 58
  freedom ride violence, 114
  march through, 13, 126–127
  Montgomery Bus Boycott, 12, 97–99, 103, 105, 110, 111
  NAACP, prohibition against, 110
Alcatraz Island, American Indian occupation of, 17, 255–258
Ali movie, 332
Ali, Muhammad (boxer), 89, 319–321
"Alice's Restaurant" (Guthrie), 297
Alliance for Progress program, 31
Alpert, Richard (Harvard psychologist and LSD experimenter), 278–279
Altamont music festival, 301
AMA (American Medical Association), 60
American Graffiti movie, 334
American Indian Movement (AIM), 17, 258–259
American Indians
  Alcatraz occupation, 255–258
  casinos, 258
  described, 17, 255

leaders in 1970s and beyond, 258–259
religion, counterculture, and, 274
American Medical Association (AMA), 60
An Loc, Vietnam, 208
Anderson, Marian (black singer), 90
Anderson naval ship sabotage, 190
androgynous fashions, 304–305
anti–Vietnam War movement
  aggression, building, 175
  Cambodian invasion, response to, 187–188, 203
  Chicago, protests at Democratic National Convention, 75, 184–186
  civil disobedience, 174
  civil rights leaders, 182–183
  college students, 15–16, 172
  described, 13, 169–170
  draft, resisting, 176–179
  early marches and demonstrations, 174
  hippies, 275
  Kent State Massacre, 188–189
  media coverage, buying, 181–182
  military, problems in, 189–190
  My Lai Massacre and, 202
  New Left, 218
  1968 turning point, 183
  Nixon's criticism of Johnson for, 74
  North Vietnamese seeing hope in, 207–208
  peace movement, 170–172
  private missions to Vietnam, 179–181
  public suicides, 174–175
  teach-ins, 173
  Tet Offensive and, 14–15
  VVAW, 190–191
appropriations measures, 92
Aptheker, Herbert (antiwar leader), 179–180
Arkansas, school integration battle in, 96–97
Armstrong, Neil (astronaut), 80
art, 316–317

ARVN (Army of the Republic of Vietnam)
  burden, shifting to, 198–199
  Cambodia, move into, 204
  coup of 1963, 152
  creation, 150
  Easter Invasion response, 208
  Laos, invasion of, 187, 206–207
  U.S. troops and, 162
Ashmore, Harry S. *(Mission to Hanoi: A Chronicle of Double-Dealing In High Places)*, 180–181
Atkinson, Ti-Grace (lesbian rights activist), 245
AWOC (Agricultural Workers Organizing Committee), 253

• B •

Baez, Joan (singer), 224, 288
Baggs, William C. *(Mission to Hanoi: A Chronicle of Double-Dealing In High Places)*, 180–181
Baldwin, Ruth Standish (Urban League founder), 109
Ball, George (Kennedy and Johnson advisor), 28, 154, 158
Barry, Marion (SNCC chairman and Washington, D.C., mayor), 113
baseball, 89, 317–318
Bay of Pigs invasion, 35
Beach Boys, 284–285, 294–295
beach movies, 310
Beatles, 19, 281–282, 289–292, 294
beats/beatniks, 268–269
Beckwith, Byron de la, 117
beer prices, 340
Belafonte, Harry (musician), 289
Berkeley, University of California at
  activism before '63, HUAC, 221
  civil rights, 221–222
  hippies, Haight-Ashbury, 225
  Oakland activities, 226
  origins, 220
  People's Park, 226–227
  protests, 222–223
  Savio, Mario, 225
  sit-in at Sproul Hall, 223–224
  student movements, 15–16
Berlin Wall, 36

bestselling books, 315–316
Birmingham, AL
  freedom riders, 114
  jailing of King and Abernathy, 115–116
  16th Street Baptist Church bombing, 120
  television coverage, 31, 32
birth control
  abortion, 248
  Catholic Church bans, 248–249
  female sexuality, unleashing, 246–247
  before Pill, 246
  Pill, introduction of, 245
  planned pregnancy, embracing, 246
Black Muslims. *See* Nation of Islam
Black Nationalism, 92
Black Panther Party
  origins, 13, 138–139
  police shootings, 230
  programs, devising and implementing, 139–140
  violent resistance, 140–142
black pride
  college campuses, 137–138
  factors leading to movement, 125
  movies about, 331–332
  music, 286
  Nation of Islam, 134–137
  Olympic athletes' gesture, 319
blacks. *See also* civil rights movement; civil rights organizations
  in entertainment, 91, 284, 285–287, 315
  in government, 93, 106
  in military, 88
"Bloody Sunday" (civil rights violence), 58, 126
Bob and Carol and Ted and Alice movie, 311
body counts, Vietnam War, 160–161
bohemians, 268
Bond, James (movie and book character), 308
books, bestselling, 315–316
Boston, school desegregation in, 96
Boudin, Kathy (Weathermen member), 230
Bowers, Samuel (Mississippi Klan leader), 123
boycott, farmworkers' rights movement, 253–255
bra burning, 241–242
Breadbasket, Operation, 132–133

Brezhnev, Leonid (Soviet premier), 79
British musical groups. *See* Beatles; Rolling Stones
Broadway, 311
Brooklyn Dodgers, 89
Brotherhood of Sleeping Car Porters, 111
Brown, H. Rap (SNCC director), 130
Brown, James (musician), 286
Brown, Jim (athlete), 89
Brown, Pat (California governor), 73, 129, 223
Brown v. Topeka Board of Education decision, 95–96, 109, 117
Brown, Willie (San Francisco mayor and protesters' lawyer), 222
Bruce, Lenny (comedian), 315
Brucker, Herbert (Green Beret designer), 33
Buckley, William F. Jr. (conservative magazine founder), 262
Buddhism, 274
Buddhist monks' suicide protests in Vietnam, 152–153, 174–175
buddy films, 308
Bunche, Ralph (U.N. leader), 92
Bundy, McGeorge (Kennedy and Johnson advisor), 28, 157
bus boycott, 97–99
busing, school desegregation and, 80–81, 96
Butch Cassidy and the Sundance Kid movie, 308
Byrnes, John (senator), 60

• C •

California, University of. *See* Berkeley, University of California at
"Call to Conscience" article (Schweitzer), 170–171
Calley, William (My Lai Massacre lieutenant), 201–202
calypso music, 289
Cambodia, extending Vietnam War into antiwar backlash, 187–188, 204–205
Congress, fallout over, 205–206
Khmer Rouge, 205
Camelot Broadway musical, 26
campus. *See* college students

Canada, draft dodgers in, 177–178
capitalism, 214
Carlos, John (Olympic athlete), 319
Carmichael, Stokely (black activist), 113, 138, 240
Carson, Johnny (talk-show host), 312
Carter, Jimmy (president), 178
casinos, American Indian, 258, 259
Castro, Fidel (Cuban dictator), 34–37
Catholic Church bans birth control, 248–249
Central Intelligence Agency. *See* CIA
Chambers, Whittaker (accused Alger Hiss of spying), 70
Chaney, James (slain civil rights worker), 122
Charles, Ray (musician), 91
Charlie Company, My Lai Massacre, 201–202
Chavez, Cesar (farmworkers' rights leader), 16–17, 251–255
Chavez, Helen Fabela (wife of Cesar), 253
Checkers speech, Nixon's, 71–72
Chicago Freedom Movement, 132
Chicago, violence in, 75, 184–186, 230
China, 76, 79, 208
Christmas bombing of North Vietnam, 210
CIA (Central Intelligence Agency)
Castro, attempts on, 34–35
Communists in South Vietnam, Phoenix Program targeting, 200–201
Cuban Missile Crisis, 37
Kennedy assassination, 43
LSD experiments, 278
OSS relationship with Viet Minh, 145–146
Watergate, 82
civil disobedience
antinuclear proliferation, 171
anti–Vietnam War movement, 174
New Left, 219, 222
Civil Rights Act
of 1957, 49, 99–100
of 1968, 127
of 1964, 12, 57, 123–124, 236
civil rights movement.
anti–Vietnam War movement, 182–183
Berkeley students, 221–222
Birmingham, 31, 32, 114, 115–116, 120
black pride, 125, 134–138, 319

civil rights movement *(continued)*
  economic empowerment, seeking,
      131–134
  factors leading to, 11–12, 85–87
  freedom rides, 113–115
  Freedom Summer, 120–123
  government and, 92–93
  Kennedy and, 25, 31–32, 43
  legacy of 1960s, 142
  lunch counter sit-ins, 31, 106–108
  March for Jobs and Freedom, 104,
      117–118
  marching from Selma to Montgomery,
      13, 126–127
  Montgomery Bus Boycott, 97–99
  New Left, 218
  Nixon's attempts to delay desegregation,
      80–81
  nonviolence movement, 102–105, 118
  performing arts, 90–92, 309–310
  pushing for change, 12–13, 88–89, 101
  racial violence, 93–94
  radical groups, 13
  riots, 128–131
  school integration, 80, 95–97, 109, 117
  sports, 89–90, 319
  statewide protests, acknowledging, 31–32
  Voting Rights Act of 1965, 127
  "We Shall Overcome" song, 294
  women, 240
civil rights organizations
  Black Panther Party, 138–142
  CORE, 103,106-107, 110–111, 112, 113, 120
  Deacons for Defense, 112
  NAACP, 32, 93, 95, 98, 108–110
  SCLC, 103, 111–112, 126–127,
      131, 132, 133–134
  SNCC, 113, 125
  Urban League, 109
Clark, Jim (Selma, AL, police chief), 126
Clark, Mark (slain Black Panther), 140
Clay, Cassius Marcellus (original name of
      Muhammad Ali), 319–320
Cleaver, Eldridge (Black Panther), 142
closet, coming out of, 259–260
CNVA (Committee for Nonviolent
      Action), 171

COFO (Council of Federated
      Organizations), 121
cold war
  Berlin Wall, 36
  Castro, targeting, 34–35
  containment strategy, 33, 155
  Cuban Missile Crisis, 36–40
  described, 32
  Goldwater's rhetoric against Soviet
      Union, 53
  Indochina, 147
  Kennedy, John F., 32–41
  movie themes, 307
  1963 Limited Test Ban Treaty, 40
  peace movement, 170–172
  social problems as reaction to, 21
  space race, 29
  Vietnam War, 13, 40–41, 161–162, 196–197
Cole, Nat "King" (singer), 91
college students. *See also* FSM
  black pride, 137–138
  campus issues, 137, 217–218
  folk music, 287
  lunch counter sit-ins, 106–108
  Vietnam War protests, 14
  women, growing number of, 237
Columbia University protests, 229
comedians, 314–315
Committee for a Sane Nuclear Policy
      (SANE), 170–171, 175
Committee for Nonviolent Action
      (CNVA), 171
Committee to Re-Elect the President
      (CREEP), 82
communes, rural, 18, 273
Communism. *See also* cold war
  in Cambodia, Khmer Rouge, 203, 205
  civil rights movement, Hoover's
      approach to, 106
  conservative movement and, 261–263
  eliminating in South Vietnam, Phoenix
      Program, 200–201
  HUAC, 70, 215–216
  1930s and 1940s, 215
  Nixon's goodwill tours as vice
      president, 72
  North Vietnam, 146, 151
  redbaiting/Red Scare, 48, 91

Community Service Organization (CSO), 253
Congress. *See also* HUAC
  Cambodia, extending Vietnam War into, 205–206
  My Lai Massacre investigation, 201
  Tonkin Gulf Resolution, 156, 157
Congress of Racial Equality. *See* CORE
Connor, "Bull" (Birmingham, AL, police chief), 114
The Conscience of a Conservative (Goldwater), 53
conscientious objector status, 176–177
conservative movement
  gay rights, 261
  Great Society programs, 60
  hippies, 271–272
  John Birch Society, 262–263
  Nixon and, 263–264
  Republican Party shift in 1964 presidential race, 52–54
  rise of, 17–18, 261–262
  segregation, supporting, 263
  social programs and blacks, 142
  women's movement backlash, 249–250
Constellation aircraft carrier, 156
consumer co-ops, 272
containment strategy, 33, 63, 146
Cooper, Chuck (basketball player), 89
cooperative living, 271–273
Cooper-Church Amendment, ground forces restriction in Vietnam, 206
CORE (Congress of Racial Equality)
  lunch counter sit-in, 106–108
  nonviolence of, 103, 113
  segregation, battles against, 110–111
The Cotton Club, 91
Council of Federated Organizations (COFO), 121
counterculture
  cooperative living, 271–273
  described, 18, 267–268, 269–270
  drugs, 277–280
  flower power, 280–281
  hippie style, 270–271
  before hippies, 268–269
  Manson murders, 281–282
  non-work ethic, 271

politics, 275
  sexual revolution, 273–274
  spiritualism, 274–275
  underground press, 275–277
counterinsurgency, 33
CREEP (Committee to Re-Elect the President), 82
Cronkite, Walter (news anchorman), 65, 166, 168
CSO (Community Service Organization), 253
Cuban American community, 43
Cuban Missile Crisis
  Castro and Khrushchev's motives, 36–37
  conclusion, 39–40
  diplomatic approach, 38–39
  evidence, gathering, 37
  movie about, 332
  options, outlined, 37–38

• *D* •

Daley, Richard (Chicago mayor), 75, 184, 185
Dallas, Kennedy's assassination in, 41–43
DAR (Daughters of the American Revolution), 90
Darin, Bobby (musician), 293
DDB (Doyle, Dane, Bernbach) advertising agency, 55
De Gaulle, Charles (French president), 147
Deacons for Defense, 112
Dead Heads, 295
Debs, Eugene (American Railway Union and Socialist Party of America founder), 214
deferment, student, 218
Democratic Party
  alternative in Mississippi, 121–122
  Chicago convention protests, 184–186
  primary races, 1968, 195–196
Democratic Republic of Vietnam (DRV). *See* North Vietnam
Department of Housing and Urban Development (HUD), 62
Department of Transportation (DOT), creation of, 62
deserters, 189

DeSoto patrols, 155
détente, 79
Detroit
  Motown music, 285–287
  riots, 129–130
Dewey Canyon III, Operation, 191
Dewey, Thomas E. (presidential
    candidate), 71
The Dick Van Dyke Show, 243
Diem, Ngo Dinh (South Vietnamese leader)
  execution, 153
  granted power, 13, 149–150
  leadership crisis, 152–153
  military assistance, requesting, 154
Dien Bien Phu, French defeat at, 148
The Diggers, 280
Dillon, C. Douglas (secretary of the
    treasury under Kennedy), 28
Dirksen, Everett (Senate minority
    leader), 57
divorce, 250
Dohrn, Bernadette (Weathermen
    leader), 229
domestic policies. *See also* Great Society
  Kennedy, 28–29
  Nixon, 80–81
domino theory, 147
Doors music group, 296
doo-wop music, 284
DOT (Department of Transportation),
    creation of, 62
Douglas, Helen Gahagan (senator), 70–71
Doyle, Dane, Bernbach (DDB) advertising
    agency, 55
*Dr. Strangelove, or: How I Learned to
    Stop Worrying and Love the Bomb*
    movie, 332
draft, military
  blacks, 88
  deferments, 218
  lottery, 77
  resistance methods and consequences,
    176–178
  Stop the Draft Week, 178–180
drug use
  earlier use, 277
  hippies, 18, 269
  LSD, 277–279

Manson "family," 281
marijuana, 279–280
military in Vietnam War, 77, 189
music, 19, 291, 296
spiritualism and, 274
DRV (Democratic Republic of Vietnam).
    See North Vietnam
Dylan, Bob (musician), 288, 289, 295
dynasties, sports, 317–318

• *E* •

Easter Offensive, North Vietnamese
    (Nguyen Hue), 207–209
Eastern religions, 274
Easy Rider movie, 308, 334–334
economic empowerment
  American Indian casinos, 258, 259
  Chicago Freedom Movement, 132
  Operation Breadbasket, 132–133
  Poor People's Campaign, 133–134
  riots, 131
Economic Opportunity Bill, 51
economic programs
  Great Society, 62
  Johnson, 62
  Kennedy and Keynesian policy, 30
  Nixon, 81
  Vietnam, 162–163
Ed Sullivan Show, 289–290
education, federal funding of, 58–61
Ehrlichman, John (Nixon advisor), 76
Eisenhower, Dwight "Ike" (president)
  cabinet, 26
  Castro, CIA targeting, 34–35
  Civil Rights Act of 1957, 99
  cold war "New Look" policy, 33
  described, 10
  National Guard, federalization of
    Arkansas, 96–97
  Nixon, choosing as vice president, 71
Eisenhower, Mamie (first lady), 304
elderly, medical insurance for, 60–61
Electric Kool-Aid Acid Tests (Wolfe), 279
Elementary and Secondary Education Act
    (ESEA), 59
English, Major General Lowell (marines
    commander, Vietnam War), 165

entertainment. *See also* movies; music
blacks, early breakthroughs, 90–92
cultural changes, 19–20
National Endowment for the Arts, 59–60
racism, opposition to, 109
women, portrayal of, 243
EPA (Environmental Protection Agency),
creation of, 81
Equal Pay Act, 235–236
ERA (Equal Rights Amendment), 239, 249
ESEA (Elementary and Secondary
Education Act), 59
establishment, 270
Evers, Medgar (slain civil rights worker),
32, 117
ExComm (Executive Committee) on
national security, Kennedy's, 37–38, 39
Executive Order 11246 (federal
contractor/subcontractor
discrimination), 127

• *F* •

Fair Housing Act, 127
Fard, W. D. (Nation of Islam founder),
134–135
Farmer, James (CORE founder), 110–111
farmworkers' rights movement
described, 16–17, 251–252
grape boycott, 253–255
picket lines, 252–253
fashion
African American, 138
cultural changes, 19
hair, 306
hippie style, 306
men's clothing, 305
paper dresses, 339–340
social upheaval, reflecting, 303–304
women's clothing, 304–305
Faubus, Orval (Arkansas governor), 96, 97
FBI (Federal Bureau of Investigation) probes
of civil rights movement leaders, 112, 140
16th Street Baptist Church bombing,
119–120
slain civil rights workers, 122–123
Federal Reserve Board, 81
female sexuality, unleashing, 246–247
feminine mystique, exposing, 232–234

The Feminine Mystique (Friedan),
16, 233–234, 237
Ferlinghetti, Lawrence (poet and San
Francisco bookstore owner), 269
festivals, music
Altamont, 301
folk, 289
Monterey, 280, 297–298
Newport, 297
Woodstock, 298–301
15th Amendment, 86
film. *See* movies
flexible response defense strategy, 33
flower power, 280–281
folk music, 287–289
Fonda, Jane (actress and antiwar
activist), 228
Food for Peace Program, 31
food prices, 338
football, 318
Force Acts, 86
Ford, Gerald (president), 82, 210
foreign aid
Kennedy, 24, 31
South Vietnam, 150, 162–163
wheat sales to Soviet Union, 50
Foreman, George (boxer), 320–321
Forman, James (SNCC leader), 120
Fort Laramie Treaty of 1868, 256, 258
14th Amendment, 86
fragging officers, 77, 189
France
Dien Bien Phu, defeat at, 148
Geneva Conference of 1954, creating two
Vietnams, 148–149
Indochina, colonialism in, 145, 147
withdrawal from Vietnam, 151
Franklin, Aretha (singer), 286
free speech movement. *See* FSM
freedom rides, 113–115
Freedom Schools, 122
Freedom Summer
background, 120
Democratic Party, alternative in
Mississippi, 121–122
described, 12, 57
Freedom Schools, 122
volunteers, Klan murder of, 122–123
voter registration drives, 120–121

free-fire zones, Vietnam War, 163
Frey, John (slain police officer), 141
Friedan, Betty *(The Feminine Mystique)*, 16, 233–234, 237
Frye, Marquette (Watts Riots instigator), 128
FSM (free speech movement)
  Baez, Joan, 224
  civil rights, 221–222
  hippies, Haight-Ashbury, 225
  Oakland activities, 226
  origins, 16, 220
  People's Park, 226–227
  pre-1963 activism, 221
  protests, 222–223
  Savio, Mario, 225
  sit-in at Sproul Hall, 223–224
Fulbright, J. William (senator), 157, 182, 206

• *G* •

Gagarin, Yuri (first man in space), 29
Gandhi, Mahatma (leader in India), 103, 254
Garcia, Jerry (musician), 295
Garvey, Marcus (Black Nationalism leader), 92, 134
gasoline prices, 337
gay and lesbian social rights movement
  coming out of the closet, 259–260
  described, 17, 259
  Ginsberg, Allen, 269
  Stonewall Riots, 260–261
  in 21st century, 261
  women's movement, 245
Gay Liberation Front (GLF), 260–261
gender-neutral language, 241
generation gap, 217
Geneva Conference of 1954, creating two Vietnams, 148–149
Gibson, Hoot and Annie (musicians), 288
Ginsberg, Allen (poet), 269
Glenn, John (astronaut and senator), 29
GLF (Gay Liberation Front), 260–261
go-go boots, 304–305
Goldman, Eric (Johnson advisor), 52
Goldwater, Barry M. (senator)
  The Conscience of a Conservative, 53
  1964 presidential campaign, 52, 53, 55–56

Republican Party shift, 261–262
  Vietnam War, position on, 154
Good Morning, Vietnam movie, 333–334
Goodman, Andrew (slain civil rights worker), 122–123
Goodwill ambassadors, Nixons as, 72–73
Goodwin, Richard (Johnson speech-writer), 52
Gordy, Berry Jr. (Motown label founder), 285–287
The Graduate movie, 334
grape boycott, 253–255
Grateful Dead, 279, 295
Great Depression, 215
Great Society
  Civil Rights Act of 1964, 57
  conservative opposition to, 17–18
  Democratic Congress in Nixon years, 81
  described, 45–46, 51–52
  economic revitalization, 62
  education, federal funding of, 58–60
  immigration policies, 61–62
  Medicare, 60–61
  post-election momentum, 56
  Project 100,000, 164
  spending undermined by Vietnam War, 62–63, 65
  Voting Rights Act of 1965, 57–58
  War on Poverty, 61
Green Berets, 13, 33, 154
The Green Berets movie, 333
Greensboro, NC, 31, 106–108
Gregory, Dick (comedian), 315
Gruening, Earnest (senator), 206
Guthrie, Arlo (musician), 297

• *H* •

Haight-Ashbury, 225, 280–281
Haiphong bombing, 208
Hair! — The American Tribal Rock-Love Musical, 19, 311
hair fashions, 19, 306
Haldeman, H. R. (Nixon advisor), 76
Hamburger Hill movie, 333
Hampton, Fred (slain Black Panther), 140
Hanoi, 179–181, 208
Harlem Renaissance, 91–92

Harrison, George (musician), 290–292

Harvard LSD experiments, 278–279

Hayden, Tom (antiwar leader and author of *The Other Side*), 179–180, 185, 186, 228

Hayes, Rutherford B. (president), 87

Haynes, Dr. George Edmund (Urban League founder), 109

Hays Code, 309

HEA (Higher Education Act), 59

Head Start Program, 61

Heanes, Cliff (police officer), 141

Hell's Angels, 301

Hendrix, Jimi (musician), 296, 299–300

Herz, Alice (Vietnam protest suicide), 174

Higher Education Act (HEA), 59

Highway Beautification Act, 62

Highway Safety Act, 62

Hilliard, David (Black Panthers founder), 138

Hinduism, 274

hippies
described, 18, 19, 267–268
fashions, 306
FSM and, 225
style, 270–271
Woodstock, 298–300

Hiss, Alger (accused spy), 70

hit songs, listed by year, 325–329

Ho Chi Minh City, 210

Hoffman, Abbie (antiwar leader), 186

Hofmann, Albert (LSD creator), 278

Holmes, John Clennon (novelist), 268

home decor prices, 340

homosexuals. *See* gay and lesbian social rights movement

hootenannies, 288

Hoover, J. Edgar (FBI director), 106, 140, 215

Houser, George (CORE founder), 110

Housing Act, 29

"Howl" (Ginsberg), 269

HUAC (House Un-American Activities Committee)
Berkeley activism against, 221
entertainment blacklists, 288
Hoover and, 106

Nixon, 70
purpose, 70, 215–216

HUD (Department of Housing and Urban Development), 62

Human Sexual Response (Masters and Johnson), 247

Humanae Vitae (Of Human Life) encyclical, 248

Humphrey, Hubert (vice president)
1963 election, 52, 55
1968 election, 75, 186, 195–196

Hunter, Meredith (slain Altamont festival-goer), 301

• I •

Ickes, Harold (secretary of the interior), 90

IGRA (Indian Gaming Regulatory Act), 258

immigration policies, 61–62

Indians. *See* American Indians

Indochina. *See* Vietnam; Vietnam War

inflation, 81

integration
Arkansas, National Guard sent to, 96–97
busing, forced, 80–81, 96
Nation of Islam's position, 134–135
Plessy v. Ferguson case, 87, 95
separate but equal doctrine overturned, 95–96, 117

interracial marriage, 127

IOC (International Olympic Committee), 319

Islam, Nation of. *See* Nation of Islam

• J •

Jackson, Jimmy Lee (slain civil rights worker), 126

Jackson, Rev. Jesse (black leader), 133

Jackson State College campus attacks, 188–189

Jenkins, Walter (Johnson aide), 56

Jim Crow Laws, 12, 87

Jimenez, Perez (Venezuelan dictator), 72

John Birch Society, 262–263

Johnson, Claudia Alta Taylor (Lady Bird), 47, 56

Johnson, Lyndon B. (president)
Civil Rights Act, 57, 100, 104
described, 10–11, 45
failures, 46
Great Society, 45–46, 51–52, 56–62
House and Senate years, 46–49
Kennedy assassination, 42, 49–50
1964 campaign, 52–56, 121–122, 154–155
Supreme Court appointment, 93
Vietnam War de-escalation, 193, 194–195
Vietnam War escalation, 14, 62–65,
154–164, 167
Voting Rights Act, 127
War on Poverty, 50–51
wife Lady Bird, 47
Johnson, Virginia *(Human Sexual
Response)*, 247
Joplin, Janis (musician), 296

• K •

Kaline, Al (baseball player), 318
Kennedy, Jacqueline (first lady),
25, 26, 27, 304
Kennedy, John F. (president)
assassination, 41–43, 49–50, 136
cabinet members and advisors, 27–28, 49
Camelot image, 22, 25–27
civil rights, support for, 12, 31–32, 104,
116, 117–118, 123
cold war, 32–41, 63, 116
described, 10, 21–22
domestic policies, 28–29
family heritage, 23–24
foreign policies, 30–31
1960 presidential race, 24–25, 73
rhetorical prowess, 22
Vietnam War, 13, 154
women's rights, 234–236
Kennedy, Joseph P. (father of JFK and
RFK), 23
Kennedy, Robert F. (senator)
assassination, 75, 134, 196
as attorney general in brother's
administration, 28, 31, 32
Democratic primary, 1968, 74, 195–196
farmworkers' rights, 254
1964 presidential campaign, 55

Kennedy-Nixon debates, 25
Kent State Massacre, 188–189
Kerner Report on race riots, 131
Kerouac, Jack *(On the Road)*, 269, 271
Kerry, John (senator), 191
Kesey, Ken
Merry Pranksters' acid test, 279
One Flew Over the Cuckoo's Nest, 271
Keynes, John Maynard (economist), 30
Khmer Rouge (Cambodian Communists),
203, 205
Khrushchev, Nikita (Soviet leader)
Berlin Wall, 36
Cuban Missile Crisis, 36–40
"kitchen debate" with Nixon, 73
kill ratios, 161, 189
King, Dr. Martin Luther Jr. (civil rights
leader)
anti-Vietnam War movement, 182–183
assassination and reaction, 74, 131
Birmingham, AL, work, 115–116
on blacks in military, 163–164
"Bloody Sunday," 58, 126
Chicago Freedom Movement, 132
freedom rides, 115
"I have a dream" speech, 118
march on Washington, 32
Nation of Islam's attitude toward, 136
nonviolence movement, 12, 102–105
Poor People's Campaign, 133–134
riots, reaction to, 129, 131
Selma to Montgomery, Ala., march,
126–127
television and, 31
Kingston Trio, 287
Kinsey, Alfred *(Sexual Behavior in the
Human Male)*, 17, 247, 259
Kissinger, Henry (Nixon advisor)
background, 76, 197
foreign policy successes, 79
peace talks, Vietnam War, 209
"kitchen debate," Nixon-Khrushchev, 73
Kleberg, Richard (congressman), 47
Ku Klux Klan
Birmingham, AL, 115, 116
civil rights workers, murder of, 122–123
origins, 86
rebirth, 94

• L •

La Porte, Roger (Vietnam protest suicide), 175
labor unions
  farmworkers, 16–17, 251–255
  socialist leanings, 213–214, 215
Laird, Melvin (Nixon's secretary of defense), 76, 208
Lam Som, Operation, Laos, 206–207
Laos, extending Vietnam War into, 206–207
late-night talk shows, 312
Latino rights movement. *See* farmworkers' rights movement
LDF (Legal Defense and Educational Fund) of NAACP, 110
Le Duc Tho (North Vietnamese politburo representative), 209
Leary, Timothy (Harvard psychologist and LSD experimenter), 278–279
left-wing politics
  FSM, 220–228
  liberal and socialist politics before 1960s, 213–216
  New Left, 216–220
  SDS, 228–230
Legal Defense and Educational Fund (LDF) of NAACP, 110
Lehrer, Tom (musician), 297
Leitsch, Dick (gay rights leader), 260
Lennon, John (musician), 290–292
Lerner, Alan Jay (writer of *Camelot*), 26
lesbians. *See* gay and lesbian social rights movement
liberal and socialist politics before 1960s, 213–216
Libertarian, 262
Lichtenstein, Roy (pop artist), 316–317
Limited Test Ban Treaty of 1963, 40
Linebacker II, Operation, bombing of North Vietnam, 210
Little, Malcolm (Malcolm X's original name), 104, 118, 135–137
Little Rock, AR, school integration, 96–97
Lodge, Henry Cabot (U.S. ambassador), 64
Loewe, Frederick (composer of *Camelot*), 26
Lon Nol (Cambodian prime minister), 204, 205

London fashions, 304–305
lottery, draft, 176
Loving v. Virginia case, 127
loyalty oath program, 215
LSD (lysergic acid diethylamide), 277–279
lunch counter sit-ins, 31, 106–108
lynch mobs, 94
Lynd, Staughton (antiwar leader and author of *The Other Side*), 179–180

• M •

Madame Nhu (Vietnamese aristocrat), 153
Maddox, U.S. destroyer in Tonkin Gulf, 156
"madman theory," 199
mafia, 42, 43
Malcolm X (black leader), 104, 118, 135–137
Malcolm X movie, 331
Mankiller, Wilma (American Indian leader), 258
Mann, Woodrow (Little Rock, AR, mayor), 97
Manson, Charles (murderer), 281–282
Mantle, Mickey (baseball player), 317–318
marches
  of Death, 188
  farmworkers', 253–254
  gay rights, 261
  for Jobs and Freedom in Washington, D.C., 104, 117–118
  on the Pentagon, 178
  from Selma to Montgomery, AL, 13, 126–127
marijuana, 279–280
Maris, Roger (baseball player), 317
Marshall, Thurgood (Supreme Court justice), 93, 105, 109
Masters, William (*Human Sexual Response*), 247
Mattachine society, 260
McCarthy, Eugene (presidential candidate), 75, 195, 216
McCarthy, Joseph (senator), 215–216
McCartney, Paul (musician), 290–292
McGovern, George (senator and presidential candidate), 82
McKissick, Floyd (CORE leader), 111

McNamara, Robert (secretary of defense under Kennedy and Johnson)
background, 27–28
false statements, 205
fears of march on the Pentagon, 178
Pentagon Papers, commissioning, 195
suicide protest outside office, 175
Meader, Vaughn (comedian), 314
meal prices, 338
Means, Russell (American Indian leader), 17, 258
Medicare, creation of, 60–61
medicine prices, 339
men's clothing, 305
Menu, Operation (Cambodian bombing), 203–204
Meredith, James (slain civil rights leader), 110, 112, 117
Merry Pranksters acid test, 271, 279
MFDP (Mississippi Freedom Democratic Party), 121–122
MIA (Montgomery Improvement Association), 98–99, 111–112
Middle East, 79
migrant workers, 253
military service
blacks, 88–89, 163–164
Johnson, 48
Kennedy, 23
military, Vietnam War problems
anti–Vietnam War movement, 77, 168, 189–190
fragging officers, 77, 189
mistrust of South Vietnamese army, 162
My Lai Massacre, 201–202
military/industrial complex, protests against, 216, 218, 222
Minh, Ho Chi (North Vietnamese leader), 146, 151, 181, 199
minimum wage increase, 29
Miss America 1968 protest, 241–242
missile gap, 33
Mission to Hanoi: A Chronicle of Double-Dealing In High Places (Ashmore and Baggs), 181
Mississippi Freedom Democratic Party (MFDP), 122
Mississippi voter registration drive, 121
Mitchell, John (Nixon's attorney general), 76

Mobes (anti–Vietnam War organizations), 275
Mobilization of November 1969, 187–188
Mongoose, Operation, 35
Montagnards forces in Vietnam, 154
Monterey music festival, 280, 297–298
Montgomery, AL, bus boycott
described, 12, 98–99
organizations behind, 103, 105, 111
Montgomery Improvement Association (MIA), 99, 111–112
moon, first man on, 80
Moratorium of October 1969, Vietnam War, 187
Morgan, Robin (underground newspaper editor), 277
Morrison, Jim (musician), 296
Morrison, Norman (Vietnam protest suicide), 175
Morse, Wayne (senator), 206
movies
Beatles, 290
marijuana use during screenings, 280
McCarthyism, 70, 216
1950s, revisiting popular themes and characters, 307–308
1960s hits, 19
sex and violence (Hays) code, 309
social and political issues, confronting, 309–311
studio system, end of, 307
visions of life in 1960s, 331–335
Muhammad, Elijah (Nation of Islam leader), 136
music
British groups, 289–294
cultural changes, 19
festivals, 297–301
folk, 287–289
hit songs, listed by year, 325–329
Motown, 285–287
1950s rock 'n' roll, 283–284
psychedelic rock, 294–295
rock protest, 295–297
soul, 285–287
surf, 284–285
Muslim Mosque, Inc., 136
mutiny, 190
My Lai Massacre, 78, 190, 201–202

• N •

NAACP (National Association for the Advancement of Colored People)
activities, 32, 108–110
Brown v. Board of Education case, 95–96
Evers, Medgar, 117
Marshall, Thurgood, 93
Rosa Parks case, 98
voter registration, 120
Namath, Joe (football player), 318–319
NASA (National Aeronautics and Space Administration), 29, 80
Nation of Islam
appearance, 135
beginning, 134–135
community, engendering feeling of, 135
confrontation, emphasis on, 104
Malcolm X, 135–137
March on Washington, derision of, 118
Muhammad Ali, 320
National Advisory Commission on Civil Disorders, 131, 183
National Aeronautics and Space Administration (NASA), 29, 80
National Association for the Advancement of Colored People. *See* NAACP
National Endowments for the Arts/Humanities, 59–60
National Guard
college campuses, deaths on, 188–189
enforcing integration, 96–97
enrollment to avoid draft, 218
People's Park, Berkeley, 227–228
National Liberation Front (NLF). *See* VC
National Organization for Women. *See* NOW
National Rainbow/PUSH Coalition (RPC), 133
Native Americans. *See* American Indians
NATO (North Atlantic Treaty Organization), 147
Nazi Germany, Olympics in, 89–90
negotiations with North Vietnam, 194–195, 209–210
Negro Leagues (baseball), 89
New Deal programs, 48

New Frontier
domestic policies, 28–30
foreign policies, 30–31
New Left
anti–Vietnam War movement, 218
campus issues, 217–218
civil rights, 218
described, 216–217
direct action, 219–220
McCarthy presidential candidacy, 216
military/industrial complex, battling, 218
sexism, 277
"New Look" policy (Eisenhower), 33
New Negro Movement, 91
New York State Liquor Authority (SLA), 260
Newark Riots, 130–131
news programs, 314
newspaper prices, 339
Newton, Huey (Black Panthers founder), 138, 140–142
Nguyen Hue, Operation (North Vietnamese Easter Offensive), 207–209
19th Amendment, 231
Nixon, Richard M. (president). *See also* Vietnamization policy, Nixon's
Cambodian bombing, 187–188, 203–204
conservative movement, 263–264
described, 11, 67–68
domestic successes, 80–81
early life, 68
foreign policy successes, 79
1960 presidential race, 24–25, 73
1968 presidential race, 73–76, 196
1972 reelection campaign, 82
redbaiting, 68–71
silent majority and, 18, 263–264
Six Crises, 73
vice presidency under Eisenhower, 71–73
Vietnam War, strategy toward, 15, 76–77, 196–197
Watergate scandal, 67, 82
Nixon, Thelma Catherine Ryan (first lady), 68, 69
NLF (National Liberation Front). *See* VC
nonviolent protests
civil rights, 102–106, 118
CNVA, 171
farmworkers', 17, 254

nonviolent protests *(continued)*
  New Left, 219, 223–224
  SNCC, 113
North Atlantic Treaty Organization
    (NATO), 147
North Vietnam
  bombing and attrition strategies against,
      77, 160
  in Cambodia, 203–204
  creating, 148–149
  leadership, 149–150
  Minh, Ho Chi, 151
  negotiations with, 194–195, 199, 209–210
  Phoenix Program, success of, 201
  swift boat campaigns, 155
North Vietnamese Army. *See* NVA
NOW (National Organization for Women)
  described, 16
  origins, 232, 237–238
  protests, 238
  working women, 238–239
nuclear explosion advertisement, 1963
    presidential campaign, 55
nuclear weapons
  Cuban Missile Crisis, 36–40
  peace movement, 170
  tensions, easing with Soviet Union, 79
NVA (North Vietnamese Army),
    152, 160–161, 166

• *O* •

Oakes, Richard (American Indian leader),
    256, 257
Oakland Induction Center, California,
    shutdown of, 178, 226
Office of Economic Opportunity, 61
Olympic games, 89–90, 319
On the Road (Kerouac), 269, 271
op (optical) art, 317
Operation Abolition HUAC movie, 221
Operation Breadbasket, 132–133
Operation Dewey Canyon III, 191
Operation Lam Som, Laos, 206–207
Operation Menu (Cambodian bombing),
    203–204
Operation Mongoose, 35

Operation Nguyen Hue (North Vietnamese
    Easter Offensive), 207–209
Operation Rolling Thunder (Vietnam War),
    157–159, 161
Oplan 34A swiftboat campaign, 155
OSS relationship with Viet Minh, 145–146
Oswald, Lee Harvey, 41–42
The Other Side (Lynd and Hayden), 179
Owens, Jesse (Olympic track star), 89–90

• *P* •

Palmer, Mitchell (attorney general), 214
Paris Peace Talks, 194–195, 209–210
Parker, John (Supreme Court
    nominee), 109
Parks, Rosa (civil rights icon), 97–99
participatory democracy, SDS, 229
Paul, Alice (ERA introducer), 239
Peace Corps, 30
peace movement, 170–172
Pentagon Papers, 78, 195
People's Park, 226–227
performing arts. *See* entertainment
Peterson, Esther (Kennedy advisor),
    234–235
picket lines, 252–253
The Pill
  birth control before, 246
  introduction of, 245
planned pregnancy, embracing, 246
Platoon movie, 333
Playboy magazine, 316
Pleiku airbase attack, Vietnam War, 157
Plessy v. Ferguson case, 87, 95
"plumbers," White House, 78, 82
Pol Pot (Cambodian prime minister), 205
police confrontations
  Chicago, Democratic National
      Convention, 184–186
  HUAC session at Berkeley, 221
  Stonewall bar, New York City, 260
poll taxes, 87, 120
Poor People's Campaign, 133–134
pop art, 316–317
pop culture
  art, 316–317
  books and magazines, 315–316

Broadway, 311
comedians, 314–315
fashion, 303–306
movies, 307–311
slang, 321–322
sports, 317–321
television, 312–314
Pope Paul VI, 248
Port Huron Statement, SDS, 228, 229
postage stamps, 337–338
Powell, Adam Clayton Jr. (congressman), 92
presidents. *See individual presidents listed by name*
President's Commission on the Status of Women, 234–235
Profiles in Courage (Kennedy, ghostwritten by Theodore Sorenson), 23
Progressive Age, 214
Project 100,000, Great Society, 164
protests. *See also* anti–Vietnam War movement
farmworkers' rights picket lines, 252–253
FSM, 222–223
lunch counter sit-ins, 106–108
Miss America 1968, 241–242
music inspiring, 287
New Left, 219
NOW, 238
school desegregation, 96
underground press, 275–276
proxy wars, 32–33
psychedelic art, 279, 317
psychedelic rock, 294–295
public suicide, 152–153, 174–175
Public Works and Economic Development Act, 62

• Q •

Quant, Mary (designer), 304–305
quarantine, Cuban Missile Crisis, 38–39

• R •

R & B (rhythm and blues) music, 284
racial violence
Chicago Freedom Movement, 132
civil rights movement, 93–95

Emmett Till, murder of, 94–95
lynch mobs, 94
motivations, 93
Rado, James *(Hair)*, 311
Ragni, Jerome *(Hair)*, 311
Ram Dass (Harvard psychologist and LSD experimenter), 278–279
Ramparts magazine, 276
Randolph, A. Philip (civil rights leader), 111, 117
Ranger aircraft carrier sabotage, 190
Rat magazine, 277
Ray, James Earl (King assassin), 105
Reagan, Ronald (president and governor of California), 129, 224, 227–228, 262
recession, 81
Reconstruction Act, 86
Red Scare, 215–216
redbaiting, 48, 68–71
red-diaper babies, 217
Reed, Donna (television star), 243
Regional Medical Program (RMP), 60
Republican Party, conservative shift in 1964, 52–54. *See also individual presidents and candidates listed by name*
Resurrection City, 134
revolutionary music, 294–297
rhetoric, Kennedy's power, 22
rhythm and blues (R & B) music, 284
Ridenhour, Ronald (My Lai Massacre letter-writer), 201
riots
after King's murder, 131
Detroit, 129–130
economic empowerment, 131
investigating, 131
Newark, 130–131
Stonewall bar, New York City, 260
Watts district of Los Angeles, 128–129
RMP (Regional Medical Program), 60
Robeson, Paul, in theater, 91
Robinson, Jackie (baseball player), 89
Rock, Dr. John (Pill codeveloper), 249
rock music, 19
rock musicals, 311
rock protest music, 295–297
rockabilly music, 284

Rockefeller, Nelson (vice president and Republican presidential candidate), 53–54

Roe v. Wade decision, 248

Rogers, William P. (Nixon's secretary of state), 76

Rolling Stones, 19, 201, 292–294

Rolling Thunder, Operation (Vietnam War), 157–159, 161

Roosevelt, Eleanor (first lady), 90, 235

Roosevelt, Franklin D. (president), 147, 215

Rosenberg, Julius and Ethel (executed for treason), 216

Rowan & Martin's Laugh-In television show, 312, 313

RPC (National Rainbow/PUSH Coalition), 133

Rubin, Jerry (antiwar leader), 186

Ruby, Jack (Dallas nightclub owner who killed Lee Harvey Oswald), 41–42

Rudd, Mark (Weathermen leader), 229

Rudolph, Wilma (Olympic track star), 90

rural relocation, South Vietnamese, 163

Rusk, Dean (secretary of state under Kennedy), 27, 205

Rustin, Bayard (civil rights leader), 111

• *S* •

sabotage, military, 190

Sahl, Mort (comedian), 314–315

Saigon, 166, 210

Salinger, Pierre (Kennedy press secretary), 28

Salisbury, Harrison (writer), 180

SALT 1 (Strategic Arms Limitation Treaty), 79

San Francisco, 221, 281

San Francisco State University, 138

SANE (Committee for a Sane Nuclear Policy), 170–171, 175

Sanger, Margaret (Planned Parenthood founder), 246

Savio, Mario (FSM leader), 222, 223, 225

Schenley growers, 254

Schlesinger, Arthur Jr. (Kennedy advisor), 28

school integration
Arkansas, National Guard sent to, 95–97
Plessy v. Ferguson ruling, 80, 87, 95

Schweitzer, Dr. Albert ("Call to Conscience" article), 170–171

Schwerner, Michael (slain civil rights worker), 122–123

science fiction films, 308

SCLC (Southern Christian Leadership Conference)
described, 111–112
economic issues, turn towards, 131
nonviolence of, 103
Operation Breadbasket, 132
Poor People's Campaign, 133–134
Selma to Montgomery march, 126–127

Scott, Lawrence (CNVA founder), 171

SDS (Students for a Democratic Society)
described, 16, 172, 174
origins, 228
participatory democracy and direct action, 229
Weathermen splinter group, 229–230

Seale, Bobby (antiwar leader and Black Panthers founder), 136, 186

segregation
conservatives supporting, 263
CORE's battles against, 110–111
Johnson's view of, 57
military, 88, 163–164
Nixon's view of, 80
northern, 128–129, 132
"separate but equal" doctrine, 87

segregationists, 17, 120, 121

Selective Service, 176

Selma, AL
"Bloody Sunday" civil rights violence, 58
march to Montgomery, 13, 126–127

separatism, black, 104

sex in movies, 309, 310–311

Sexual Behavior in the Human Male (Kinsey), 17, 247, 259

sexual revolution, 245, 273–274

Shriver, Sargent (Peace Corps head), 30

Shuttlesworth, Rev. Fred (civil rights leader), 110, 111

Sihanouk, Norodom (Cambodian prince), 203, 204, 205
silent majority, 75–76
sip-in, 260
sitcoms, 313
sit-ins
  civil rights movement, 106–108
  New Left, 219, 223–224
Six Crises (Nixon), 73
16th Street Baptist Church, bombing
    of, 118–119
SLA (New York State Liquor Authority), 260
slang, 321–322
Smith, John (symbol of Newark Riots),
    130–131
Smith, Tommie (Olympic athlete), 319
Smothers Brothers Comedy Hour television
    show, 312–313
SNCC (Student Nonviolent/National
    Coordinating Committee), 113, 225
social rights movements
  American Indians, 17
  backlash, 75
  conservatives, 17–18
  gays and lesbians, 17
  Latinos, 16–17
  movies, 309–311
  1968 presidential campaign, 75–76
  university students, 15–16
  women, 16
Socialism
  early 20th century, 213–214
  Great Depression and World War II, 215
  Nixon's first political opponent, 69
  Palmer Raids, 214–215
sodomy laws, 261
Sorenson, Theodore (ghostwriter of
    Profiles in Courage), 23
soul music, 284, 285–287
South America, Nixon's vice presidential
    trip to, 72
South Vietnam. *See also* ARVN
  agitation, Gulf of Tonkin, 156
  cold war, 13, 40–41
  Communists, eliminating through
    Phoenix Program, 200–201
  coup of 1963, 152–153
  creating, 148–149

Diem, Ngo Dinh, 149–150
  hearts and minds of population, failure to
    win, 162–164
  politics, 149–150
  Vietnamization, reassuring, 198
  withdrawal, 15, 198–199
Southern Christian Leadership Conference.
    See SCLC
Soviet Union. *See also* cold war
  Kennedy assassination, 43
  Nixon foreign policy advances, 76, 79
  Nixon's vice-presidential visit, 72–73
  Vietnam, objections to war in, 208
space travel, 29–30, 80
Special Forces, 13, 33, 154
spiritualism, 274–275, 291–292
sports
  Ali, Muhammad, 319–321
  baseball, blacks in, 89
  civil rights movement, 89–90
  dynasties, 317–318
  Olympic games, 89–90, 319
  underdogs, 318–319
  women's, 250
Sproul Hall, University of California at
    Berkeley
  People's Park protest, 227
  sit-in, 219, 222, 223–224
Sputnik I space satellite, 29
stagflation, 81
Star Trek television show, 243
steel industry, 28–29
Steinem, Gloria (feminist leader), 244
Stonewall Riots, 17, 260–261
Stop the Draft Week, 178–180, 226
Strategic Arms Limitation Treaty
    (SALT 1), 79
Strong, Edward (Berkeley chancellor), 223
student movement, 172
Student Nonviolent/National Coordinating
    Committee (SNCC), 113, 225
Students for a Democratic Society. *See* SDS
studio system, end of, 307
Summer of Love, 280–281
Super Bowl, 318
Supreme Court decisions
  abortion, 248
  affirmative action, 81

Supreme Court decisions *(continued)*
  conscientious objector status, 177
  interracial marriage, 127
  interstate travel, desegregation of, 114
  Montgomery bus segregation, 99
  Pentagon Papers, release of, 78
  school integration, 80, 95–96, 109
  "separate but equal" doctrine, 87, 95
Supremes, 285, 286
surf music, 284–285
survival programs, Black Panther, 140

• T •

Tate, Sharon (murdered movie star), 282
Taylor, Maxwell (ambassador to South
    Vietnam), 175
Tchepone, Laos, invasion of, 206–207
teach-ins, 173
television
  black performers, 91
  growth of, 9, 20
  Kennedy-Nixon debates, 25
  late-night talk shows, 312
  media coverage of Vietnam War,
    buying, 181–182
  music, promoting, 288, 289–290, 296
  news programs, 31, 32, 314
  1963 election, 55
  Nixon's "Checkers" speech, 72
  sex, 247
  sitcoms, 313
  variety shows, 289–290, 312–313
  Vietnam War, effect on support, 167
  women, portrayal of, 243
Tet Offensive, North Vietnamese
  described, 164–168
  goals, 65
  impact on American public, 14–15, 65
  Johnson credibility gap, 64
  Johnson strategy, change after, 194
  Khe Sanh, diverting attention at, 165
  surprise attacks, 166
That Girl television show, 243
Thieu (South Vietnamese president), 209
Thirteen Days movie, 332
Thompson, Hugh (My Lai Massacre
    rescuer), 201

Ticonderoga aircraft carrier, 156
Tilden, Samuel (1876 presidential
    candidate), 87
Till, Emmett, murder of, 94–95
Tindley, Charles ("We Shall Overcome"
    song), 294
toiletry prices, 338–339
Tonkin Gulf, Vietnam
  confrontation in, 14, 63, 155–157
  false statements about, 205
  Pentagon Papers revelations, 78
Trade Expansion Act of 1962, 29
Traffic Safety Act, 62
triangular diplomacy, 197
troop withdrawals, Vietnam War,
    198–199, 206
Trudeau, Pierre (Canadian prime
    minister), 177
Truman, Harry (president), 88, 147
Turkey, U.S. missiles in, 39
Tuskegee Airmen, 88
Twiggy, 305

• U •

underdogs, sports, 318–319
underground press, 275–277
unions. *See* labor unions
United Farm Workers. *See* farmworkers'
    rights movement
University of Alabama, 263, 264
University of California. *See* Berkeley,
    University of California at
university student movements, 15–16
Urban League, 109

• V •

variety shows, 289–290, 312–313
VC (Viet Cong)
  body counts, 160–161
  Cambodia, 205
  creation, 152
  leadership, attacking, 200–201
  peace negotiations, 194–195, 210
  South Vietnamese villagers, relationship
    with, 162–163
  Tet Offensive, 166, 167

VDC (Vietnam Day Committee), 224, 226
Venezuela, Nixon's vice presidential
    trip to, 72
veterans' Winter Soldier Investigation, 190
Viet Cong. *See* VC
Viet Minh, 148, 151
Vietnam. *See also* North Vietnam; South
    Vietnam
  French colonialism in, 147–148
  Geneva Conference of 1954 creating two
    nations, 148–149
Vietnam Day Committee. *See* VDC
Vietnam Peace Parade on Fifth Avenue,
    New York, 175
Vietnam Veterans Against the War (VVAW),
    190–191
Vietnam War. *See also* anti–Vietnam War
    movement
  black soldiers' deaths in, 88–89, 140
  Easter Offensive, 207–209
  escalation, 14–15, 46, 62–63, 154–164
  factors leading to U.S. involvement,
    13, 145–153
  fall of Saigon, 210
  Johnson's credibility gap, 63–65
  King's opposition to, 104
  movies about, 333–334
  negotiations with North Vietnam,
    194–195, 209–210
  1968 presidential race, 195–196
  Nixon's strategy, 76–77
  peace talks, 209–210
  as proxy war, 33
  Tet Offensive and affects on U.S. attitude,
    65, 164–168, 193, 194
  widening to Cambodia and Laos, 202–207
  withdrawal, 15
Vietnamization policy, Nixon's
  ARVN, using in Laos, 206–207
  described, 15
  North Vietnam, negotiating with, 199
  South Vietnam, reassuring, 198
  troop withdrawals, 76–77, 198–199
Village Voice newspaper magazine, 276
violence in movies, 309
violent resistance
  Black Panther Party, 140–142
  to civil rights movement, 12
  to Reconstruction, 86

Voorhis, Jerry (congressman), 68–69
voter registration
  Freedom Summer drive, 1964, 120–121, 225
  Jim Crow Laws, 12, 87
  Voting Rights Act, changes from, 127
Voting Rights Act of 1965, 57–58, 80, 127
voting rights, women's, 231
VVAW (Vietnam Veterans Against the War),
    190–191

• W •

wage, increasing minimum, 29
Wallace, George (Alabama governor and
    presidential candidate), 75, 82, 126,
    263, 264
War on Poverty, 50–51, 61
war protesters. *See* anti–Vietnam War
    movement
Warhol, Andy (pop artist), 317
Warren Commission, 42
Warren, Earl (Supreme Court Chief
    Justice), 96
Washington, Kenny (football player), 89
Watergate scandal, 67, 78, 82
Watts Riots, 13, 128–129
"We Shall Overcome" song (Tindley), 294
Weathermen splinter group, 229–230
Welch, Robert Jr. (John Birch Society
    founder), 262
Westmoreland, General William C.
    (Vietnam War leader)
  combat troops, requests for more,
    158, 165, 194
  progress claims belied by Tet Offensive,
    167, 183
  Tonkin Gulf confrontation, 155
White House "plumbers," 78, 82
Wilson, Dagmar (WSP founder), 171
Wilson, Woodrow (president), 146
Wolfe, Tom (*The Electric Kool-Aid Acid
    Tests*), 279
women's clothing, 304–305
women's lib/liberation, 242
women's rights movement
  backlash, 249–250
  birth control, power of, 245–249
  described, 16, 231–232
  fashion, 305

women's rights movement *(continued)*
 feminine mystique, exposing, 232–234
 gender-neutral language, 241
 government actions, 234–236
 homoscxual rights and, 17
 legacy, 250
 NOW, 237–239
 radical, 240–245
 underground newspaper, 277
Women's Strike for Peace. *See* WSP
Woodstock: 3 Days of Peace & Music
  movie, 335
Woodstock music festival, 298–301
Woolworth's lunch counter sit-ins,
  31, 106–108
working women, 232–233, 238–239
World War II
 Socialism, 215
 Vietnam, 145–146
 women in work force, 232

WSP (Women's Strike for Peace), 171–172
WTO (World Trade Organization), protests
  against, 220

X, Malcolm (black leader), 104, 118,
  135–137

YAF (Young Americans for Freedom), 262
yippies, 184–185
youth counterculture, 18

• *Z* •

Zen Buddhism, 274